Can Latin American Firms Compete?

Can Latin American Firms Compete?

Robert Grosse and Luiz F. Mesquita

OXFORD

UNIVERSITY PRESS

A 29953510

OXFORD

UNIVERSITY PRESS

Great Clarendon Street, Oxford ox2 6DP

Oxford University Press is a department of the University of Oxford.
It furthers the University's objective of excellence in research, scholarship,
and education by publishing worldwide in

Oxford New York

Auckland Cape Town Dar es Salaam Hong Kong Karachi
Kuala Lumpur Madrid Melbourne Mexico City Nairobi
New Delhi Shanghai Taipei Toronto

With offices in

Argentina Austria Brazil Chile Czech Republic France Greece
Guatemala Hungary Italy Japan Poland Portugal Singapore
South Korea Switzerland Thailand Turkey Ukraine Vietnam

Published in the United States
by Oxford University Press Inc., New York

© Oxford University Press 2007

The moral rights of the authors have been asserted
Database right Oxford University Press (maker)

First published 2007

British Library Cataloguing in Publication Data

Data available

Library of Congress Cataloging in Publication Data

Can Latin American firms compete? / [edited by] Robert Grosse and Luiz F.
Mesquita.
  p. cm.
Includes bibliographical references and index.
ISBN 978–0–19–923375–5 (alk. paper)
1. International business enterprises—Latin America. 2. Competition,
International. I. Grosse, Robert E. II. Mesquita, Luiz F.
HD2810.5.C36 2007
338.8'898—dc22   2007018476

Typeset by SPI Publisher Services, Pondicherry, India
Printed in Great Britain
on acid-free paper by
Biddles Ltd., King's Lynn, Norfolk

ISBN 978–0–19–923375–5

1 3 5 7 9 10 8 6 4 2

Contents

Part I. Themes in the Competitiveness of Latin American Firms

Part II. Micro-Level Strategies of Firms in Specific Sectors

Contents

List of Figures

List of Figures

List of Tables

Notes on Contributors

Miguel Caldas is the current holder of the Gerald N. Gaston Chair in International Business, and an Associate Professor of International Business at the College of Business at Loyola University New Orleans since 2003. He holds a BA in business degree from Brasilia Federal University and earned a Master in Science and a Ph.D. from FGV-EAESP, Brazil's most prestigious and only AACSB-accredited institution. Prior to joining Loyola, he served for 5 years as a professor at FGV-EAESP, and before that as an adjunct for 10 years at ESPM business school, both in São Paulo, Brazil. He has been a Visiting Professor at Northwestern University's GIM program (Chicago) and at ICESI's International MBA (Cali, Colombia), and a Visiting Scholar at UT-Austin.

Prior to joining academia full time, he had a 15-year career in consulting, reaching partner status at Coopers & Lybrand, Andersen Business Consulting, and PricewaterhouseCoopers. As a consultant he concentrated on organizational change and was responsible for cross-country assignments and client accounts with multiple MNCs, mostly assisting them with their operations in Latin America.

Professor Caldas is a prolific author about international business in Latin America. He has authored, coauthored, or coedited seven books in Portuguese, written more than twenty-five articles in scholarly journals (including six awarded papers, two of which won Academy of Management divisional awards) and several book chapters. His research agenda has recently been concentrated mostly on international and comparative management and ethics, as well as organizational and national (Brazilian, Latin American) culture, and lastly the professional service firms (typically consulting) industry.

Keum-Young Chang is a doctoral candidate in Strategy and International Business at Seoul National University. Her academic advisor is Professor Dong-Sung Cho. She received an MBA from the University of Washington in 2001. She has worked at the Ministry of Commerce, Industry and Energy in Korea since 1996. She has been involved in trade and industrial policy making in Korea and currently she is a director at the Unfair Trade Investigation Division.

Dong-Sung Cho is Professor of Strategy, International Business and Management Design at Seoul National University. He received a doctoral degree from Harvard Business School in 1976, and worked at Gulf Oil's Planning Group before joining SNU in 1978. He was a visiting professor at HBS, INSEAD, Helsinki School of Economics, the University of Tokyo, Hitotsubashi University, University of Michigan, Duke, Peking, Zhejiang and Nankai University. Among the forty-two books he has published are *The General Trading Company* by Lexington Books (1986), *Tiger Technology: The Rise of the Semiconductor Industry in Asia* by Cambridge University Press (1999), and *From Adam Smith to Michael Porter: Evolution of Competitiveness Theory* by World Scientific (2000).

He was Dean of the College of Business Administration, SNU, 2001–3, and Dean of the Graduate School of International and Area Studies, SNU, 1999–2001. He has been on the Board of Directors at fifteen multinational companies and research organizations. He is Honorary Consul General of the Government of Finland in Korea. He was President of Korean Academic Society of Business Administration, which is the flagship organization in Korea representing thirty-four functionally oriented academic societies in business administration. He is now Chair the of Korean Association of Academic Societies, which is the umbrella organization of 620 academic societies that encompass humanities, social sciences, natural sciences, engineering, and others. He also chairs the Committee for Government Innovation Management, and the Committee for Synergistic Cooperation between Big and Small Corporations jointly with the Prime Minister of Korea.

Guillermo D'Andrea is Professor of Business Administration at IAE, the Business School at the Austral University in Buenos Aires, Argentina. Professor D'Andrea obtained his Ph.D. from IESE, in Barcelona, Spain. His fields of research deal with retail strategy and management, and the process of shaping business for the Base of the (Socioeconomic) Pyramid. He has written over fifty cases and teaching materials and is coauthor of *Cases in Strategic Marketing in Latin America*, 2001 (Spanish version in 2002), *Administración de Servicios (Services Management)*, and *Retail Management*, both published during 2004. His articles have been published in the *Harvard Business Review*, Booz Allen's *Strategy & Business*, and the *McKinsey Quarterly*.

Professor D'Andrea is the Research Director of the Coca-Cola Retailing Research Center—Latin America. He teaches at Babson College's Strategic Planning and Management in Retailing Program, and is a visiting professor at Instituto Politecnico di Milano, Italy. He has been visiting professor at the Instituto Internacional San Telmo, Seville, Spain, the Darden Graduate School of Business Administration of the University of Virginia, and IEDC, Lubljana, Slovenia.

Professor D'Andrea combines his academic activity with active consulting, having collaborated with companies in many fields including retailing, market research, textiles, pharmaceuticals, medical services, food manufacturing, and distribution. He works with companies such as Exxon (On the Run C-Stores), Exito-Casino in Colombia, La Polar in Chile, Mr. Price Group in S. Africa, IPSOS France, Easy Home-Center, Siemens, Unilever, Best Foods, Bayer, Osram, and 3M. He specializes in process consulting in long-range projects dealing with strategic marketing problems.

John C. Edmunds is Professor of Finance and Research Director of the Institute for Latin American Business Studies at Babson College. He has taught extensively at overseas MBA programs, including Instituto de Empresa in Madrid, Spain, INCAE in Central America and the Universidad Católica Madre y Maestra in the Dominican Republic, and two universities in Chile. He has also taught at other schools in the Boston area, including the Arthur D. Little School of Management, Boston University, the Fletcher School of Law and Diplomacy, Harvard University, Hult International Business School, and Northeastern University. He is a member of the Golden Key Society and at Arthur D. Little he was voted Professor of the Year. He has lived in six countries and spent 18 years abroad. He is fluent in Spanish and also speaks French.

Dr Edmunds's areas of interest are international finance, derivatives, capital markets, and emerging markets. He is the author of over 170 articles and cases published both in academic and practitioner journals. He has published four books.

Dr Edmunds holds a D.B.A. in International Business from Harvard Business School, an MBA in Finance and Quantitative Methods with honors from Boston University, an MA in Economics from Northeastern University, and an A.B. in Economics cum laude from Harvard College. He has consulted with the Harvard Institute for International Development, the Rockefeller Foundation, Stanford Research Institute, and numerous private companies.

Eduardo Fracchia is the Director of Department of Economics at IAE Business School, Universidad Austral. He is an engineer and an economist from the Universidad de Buenos Aires and holds a Ph.D. in Management from IESE, Barcelona. He has taught Economics at the Universidad de Buenos Aires (1987–95) and at the IAE since 1990 in all the programs offered.

He offers courses on international economics, domestic economics, and applied macroeconomics at the MBA. He has developed specific studies on the evolution of economic groups in Argentina. His principal area of interest is competitiveness.

He participates in the initiative to develop public leaders at the IAE and is the coordinator of the program oriented to young people working in public issues. He has written several case studies and papers on the evolution of the domestic macroeconomics and writes often in the local newspapers regarding economic matters.

Andrea Goldstein is senior economist at the OECD in Paris. A graduate of Bocconi University in Milan and Columbia University in New York, he has also worked for the OECD Economics Department, the World Bank Group, and the Italian Securities and Exchange Commission. He has also consulted for the Department for International Development and the Inter-American Development Bank.

His research on international investment, regional integration, and privatization has been published on the *Cambridge Journal of Economics*, *CEPAL Review*, *Economia Internazionale*, *Industrial and Corporate Change*, the *Journal of Chinese Economic and Business Studies*, and other journals. In 2007, Andrea published a book on multinationals from emerging economies (with a foreword by Lou Wells) and one other on multinationals with Lucia Piscitello.

Robert Grosse is Director of the Global Leadership Centre at Standard Bank in Johannesburg, South Africa. He holds a BA degree from Princeton University and a doctorate from the University of North Carolina, both in international economics. He has taught international finance in the MBA programs at Thunderbird, the University of Miami, the University of Michigan, and at the Instituto de Empresa (Madrid, Spain), as well as in many universities in Latin America. As a consultant in international business he has worked for the US Commerce, State, and Treasury Departments, the Organization of American States, and the United Nations. Among the many companies he has served are: American Express, Anaconda, Banco Ganadero, Chase Manhattan Bank, Citibank, EXXON, IBM, Merrill Lynch, Raymond James, Texaco, YPF, and Xerox.

Professor Grosse is a leading author on international business in Latin America. He has written about global firms' strategies in the region (*Multinationals in Latin America*, Routledge, 1989), the financial crises of the 1980s and 1990s and strategies of banks and firms to deal with them (three books and a dozen articles) and the strategies of Latin American firms in international competition (cases on Enersis, Banco Ganadero, YPF, and LanChile, among others). He wrote a section on 'International Business in Latin America' for the *Oxford Handbook of International Business* (Oxford, 2001). He is a Fellow of the Academy of International Business.

Professor Grosse has worked as Chair in Capital Markets at the Instituto de Empresa (Madrid), and as Visiting Professor of International Finance at ICESI (Cali, Colombia), Universidad del Norte (Barranquilla, Colombia) and at the Universidad Gabriela Mistral (Santiago, Chile). He has taught executive programs in international finance and global business strategy in Argentina, Bolivia, Chile, Colombia, Costa Rica, Ecuador, México, Panama, Perú, Puerto Rico, Spain, Trinidad, Uruguay, and Venezuela. He was President of the Business Association of Latin American Studies in 2005–6.

Andrés Hatum is Associate Professor in Human Resource Management at IAE Business School, Austral University, Argentina. He received his Ph.D. in Management and Organization at Warwick Business School (University of Warwick), England. He also obtained a BA in Politics and International Relationships at the Catholic University in Argentina.

His professional experience in management began as Assessor of the Home Office and later in the Economy Ministry in Argentina. Later he became the HR Manager at Transportes Furlong. Professor Hatum's academic activities started in 1992 when he was named Associate Professor at the Catholic University. Since 1995 he has been a full-time faculty member in Human Resources at IAE Business School.

He has published articles in journals such as *British Journal of Management*, *Management Research*, *Harvard Business Review*, and *Family Business Review*. He has also published books in Spanish (Dirigiendo Personas, Temas, 2004; Organizaciones que Crecen, Temas, 2006) and English (Adaptation or Expiration in Family Firms: Organizational Flexibility in Emerging Economies, Edward Elgar Publishing, forthcoming 2007).

Jorge Katz was born in Buenos Aires, Argentina in 1940. He received a First Degree in Economics at the University of Buenos Aires and completed his Doctorate at Balliol College, Oxford in 1967 with a dissertation entitled 'Production Functions, Foreign Investment and Growth' which was published by North Holland Publishing Company in 1969.

He was Professor on Industrial Economics at the University of Buenos Aires during the period 1968–92 and is former Director of the Division of Production, Productivity and Management, at the United Nations ECLAC in Santiago, Chile. He teaches a Graduate Course on Technology and Innovation at the University of Chile. He has published extensively both on the subject of Technology and Industrial Restructuring in Latin America and also on Issues Related to the Structure and Behavior in the Health Sector.

Gerald A. McDermott is Assistant Professor of Management at the Wharton School of the University of Pennsylvania and holds a secondary appointment in the Department of Political Science. He specializes in international business and political economy. McDermott received his Ph.D. from the Department of Political Science at MIT. His first stream of research has mainly focussed on the impact of industrial networks on the creation of economic governance institutions in postcommunist countries. His current research in South America uses both comparative and statistical survey methods to examine the sociopolitical conditions under which societies build new innovative capacities to achieve sustained upgrading in their industries.

He has also recently launched a project about the impact of international integration regimes on local institutional development via a comparison of the EU accession, NAFTA, and Mercosur. His publications include articles in such scholarly journals as *Comparative Political Studies, Industrial and Corporate Change, Review of International Political Economy, Academy of Management Review,* and *Organization Studies* as well as his book, *Embedded Politics: Industrial Networks and Institutional Change in Post-Communism* (University of Michigan Press, 2002). McDermott has also consulted the multilateral lending institutions and the governments of the Czech Republic and Argentina. He lived in Prague for over 4 years and in Buenos Aires for over 6 years, being fluent in both Czech and Spanish.

Luiz F. Mesquita is Assistant Professor of Business Policy & Strategy, at the School of Global Management and Leadership, Arizona State University. He holds a masters degree in Applied Economics (1997) and a Ph.D. in Strategy from Purdue University. His research interests evolve around *alliances among firms, and their effect on supply chain product exchanges.* Professor Mesquita's research also encompasses topics in international management such as the impact of *interfirm ties within industrial clusters, especially those in emerging markets such as Argentina and Brazil, and their effect on export performances.* Additionally, Professor Mesquita has analyzed the *corporate strategies of business groups in emerging economies,* as well as *the factors that impact the effectiveness of trust-facilitators in cluster development projects.* This research has been published in prestigious outlets, such as the *Academy of Management Review, International Journal of Production and Operations Management, Academy of Management Executive,* and *Harvard Business Review.* Professor Mesquita is coeditor of the book *The New Entrepreneurs,* by Blackwell, a book focussing on the alternative entrepreneurial strategies used in emerging economies.

Previous to joining Arizona State University, Professor Mesquita taught strategy, entrepreneurship and international management courses at the undergraduate and graduate programs at Purdue University, as well as the IAE School of Management and Business, Austral University in Argentina. In 2000, Professor Mesquita was inducted into the prestigious Purdue University's Teaching Academy, a society which gathers the top 3 per cent instructors of that University. Professor Mesquita is a Brazilian national. He has lived several years in the United States, Brazil, and Argentina. He has worked at and lectured for Fortune 500 companies such as Deere & Co, Caterpillar, Monsanto, and Microsoft. He has also worked as Project Director and consultant for the Inter-American Development Bank. Professor Mesquita is an active member of the Strategic Management Society, the Academy of Management, and Purdue University's Teaching Academy. He is fluent in English, Portuguese, and Spanish.

Héctor Ochoa is Dean of the Management and Economics School, ICESI University, in Cali, Colombia. Professor Ochoa studied Economics at Universidad de Antioquia, in Medellin, Colombia, and earned his MBA and Ph.D. degrees at Syracuse University. He was President at Universidad EAFIT, in

Medellin, for 9 years; and Advisory to the President of Colombia from 1983 to 1986.

At Universidad Icesi, where he has been for 16 years, Professor Ochoa teaches Macroeconomics and Management Strategies. He is part of a research team whose objective is the study of public policies in Colombia. His most recent article is: 'The effects of a monopolistic market structure on the assessment of privatized companies: The Colombian case'. Recently, he participated with other authors in the preparation of the book 'The social effects of the Paez Law in the Cauca Region in Colombia'.

Currently, for the period 2006–8, Professor Ochoa is President of the Latin American Council of Business Schools, CLADEA.

Michael Penfold is currently an associate professor at IESA (Caracas, Venezuela), one of the leading business and public policy schools in Latin America, and holds a Ph.D. in Political Science from Columbia University. In 2005, he was Columbia University's Tinker Professor at the School for International and Public Affairs. His research interests are centered on public policy and political economy in Latin America. He was the executive director of Venezuela's Investment Council (CONAPRI) between 1999 and 2003 in charge of collaborating in the opening of the telecommunication and gas sector. He is the author of several books and journal articles published both in Spanish and English, including *Harvard Business Review, Journal of Democracy,* and *Latin American Politics and Society.* Dr Penfold is also the board member of Rum Santa Teresa and was director of Venezuela's Export Bank (BANCOEX). He has worked as a consultant for the Carter Center, Open Society Institute, CAF, World Bank, and the IADB.

Andrew Pettigrew is Dean of the University of Bath School of Management. Professor Pettigrew received his training in sociology and anthropology and conducted his first research among the Sebeii people in Uganda. He received his Ph.D. from Manchester Business School in 1970, and has held academic appointments at Yale, Harvard, London Business School, and Warwick Business School.

His long-term research interests have been in the study of decision-making, power, strategy development, change, performance, and corporate governance in private and public sector organizations in the United Kingdom and beyond. He has written, coauthored, or edited sixteen books, and has published in most of the top management journals in the United States and Europe. His current research interests include studies of the boards and directors of the UK's top 500 companies, and new forms of organizing and company performance in major corporations in Europe, Japan, and the United States.

Over the years Professor Pettigrew's consultancy clients have included: BP, ICI, Shell, PA Management Consultants, Unilever, IBM, Lloyds TSB,

McKinsey & Company, PricewaterhouseCoopers, The Cabinet Office, the Department of Health, various levels in the NHS, the Department of Trade and Industry, the National Board of Education in Sweden, the Korean Chaebol LG, and Instituto de Altos Estudios Empresariales, Argentina. He has also advised a number of government departments including: the Cabinet Office, DTI, Department of Health and the Department for Education and Employment.

Márcia Tavares is Economic Affairs Officer at the United Nations Economic Commission for Latin America and the Caribbean, ECLAC. She works for the Investment Unit of ECLAC in Santiago, Chile. She is part of the team that produces ECLAC's annual report on Foreign Investment in Latin America and the Caribbean. Her latest research topic has been on the internationalization of Latin American companies.

Ms Tavares holds a degree in Economics from the University of Geneva and a Master of Science in Politics of the World Economy from the London School of Economics and Political Science, focussing on international business and the environment. She also has training in public management and environmental economics. Before joining ECLAC, she worked for the Brazilian government and for a private consulting firm, dealing with competition policy and regulation.

Doug Thomas is Assistant Professor of Management at the University of New Mexico's Anderson School of Management. He earned his Ph.D. in Strategic Management from Texas A&M University. He holds a BA in economics from BYU, where he also has served as a visiting lecturer at the Marriott School of Management. In addition he has taught strategy and international business courses at Texas A&M University and the University of Texas at San Antonio. He is fluent in Spanish and previously worked as an internal consultant to American Express in Mexico City. He has published articles on strategy in *Management International Review, Journal of Business Research, International Journal of Management, Journal of International Management, Journal of Managerial Issues,* as well as several other academic publications. While at the Anderson School, he has consulted for a variety of organizations including start-ups, nonprofits and governmental agencies.

Omar Toulan is Associate Professor and Head of the Strategy Department at the Desautels Faculty of Management at McGill University. He holds a Bachelors degree from Georgetown University's School of Foreign Service and a Ph.D. in Strategy from the Sloan School of Management at MIT. He teaches international strategy in the MBA and B.Com programs at McGill. In addition, he has taught at the Stockholm School of Economics. He has been a visiting scholar at INSEAD, London Business School, Imperial College, and Universidad Torcuato di Tella in Argentina.

Dr Toulan's research revolves around different aspects of International Business. One of his primary streams focusses on the impact of globalization on emerging markets, and in specific firms based in those countries. In different projects he has looked at the impact of liberalization on firm internationalization patterns as well as horizontal and vertical strategies. From a regional perspective most of this work has been conducted in Latin America. Professor Toulan's work has been published in a variety of academic and managerial journals including the *Strategic Management Journal, Journal of International Business Studies, California Management Review, Journal of Latin American Studies, Industrial and Corporate Change*, and the *International Trade Journal*.

Prior to entering academia, Dr Toulan worked as a management consultant for McKinsey & Company in its New York office, as well as at its Global Institute in Washington, DC. He has also worked as a researcher at the US President's Council of Economic Advisers.

Thomaz Wood, Jr. teaches business strategy and organizational theory at FGV-EAESP and is a partner with Matrix/CDE, a management consulting firm. From 2001 to 2004, he served as director and editor for RAE-Revista de Administração de Empresas, a 46-year-old, leading academic journal in Brazil. During his tenure, he created two new journals—RAE-eletronica, for academics, and GV-executivo, for practitioners. In the same period, he served as Vice-President at the Iberoamerican Academy of Management.

He has authored/edited eighteen books and over fifty academic papers in the field of organization studies. His research work can be broadly located in the realm of organizational discourse and symbolism. Currently, his research interests include: new organizational forms and the emergence of symbol intensive organizations, the study of the 'spectacularization' of organizational life, and creative industries. He is also involved in the development of a research group focussing on organizational change in transforming societies.

Professor Wood holds a doctoral and a master's degree in Business Administration, from Fundacao Getulio Vargas-EAESP, and a degree in Chemical Engineering, from UNICAMP. He is also an 'accidental journalist' and publishes regularly at *CartaCapital*, a Brazilian magazine.

1

Introduction: Can Latin American Firms Compete?

Robert Grosse

1.1. Introduction

The chapters in this project seek to answer the question: How can Latin American firms compete against domestic and foreign rivals in the twenty-first century? The answer is stated as a question in our project title, since it seems that most observers do not see specific competitive strengths that will indeed enable firms from Latin America to beat out the competitors from abroad—in their own Latin American markets or elsewhere in the world. Our intent is to identify those characteristics and strategies of such firms that will enable them to compete successfully in domestic and foreign markets in the years ahead.

This project was born out of frustration—frustration that North and South American writers and analysts have not been able to identify particular capabilities of firms from Latin America that will enable them to compete successfully in the increasingly open markets around the world. It seems that Latin American firms are generally viewed as less-efficient outgrowths of the US company model. That is (except for the remaining government-owned firms), the leading Latin American firms tend to be smaller than their US counterparts, while their competitive advantages and strategies tend to mimic those of the US firms.[1] Is there anything special about Latin American firms? Are there particular capabilities that distinguish them in domestic or foreign competition that may lead to sustainable advantages and can be transferred to other contexts? These are the questions that launched the project.

To put the discussion in context, Latin America makes up a major part of the emerging market world. If we ignore China and India, Latin America constitutes about 1/6 of the population of the rest of the emerging world, and a slightly larger percentage of GDP. Table 1.1 compares

Table 1.1. Latin America compared to other regions

	GDP 2004 (US$ M)	Per capita GDP 2004 (US$)	Population 2005 ('000)	Exports 2004 (US$M)	Outward FDI 2004 (US$M)	Corruption rating & rank
	http://siteresources.worldbank.org/DATASTATISTICS/Resources/GDP.pdf	http://siteresources.worldbank.org/DATASTATISTICS/Resources/GNIPC.pdf	http://www.census.gov/cgi-bin/ipc/idbrank.pl	http://devdata.worldbank.org/data-query/; http://www.census.gov/foreign-trade/statistics/historical/gandsexp.pdf; http://www.wto.org/english/res_e/statis_e/its2005_e/its05_byregion_e.htm	http://stats.unctad.org/FDI/TableViewer/tableView.aspx?ReportId=5; http://www.fdi.gov.cn/common/info.jsp?id=ABC000000000028177	TI 2005 Corruption Perceptions Index* http://ww1.transparency.org/cpi/2005/cpi2005_infocus.html#cpi
Latin America	2,018,715	7,660	561,825	538,997	10,943	1–4 (Argentina −2.8, Brazil −3.7)
China	1,649,329	5,330	1,306,314	663,030	60,630	3.2
India	691,876	3,100	1,080,264	10,586	2,222	2.9
Rest of Asia	2,367,508	5,070	1,301,404	1,063,011	103,410	1.7–9.4 (Taiwan −5.9, Bangladesh −1.7)
Eastern Europe	3,246,293	8,360	325,715	564,020	9,707	2–4 (Bulgaria −4.0, Russia −2.4)
Africa	1,422,775	5,760 (North Africa) / 1,850 (Sub-Saharan Africa)	910,850	350,815	5,134	1.7–5 (South Africa −4.5, Egypt −3.4, Nigeria−1.9)
European Union	11,871,288	27,840	396,340	4,731,600	309,498	5–10 (Iceland −9.7, German −8.2, Spain −7.0, Italy −5.0)
United States	11,667,515	39,710	295,734	1,151,448	152,130	7.6

* **CPI Score** relates to perceptions of the degree of corruption as seen by business people and country analysts and ranges between 10 (highly clean) and 0 (highly corrupt).

Latin America and the Caribbean with the rest of the world along several dimensions.

Note that Latin America's per capita income is quite high relative to other emerging markets, while its exports and outward foreign direct investment (FDI) are relatively small in comparative terms.

The challenge for Latin American firms is clear. If we compare the global competitiveness of Latin American firms with other emerging market firms (e.g. measured by the firms' foreign direct investment value), the results are quite unfavorable, as shown in Table 1.2.

The Latin American firms are few (7) on the list, and all from Mexico and Brazil. Almost all of the firms are in raw materials industries, such as oil, steel, and cement. The technological weakness of Latin American firms is evident from that picture alone. Further support for this claim of technology/innovation weakness is shown by many other indicators, including this measure of the number of science and engineering articles published by authors from various regions of the world (see Figure 1.1 below).[2]

Thus, on the basis of measured innovation in emerging markets, Latin America falls far behind Asian and Eastern European countries—not to speak of the gap with respect to industrialized countries. There is an enormous challenge here to find ways for Latin American firms to compete.

By looking at the experiences of some of the largest Latin American firms—such as Embraer in Brazil, Quiñenco (Luksic) in Chile, Techint in Argentina, Carso in Mexico, Cisneros in Venezuela, and Grupo Empresarial Antioqueño (GEA) in Colombia, along with a number of other firms in key industries—we are able to identify a set of factors that appear to have contributed to these firms' survival up to now. The analyses demonstrate factors that have led to these firms' successes but also some reasons why those factors may be insufficient to ensure the firms' continuing competitiveness in the twenty-first century. Our project aims to illuminate the key reasons why some Latin American firms succeed at home and abroad, while others seem unable to compete in foreign (and often domestic) markets, often ending up as takeover targets or just lingering on with substandard performance.

This set of analyses demonstrates the ways in which successful Latin American firms are responding to the new challenges of competition in the region and in the United States, Europe, and Asia. These challenges include the reduction of trade and investment barriers, which allows foreign multinationals to enter Latin American markets and to compete with the local firms on their own turf. The challenges also include technological innovation, such as the use of the internet and of high-powered computing capabilities, as well as biotechnology and even management technology, which allow tech-savvy foreign firms to have a competitive edge against 'tech-challenged' domestic firms in Latin America. The competitive threats are very clear; the viable responses for dealing with these threats are not so clear.

Table 1.2. World's 50 largest MNEs from emerging markets

Ranking by: Foreign assets	TNI[b]	II[c]	Corporation	Home economy	Industry[d]	Assets Foreign	Assets Total	Sales Foreign[e]	Sales Total	Employment Foreign	Employment Total	TNI[b] (Per cent)	No. of affiliates Foreign	No. of affiliates Total	II[c]
1	7	41	Hutchison Whampoa Limited	Hong Kong, China	Diversified	59,141	80,340	10,800	18,699	104,529	126,250	71.4	1900	2350	80.85
2	27	39	Singtel Ltd.	Singapore	Telecommunications	17,911f	21,668	4,672	68,848	8,642g	21,716	43.1	23	30	76.67
3	42	35	Petronas - Petroliam Nasional Bhdh	Malaysia	Petroleum expl./ref./distr.	16,114	53,457	8,981	25,661	3,625	30,634	25.7	167	234	71.37
4	26	48	Samsung Electronics Co., Ltd.	Republic of Korea	Electrical & electronic equipment	12,387	56,524	41,362	54,349	19,026g	55,397	44.1	80	89	89.89
5	12	36	Cemex S.A.	Mexico	Construction Materials	11,054	16,021	5,189	7,167	17,051g	25,965	69.0	35	48	72.92
6	23	37	América Móvil	Mexico	Telecommunications	8,676	13,348	3,107	7,649	8,403g	18,471	50.4	12	16	75.00
7	31	24	China Ocean Shipping (Group) Co.(f)	China	Transport and storage	8,457f	18,007	6,076i	9,163	4,600	64,586	40.1	22	56	39.29
8	46	7	Petroleo Brasileiro S.A. - Petrobras	Brazil	Petroleum expl./distr.	7,827	53,612	8,665	42,690	5,810	48,798	15.6	13	79	16.46
9	25	47	LG Electronics Inc.	Republic of Korea	Electrical & electronic equipment	7,118j	20,173	14,443j	29,846	36,268	63,951	46.8	134	151	88.74
10	16	34	Jardine Matheson Holdings Ltd	Hong Kong, China	Diversified	6,159k	8,949	5,540k	8,477	57,895g	110,000	62.3	16	23	69.57
11	10	14	Sappi Limited	South Africa	Paper	4,887f	6,203	3,287	4,299	9,454g	16,939	70.4	115	456	25.22
12	33	45	Sasol Limited	South Africa	Industrial chemicals	4,226	10,536	5,033	9,722	5,643	31,150	36.7	21	25	84.00
13	50	30	China National Petroleum Corporation	China	Petroleum expl./ref./distr.	4,060f	97,653	5,218	57,423	22,000	1,167,129	5.0	119	204	58.33
14	22	2	Capitaland Limited	Singapore	Real estate	3,936	10,316	1,449	2,252	5,033g	10,175	50.7	2	61	3.28
15	8	43	City Developments Limited	Singapore	Hotels	3,879j	7,329	703l	930	11,549f	13,703	70.9	228	275	82.91
16	4	49	Shangri-La Asia Limited	Hong Kong, China	Hotels and motels	3,672	4,743	436	542	12,619m	16,300	78.4	29	31	93.55
17	15	33	Citic Pacific Ltd.	Hong Kong, China	Diversified	3,574f	7,167	2,409	3,372	8,045	12,174	62.5	2	3	66.67
18	45	16	CLP Holdings	Hong Kong, China	Electricity, gas and water	3,564	9,780	298	3,639	488f	4,705	18.3	3	11	27.27
19	41	21	China State Construction Engineering Corp.	China	Construction	3,417	9,677	2,716	9,134	17,051	121,549	26.4	28	75	37.33
20	24	22	MTN Group Limited	South Africa	Telecommunications	3,374	4,819	1,308	3,595	2,601	6,063	49.8	6	16	37.50
21	2	26	Asia Food & Properties	Singapore	Food & beverages	3,331	3,537	1,232	1,273	32,295n	41,800	89.4	2	4	50.00

22	11	46	Flextronics International Ltd.	Singapore	Electrical & electronic equipment	3,206	5,634	4,674	8,340	80,091[g]	82,000	70.2	92	106	86.79
23	30	17	Companhia Vale do Rio Doce	Brazil	Mining & quarrying	3,155[f]	11,434	6,513	7,001	224	29,632	40.5	16	55	29.09
24	29	10	YTL Corp. Berhad	Malaysia	Utilities	2,878	6,248	489	1,060	1,518[g]	4,895	41.1	24	115	20.87
25	20	38	Hon Hai Precision Industries	Taiwan Province of China	Electrical & electronic equipment	2,597	6,032	4,038	10,793	78,575[n]	93,109	54.9	25	33	75.76
26	9	11	China Resources Enterprises[h]	Hong Kong, China	Petroleum expl./ref./distr.	2,364	4,034	2,542	4,450	76,364[g]	80,000	70.4	4	19	21.05
27	49	1	Oil & Natural Gas Corp.	India	Petroleum expl./ref./distr.	2,328	15,249	648[d]	9,370	4,515[n]	38,033	11.4	1	40	2.50
28	5	31	Neptune Orient Lines Ltd.	Singapore	Transport and storage	2,266	4,064	4,705	5,523	10,367[g]	11,322	77.5	6	10	60.00
29	37	4	United Microelectronics Corporation	Taiwan Province of China	Electrical & electronic equipment	2,251	10,302	1,891	2,781	1,045[g]	10,576	33.2	7	75	9.33
30	44	20	Singapore Airlines Limited	Singapore	Transport and storage	2,118	11,278	2,932	6,182	2,465[n]	29,734	24.8	4	11	36.36
31	32	19	Metalurgica Gerdau S.A.[h]	Brazil	Metal and metal products	2,056[f]	4,770	2,096	4,531	5,334	19,597	38.9	19	53	35.85
32	21	27	Barloworld Ltd	South Africa	Diversified	1,967	3,482	2,380	4,574	10,514	22,749	51.6	2	4	50.00
33	40	50	Quanta Computer Inc	Taiwan Province of China	Computer and related activities	1,934	4,593	737	8,657	5,772[n]	17,318	28.0	4	4	100.00
34	1	42	First Pacific Company Limited[h]	Hong Kong, China	Electrical & electronic equipment	1,910	2,074	2,162	2,162	46,926	46,951	97.3	28	34	82.35
35	43	40	Hyundai Motor Company	Republic of Korea	Motor vehicles	1,780[o]	20,334	12,008	20,935	4,825	51,837	25.1	8	10	80.00
36	36	18	Taiwan Semiconductor Manufacturing Co Ltd	Taiwan Province of China	Computer and related activities	1,539[f]	11,957	3,787[f]	6,067	4,442	16,997	33.8	4	12	33.33
37	17	3	Benq Corp.	Taiwan Province of China	Computer and related activities	1,497	2,778	1,838	3,774	11,100	14,911	59.0	1	14	7.14
38	48	23	China National Offshore Oil Corp.[h]	China	Petroleum and natural gas	1,467	14,479	1,877	6,507	1,000	24,000	14.4	41	105	39.05
39	19	28	Fraser & Neave Limited	Singapore	Food & beverages	1,395	4,536	1,232	2,140	9,951[g]	12,878	55.2	80	148	54.05
40	39	25	Swire Pacific Limited[h]	Hong Kong, China	Business services	1,387[f]	12,060	1,042	2,263	18,791	56,700	30.2	231	470	49.15
41	35	9	Keppel Corporation Limited	Singapore	Diversified	1,361	5,928	898	3,496	11,364	20,402	34.8	10	53	18.87
42	3	29	Yue Yuen Industrial Holdings Limited[h]	Hong Kong, China	Textile and leather	1,317	2,569	2,470	2,520	241,800	242,000	83.1	18	33	54.55
43	13	32	Acer Inc.	Taiwan Province of China	Electrical & electronic equipment	1,244	3,451	3,637	4,640	5,374[n]	6,368	66.3	9	14	64.29
44	28	8	Delta Electronics Inc.	Taiwan Province of China	Electronics	1,219	1,861	266	1,458	1,356[l]	3,238	41.9	13	78	16.67

(Cont.)

Table 1.2. (Continued)

Ranking by:						Assets		Sales[e]		Employment		TNI[b]	No. of affiliates		II[c]
Foreign assets	TNI[b]	II[c]	Corporation	Home economy	Industry[d]	Foreign	Total	Foreign[e]	Total	Foreign	Total	(Per cent)	Foreign	Total	
45	38	12	Grupo Bimbo SA De Cv	Mexico	Food	1,156	2,716	1,417	4,153	15,525	70,644	32.9	50	232	21.55
46	14	5	China Minmetals Corporation[h]	China	Metals mining and processing	1,150	5,352	1,933	1,168	973	33,000	63.3	22	162	13.58
47	6	44	The MUI Group	Malaysia	Hotels	1,135	1,840	499	621	9,022[n]	11,000	74.7	166	199	83.42
48	18	13	Gruma S.A. De C.V.	Mexico	Food & beverages	1,086	2,081	1,396	2,051	8,519	15,104	58.9	12	52	23.08
49	47	6	Hongkong Electric Holdings Limited	Hong Kong, China	Electricity, gas and water	1,074	7,305	258	1,449	295[m]	2,092	15.5	1	7	14.29
50	34	15	Nan Ya Plastics Corporation	Taiwan Province of China	Rubber and plastics	1,030	8,576	936	5,052	16,478[n]	22,027	35.1	3	11	27.27

Source: UNCTAD, World Investment Report 2005, pp. 270–1.

a All data are based on the companies' annual reports unless otherwise stated.

b TNI is calculated as the average of the following three ratios: foreign assets to total assets, foreign sales to total sales and foreign employment to total employment.

c II is calculated as the number of foreign affiliates divided by number of all affiliates (note: affiliates counted in this table refer to only majority-owned affiliates).

d Industry classification for companies follows the United States Standard Industrial Classification as used by the United States Securities and Exchange Commission (SEC).

e Foreign sales are based on the origin of the sales. In a number of cases companies reported sales only by destination.

f In a number of cases, companies reported only partial foreign assets. In these cases, the ratio of the partial foreign assets to the partial (total) assets was applied to total assets to calculate the total foreign assets.

g Foreign employment data are calculated by applying the share of foreign employment in total employment of the previous year to total employment of 2003.

h Data were obtained from the company in response to an UNCTAD survey.

i Foreign sales data are calculated by applying the share of foreign sales in total sales of the previous year to total sales of 2003.

j Foreign assets data are calculated by applying the share of foreign assets in total assets of the previous year to total assets of 2003.

k Data for outside Hong Kong (China) and mainland China.

l Data for outside Asia.

m Foreign employment data are calculated by applying the share of foreign assets in total assets to total employment.

n Foreign employment data are calculated by applying the average of the shares of foreign employment in total employment of all companies in the same industry (omitting the extremes) to total employment.

o Foreign assets are calculated by applying the share of foreign employment in total employment to the balance of total assets.

Thousands of articles

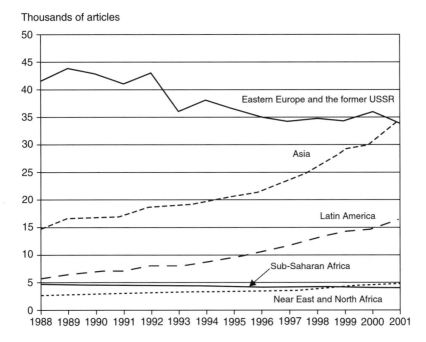

Figure 1.1. Science and engineering article output of emerging and developing countries by region: 1988–2001

Notes: Developing and emerging countries consist of countries classified as low or middle income by the World Bank. Article counts are assigned to the country on the basis of the institutional address(es) listed on the article. For articles with multiple-country authors, counts are apportioned to each country on the basis of the proportion of authors from each country. Articles with institutional authors in Hong Kong are included in China.

Source: National Science Foundation, *InfoBrief*, Science Resources Statistics, NSF 04-336, August 2004, p. 2.

As we discuss below, the contribution of our project is that it explores the responses of successful Latin American firms based on a four-level theoretical perspective that brings together previously dispersed perspectives on firm-competitiveness, industry environment, market institutional structure as well as international competitive engagements. The emerging picture throughout this book, and distilled in practical lessons in Chapter 16, will enable Latin American entrepreneurs and executives, academic analysts, and policymakers, to better devise future responses for dealing with the threats discussed above.

1.2. Perspectives on Competitive Strategy

A variety of perspectives have been developed in the post–World War II period, from Joe Bain's *Barriers to New Competition*[3] (1956) to the latest ideas in game theory. Several of them are discussed here, to suggest avenues of inquiry toward understanding the competitive advantages that may accrue to Latin American firms. The goal is not to present a broad survey of the competitive strategy literature, but rather to identify and put together lines of thought that we believe are helpful toward gaining a more integrated understanding of the competitiveness of Latin American firms.

After Bain, many conceptual frameworks have been developed to explain both domestic and international competitiveness. On the domestic side, or focussed on competitive strategy without emphasizing national boundaries, a wide range of ideas have been developed in recent years.

Michael Porter (1980, 1985) developed a theory of competitive advantage that emphasizes companies' internal capabilities relative to rivals at each step of the value chain. His well-known idea of competitive advantage is that superior performance comes from possession of proprietary skills and capabilities, which in turn may be available at any stage(s) of the production and distribution process. These capabilities can be used to enable the firm to establish a superior position relative to rivals based on cost leadership, differentiation, or focus on a particular market segment.

Birger Wernerfelt (1984), Jay Barney (1986) and others developed a resource-based view (RBV) of the firm. They focus on the kinds of attributes that can be classified as competitive resources, namely resources that are valuable and rare (e.g. proprietary technology; controlled distribution channels; relationships with clients and other key actors). These resources are seen as producing the potential for sustainable competitiveness if they are difficult to imitate, transfer, or substitute. Finally, if the possessor firm has the ability to exploit the resources and to leverage them in business activities, then the resource-based advantage exists.

Gary Hamel and C. K. Prahalad (1990) took a further step by arguing that it is more than a sum of resources that leads to competitiveness. They focus on the use of resources to develop the 'core competence of the corporation', the ability to realize business activities in a way superior to key competitors. The emphasis of this view is on implementation of a firm's strengths in business activities that are realized more successfully than those of competitors. While the emphases are different, the applications of the ideas in all three of these perspectives are complementary.

Building on this resource-based tradition, a number of authors coming from economics, political science, and sociology have analyzed the firm from an institutional perspective. They do not necessarily focus on competitiveness, but rather on reasons for the firm's existence, reactions of the firm to institutional constraints, and other issues. These views add to the ability to explain company behavior and success as well. For example, Oliver Williamson (1975) used economics-based concepts to create an institutional, transaction-cost, theory of the firm. In this view firms try to minimize transaction costs of contracting for production inputs and dealing with outputs, based on conditions of limited information, opportunism by market participants, and other market imperfections. The other disciplines similarly use elements of their models to apply to the institutional relationships between individuals in an organization, between companies and governments, and between companies. Our view in the chapters below comes largely from this institutional grounding.

Looking specifically at the international context, Stephen Hymer (1960) identified the characteristics of international firms that enabled them to compete in foreign markets through direct investment. He emphasized the monopolistic advantages that firms sought through utilizing their proprietary technology, lowering production costs by moving abroad, and borrowing in lower-cost capital markets. Raymond Vernon (1966) laid out an international product cycle, arguing that firms will be able to undertake exports and FDI based on technological and marketing advantages over domestic and foreign rivals. John Dunning (1977) presented an 'eclectic' view, pointing out that international firms gain competitive advantage through their own skills and capabilities, through location advantages of their facilities locations, and through internalizing business activities. One could argue that Dunning's view is a useful complement to Porter's theory (below), *post hoc*, extending it to the international context.

1.3. A Conceptual Overview

The basic elements reviewed above illustrate facets of the competitive game which so many Latin American firms have found so difficult to win. What is lacking there is a more integrated view of how each of the above particular parts influences the others. Such integration is our central proposition in this book. For example, one of the most striking aspects of the business environment in Latin America as contrasted with, for example, the United States, is that 'market institutions', that is organizations created to organize markets and exchanges, are often lacking, and therefore their absence is felt much more deeply. Even as US business literature in recent years has come increasingly to recognize the importance of institutions in driving company strategies and performance, the fact remains that similar institutions are either nonexistent or at best emerging in Latin America. As a result of such conditions, the resources and capabilities which would be deemed as irrelevant in 'institution-strong' markets are found to be vital for competition in Latin America. Moreover, as different sets of resources and capabilities become necessary in these contexts, the industry environment is shaped by a different collection of competitive threats and players, thus changing the way firms interact and aggressively pursue market positions at home and abroad. As

Latin American firms structure their competitive behavior departing from a different paradigm of institutions, competitive landscape, and need for idiosyncratic resources, their ability to compete with foreign firms in markets which do not resemble those of their home turf needs to be reevaluated.

In recognizing the above, we propose a 4-level perspective on Latin American companies to help understand their activities. This integrated view calls for examination of the ***company*** itself, the conditions in the ***industrial sector*** in which the firm operates, conditions at the ***national*** level, which includes the *institutional* perspective we discussed above, and finally conditions at the ***international*** level (in the sense that the country is involved in international relations with other countries and the companies are involved in international competition with firms from other countries.

Figure 1.2 portrays this multilevel environment in which the firm operates.

To illustrate our model, as shown in the Figure, Grupo Bimbo from Mexico competes in its home market against domestic and foreign firms such as Holsum and Wonder bread. At the same time, Bimbo competes against similar rivals in the United States and other Latin American countries. Bimbo's competitiveness—or lack of competitiveness—derives from the company's own internal characteristics (resources or competitive advantages). And Bimbo's competitiveness also depends on the competition in its industry, the bread business in particular. (How monopolistic or competitive is the sector; how technology-intensive is it; how large are barriers to entry by new, especially foreign, competitors?) Additionally, Bimbo's ability to compete depends on institutional conditions in Mexico. These include the level of government

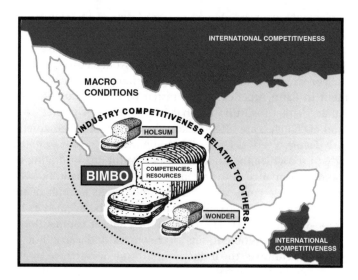

Figure 1.2. Bimbo in the 4-level institutional context

intervention in the functioning of the economy and the bread business in particular, the way in which labor relates to corporations, the characteristics of corporate governance, the level of infrastructure development (for delivering bread), and even macroeconomic conditions—whether the economy is in boom or recession. And finally, Bimbo may compete overseas against other bread companies, so competitive conditions there are relevant to evaluate Bimbo's strengths and weaknesses in that context as well.

This four-level approach enables the analysis to capture the institutional characteristics of countries such as Mexico, with different amounts of government protectionism, macroeconomic weakness, corruption, technology availability, labor flexibility, etc. relative to the United States or to other home countries of multinational firms. Clearly, Bimbo's competitive conditions in the home-country market, Mexico, are quite different from those conditions in Holsum's home market, the United States. This fact may give Bimbo an advantage over Holsum in other Latin American countries—or not. It may imply that Bimbo can better defend itself in Mexico against the US-based Holsum and Rainbo, as compared with a local rival or another bread company from Latin America.

As will become apparent in the chapters below, this four-level perspective helps to understand the competitive capabilities of Latin American firms, and it also helps to organize the various authors' viewpoints, which focus on different levels of these four.

1.4. Summary of Chapter Contents

The set of chapters is organized into four sections, beginning with several of the broader-scope analyses, and then following with groups of chapters that focus on individual firms, firms from specific home countries, and finally issues related to competing in emerging markets.

1.4.1. *Section I: Themes in Competitiveness of Latin American Firms*

The first chapter in this section, by **Robert Grosse**, establishes some terms of reference for the firms that play the greatest role in our analysis. These are large Latin America-based firms, often organized in the form of Grupos Económicos, or economic groups. These groups generally have narrowly held control, in the hands of one or two families, even though minority shares may be traded in domestic and foreign stock exchanges. The groups are quite heterogeneous, with some holding diverse portfolios of businesses (e.g. Carso and Luksic), while others have a single-industry focus (e.g. Cemex, Gerdau). This initial chapter describes some of the groups' characteristics and takes an initial step into exploring their competitive strengths.

Based on prior studies that have appeared in the literature, Grosse notes that the key competitive strengths of Latin American firms have been attributes such as dominance of local distribution channels, ability to use financial resources quickly to take advantage of opportunities in local markets, and ability to produce at low unit cost. These characteristics appear in Latin American firms that have succeeded in defending their home markets against domestic and foreign competitors. In competing overseas, the few large Latin American firms that have made significant headway in foreign markets tend to base their competitiveness on low-cost production, links to existing clients (ethnic or industrial clients), and superior technology in comparison with the relevant competitors in the foreign markets.

Based on new interview information, Grosse found that managers in large Latin American firms frequently claimed that their competitiveness was due to their ability to produce high-quality products and services; low production costs; relations with existing clients; and superior marketing capabilities. These advantages largely overlap with those noted previously, and they confirm these advantages in the early 2000s. The unanswered question is whether these advantages are sustainable in the open market competition that characterizes the internet age.

The second chapter in this section, by **Márcia Tavares**, takes a broad look at FDI activity by Latin American firms. Using data collected by the United Nations Center on Latin America and the Caribbean, she shows that half a dozen firms are among the largest emerging market multinationals (viz. Cemex, America Movil, Petrobras, CVRD, Gerdau, and Bimbo) when measured this way. The largest thirty-six foreign direct investors from Latin American countries include more than half in extractive industries such as oil and gas and mining, and only a couple in high-tech businesses (viz. Embraer airplanes and Bagó pharmaceuticals).

The interview data show that these large direct investors from Latin America tended to have advantages when competing in their domestic markets based on superior quality and better technology of their products and services. In international markets, the firms tended to have the advantages of experience operating in one emerging market that is transferable to another, as well as cultural/linguistic proximity to customers in other similar markets, and the same quality and technology advantages noted in the domestic context. This is quite similar to the findings of Grosse in the previous chapter, based on a sample of firms that are only slightly overlapping.

Tavares concludes that these advantages are not necessarily sustainable as Latin American firms move into industrialized countries, and as industrial-country MNEs move into the markets served by the Latin American firms. The benefits of cultural proximity that help companies in their efforts to expand abroad into culturally similar countries sometimes have paradoxically turned into barriers when the cultures were actually different from each other, even between two Latin countries. The key challenge to Latin American firms is to sustain their competitive advantages through finding and retaining skilled professionals and to avoid diminishing the advantages by overextending themselves overseas.

The third chapter in this section, by **Jorge Katz**, takes a macro view of Latin American firms' generation of competitive advantages. His analysis looks at the past few decades of historical experience, in which the Latin American countries have experienced a sequence of booms and busts, or in his terms 'cycles of creation and destruction'. These cycles have not been the Schumpeterian kind, which lead to [rapid] economic development, but rather they have produced major shocks to the productive systems of Latin American countries, making it difficult for firms to survive the turbulence.

Katz looks at the environmental conditions that surround business in the region, and he notes that the policy environment has not been conducive to sustained development because of the dramatic shifts from inward-looking, import substitution policies, to outward-looking export oriented policies, and with varying degrees of private-sector participation in the overall economy. He emphasizes the fact that the policies and the company strategies that have existed during the past twenty years have not produced anywhere near the degree of technological development seen in the emerging economies of Asia. Neither company strategies nor government policies have produced sustained competitive advantages in technology, though some firms such as Embraer have proven exceptions to the general rule.

His normative conclusion is that Latin American governments should inter-vene more extensively in industrial policy to promote investment in R&D, as the Asian newly industrializing countries such as Korea, Taiwan, Singapore, and even Malaysia, Indonesia, and Thailand have done. It is certainly true that the measures of innovation that are commonly collected show Latin American countries and companies lagging far behind their Triad counterparts, and also far behind their emerging market counterparts in Asia and Eastern Europe. He also recommends additional policies to strengthen National Innovation Systems, such as support for development of technology parks and incubators, government investment in the information infrastructure, and subsidies to R&D by small and medium-sized firms.

The final chapter in this section, by **Gerry McDermott**, focusses on a particular sector (wine) in Argentina, looking at the relationship between government and companies that have combined to upgrade the wine pro-duction and export activity in that country during the past decade. This chapter follows the Katz one in emphasizing the importance of government institutions, and it moves to the micro level in analyzing the wine producers in the Mendoza and San Juan provinces of Argentina. His chapter explores the process through which public sector and private firms have collaborated in this context, with much greater success in Mendoza than in San Juan.

McDermott's reasoning for the relative success of Mendoza province in generating internationally competitive wine producers was a collaboration among the producers and between the producers and the provincial government. Mendoza and San Juan had fairly similar preconditions as far as land, climate, skilled people, numbers of companies, and even local governments were concerned at the time of the divergence of their wine-growing fortunes in the 1990s. Mendoza's wineries were able to partner more successfully with government agencies by taking better advantage of the privatization of the state-owned local winery than San Juan had done a couple of years earlier. Mendoza province transformed the state-owned Giol winery into a federation of cooperatives (Fecovita) that collaborated with small and medium-sized grape farmers, rather than dealing only or largely with the major growers. This federation then offered training, credit, and other services to the members, which reinforced the build-up of production and quality of the wines.

McDermott details a range of differences in the strategies of the two provinces and their fortunes as wine-producing centers in Argentina. The primary driver of Mendoza province's success, according to McDermott, is the dense network of public/private organizations like Fecovita, in which community cooperation has been generated toward goals of economic development and civic stability. His analysis is a very compelling example of the use of a pair of comparable situations (Mendoza and San Juan Provinces) to try to illuminate the reasons for which the successful Mendoza wine experience has taken place. Starting from extremely similar conditions, the two provinces have experienced very different results, and McDermott's effort to explain why is an excellent example of precisely how 'institutions matter' in business.

1.4.2. Section II: Micro-Level Strategies of Firms in Specific Sectors

Héctor Ochoa studied the large Colombian group called the Grupo Empresarial Antioqueño, or GEA. This group is similar to a number of others that are discussed here, in that it possesses a diversified set of major companies in Colombia, including the largest chocolate company, Nacional de Chocolates; the largest cookie and cracker company, Noel; a major financial institution, Sudamericana de Seguros; the largest cement company, Cementos Argos; and several other large businesses. All three of the GEA's main businesses—foods, financial services, and cement—have operations overseas and are important multinational competitors in Latin America. The group is different from most of the others studied here in that ownership is widely held, though mostly by investors on the Medellin stock exchange.

Ochoa explains the sprawling conglomerate that is the GEA, along with a historical view of its development. The main part of the article looks specifically at the food division of GEA, which has recently consolidated thirty-three food companies, from crackers to meats to coffee, under the

Chocolates name. He explains the series of steps that have been taken in recent years to streamline the overall business and to manage this business. Notably, the new Chocolates division of GEA is managed as a holding company itself, allowing the individual food companies under it to operate relatively independently. Senior managers in this division explained that their domestic production network (especially in chocolates and crackers), along with their international distribution network (using what they call 'cordialsas', local food distribution companies in each country), have enabled Chocolates to compete successfully in over seventy countries worldwide. For five years a strategic alliance with Danone gave the company access to international distribution and marketing knowledge. The alliance was dismantled in 2005, and now Chocolates operates independently throughout Europe.

Ochoa paints a fascinating picture of this Colombian multinational that is increasingly competing at the global level with Nestlé, Kraft, and other food giants. The competitive strengths in Latin American countries that enable Chocolates to survive in competition with the US-based and European multinationals are the direct distribution system that they initiated in Colombia and extended abroad, plus the high-quality, frequently updated products that they produce in Colombia and abroad. In line with the editors' normative hopes for sustainable advantages in Latin American firms, the CEO of Chocolates said: '*We are not available for sale, we're here to purchase!*'

Michael Penfold examines the shrimp industry in Venezuela. This is a new industry, similar to salmon in Chile and tilapia in Mexico, which was established a few years ago to take advantage of world demand for the fish and the Venezuelan growing conditions that favor such a sector. It is an especially positive story in the context of Venezuela, which has suffered through disastrous management during the Chavez regime, while benefitting from high oil prices that mask the other growing weaknesses in the economy. The success of the shrimp industry in Venezuela, despite the much less supportive institutional environment in comparison with Chile or Mexico, is particularly striking.

The shrimp-growing business in Venezuela arose as an outgrowth of tuna fishing in the late 1980s, which alerted Venezuelan fishing firms to the opportunity to serve the US market for fish such as shrimp through a farming process rather than through simple wild shrimp harvesting. The major Venezuelan food company, Mavesa, made an initial investment in developing this business, but withdrew after a short experience with unsatisfactory results. However, the initial steps were followed by other, smaller Venezuelan firms entering the fresh-water shrimp-farming business in Lake Maracaibo in the western part of the country, and the salt-water shrimp farming business along the Caribbean coast in the eastern part of the country. Over the course of the 1990s, two clusters of shrimp-growing activity developed in these two distinct locations.

Penfold describes the development of the clusters, and the lack of government support along with rivalry among the firms, each of which failed to stimulate cooperation in the clusters. A case of a virus (Taura) that harmed shrimp, entering through imports of shrimp larvae, demonstrated that cooperation among the firms was important to the continuing success of the cluster—though Penfold expresses doubts about whether the firms have achieved the degree of cooperation needed in this regard (different from the more-cooperative experience in McDermott's study of Argentinian wine producers).

As in the case of Chilean salmon production, foreign fishing companies have entered the Venezuelan shrimp business, acquiring some of the local firms. Today the foreign firms hold more than half of the industry's production, and their participation is leading to greater integration of the Venezuelan firms and industry into the global shrimp business. Indeed this participation of nonlocal firms may be the stimulus that produces a sustainable competition/cooperation environment in the Venezuelan shrimp clusters.

The final chapter in this section, by **Joseph Ganitsky**, takes a different tack, looking at Latin American entrepreneurs and their successes overseas.

1.4.3. *Section III: Competitiveness of Firms from Selected Countries*

Eduardo Fracchia and **Luiz Mesquita** begin this section with a study of Argentinian business groups. They analyzed twenty-five large, diversified Argentinian groups in light of those firms' reactions to the process of economic opening in the 1990s. This chapter is based on a wealth of information collected in personal interviews at the firms, along with publicly available data from other sources. The authors assert that the firms were likely to react differently to the more open, competitive economic conditions of the 1990s, depending on the speed and breadth of reform impacts across particular economic segments, the path dependency of investments in resources and capabilities of given economic groups, as well as the decision-making style of particular firms. Rather than expecting a generalized move to focus on more competitive business lines, and to look to foreign markets (the standard solutions for dealing with the challenge of market opening), the authors anticipated diverse strategies depending on the industries in which the firms were concentrated and the decision-making styles of their leaders.

They found, among other things, that firms tended to react to the economic opening that began in 1990 by expanding their business dispersion, often taking advantage of privatizations of utilities and other state-owned firms. Then later in the decade, they tended to reduce the number of business sectors in which they operated, presumably as they took short-term profits on the privatized firms and/or refocussed where their competitive advantages were stronger. The net result was no significant change in overall business line diversification from the beginning to the end of the decade. As far as internationalization is concerned, the firms almost all expanded their overseas activities through the 1990s, citing reasons from economies of scale to the need to diversify their Argentina country risk.

Fracchia and Mesquita then divided the firms into four categories of greater foreign or domestic focus and greater or lesser product line diversification. They found that about half a dozen firms fell into each of the categories, and they then tried to explain why these strategic responses occurred. For example, firms with greater family control and dominant leadership were more likely to focus on the domestic market. These firms pursued greater product line diversification if they were involved more as suppliers to the government or to government-owned companies (especially when opportunities arose to buy privatizing firms). When such firms were in more open industries, subject to greater entry by foreign competitors, they tended to focus more narrowly on a smaller number of domestic product lines. The firms that were more internationally oriented tended to focus more narrowly if they were able to achieve process improvement and scale economies in their existing businesses; other firms entered more diverse foreign business activities if they were less dependent on scale economies and less dominated by family decisions of the leading family owners. Overall, this disaggregation of the economic groups into subcategories shed valuable additional light on the strategic decisions of such firms.

Thomaz Wood and Miguel Caldas analyze the situation of Brazil's companies during the past decade, facing the same kinds of turmoil as existed in Argentina, though with more notable examples of successful international firms (such as Embraer, Banco Itau, Votorantim, and Aracruz). They describe the recent economic history of Brazil, with the various inadequate stabilization plans that produced a very volatile environment for firms to operate in. They also note the relative uncompetitiveness of Brazil in a variety of country rankings in recent years.

From this national perspective they move to discuss some industry-specific factors that help to understand Brazilian companies' relatively low international competitiveness. And then they focus on firm-level characteristics that contribute to individual companies' abilities to compete against foreign rival firms. At the firm-specific level they lay out a model of sustainability, cost, attractiveness, and return (SCAR) which can help to identify individual companies' strengths and weaknesses versus foreign rivals. This model is applied in the cases of ten large Brazilian multinationals to demonstrate the usefulness of this perspective and the possible directions for the firms to improve their competitiveness.

The firms that are examined include the most commonly discussed global Brazilian firms such as Embraer (airplane manufacturer), Aracruz Celulosa (paper producer), and Banco Itau (financial institution), as well as less-known but highly competitive firms such as Natura (cosmetics), Promon (construction), and Sabó (auto parts). The authors conclude that the main challenge for Brazilian firms is to find internal configurations that not only assure domestic survival, but provide exceptional capabilities to overcome environmental limitations, and even enable them to survive in the international context.

Robert Grosse and Doug Thomas move the discussion to Mexico, looking at a group of fifteen of the largest economic groups in that country and their activities and performance over the past decade. They focussed on the strategies of these firms as explained by senior managers at each firm, accessed through an interview survey. The intent of the interviews was to illuminate the factors that top managers viewed as most compelling for their firms' competitiveness, along with weaknesses, challenges, and other concerns.

Grosse and Thomas found that the large Mexican groups saw their common competitive strengths as being in the areas of superior distribution capabilities in Mexico relative to domestic and foreign rivals and also lower-cost, higher-quality production of goods and services than their key rivals.

They found that differences existed in how the Tequila Crisis of 1994–5 affected the firms, with those having greater overseas diversification being hurt less than the more domestically focussed firms. Product diversification did not have a significant effect on the firms' ability to survive the crisis. The generalized economic opening of Mexico during the 1990s also affected firms differentially, with the more diversified firms achieving better financial performance than the more narrowly focussed firms. International diversification did not appear to improve financial performance across the period of economic opening. Overall, these authors found that traditional competitive advantages (distribution and efficient, high-quality production) were more important to the large Mexican firms' strategies than either type of diversification.

Andres Hatum and Andrew Pettigrew take the discussion back to Argentina, this time using two companies to explore how specific company characteristics enabled the firms to cope more flexibly with the turbulent 1990s. The firms are in the pharmaceuticals (Sidus) and edible oils (AGD) businesses. These firms were selected because they had demonstrated a high degree of flexibility in their responses to changing business and economic conditions in Argentina, and thus they may be useful examples of the kinds of characteristics that will enable firms to compete successfully in this environment. Through a series of interviews, the authors explored a wide range of organizational characteristics and responses to conditions during the 1990s.

The main proposition that the authors sought to examine was the idea that organizational flexibility would lead to greater ability to respond to changing conditions—in competition, in technology, in regulation, and in the macroeconomic environment. They were able to identify five areas in which the two firms distinguished themselves relative to competitors. Both firms demonstrated a relatively low level of 'industry embeddedness', meaning that they were not constrained to follow the pack in business practices and management styles. Each one challenged the existing orthodoxy in its sector, by bringing in new competitive methods (e.g. acquisition of other firms; entry into generic drugs) and by learning from examples in other industries and countries. Both firms had a strong organizational identity, which gave them stability internally as a base to operate from in an extremely unstable external environment. And both firms used informal methods of environmental scanning, rather than being tied down to traditional methods such as benchmarking with competitors. Both firms also showed managerial diversity at the top level. This feature helped the companies to bring new ideas and achieve cognitive diversity. Finally, both firms scanned the environment frequently, therefore, they were able to anticipate industry changes and take advantage of new opportunities. That is, they looked further into the value chain of their industries for new opportunities upstream and downstream and in related businesses. These five organizational characteristics appeared to be significant factors underlying the superior flexibility of Sidus and AGD relative to competitors.

1.4.4. *Section IV: Competing in Emerging Markets*

This final section of the book broadens the perspective to consider firms competing in emerging markets both in and outside of Latin America. Two chapters consider firms competing in Asia, while one looks particularly at serving low-income customers, and the final one looks particularly at the financial markets as contributing to or hindering competitiveness of firms from Latin America. Each of these analyses provides additional perspective on the ability of Latin American firms to compete at home and abroad.

Andrea Goldstein and Omar Toulan use two Latin American firms, Embraer and Techint, to demonstrate their abilities to compete in the most dynamic market of the new century, China. This chapter, and the one by Cho and Chang on Korean multinationals, expand the geographic scope of our analysis to focus specifically on Asian emerging markets. The current authors explore the attempts by two Latin American multinationals to enter the Chinese market. Their article describes the prior development of each company in Argentina and elsewhere, detailing organizational structure and competitive strengths and weaknesses. They then analyze each company's entry into production in China, which in both cases has been slow and complicated.

Embraer, the formerly state-owned manufacturer of small commercial aircraft for regional use, really only began its concerted effort to penetrate the Chinese market in the year 2000, setting up a sales office in Biejing. Embraer found that the Chinese government resisted its applications for permission to sell airplanes in China until Embraer would guarantee to incorporate locally produced content. In 2001, the company proceeded to contract with the China Aviation Supplies Import and Export Corporation to buy parts and warehouse them for Embraer in China. This step was followed by the decision in 2002 to establish a final assembly line for Embraer regional jets in China, through a joint venture with a government-owned company. Thus, Embraer followed the model of many US and other non-Chinese companies of battling for permission to operate locally and eventually giving in to accept a joint-venture partner and to produce some of the product locally in China. The time line for these steps, essentially three years, was extremely rapid in comparison with the experiences of other non-Chinese companies, and it may reflect the fact that Embraer is used to dealing with emerging market governments and conditions, and thus was able to react quicker and more successfully than many other firms. (Bombardier, Embraer's main competitor worldwide, had not been able to enter the Chinese market by 2005.)

Techint has two main divisions: Tenaris, which makes steel pipe, especially for oil pipelines; and Ternium, which makes steel sheet. The flat steel business has proven much more difficult globally, with many regional and local competitors as well as multinationals providing Techint with rivals to overcome—and Techint has limited its activities largely to the Americas in this division. In steel pipe production and pipeline construction, Tenaris has found greater ability to enter foreign markets elsewhere, especially where oil is being produced and shipped. As early as 1976, Tenaris had export sales to China of steel pipe for constructing oil pipelines. By the early 2000s, Tenaris had local sales representatives permanently in China, and was one of the leading foreign suppliers of steel pipe in the country. Tenaris was negotiating to participate in major construction projects with several potential Chinese partners, but without a major success by 2005. The firm also has been selling consulting services to Chinese construction companies and pipeline developers.

These two examples show how Latin American companies have been able to enter the Chinese market, probably no less successfully than their US and European counterparts. The successes of Embraer and Techint have not been total, but both companies have found that their Latin American roots have provided some benefits—in dealing with an emerging market government and in facing demands for local production presence, as occurs in Latin America. In both cases, the companies are relatively high-tech, and not suppliers of raw materials or slightly processed goods. This fact points to the positive conclusion that some Latin American firms can compete in this type of business and to the negative conclusion that most Latin American multinationals are not in such businesses, and thus may not be able to benefit from operating in China as Embraer and Techint.

Dong-Sung Cho and Keum-Young Chang use the example of a joint venture in Korea to offer lessons that may be useful to Latin American firms in building sustainable competitive advantages at home and abroad. The joint venture is Yuhan–Kimberly, joining US-based Kimberly Clark with a Korean firm in producing tissue, diapers, paper towels, sanitary pads, and other paper products for local sales. This firm in the past decade has become the most-admired company in Korea, with outstanding evaluations by consumers and employees alike. Cho and Chang show the reasons why this firm has achieved such success, and suggest that this model would apply to Latin American firms as well. The reasons are largely based in 'people management', built on a corporate culture that encourages creativity and autonomy, innovation and challenge, encouraging people-focussed management and life-long learning in the firm.

They use Cho's SER-M model, which explains competitive advantages based on Subject (or leadership), Environment, Resources, and then the Mechanism through which these factors interact. They argue that the leadership (S) of CEO Kook-Hyun Moon, the environment (E) in Korea following the economic crisis of 1997, and the resources (R) of Yuhan–Kimberly—particularly the firm's reputation for people management and ethical behavior—have been combined under very innovative management techniques (IMT) (the Mechanism), to produce outstanding performance. The chapter then provides a detailed discussion of the ways in which innovative management has been used to generate the superior results that Yuhan–Kimberly has obtained during the past half-decade.

Cho and Chang focus mainly on the Mechanism that Yuhan–Kimberly has used to take advantage of the SER conditions that it has faced in the past decade. They point to a wide range of people-management techniques and programs used by the joint venture to motivate people and to provide excellent quality and service to customers. For example, Yuhan–Kimberly set up an innovative training program, allowing employees to take time off to pursue learning activities and providing up to 183 hours per employee of training per year. They took from Kimberly-Clark a program for improving efficiency in production called the high performance work system (HPWS). As a heavy user of wood for its products, the firm launched a 'Keep Korea Green' campaign, which employs high-school students during the summer to plant trees around the country. So far, 150 million trees have been planted, and Yuhan–Kimberly has gained a very positive image in the community. In all, the people-management and environmental protection steps that this company has undertaken appear to be the bases on which market-leading respect and employee satisfaction have been built—along with sustained profitability as well. These are certainly steps that Latin American firms can follow, and they may prove to be very valuable lessons in that context.

John Edmunds varies the approach to our effort to identify character-istics of Latin American firms that may enable them to compete against foreign multinationals at home and abroad by focussing on the environment rather than on the firm. While our overall effort has been to emphasize the capabilities of firms to compete, rather than countries, it is useful nonetheless to consider some of the country characteristics that help or hurt firms in being competitive. Gerry McDermott similarly looked at country (actually province) conditions relating companies and government, to see how firms in that context were able to develop international competitiveness. John Edmunds looks at national financial systems, argues that they tend to hold Latin American firms back, and offers some suggestions about how to deal with this limiting factor.

The key features of Latin American financial markets that make them hindrances to firms rather than positive supportive infrastructure are that: (*a*) the markets are small on a global scale; (*b*) there are frequent bouts of illiquidity even in the largest markets (in Mexico and Brazil); (*c*) the markets are too focussed on financing just traditional production, exports, and imports, without offering innovative financing and especially without offering adequate equity financing. Additionally, Edmunds asserts that Latin American financial markets are too focussed on financing traditional commodity production and export, without serving the needs of diversified firms and Latin American multinationals. He explains how each of these features of the financial markets in Latin American countries has contributed to constrain local firms' ability to grow due to inadequate financial resources.

The solution to these problems, of course, is to improve financial systems in the region. This is not a foolish or unrealistic suggestion; what is needed are specific policy elements and mechanisms to get them into force. Building local equity markets is much more feasible in the early 2000s, now that national pension fund systems have been privatized in many countries of the region, and long-term investors are thus available to absorb issues of bonds and shares of stock. The small size of national capital markets is being resolved by economic opening, which permits the world's leading banks to lend more efficiently to Latin American borrowers. As well, the arrival of banks such as Santander, BBVA, and Citibank, with major local operations in Mexico, Argentina, Colombia, Chile, and elsewhere in the region means that financial resources are not lacking any more—though credit-worthy borrowers sometimes are.

Guillermo D'Andrea concludes this section with a chapter on 'serving the bottom of the pyramid', that is, on serving low-income customers in emerging markets, where they constitute the vast majority of potential customers. C. K. Prahalad (2004) argued that multinational firms should be considering ways to serve the more than four billion people who fall into this category worldwide. D'Andrea takes the logic to local firms in emerging markets as well, with an examination of the opportunities for Latin American firms in this segment of the market. He uses a survey of low-income consumers in six Latin American countries: Argentina, Brazil, Chile, Colombia, Costa Rica, and Mexico, to profile their purchasing habits and preferences.

Based on his demonstration that the consumers in Latin American countries are not far outside of the scope of customers targeted by companies in the 'formal', above-ground economy, D'Andrea then goes on to describe the opportunities that exist for firms to serve Latin America's poor market segments. Steps such as selling in small bodegas, providing product quantities less than those sold in supermarkets, focussing on low costs/prices, and other marketing ideas illustrate the ways in which firms (from Latin America and multinationals from outside the region) can penetrate this market segment.

Finally, he provides a number of examples of Latin American companies that have found success in gaining access to the bottom of the pyramid (BOP) market segments, typically through strategies that use the steps just mentioned (low prices and small quantities in particular). Cemex sells small, very inexpensive bags of cement for do-it-yourself builders across Mexico. Kola Real from Peru sells a cola priced well below Coke and Pepsi, distributed largely through small, often informal distributors, and has gained leading market share in the poorer income segments in Peru and significant market share elsewhere in Latin America. Jabon La Corona has taken the leading market share for soap in Mexico—ahead of Procter and Gamble, Colgate, and Unilever—with a strategy of selling individual, small soap bars in a wide variety of local distribution formats (i.e. outside of supermarkets). Bodegas Lopez in Argentina has developed two sets of product lines for its wines: one for high-income consumers with upper-market pricing and quality, and a second line for low-income consumers, with low prices and table-wine quality. In all, the examples clearly illustrate the ability of Latin American firms to successfully target the BOP in their own countries. One wonders how transferable these strategies are to other emerging markets around the world.

1.5. Conclusions

These individual analyses clearly emphasize the crucial role of institutions and market idiosyncrasies in shaping the competitive landscape in Latin America, and in driving the competitiveness of Latin American companies. From probably the most institution-focussed analysis by McDermott, showing key links between local government and successful development of the wine sector in Mendoza, Argentina, to the competitive-advantage focussed analyses of GEA and Embraer and Techint—the fact is clear that successful Latin American firms have first successfully competed in their home markets, with strong government intervention, weak infrastructure, and other differences from the United States and Western Europe, before entering into international competition. Their ability to deal with these structural conditions does appear to be a core competency for many of these firms, and it is often transferable to other markets.

Overall, the analyses presented here point to a set of competitive advantages that appear to be shared by many of the large and successful Latin American firms, with a few cases of unusual advantages that may be more difficult to transfer to other companies and contexts. The clear strengths that enable Latin American firms to compete successfully against domestic and foreign rivals in their home countries include:

- High-quality products and services
- Low-cost production
- Domination of distribution channels
- Ability to deal successfully with the government and other institutions.

These strengths were found in companies from Mexico to Argentina, in industries from consumer products to mining to services, in domestic competition. The first two items are not different from what has been found in many industrial countries, while the last two items tend to be more associated with conditions in emerging markets.

To compete in international markets, the Latin American companies offered fewer examples of success. As well, the list of common characteristics was shorter:

- High-quality products and services
- Low-cost production
- Existing relationships with foreign clients and suppliers.

Additional features that sometimes appeared, and which might be particular to emerging market (Latin American) firms included:

- Ability to form and manage strategic alliances with local partners
- Ability to deal with greater levels of risk and volatility in emerging markets than in industrial countries.

These features were particularly useful in the firms' ability to compete in other emerging markets, both in Latin America and elsewhere in the world.

Notes

1. The impact of European firms as models for Latin American firms has grown dramatically in the last decade, especially with the entry of the Spanish banks, telephone company, and energy companies, as well as other European firms.
2. Several additional measures are available showing Latin American countries to be far behind their emerging-market counterparts in Asia and Eastern Europe in scientific/innovative activity. For example, patent data for patents registered with the US Office of Patents and Trademarks shows that Latin American countries lag behind China and India by far, and the region overall is far behind Asia and Eastern Europe

in patent registry. See http://www.uspto.gov/web/offices/ac/ido/oeip/taf/cst_all.pdf. Also, data from the National Science Foundation concerning US companies overseas activities in R&D show that Latin American employment and spending by US affiliates on R&D are far behind that in other regions in absolute and in percentage terms. See National Science Foundation, 'Industrial R&D Employment in the United States and in US Multinational Corporations.' *InfoBrief* # NSF 05–302. December 2004.

3. Bain, Joe. (1956). *Barriers to New Competition*. Boston (MA): Harvard University Press.

References

Bain, J. S. (1956). *Barriers to New Competition*. Boston, MA: Harvard University Press.

Barney, J. B. (1986). 'Types of Competition and the Theory of Strategy: Toward an Integrative Framework', *Academy of Management Review*, 11: 791–800.

Dunning, J. (1977). 'Trade, Location of Economic Activity and the MNE: A Search for an Eclectic Approach', in Bevlil Ohlin (ed.) *The International Allocation of Economic Activity*. New York: Holmers & Meier, 395–418.

Grosse, R. (2003). 'The Challenges of Globalization for Emerging Market Firms', *Latin American Business Review*, 4(4): 1–21.

Hamel, G. and Prahalad, C. K. (May–June 1990). 'The Core Competence of the Corporation,' *Harvard Business Review*, 68(3): 79–93.

Hymer, S. H. (1960). *The International Operations of National Firms: A Study of Direct Foreign Investment*. Ph.D. Dissertation, published posthumously. The MIT Press, 1976. Cambridge, MA.

Porter, M. (1980). *Competitive Strategy*. Boston, MA: The Free Press.

—— (1985). *Competitive Advantage*. Boston, MA: The Free Press.

Prahalad, C. K. (2004). *The Fortune at the Bottom of the Pyramid*. Philadelphia, PA Wharton School Publishing.

Vernon, R. (May 1966)' International Trade and International Investment in the Product Cycle', *Quarterly Journal of Economics*, 190–207.

Wells, L. T. (1983). *Third World Multinationals*. Cambridge, MA: MIT Press.

Wernerfelt, B. (1984). A Resource-Based View of the Firm. *Strategic Management Journal*, 5: 171–80.

Williamson, O. (1975). *Markets and Hierarchies*. New York: Free Press.

Part I

Themes in the Competitiveness of Latin American Firms

2

The Role of Economic Groups in Latin America

Robert Grosse

2.1. Introduction

Economic groups (grupos económicos)—groups of companies operating under closely related management and with controlling ownership in the hands of a small number of investors (typically one or two families)[1]—have long been the leading firms in Latin America. Their names are well-known in their own countries, but often unknown elsewhere. The largest of them, such as Grupo Carso from Mexico and Grupo Cisneros from Venezuela, are known through the region, and some, such as Cemex and Embraer[2] are even known worldwide. The groups have not been a stable set, but have changed over the years as internal crises and external events have pushed some of them out of existence and others into being acquired by foreign investors. Nevertheless, the business group continues to be the leading form of large, Latin American corporate organization.

In fact, the Grupos are not the only large Latin American companies. Government-owned enterprises, especially oil companies and public utilities, have also been well-known, major competitors in the region for many years. Other than the oil companies, however, these state-owned firms have largely been privatized, wholly or partially, in the past decade. Today most of the electric power companies and telephone companies are in private-sector hands—often those of the Grupos that are our focus.

A striking feature of the Grupos is that they are a persistent feature of the competitive landscape outside of the United States and the United Kingdom, but almost unknown in those two leading markets.[3] Similar family-based, or closely held, companies are leaders in most emerging markets from Korea (the 'chaebols') to India to Turkey to Indonesia. Even in France, Spain, Germany,[4] and Australia, the largest firms tend to be controlled by a limited group of shareholders, either families or institutions such as banks.[5] It remains to be seen just how viable this grupo model is in the new century, and particularly to see whether the Latin American firms are likely to be able to compete against foreign and domestic rivals.

An additional feature of many of the family-based groups is that they often are widely diversified in their business activities. Diversification into unrelated businesses (conglomerate diversification) is another aspect of many Latin American large firms that differs quite strikingly from the US model. Again, this is less different from the realities in Asia, Eastern Europe, and other emerging markets. The conglomerate form of enterprise for very large firms seems to be the global rule (i.e. it is common in most countries) rather than the exception.[6] Our interest is in both diversified and more focussed groups, and when talking about grupos, the discussion means closely held large firms that may or may not be widely diversified.

2.2. The Reality: Leading Firms from Latin America are Grupos Económicos

According to the annual survey of firms in Latin America by *América Economía* magazine, the largest fifty companies in 2004 can be seen in Table 2.1.

Table 2.1. The largest firms in Latin America, 2004

No.	Company name	Nationality	Firm type	Main business	Sales ($billion)
1	Petroleos Mexicanos (Pemex)	Mex.	SOE	Oil	69,834.0
2	PDVSA	Ven	SOE	Oil	63,200.0
3	Petrobras	Brasil	SOE	Oil	40,763.1
4	Pemex Refinacion	Mex.	SOE	Oil	28,350.8
5	Comision Federal de Electricidad (CFE)	Mex.	SOE	Electricity	14,641.6
6	Wal-Mart de Mexico	Mex.	MNE	Retail sales	12,597.9
7	Telefonos de Mexico (Telmex)	Mex.	grupo	Telecom	12,449.2
8	America Movil	Mex.	grupo	Telecom	12,085.5
9	General Motors	Mex.	MNE	Autos	22,068.0
10	Petrobras Distribuidora	Brasil	SOE	Oil	11,493.3
11	Pemex Gas y Petroquimica Basica	Mex.	SOE	Oil & Gas	10,407.1
12	Vale do Rio Doce (CVRD)	Brasil	grupo	Mining	10,376.8
13	DaimlerChrysler	Mex.	MNE	Autos	9,573.6
14	Fomento Economico Mexicano (FEMSA)	Mex.	grupo	Beverages	8,425.8
15	Empresas Petroleo Ipiranga	Brasil	grupo	Oil	8,393.8
16	Odebrecht	Brasil	grupo	Conglom.	8,206.8
17	Codelco	Chile	SOE	Mining	8,203.7
18	Cemex	Mex.	grupo	Cement	8,142.4
19	Bunge Brasil	Brasil	grupo	Agriculture	8,105.6

(Cont.)

Table 2.1. *(Continued)*

No.	Company name	Nationality	Firm type	Main business	Sales ($billion)
20	Eletrobras	Brasil	SOE	Electricity	7,501.8
21	Gerdau	Brasil	grupo	Steel	7,382.9
22	Distribuidora de Productors de Petroleo Ipiranga	Brasil	grupo	Oil	7,200.0
23	Telefonica	Brasil	MNE	Telecom	7,133.2
24	YPF	Arg.	MNE	Oil	6,665.9
25	Org. Techint	Arg.	grupo	Construction	6,421.0
26	Telcel	Mex.	grupo	Telecom	6,351.2
27	Grupo Carso	Mex.	grupo	Conglom.	6,253.3
28	Cia. Brasileira de Petroleo Ipiranga	Brasil	grupo	Oil	6,121.3
29	General Motors	Brasil	MNE	Autos	5,990.0
30	Telemar Participacoes	Brasil	grupo	Telecom	5,968.1
31	Telemar Norte Leste	Brasil	grupo	Telecom	5,882.3
32	Grupo Votorantim	Brasil	grupo	Conglom.	5,809.2
33	Empresas Copec	Chile	grupo	Conglom.	5,718.9
34	Bunge Alimentos	Brasil	grupo	Agriculture	5,679.2
35	Volkswagen	Mex.	MNE	Autos	5,542.6
36	Ecopetrol	Col	SOE	Oil	5,440.0
37	Volkswagen	Brasil	MNE	Autos	5,284.1
38	Grupo Alfa	Mex.	grupo	Conglom.	5,274.6
39	Shell	Brasil	MNE	Gas	5,118.3
40	Telesp	Brasil	MNE	Telecom	5,013.8
41	Enersis	Chile	MNE	Electricity	4,863.4
42	Cargill	Brasil	MNE	Agriculture	4,853.8
43	Hewlett-Packard	Mex.	MNE	Computers	4,850.0
44	Nissan Mexicana	Mex.	MNE	Autos	4,760.0
45	Grupo Pao de Acucar, CBD	Brasil	grupo	Retail sales	4,733.7
46	ENAP	Chile	SOE	Oil	4,704.4
47	Grupo Bimbo	Mex.	grupo	Food, bread	4,623.1
48	Usiminas	Brasil	grupo	Steel	4,607.4
49	Braskem	Brasil	grupo	Petrochem	4,593.1
50	Carrefour	Brasil	MNE	Retail sales	4,562.2

Source: America Economia (July 15, 2005), p. 84.

These firms include:

- Eleven state-owned enterprises (SOE), mainly oil companies
- Fifteen foreign multinational firms (MNE), based mostly in the United States
- Twenty-four grupos económicos, locally based firms with typically one or two controlling shareholders.

So, if we ignore the foreign-owned firms, the majority of the largest Latin American-owned firms are Grupos, and also a strong plurality of the firms are SOE. If we additionally ignore the oil sector, then almost all of the firms are Grupos, covering a wide range of industries. And if we move further down the list of the largest 500 firms in Latin America (not shown in

Table 2.1), they are fairly evenly split between local Grupos and foreign MNE affiliates.

This evidence demonstrates the prevalence of business groups as the leading firms in Latin America (again, ignoring affiliates of foreign multinational firms). It may appear wildly different from business conditions in other countries, but one quickly realizes that the exceptions are the United States and the United Kingdom, and that firms in most countries of Europe, Asia, and other parts of the world also tend to be dominated by local, often family-based groups (Faccio and Lang 2001; Morck, Wolfenzon, and Yeung 2005). The reasons for this difference are many, but one clear feature of the United States and the United Kingdom is the advanced development of the stock market, in which company ownership is shared by often thousands or millions of investors.[7] The lack of strong stock markets in most countries, related weak protection of minority shareholders' rights (La Porta, Lopez-de-silanes, and Schleifer 1999) where stock markets do exist, and various other factors, especially cultural ones, lead to the predominance of business groups as leaders in the markets of most countries today and in the past.

For brief comparison, note the ownership of large publicly traded firms around the world, as measured by Morck, Wolfenzon, and Yeung (2005). Table 2A.1 in the appendix to this chapter shows the striking similarity of these other countries to the Latin American examples presented above. Countries from Switzerland to Singapore demonstrate a high degree of family ownership of major publicly traded companies, similar to our findings in Latin America.

A key question that remains, based on this reality, is: why aren't Latin American firms more extensively represented on the list of the world's largest firms? If firms from these other countries can compete in size with the American and British multinationals, why are Latin American firms so underrepresented on that list (i.e. the *Fortune* Global 500) (Table 2.2) With a population of more than 550 million people, Latin America and the Caribbean as a region is larger than the United States and Canada, and also larger than the European Union. In terms of GDP, the region had combined income of approximately two trillion dollars in 2004. This is approximately one-sixth of the size of the US economy or the European Union economy. This comparison of productive size might imply that Latin America should have about 1/6 as many companies on the global list of large firms in comparison with the United States or the European Union. In fact, in the *Fortune* Global 500, Latin America has five members, far less than proportional to the region's economic size. This question of the disproportionately small number of Latin American firms among the global leaders is explored in more detail below.

Table 2.2. Latin American firms in the *Fortune* Global 500

Company	Ranking in Global 500	Revenues (US$ million)
Pemex (Mexico)	51	63,691
Petrobras (Brazil)	125	36,988
Banco Bradesco (Brazil)	376	15,899
Banco do Brasil (Brazil)	419	14,769
CFE (Mexico)	426	14,465

Source: *Fortune* magazine, July 25, 2005.

2.2.1. Why are the Firms Organized as Grupos?

Latin American large and successful firms tend to be organized as business groups for a variety of reasons. In recent years, these have been identified by Grosse, Guillen, Khanna, and Palepu, and others as:

- To overcome weak local capital markets, that favor internal financing for expansion (Khanna and Palepu 1997)
- To take advantage of knowledge of local market conditions, which gives local firms an ability to identify and pursue opportunities in other sectors locally (Guillen 2000; Grosse 2004)
- To take advantage of low cost conditions, enabling local firms to operate more profitably than foreign entrants, assuming some degree of barriers to foreign entry (Peres 1998; Guillen 2000)
- To internalize market failure, as entrepreneurs seek to overcome the difficulties of obtaining capital, labor, raw materials, components, and technology (Khanna and Palepu 1997)
- Part of the interaction between business and government. Other analysts have discussed the impacts of social and political conditions that favor local firms versus foreign ones, and the extension of some local firms into new business activities (Amsden 1989).

The first logic listed above, to **overcome weak local capital markets**, has been noted for many years (e.g. Leff 1978). The fact that financing in emerging markets generally comes from an entrepreneur's own family wealth and/or from short-term commercial bank loans makes it very difficult to support the growth of large firms. If a business group can operate its own internal capital market, sharing available funds among member companies in the group, then greater long-term commitment of funds is possible. This feature alone could explain much of the prevalence of Grupos in emerging markets.

The issue is perhaps not as clear as this brief commentary makes it appear. When Grupos set up commercial banks or other financial institutions, the financial firms are generally limited by banking laws as to how much lending they can do to related firms. Funding of related firms cannot be simply through the group bank lending to other members of the same group. The sharing of available funds among group members may take place through investments by members of the group in each other, in addition to some [limited] direct lending to members by the 'captive' financial institution. The key point is that financial resources can be obtained within the group, without resorting to outside financial markets, which traditionally have not been willing or able to lend for the long-term needs of their clients, and also may be limited in the amounts they can lend as the borrowing firms get larger.

The second source of emerging market companies' competitiveness arises from the firms' **greater knowledge and understanding of local market (and nonmarket) conditions** in their home country. Thus, when local conditions offer opportunities for investing in, say, a temporarily weakened firm, the Grupo that recognizes this situation rapidly and can move funds to take advantage of the investment opportunity quickly, will be able to build a portfolio of businesses on this basis. The Luksic group in Chile even identifies its strategy in this way: they look for opportunities to 'buy low and sell high', profiting from the ability to identify these opportunities and exploit them.[8] This advantage is especially relevant for the diversified (conglomerate) groups.

A third source of competitiveness for emerging market firms is their general **ability to produce at low cost**. Because of lower labor costs than in industrial countries, the emerging markets can produce some products, especially commodities, at lower cost. This advantage has been seen to extend to more and more production, from computer chips (Intel in Costa Rica and China) to software (the development of Bangalore in India as a global software development hub) to assembly of a wide range of manufactured goods (maquila production of autos, electronics, and clothing in Mexico). Of course, foreign multinationals may take advantage of the low local costs to achieve the same advantage, but in general the emerging market firms start from this favorable position (Garrido and Peres 1998; Grosse 2004).

Khanna and Palepu (1999) identified **internalizing market failure** as another source of competitiveness in local competition for the large grupos. This idea is somewhat related to the superior knowledge that emerging market firms may have of local conditions in comparison with their foreign rivals—and it focusses on the point that large grupos may have the financial wherewithal to take advantage of underpriced acquisition opportunities in an imperfect capital market. Unquestionably, the market for corporate control in Latin American countries is not particularly open or transparent, so 'inside information', or simply better knowledge may be available about local firms for some companies (such as local grupos) than others (smaller firms and foreign firms).

A final point that helps explain why large Latin American firms are often organized as grupos is that ***monopoly in one business may favor expansion into others***. That is, a monopoly or heavily dominant position in one business may generate profits sufficient to invest in other activities when the dominant sector is saturated. If local conditions permit the monopoly to operate without government sanctions or intervention, then the possessor of this favorable situation can take advantage of it by utilizing funds generated there to enter other businesses and compete using this presumably low-cost, low-risk funding source. This advantage clearly favors the development of diversified groups.

2.2.2. *Key Competitive Advantages of Groups in Latin America*

Taking a slightly different perspective from the one above, in which reasons for grupos' existence were identified, the key competitive advantages that characterize many of the large groups may be explored as well. Based on previous studies of large Latin American firms, key competitive advantages have been shown to include those in Table 2.3.

These competitive advantages are divided into those that apply primarily in the domestic context—competing against local rival firms and foreign multinationals in the home country—and those advantages that apply in the overseas context, competing against multinationals and local firms in their own countries and in third countries. The key advantages have migrated over time. They used to be based on conditions in fairly isolated, protectionist economies in the post–World War II period, such as government protection and knowledge of the local market's idiosyncrasies. They have shifted to those based on conditions in relatively open, globalized economies, such as superior product quality and more extensive distribution channels. In any event, our interest in the present analysis is to explore the advantages that have led to competitiveness of selected major groups in the region in the past decade or so.

2.2.3. *Examples of Major Groups in Latin America*

The **Luksic** Group has been one of the two or three largest business groups in Chile for almost three decades. The group began in the copper business, with Andrónico Luksic's purchase of small mining areas in Antofagasta in 1954. While that business has remained in the Luksic portfolio for decades, it did not become the major player that it is today until the purchase of the

Table 2.3. Key competitive advantages

Competitive advantage	Description	Examples	Sources
Key advantages in domestic competition			
Government protection	Tariffs against imports; subsidies; 'buy local' policies; local ownership rules	Electric power in Mexico;	Amsden
Access to local distribution channels	Preferential access to local physical distribution or promotional vehicles	YPF; GEA	Dawar & Frost; Grosse
Membership in a conglomerate economic group	Conglomerate spread of activities	Grupo Luksic; Grupo Carso; GEA; Grupo Cisneros	Peres
Internal capital market	Internal financing availability		Khanna & Palepu
Superior quality products/services		LanChile; CSAV; Grupo Cisneros	
Key advantages in overseas competition			
Low-cost production	Based on small-scale manufacturing or low wages	Mexican firms	Wells; Thomas & Grosse; Peres
"	Based on offshore production for industrial-country clients		Wells
Ties to existing clients	Suppliers to MNEs		Wells
Ethnic connections		Indian firms; Mexican firms	Lall
Technology		Mexican firms	Lall; Grosse & Thomas
Membership in a conglomerate economic group	Ability to realize economies of scope		Lall; Khanna & Palepu
Experience		Hong Kong firms	Lall

Los Pelambres mine in 1986, and the major development of that resource beginning in 1996. That production made the Luksic group into the second largest copper producer in Chile, after the state-owned Codelco. The group's founder, Andrónico Luksic, saw additional opportunities in other sectors, and built up a pasta business (Lucchetti), a beer business (CCU, acquired in 1986), and a metal fabricating business (Madeco, acquired in 1970). In addition, he added a financial institution, initially the Banco de Santiago, which was sold to Banco Santander in 1999, and more recently the Banco de Chile, which has become the second-largest bank in Chile.

The Luksic group grew during the 1980s into the largest Chilean private-sector company (still much smaller than the government-owned copper company, Codelco, however). It is a classic conglomerate grupo, with family control of the diverse businesses, and a set of quite unrelated sectors in the portfolio. The group has 'modernized', with a holding company, Quiñenco, now publicly traded and owning a minority share in the family's businesses.

The **Grupo Diego Cisneros** has long been the largest business group in Venezuela. As in Chile, a government-owned natural resource company (PDVSA oil company) is much larger than this largest private-sector firm, but the Cisneros Group is still a multibillion dollar company. The Cisneros group began as a small transportation company in the 1930s. Responding to a government decision to nationalize the bus system in Caracas, the Cisneros moved into other businesses, including an exclusive distribution agreement with Pepsi-Cola in Venezuela in the 1940s. In 1961, the group bought the national television station, renamed Venevision, from the government in a privatization process. In the 1970s and 1980s, the group expanded into additional sectors, from a Burger King restaurant franchise to operating a chain of supermarkets (Puebla). A beermaker, Cerveceria Regional, was added in 1992.

Beginning with the television station, the Cisneros group had developed largely into a media company by the end of the 1990s. In 1995, Cisneros joined Hughes Electronics to form DirecTV Latin America, a satellite-based TV broadcasting service. In 1997, the group joined in a 50-50 partnership with Hicks, Muse, Tate & Furst, to form Ibero-American Media Partners, which owns pay-TV and radio assets in Latin America. In 1998, the group joined AOL to form AOL Latin America, a 50-50 joint venture to provide the same internet services that AOL offers in the United States and elsewhere in the world.[9] Overall, by the early 2000s the Cisneros Group had greatly concentrated its activities in the media sector, though without eliminating its major presence in the various food businesses.

The organization that eventually became the **Grupo Ardila Lulle** was founded in 1904 by two entrepreneurs, Posada y Tobon. (The name was later shortened to Postobon.) The firm began as a producer of soft drinks, with a locally produced cola product. The company grew from its base in Medellin to cover the entire country through acquisition of other local companies as well as internal expansion. Postobon became the distributor of Coca-Cola for Colombia in 1927, later switching to be the distributor of Pepsi-Cola as it remains today.

When Carlos Ardila Lulle became President of Postobon in 1968, he began a new era of expansion, into additional industrial sectors as well as into greater vertical integration of Postobon, from sugar mills to glass bottle fabrication. Today the group is the second-largest sugar producer in Colombia through its Cali-based Ingenio del Cauca. This control over the raw material gives Ardila Lulle a major competitive advantage over soft drink competitors, who have to purchase sugar from outside sources.[10]

In 1973 the group, under the holding company name of Grupo Ardila Lulle, acquired one of Colombia's leading radio/television broadcasting stations,

RCN. This was followed in 1978 by the acquisition of Colombia's leading textile manufacturer, Coltejer, which remains one of Latin America's largest clothing manufacturers. In the early 2000s, the group comprises the beverages business, including upstream integration of sugar mills and bottle and cap production, along with clothing manufacture, TV and radio broadcasting, and some smaller businesses in commercial financing, physical distribution, and forestry.

Grupo Carso is the largest Mexican conglomerate with six main subsidiaries and more than 200 smaller subsidiaries. The family of Carlos Slim owns about 65 percent of the group. Key industrial holdings include (*a*) Condumex, a producer of mostly cable and wire products (for the telecommunications, power, and mining industries) and autoparts; (*b*) Nacobre, a brass mill that produces copper-, copper-alloy-, and aluminum-based products predominantly for the construction industry; (*c*) Porcelanite, Mexico's leading producer of ceramic tiles; and (*d*) Frisco, a holding that is involved in mining (gold, silver, copper, zinc, and lead), railroads (via Ferrosur), and hydrofluoric acid. Complementing Carso's strong industrial base is its participation in the consumer and retail sectors, including Cigatam (cigarettes), Sanborns (holding specialty retail company), Sears de Mexico, and Pastelería Frances (bakery chain).

In addition to the holdings within this corporate entity, the Slim family owns a controlling interest in Telmex, the main Mexican fixed-line telephone company, and America Movil, its related wireless telephone service company. America Movil operates throughout Latin America and is the largest or second largest wireless operator in most countries of the region. These telephone holdings were part of Grupo Carso, but were spun off into a separate corporate entity in 1996.

Similarly, the family controls the financial organization, Grupo Financiero Inbursa, which includes an insurance company, a large stockbroker, and a commercial bank. The most important competitive strengths of the Carso group, according to senior management, include a superior knowledge of the Mexican market and of key clients in foods, and in general in retail sales. At the Latin American level the group has superior knowledge of the market and superior distribution for telephone service relative to local and international rivals (although Telefonica is a direct and equally strong competitor in several markets).

Grupo Techint in Argentina has been a leading steel pipeline builder and general construction company since the 1940s. The company was founded by Agostino Rocca, a former head of the Italian steel company, Dalmine. From the beginning Techint had branches in both Italy and Argentina. His family continues to maintain controlling ownership in the early 2000s. The firm's business is significant in both Europe and Latin America, though the Latin American activities dominate today.

The company has produced a wide range of steel products over the years, from railroads to power plants to bridges and tunnels. During the 1990s and more recently, Techint's largest projects have been oil and gas pipeline construction ventures. Projects in Argentina and Brazil were followed by major pipelines in Ecuador and Peru. These latest projects involved design and construction of almost 2,000 km of oil and natural gas pipelines in the two countries.

Techint has developed technical expertise superior to other construction companies, which it has exploited in projects in both Europe and Latin America in recent years. The company has also developed an ability to negotiate successfully with Latin American governments to win privatization projects and gain permissions for major construction ventures such as the oil and gas pipelines.

These descriptions of a handful of the largest economic groups in Latin America today demonstrate the variety of businesses they pursue and the range of focussed versus diversified strategies that they are following. The question that arises from this diffuse set of companies is: what kinds of competitive strengths may be common to them all, such that other Latin American firms could find lessons for their own strategy-building?

2.3. Common Sources of Competitive Advantage among Economic Groups in the Early 2000s

Based on personal interviews with senior managers at twenty-three of the economic groups in Latin America during 2003–5, Table 2.4 notes the most commonly identified sources of competitive advantage:

Table 2.4. Key competitive strengths of Latin American economic groups, 2005

Competitive strength	Industry	Country
Production of high-quality products and/or services	Auto parts; publishing; construction; TV; telephone	Argentina; Bolivia; Colombia; Mexico
Production of low-cost products	Auto parts; beverages; books; retail stores	Colombia; Mexico
Relations with existing clients	Auto parts; beverages	Mexico
Superior distribution network	Airline; beverages; conglomerate; publishing; retail stores; telephone	Bolivia; Chile; Colombia; Mexico; Venezuela
Superior service	Airline; retail stores; telephone	Chile; Mexico
Diversification	TV; conglomerate	Chile; Mexico
Superior knowledge of the market	Conglomerate; construction	Argentina; Bolivia; Chile

Source: Interviews at twenty-three large economic groups in Argentina, Bolivia, Chile, Colombia, Mexico, and Venezuela, 2003–5.

39

This set of competitive strengths is not unique to Latin America—that is, several of the capabilities listed here are the same ones that enable US or European firms to establish competitive advantages in their business activities. What is somewhat different about Latin American firms in comparison with US or European multinational firms is their emphasis on superior knowledge of the market and of course production of low-cost products. These characteristics are noted in analyses of Asian and Eastern European large firms as well, so they are not unique to Latin America but rather to emerging market firms.

2.4. Relation of the Groups to Economic Development in Latin America

While the economic size of the large groups is generally not dominant in any Latin American economy, still these organizations are major participants in national economies, and have enormous impact on employment, exports, technological development, and other key economic indicators. In a country such as Mexico, once the national oil company has been put aside, the main firms that dominate industries are large groups and foreign multinationals. This is likewise true for Brazil, Chile, Colombia, and Peru, as well as for the smaller countries in the region.

Argentina is an exception because even the national oil company, YPF, was privatized in the early 1990s. The key remaining 'national champion' firms are just a bank (Banco de la Nación) and a newly created energy company, which is not a major force in the economy. And Venezuela is an exception, because the government of Hugo Chavez has used oil revenues from state-owned PDVSA to finance other public-sector build-up, and attacks on private-sector firms, local and multinational. So, broadly speaking, the grupos are major participants in every Latin American country, and they dominate many industries outside of the petroleum sector.

If we look back at the past half-century of economic development in Latin America, the domestic firms that have built and buoyed the economies have been SOE and economic groups. This itself may be a source of one problem in the region, namely a very low rate of internal technological development. The rate of innovation as measured by patents, scientific articles published, R&D spending by firms, and other indicators of technological progress demonstrates that Latin American firms have been followers rather than leaders in global comparison.[11] Perhaps the grupo form of organization contributes to this weakness, though similar forms in Korea and other Asian tiger countries have not held back the rate of scientific development there. In Latin America at least it can be said that the economic groups have not been a solution to this problem of technological weakness.

Given that the groups are a feature of the Latin American business land-scape, it would be difficult to separate out their impact on the rate of economic development versus the impacts of other factors such as government policies, social conditions, and general technological progress. A model of economic development, or growth rate of national income, would include factors such as the following:

Rate of growth of GDP = f (economy size; tech development; corruption;

% of GDP of grupos; government type; economic

openness; economic volatility; aggregate savings;

capital formation; inward FDI; ...)

While this kind of modeling would be attractive if data were available for all of the key factors involved, an underlying problem is that the grupos themselves are heterogeneous. If we measure the percentage of GDP created by grupos, it would be necessary to draw a line at some minimum size of the group—otherwise all family-based businesses would be included, from tiny bodegas to the large and powerful groups discussed here. Our question is not whether family-based firms make a difference, but rather whether large, often family-based grupos make a difference. In the present context, this question cannot be answered simply.

2.5. Are Economic Groups the Key Firms for the Twenty-first Century in Latin America?

The historic dominance of grupos as the leading firms in Latin America, along with state-owned firms and affiliates of foreign multinationals, has not changed in the past 30 years. Fewer state-owned firms now exist, but the typically family-based grupos remain as the leading competitors in many industries, including ones where state-owned firms were privatized. The pos-sibility of local stock markets to grow and become sources of long-term equity finance that could replace grupos is not increasing very rapidly, though there is evidence of growth of local stock markets from Mexico to Argentina. It is a very safe bet to say that the grupos will remain as key players in Latin American business for at least the next decade.

The grupos have developed a set of core competencies that enable them to survive the onslaught of foreign multinationals. These capabilities include superior knowledge of and ability to navigate local markets, which in turn have inefficiencies and imperfections that more open competition has not resolved.

Appendix

Table 2A.1. Widely vs. family-held firms as a percentage of large corporations

Country	Control inferred at 10%		Control inferred at 20%	
	Widely held	Family control	Widely held	Family control
Argentina	0	65	0	65
Australia	55	10	65	5
Austria	5	15	5	15
Belgium	0	50	5	50
Canada	50	30	60	25
	17.54	46.67	36.24	26.18
Denmark	10	35	40	35
Finland	15	10	35	10
France	30	20	60	20
	8.92	70.44	17.79	64.83
Germany	35	10	50	10
	5.61	71.64	14.02	64.62
Greece	5	65	10	50
Hong Kong	10	70	10	70
	0.6	64.7	7	66.7
Indonesia	0.6	68.6	5.1	71.5
Ireland	45	15	65	10
Israel	5	50	5	50
Italy	15	20	20	15
	7.83	64.87	15.86	59.61
Japan	50	10	90	5
	42	13.1	79.8	9.7
Korea	40	35	55	20
	14.3	67.9	43.2	48.4
Malaysia	1	57.5	10.3	67.2
Mexico	0	100	0	100
Netherlands	30	20	30	20
New Zealand	5	45	30	25
Norway	5	25	25	25
Philippines	1.7	42.1	19.2	44.6
Portugal	0	50	10	45
Singapore	5	45	15	30
	1.4	52	5.4	55.4
Spain	15	25	35	15
	12.74	67.33	28.06	55.79
Sweden	0	55	25	45
Switzerland	50	40	60	30
Taiwan (China)	2.9	65.6	26.2	48.2
Thailand	2.2	56.5	6.6	61.6
United Kingdom	90	5	100	0
	27.06	33.75	69.08	19.88
United States	80	20	80	20
	38.95	23.37	69.26	6.13

Notes

1. Nathaniel Leff (1978: 663–4) characterized the Grupo as: 'a multicompany firm which transacts in different markets but which does so under common

entrepreneurial and financial control.' Two key features of a Grupo are that it 'draws its capital and high-level managers from sources which transcend a single family', and 'the groups invest and produce in several product markets rather than in a single product line'.

2. Embraer might not qualify as a Grupo in the sense that its controlling ownership is not held by a small set of key investors/families, but rather by a diverse group of institutional investors. Brazilian interests—investment conglomerate Cia. Bozano and pension funds PREVI and SISTEL—control 60 percent of the voting shares. The Brazilian government still retains a 'golden share' in the company, giving it the right to disallow any major changes in corporate activities and also requiring majority Brazilian ownership.

3. Interestingly, one of the most successful US giant companies in recent years, Microsoft, remains largely a family-based company, with Bill Gates owning 10 percent of outstanding shares (and with Paul Allen holding 5% and Steve Ballmer another 4%).

4. In the case of Germany, the traditional financial-institution-based economic groups have been disintegrating in the past several years. With the dismantling of Deutsche Bank and Dresdner Bank ownership networks in large corporations such as Daimler-Chrysler, Thyssen, and others, the German system is becoming more similar to the Anglo-Saxon model.

5. In the industrialized countries of the Triad, reasons for pursuing conglomerate diversification may be more related to financial benefits of such pursuit, rather than the emerging market emphasis on the ability to rapidly move to take advantage of market imperfections (e.g. mispricing). Also, the emerging market conglomerates tend to be closely managed, while the Triad conglomerates tend to be managed as a portfolio, with fairly independent decision-making in the diverse divisions (See Guillen 2000.)

6. This statement has been debated by a number of authors recently, arguing that the conglomerate form is a response to weak and inefficient markets, which will be replaced by more focussed firms as markets become more efficient and as market imperfections are reduced. There does appear to be a generalized movement toward more focussed firms in the European Union countries, but the trend is not at all clear in Latin America.

7. See, for example, Demirguc and Levine, 'Stock market development and financial intermediaries: stylized facts', *World Bank Working Paper #1462*. Washington, D.C.: World Bank, May 1995.

8. Interview with Guillermo Luksic (July 2004); 'The Luksic Group', INSEAD case #302-059-1. 2002.

9. In 2005, the AOL Latin America business went into bankruptcy, after never gaining the market penetration that had been anticipated.

10. The sugar business has also been expanded into production of 'gasohol', the sugar-based ethanol used for auto fuel in Brazil and increasingly in the United States and elsewhere.

11. See Grosse (2005) for an analysis of company-based R&D activity in Latin America. The analysis shows that this activity is much less than in the Triad countries, and also much less than in Eastern Europe, China, and Southeast Asia.

References

Amsden, A.H. (1989). *Asia's Next Giant: South Korea and Late Industrialization*. New York: Oxford University Press.

—— and Hikino, T. (1994). 'Project Execution Capability, Organizational Know-how, and Conglomerate Corporate Growth in Late Industrialization', *Industrial and Corporate Change*, 3: 111–47.

Aulakh, P., Koabe, M., and Teegen, H. (2000). 'Export Strategies and Performance of Firms from Emerging Economies: Evidence from Brazil, Chile, and Mexico', *Academy of Management Journal*, 43(3): 342–61.

Booth, L., Aivazian, V., Demirguc-Kunt, A., and Maksimovic, V. (2001). 'Capital Structure in Developing Countries', *Journal of Finance*, 106(1): 87–129.

Chudnovsky, D. and López, A. (2000b). 'A Third Wave of FDI from Developing Countries: Latin American TNCs in the 1990s', *Transnational Corporations*, 9(2): 31–73.

Dawar, N. and Frost, T. (March–April 1999). 'Competing with Giants: Survival Strategies for Local Firms in Emerging Markets', *Harvard Business Review*, 119–29.

Faccio, M. and Lang, L. (2002). 'The Ultimate Ownership of Western European Corporations', *Journal of Financial Economics*, 65(3): 365–95.

Garrido, C. and Peres, W. (1998). Las grandes empresas y grupos industriales latinoamericanos en los años noventa, in W. Peres (ed.), *Grandes empresas y grupos industriales latinoamericanos: Expansión y desafíos en la era de la apertura y la globalización*. Mexico, D.F.: Siglo XXI Editores.

Granovetter, M. (1995). 'Coase Revisited: Business Groups in the Modern Economy', *Industrial and Corporate Change*, 4: 93–130.

Grosse, R. (2004). 'The Challenges of Globalization for Emerging Market Firms', *Latin American Business Review*, 4(4): 1–21.

—— and Thomas, D. (2007). 'Sources of Competitiveness of Large Mexican Groups' in *Can Latin American Firms compete?*, chapter 11.

Guillen, M. (2000). 'Business Groups in Emerging Economies: A Resource-Based View', *Academy of Management Journal*, 43(3): 362–80.

Khanna, T. and Palepu, K. (July–August 1997). 'Why Focussed Strategies may be Wrong for Emerging Markets', *Harvard Business Review*, 41–51.

—— —— (July–August 1999). 'The Right Way to Restructure Conglomerates in Emerging Markets,' *Harvard Business Review*, 125–34.

Lall, S. (1984). *The New multinationals*. New York: Wiley.

La Porta, R., Florencia Lopez-de-Silanes, and Schleifer, A. (April 1999). 'Corporate Ownership Around the World', *Journal of Finance*, 471–517.

Leff, N. (1978). 'Industrial Organization and Entrepreneurship in the Developing Countries: The Economic Groups', *Economic Development and Cultural Change*, 661–75.

Morck, R., Wolfenzon, D. and Yeung, B. (Sept. 2005). 'Corporate Governance, Economic Entrenchment, and Growth', *Journal of Economic Literature*, 655–720.

Peres, W. (ed.) (1998). *Grandes Empresas y Grupos Industriales Latinoamericanos*. Siglo 21 Editores: Mexico.

Salas-Porras, A. (1998). Estrategias de las empresas mexicanas en sus procesos de internacionalización. *Revista de la Cepal*, 65: 133–53.

Wells, L. (1983). *Third world multinationals*. Cambridge, MA: MIT Press.

3

Outward FDI and the Competitiveness of Latin American Firms

Márcia Tavares

3.1. Introduction

Foreign direct investment by companies based in Latin America has increased significantly over the last decade and a half, reflecting the greater openness of the region's economies (ECLAC 2006). Although, despite this increase, when looked at in the aggregate and in comparison to flows from other regions, outward foreign direct investment (OFDI) flows from Latin America are still timid. When looked at from the point of view of individual companies, experiences in OFDI have had important qualitative impacts on competitiveness both at home and in the international arena.

This chapter briefly presents numbers that reflect the significance of direct investment in other countries by companies based in Latin America and shows the firms and sectors that are behind those numbers (Section 3.2); ways in which OFDI has contributed to the competitiveness of Latin American firms (Section 3.3); factors that are in some way specific to the Latin American business environment that have contributed to the success of Latin American firms in their direct investments abroad (Section 3.4); and some of the challenges faced by these companies when investing outside their home countries (Section 3.5). It is based on interviews of executives at forty firms in Argentina, Brazil, Chile, and Mexico conducted by the United Nations Economic Commission for Latin America and the Caribbean (ECLAC) (henceforth referred to as 'the ECLAC Survey'),[1] as well as publicly available corporate information and secondary sources.

3.2. How Relevant is OFDI from Latin America?

The existing literature has referred to a 'first wave' of FDI from developing countries roughly in the 1970s, and a 'second wave' in the 1980s (Chudnovsky and López 1999); or to a 'first wave' that includes both periods (Dunning, van Hoesel, and Narula 1996). In retrospect, what we see—both for Latin America and for developing countries as a group—is that these were mere ripples and that a real first wave only appeared in the 1990s. During the first 'ripple', Latin America led the way but was, by the time of the second, overtaken by developing Asia. By then, the export-led growth strategies of the Asian Tigers had led companies to invest abroad in more significant volumes, either in support systems for their exports or in production facilities in less developed countries, usually in the same region, that would maintain the competitiveness of manufacturing despite rising labor costs in the home markets (Goldstein, and Stow 2007).

In the 1990s, a number of push and pull factors came into force in Latin America that led to increased outward investment flows. Trade and investment liberalization, privatizations, deregulation, and the strengthening of competition policy created challenges for companies in maintaining their positions in local markets and opportunities abroad—many of which were within the region. OFDI from the region grew significantly, as shown in Figure 3.1, although as a percentage of GDP, OFDI from South and Central America (excluding, therefore, the main financial centers in the Caribbean) represented only 7.6 percent, compared to 15.4 percent for South, East, and Southeast Asia (UNCTAD Foreign Direct Investment Statistics).[2]

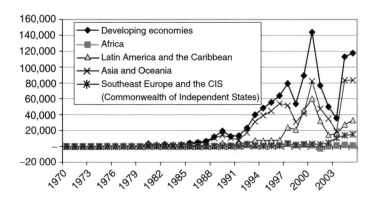

Figure 3.1. Outward FDI flows from developing countries 1970–2005 (millions of dollars)

Source: UNCTAD Foreign Direct Investment Statistics.

Much of this investment has been made with a view to expand sales in local markets either through directly producing abroad or through support to exports from the home country. In some cases plants have been built to assemble exported parts, in other cases to add value to products locally and avoid tariff and nontariff barriers, and in others still, to ensure closer relationships with clients in order to be able to either develop tailor-made products or to provide post-sales assistance. Other investments relocate production, taking advantage of free-trade agreements of host countries with major consumer markets or simply producing for local markets with local inputs. There have also been natural-resource and technological asset-seeking investments, to use the traditional categories for investment motivations based on Dunning (1993; see also ECLAC 2003, 2004, 2005). Efficiency-seeking operations— which generally refers to locating production in a lower-cost site—is not a major motivation for outward investment from Argentina and Brazil nor from other Latin American countries, which is explained by the fact that the region is itself a low-cost area. Nonetheless, some companies are starting to consider investments in China in order to take advantage of low cost inputs and place products competitively on the Chinese market and Asia in general.

As regards Latin American presence in global rankings, in 1994 there were no Latin American firms in UNCTAD's list of the top 100 nonfinancial transnational corporations ranked by foreign assets. Cemex made it to this list in 1999, and was still the only one in 2002. For 2003 and 2004 (the most recent list), there were no Latin American companies, although it is likely that with the recent acquisition of the RMC group in the United Kingdom for approximately 5.8 billion dollars, Cemex will be back for the 2005 list (to be published in 2007). In the top fifty nonfinancial transnational firms from developing countries, also ranked by foreign assets, there were fourteen companies from Latin America in 1994, with approximately 8 billion dollars in foreign assets. By 2004, there were eight companies (up from six in 2003) from the region in the top fifty from developing countries. The volume of foreign assets, however, amounted to over 47 billion dollars (UNCTAD 1996, 2001, 2004, 2005, 2006).[3]

Who are the main investors? Ranked by foreign assets, the eight companies that appear on UNCTAD's most recent list of nonfinancial transnational corporations from developing countries (UNCTAD 2006) are Cemex from Mexico, in the cement business; PDVSA (Venezuela) and Petrobras (Brazil) in oil and gas; Telmex and América Móvil, from Mexico, in telecommunications; mining company Companhia Vale do Rio Doce (CVRD) from Brazil; Gerdau, a steel producer, also from Brazil; and Femsa, a mexican beverages producer and distributor. All of these are successful transnational companies by some relevant criterion: Cemex is the world's largest producer of concrete; Telmex and America Móvil are the leading providers of wireless services in Latin America; PDVSA and Petrobras rank third and fourteenth, respectively, among

Petroleum Intelligence Weekly's 2005 list of largest oil companies (Folha de São Paulo 2005); CVRD is among the world's three iron ore giants, and Gerdau is the largest long steel producer in the Americas and controls Gerdau Ameristeel, the fourth largest overall steel company and the second largest mini-mill steel producer in North America; Grupo Bimbo is one of the most important producers of baked food products, second only to Yamazaki (Japan) (*Expansión* 2005).

Table 3.1, while far from exhaustive, shows the country of origin and industry of some of the main investors from Latin America and the Caribbean. Many have been, since the beginning of their histories as foreign investors, fully or partially acquired by players from other countries, but their experiences as Latin American companies remain relevant. As the table shows, a number of the outward investors from the region are in natural resource extraction and natural-resource-based manufacturing industries such as oil and gas, mining and steel, cement, and pulp and paper. There are, however, important companies, such as Embraer, in high-tech industries; and others in medium to high-tech manufacturing such as auto parts and components for household appliances. There are also service companies with a predominantly regional outreach—in telecommunications, retail, air travel, and entertainment—and others with a more global outreach—such as engineering.

A number of relatively large (over 1 billion dollars) intra-regional deals have been undertaken among these companies in the past few years. Some examples are the acquisition of Mexican Hylsamex by Techint for 2.2 billion dollars; of Argentinian Loma Negra by the Brazilian Camargo Correa group for approximately 1 billion dollars; of Pérez Companc from Argentina by Petrobras in 2002 for 1 billion dollars; and of Sidor in Venezuela in 1998, when it was privatized and acquired for 1.8 billion dollars by a consortium of regional companies, led by Techint. Companies from the region have also been protagonists of some of the largest recent global acquisitions: in 2006, CVRD acquired Canadian nickel producer Inco for over 17 billion dollars, and at the time of writing CSN was battling against Indian company Tata Steel for control of Corus Steel in bids of over 10 billion; CEMEX was trying to acquire Rinker in Australia for over 12 billion dollars; in 2005, Cemex acquired RMC in the United Kingdom for approximately 4.5 billion dollars in 2005, and had acquired Southdown Inc. in the United States for 2.8 billion dollars in 2000. In parallel to these acquisitions, substantial greenfield investments, especially in natural resource exploration and production, have occurred.

There are two ways of looking at this picture: one is to say that despite the boom in outward investment flows in the 1990s, in quantitative terms there is still relatively little outward investment from Latin America when compared to other regions. The other is to see that despite recent industrialization processes in their home countries, a sometimes very recent history of

Table 3.1. Main outward investors from Latin America and the Caribbean[4]

Industry	Country of origin	Company
Oil and gas	Argentina	YPF (now Repsol YPF)
		Pérez Companc (now Petrobras Energía)
	Brazil	Petrobras
	Chile	ENAP
	Venezuela	PDVSA
Mining	Brazil	Companhia Vale do Rio Doce
	Mexico	Grupo México
Agribusiness	Mexico	La Moderna-Seminis
Steel and other metals and metal products	Argentina	Techint
	Brazil	Gerdau
		Usiminas
		Belgo Mineira (part of Arcelor)
		Companhia Siderúrgica Nacional (CSN)
	Chile	Molymet
		Madeco
	Mexico	Hylsamex (now Techint)
		Grupo Imsa
Cement	Brazil	Votorantim
		Camargo Correa
	Mexico	Cemex
Pulp and paper	Brazil	Klabin
	Chile	Celulosa Arauco y Constitución (ARAUCO)
		Compañía Manufacturera de Papeles y Cartones (CMPC)
		Masisa
Glass	Mexico	Grupo Vitro
Food products	Argentina	Arcor
	Mexico	Grupo Maseca
		Grupo Bimbo
Beverages	Argentina	Quilmes (now partially owned by InBev)
	Brazil	AmBev (now InBev)
	Chile	Compañía Cervecerías Unidas (CCU)
		Embotelladora Andina
	Colombia	Bavaria (now SABMiller)
	Mexico	Femsa
		Jugos del Valle
Textiles, clothing	Brazil	Santista/Camargo Correa group
Pipes and connections	Brazil	Tigre
Auto parts and vehicles	Brazil	Sabó
		Weg
		Marcopolo
	Mexico	Dina
		San Luis Rassini
Domestic appliances and parts, electronics	Brazil	Embraco (now part of the Whirlpool group)
		Multibrás (now part of the Whirlpool group)
	Mexico	Mabe
Pharmaceuticals	Argentina	Bagó
Airplanes	Brazil	Embraer
Telecommunications	Argentina	Impsat (sold in 2002)
	Chile	Entel
	Mexico	América Móvil

(Cont.)

Table 3.1. (*Continued*)

Industry	Country of origin	Company
Engineering and capital goods for energy systems	Argentina	Impsa
Engineering and construction	Brazil	Odebrecht
		Queiroz Galvão
		Andrade Gutierrez
	Mexico	ICA
Retail	Chile	Falabella
		Cencosud
		Farmacias Ahumada
		Ripley
	Mexico	Elektra
Electricity	Chile	Compañía General de Electricidad
Air travel	Chile	Lan
Television	Mexico	Televisa
Entertainment	Mexico	CIE
Hotels	Mexico	Grupo Posadas

(and sometimes continuing) state ownership, unstable macroeconomic and regulatory environments, significant institutional barriers to competitiveness and very limited government support for foreign investment, a nonnegligible mass of companies has reacted positively and managed to grow into successful regional or global players. Foreign investment has been an important tool for these companies in maintaining and enhancing competitiveness both internationally and on their home country markets.

3.3. How Does OFDI Contribute to the Competitiveness of Latin American Companies?

Dunning (1993) summarizes literature on the main motivations for FDI in the following categories:

to acquire natural resources, the price of which (net of transportation costs) is lower and/or the quality is higher than in the investing country; to service foreign markets, particularly in the country in which the investment is being made; to restructure existing foreign value-added activities, so as to improve overall efficiency and change the range of products produced; to acquire assets which might be complementary to existing assets, or competitive to them, so as to reduce risk, capture the economies of scale or synergy, or generally strengthen the acquiring firms' competitive position in national or world markets.

It is the last category, that applies to Latin American companies as it does to others, that is especially relevant in answering how internationalization has contributed to the competitiveness of Latin American companies, beyond the simple and straightforward expansion of sales of access to natural resources. This category should in fact be looked at in a different dimension from the first three: even when the main motivation for investment is as conceptually simple as natural resource-seeking or market-seeking, these strategies are often instruments toward other goals—in Dunning's terms, risk reduction, economies of scale, etc. In other words, companies invest abroad to acquire natural resources or have access to foreign markets because, in addition to growth, they need or perceive a need to 'reduce risk, capture economies of scale or synergy', or other reasons, all of which will generally strengthen their competitive positions at home and abroad. In the next few paragraphs, we will take it as given that market access, growth, expansion of sales and revenues, and/or access to natural resources are positive results of internationalization, but we will focus on other factors *that contribute to—as opposed to being a result of—a company's competitiveness.*

The results of the ECLAC survey on Argentinean, Brazilian, Chilean, and Mexican companies show that risk diversification has been a major motivation for internationalization for only five of thirty-six firms but was claimed by seventeen firms as one of the major benefits of OFDI, ranked higher than any other. Section 3.3.1 discusses risk management as a benefit of internationalization. Growth, translated into market access, greater revenues and scale, came second, although access to markets was ranked as the main motivation for outward investment by almost all interviewed firms. The benefit here is straightforward and we have chosen to discuss two aspects of this (Section 3.3.2): (*a*) the acquisition of scale to ensure survival on the domestic market and (*b*) outward growth to overcome limits on growth in the domestic market created by competition policy and changes in regulation in the 1990s. The third main benefit identified by interviewed firms was access to knowledge and technology (discussed in section 3.3.3). Other benefits identified have been opportunities for the professional development of personnel, access to technology, the development of partnerships with international players, and the possibility of improving operations through benchmarking and the competitive pressures of the international market.

Before discussing the main competitive benefits of OFDI for the investing company itself, it is worth mentioning that OFDI from the region has also contributed to the growth of third parties, often small and medium enterprises (SMEs), not necessarily investors themselves. A number of SMEs from the region have managed to conquer space on the international market—either through exports or production abroad—by becoming initially local providers to transnational corporations in their home countries. When local companies become transnational players, there is potential for the leveraging of SMEs. The Techint group, for example, participating in a public–private program in support of small and medium companies from Argentina, identified companies among this group that could profitably supply its operations outside the country. Currently more than fifty small and medium companies export to Techint plants in Mexico, Venezuela, Brazil, Canada, and Italy. Exports of these companies increased by 73 percent in one year (Techint 2004). Brazilian engineering and construction company Odebrecht works with 1,800 Brazilian suppliers, 1,500 of which are small and medium enterprises.

3.3.1. *Risk Management*

The literature on FDI as a tool for risk diversification is practically as old as the literature on transnational firms and FDI generally. Hymer (1960, in Dunning 1993) addressed the issue of FDI as a means to diversify toward products or activities that are counter cyclically related. Although portfolio investment could be a substitute to FDI when the main motivation is risk management, Hymer states, FDI may have the advantage of greater information (Hymer 1960 in Dunning 1993). Lessard (1974) looks at the financial motivations for FDI, showing that the literature usually justifies FDI in order to diversify risk because of capital market imperfections and because of the behavior of risk-averse managers, who see international investment as a way to diversify (and reduce risk), but in the activities they know well rather than those where they have little expertise. Several other finance-oriented scholars wrote on FDI as a mechanism for the management of exchange-related risk management and of its influence on the cost of capital (Stonehill and Moffett 1993). Specifically on investment by companies based in developing countries, Wells (1983) wrote about diversification as a reaction to political risk at home, fear of nationalizations and others. Nonetheless, he stated, without competitive advantages to support the investments made abroad, portfolio investment would be a more likely means of diversification.

As mentioned above, risk management under one form or another was stated as a major benefit of internationalization by the highest number of companies, above any other benefit including market access/growth/revenues. This has been an especially important factor for Brazilian companies. 'Access to hard currency,' 'the reduction of exposure to exchange rate risk', 'protecting the firm from "Brazil risk" ',[5] an improvement of company risk with a resulting reduction in capital costs for the financing of operations, greater stability in results because of geographical diversity of markets, geographical diversity in the location of assets, and the dispersion of economic and financial risks are some of the ways in which OFDI is used as a risk management tool.

Where investments were natural resource seeking, the main motivations within the risk diversification strategy was to diversify asset location, reduce corporate risk and thus the company's capital costs; or reduce risks associated with the concentration of production in a small number of products or one main product. Companhia Vale do Rio Doce's (CVRD) is an especially interesting example of natural resource-seeking investments as an instrument for risk management. Situated among the three largest mining companies in the world, and the largest iron ore producer and exporter, CVRD is also the least diversified of these companies in terms of the geographical position of its assets and in terms of its range of products. Recent investment planning has emphasized foreign operations, which will allow the company to expand its range of products (iron ore production is still concentrated in Brazil) and the geographical distribution of its assets.

Petrobras invested abroad initially in search of natural resources as a result of uncertainty in regard to the existence and dimensions of Brazilian reserves. More recently, however, with consolidated production, reserves and exploration and production (E&P) activities within Brazil, the geographical diversification of assets has been seen as an instrument for corporate risk management. Petrobras' international strategy for the 2000–10 period, as defined in 1999, was directed at 'diversifying risk, reducing capital costs, and ensuring the growth of the company' (Petrobras 2000). The company's strategic plan was revised more than once over the past few years, often in response to political changes in the country which directly affected company management. Nonetheless, in the strategic plan drafted in April 2003, for 2003–7, one of three vectors was to expand international presence, for which portfolio diversification to reduce capital costs was still among the main motivations. In other words, despite numerous revisions of the company's strategic planning, risk diversification remained among the top motivations for outward investment (Petrobras 2004). To quote another example from the oil industry, the acquisition by YPF of Maxus in the United States in 1995 improved the company's credit risk (Kosacoff 1999).

Most other companies from Brazil interviewed through the ECLAC Survey invested in market-seeking operations for risk diversification. The objectives sought through these operations are the management of exchange rate risk and of risks associated to market cycles. These companies usually produce non-commodities or products which are difficult to export, require client proximity either for product development, maintenance or marketing, suffer trade barriers in the target markets (steel is a case in point) or that for other reasons cannot be exported. Services companies also enter this category.

Risk management was also a major motivation behind the internationalization strategy for Mexican company CEMEX, the largest transnational corporation from Latin America according to UNCTAD (UNCTAD 2005), not interviewed for the ECLAC Survey. Among motivations for CEMEX's acquisition the RMC group (United Kingdom)—a market-seeking/risk diversifying operation—was the need to balance out markets with high risk and high profit margins with less profitable but more stable markets operating in hard currency. After the RMC acquisition, Cemex has 56 percent of its cash flow originating in Mexico, the Philippines, Indonesia, and Egypt, and the remaining 44 percent in the United States and Europe (Expansión 2004). Also in the cement industry, Votorantim's investments abroad have helped the company diversify risk, allowing it to 'access financing at a fraction of the cost its parent would otherwise pay' (Latin Finance 2005).

3.3.2. Growth

3.3.2.1. SCALE TO PROMOTE SURVIVAL

One of the defining characteristics of developing country markets in the literature on developing country transnational firms in the early 1980s was their small scale (Wells 1983). This is a relative concept. Brazil, for example, is a large consumer market, and this has been pointed out as one of the dissuasive factors to OFDI by Brazilian firms (Da Rocha 2003). Nonetheless, for some industries the minimum scale to ensure competitiveness on local markets relatively recently opened to competition by foreign players required expansion beyond the limits of their home country markets. This is especially relevant in industries with relatively high R&D expenditures and where client proximity is important and sales cannot be effectively undertaken exclusively through exports. The motivation is different from that of simple growth, described above, in that it is necessary to maintain even the domestic feasibility of operations. Investments under this category are usually market-seeking.

Embraco, from Brazil, is a leading manufacturer of compressors for refrigerators. Founded in 1971 by three national refrigerator manufacturers, its original mission was to supply the national market, then strongly protected under a regime of import substitution industrialization. It started exporting in the late 1970s, in large part to ensure scale that would allow for the necessary investments in technology and innovation. Soon exports had to be complemented with investments abroad, through which the company consolidated its presence in the international market—it now has approximately 25% of the world market for domestic refrigerator compressors (Fundação Dom Cabral 2005)—and domestically. For Brazilian auto parts company, Sabó, scale acquired through its foreign operations was crucial in ensuring the company's survival once the Brazilian market was opened to competition in the 1990s. Supplier to some of the world's most important auto manufacturers, it is the only survivor among the twenty largest auto parts firms in Brazil (*Exame* 2005). For Argentinean company Impsa, whose main business line is integrated energy systems (involving both the engineering and the manufacturing of related capital goods, such as turbines), the Argentinean market was too limited to ensure the company's survival had it remained on the national scale. The nature of this company's services—often inserted in large-scale, government financed projects—would have made survival difficult had it depended on the domestic market alone.

International productive scale can also be important from a buyer's point of view. One of the benefits Techint has reaped from acquisitions outside of Argentina has been the possibility of unification of supply management. With the scale of worldwide operations, the company has the benefit of buying power associated to volume. Its procurement company now provides procurement services to third parties, as well as to the Techint group companies, processing 3 billion dollars a year in purchases.

3.3.2.2. GROWTH BEYOND THE LIMITS OF COMPETITION POLICY AND REGULATION

Competition policy has been strengthened in many Latin American countries since the 1990s, and merger reviews instituted in a number of countries. Competition authorities have imposed restrictions on the growth of companies through mergers and acquisitions, creating the need for companies to either diversify toward other product markets or direct investments at other geographical markets in product markets which they know well and where they have constructed competitive advantages. In other words, whereas the enforcement of competition policy has the effect, for companies, of further reducing the size of the 'claimable' national market, OFDI provides an opportunity for growth. One of the first cases in which the Brazilian antitrust authorities imposed restrictions on an acquisition involved Gerdau in the mid-1990s. The company then saw that to grow to the extent of its capacity in the product segments in which it specialized it would have to venture outside of Brazil.

Interestingly, outward FDI was seen as a benefit in itself and used as an argument for the approval of the merger between the country's largest brewers that produced AmBev (now merged with Belgian Interbrew). The merger, despite producing a giant by national standards, was considered necessary to enable this company to compete internationally. Restrictions on mergers and acquisitions (M&A) have also created opportunities for foreign investment by companies from the region. Restrictions by the Argentinean authorities on the acquisition of YPF by Spanish Repsol led to an asset swap with Petrobras whereby the latter entered the Argentinean downstream market; CSN acquired assets divested by Arcelor in Europe as a result of restrictions imposed by the European Commission (Corus Group 2003); and Votorantim acquired assets in Canada that were sold in response to restrictions imposed by Canadian and United States competition authorities.

Besides competition policy, regulatory changes have also motivated foreign investment by restricting possibilities for growth (or in this case, the maintenance) within the domestic market. With the imminent end of the monopoly on the oil and gas industry in Brazil, in the 1990s Petrobras intensified its investments abroad, investing in downstream segments in Bolivia and Argentina and more recently in other countries in the region through the acquisition of Shell's downstream assets in a number of countries.

3.3.3. *Acquisition of Knowledge*

A limited number of investments by Latin American firms have been *motivated* by the search for technological assets. López (1999) mentions some of the early investments by Petrobras, done in partnership with other companies in order to absorb leading-edge technology that it needed to function competitively. ENAP, the Chilean oil and gas company, undertook similar investments. Other companies invested in search of knowledge about specific markets or about international operation in general as a first step toward a more intensive internationalization process. Gerdau's first acquisition abroad, for example, was a relatively small operation in Uruguay in 1980. Uruguay was then a more open market than Brazil, with stronger labor unions and the operation provided Gerdau with important experience both about the operation of a firm under these conditions and of the complexities of an international operation. Brazilian poultry producer Sadia, which to date is more of an exporter than of an outward investor, opened a restaurant—the Beijing-Brasil 'churrascaria'— in China in 1994, in partnership with a local company, as an observatory of the local market with a view to start exporting to China (*Agência Estado* 2002).

In many more cases, however, although the acquisition of knowledge— technological, managerial, or other—was not a main motivation for outward investment, for many of the interviewed companies, it turned out to be one of the main alleged benefits of internationalization. Having been born and raised in closed and protected environments, many companies from the region were challenged by new foreign competition in the 1990s both on domestic markets and on the international markets they were trying to conquer. When exporting, companies acquired knowledge on the quality standards of the international market. When investing abroad, they additionally benefitted from exposure to new management practices, technical, technological, or logistic solutions. Beyond the interviewed companies, incorporating previously isolated operations into global production systems has been a challenge for Cemex, for example, but also a means to take advantage of a wide base of best practices (Cemex 2001).

3.4. What Latin American Characteristics Have Contributed to the Success of Latin American Firms in Their OFDI Operations?

This section addresses the flip side of Section 3.3: what is it about Latin American firms that have made their OFDI operations comparatively easier or less costly than for their counterparts in other regions.

When asked about their competitive advantages of products or services—first without regard to international operations—the most common replies by companies interviewed through the ECLAC Survey were quality of products, technological level of products, and brands. When asked about their competitive advantages derived from upstream or downstream relationships in the production chains, the most commonly quoted factor was relationships with distribution networks and with suppliers. Most companies stated that these advantages reflected broadly on their international operations. There is, however, little uniformity in these responses and little of a 'Latin American' pattern. What companies did not state, but is retrievable from the sectors in which they function and their corporate histories, is that their very existence is often related to regional characteristics such as the availability of mineral resources and state policies supporting the development of national companies in strategic industries under import-substituting industrialization; as well as to competent post-privatization restructuring.

Competitive advantages identified by companies specifically in regard to their international operations show that, to the extent that there is a group of 'Latin American' advantages, these are often of the type described by the 1980s literature on OFDI by developing countries (Lall 1983; Wells 1983). These authors identified ownership advantages of transnational firms from developing countries as access to—or capacity to develop—technology or marketing practices, low-cost factors, ethnic factors, and management skills that would allow them to function competitively mostly in other developing countries (Lall 1983; Wells 1983, although these authors diverge in relation to the sources of advantages and to these firms' innovation capacities). Some of the firms interviewed through the ECLAC Survey effectively claim advantages that can be classified among these traditional ones.

The 'ethnic' or, more specifically, cultural and linguistic, aspect is seen as an advantage when the target country is either within Latin America, in Portuguese-speaking African countries or in Portugal or Spain, although, sharing language or cultural heritage are not an assurance of lack of cultural conflict as one Brazilian company has stressed in regard to its operations in Portugal, or a Mexican company has said in regard to its Brazilian operations, and indeed culture and language were reported as one of the main barriers to outward investment (see below). Another company stated that being Brazilian has ensured a positive image and receptiveness in African countries where, differently from European counterparts, it is not associated to a not so distant colonial past. This source of advantage is, however, obviously limited in geographical scope—and to developing countries were it not for Spain and Portugal—and has not been among the main ones highlighted by interviewed firms. Moreover, cultural and linguistic factors are also among the main difficulties to investment, as described below. What can be said generally about the ethnic factor is that when there was a choice between locations in which to invest or regions in which to focus internationalization strategies, cultural proximity has been an asset, but not a determinant. An exception to this is the case of companies that have invested in search of specific ethnic markets, such as Mexican companies that first exported then started investing in the United States to cater to the Mexican community in that country.

A second traditional category refers to the ability of firms to function in high risk, unstable macroeconomic environments as well as with changing sets of rules, what Lall (1983) called 'management adapted to Third World conditions'. This has been explicitly quoted by interviewed companies as relevant in investments within the region or in other developing areas—namely Africa. One interviewed company raised a plausible Darwinian hypothesis that the companies that have been able to survive and thrive in developing country environments have developed resilience and flexibility, among other assets, that will give them an advantage in operating in diverse environments, developing or developed.[6]

Another similar advantage quoted has been know-how in company turnarounds. Having acquired expertise in these processes through multiple acquisitions in their domestic markets (often through privatization), a small number of companies have been able to take advantage of this and turnaround unprofitable operations in developed country markets.

It is unclear, however, how the 'Latin American' or the 'developing' conditions are determinants of this advantage and to what extent these are company-specific characteristics. The fact that quality and technological level have been quoted as competitive advantages, in both home and foreign operations, may be related to the 'developing' condition of host countries. Mastering distribution networks in complex home country infrastructure situations has also doubtlessly given companies an edge in managing similar situations within the region. Nonetheless, in some cases companies have ensured important global leadership in markets (and success in investments) where they compete with transnational firms from developed countries.

Among the companies that claim technological advantages are formerly state-owned companies such as Embraer, as well as still majority state-owned Petrobras. These companies obviously benefitted at least for a significant period of time from government support as national champions or as local monopolists, but what is relevant is that, during this period they were able to develop unique capacities—such as offshore drilling technology in the case of Petrobras—and once privatization, liberalization, and/or deregulation in the 1990s threatened established positions and government support, these companies reacted and were able to ensure capacity to produce world class products and technology. There are other companies on this list that do not have a state-owned past but that also grew in a closed economy environment. Again, they stand out as having had the capacity to adapt to new market conditions and aggressively take advantage of international opportunities. Beyond country-specific advantages—of which there seem to be few—both categories of companies have developed firm-specific advantages, suggesting they are moving closer to what Dunning, van Hoesel, and Narula (1996) call 'conventional' transnational firms, with a capacity to operate globally.

The answer to the introductory question to this section is, then, (a) that when investing in other countries, many Latin American companies claim advantages that are related to the 'developing' condition of their home countries, and to their own 'Latin American' condition only in what relates to culture and language, although culture and language are a barrier as much as they are an advantage even when countries invest within the region (see below); and (b) that a select number of players have managed to develop global competitive advantages often based on a period of state-supported 'incubation' followed by a competent relay in post-privatization or post-'apertura' management.

3.5. The Challenges

The results of the ECLAC Survey show that (a) cultural or language differences; (b) adaptation to the idiosyncrasies of business environments—legislation and regulation, legal and tax systems, etc.; and (c) the availability of internationally functional human resources are the main challenges to outward investment across countries. Access to financing or credit was stated by very few of the interviewed companies as an obstacle to internationalization. Brazilian firms referred to the difficulties in access to financing as a major motivation for, rather than obstacle to, foreign direct investment, by allowing improvement of credit ratings and access to international capital markets.

Johanson and Vahlne (1977, 1990) highlighted the cost of the acquisition of information on foreign markets and coined the concept of 'psychic distance' which considers the importance of language and cultural barriers in internationalization (Johanson and Vahlne 1990).[7] What is interesting from the results of the ECLAC Survey is that cultural barriers were identified even when there was a common language and even within Latin America. In some cases they took subtle forms, albeit with strong repercussions on business. In other cases outright xenophobia was reported. The fact that cultural identity and language were also quoted by firms as an advantage (see above) shows the importance—both positive and negative—of the management of this issue. Through many of the accounts of the interviewed executives, it became clear that the importance of cultural or linguistic differences in the success of foreign ventures had been underestimated at least in companies' first experiences.

Dealing with local business environment idiosyncrasies, including tax systems and legislation, legal systems, and local business practices, among other factors, were the second most quoted difficulties. They have often been at least partially overcome by operating with local partners. These difficulties have translated into a relatively uniform voice by firms when asked to make public policy suggestions to host countries: transparency, stability in the rules of the game, and level-playing fields. Again, as mentioned above, knowing how to deal with developing business environments has also been quoted as a significant competitive advantage in outward investment, against firms from other regions (see above).

Both factors—cultural/linguistic differences and difficulties with idiosyncrasies of local markets—are intrinsically related to the third factor—the availability of internationally functional human resources. These have been reported as 'scarcity of human capital qualified to function on a global market', 'difficulties in forming a team capable of functioning in the international market' or of 'dealing with international expansion'; and 'recruitment and development of human resources with an international profile', among others.

Ideally, adequately recruited and trained personnel would be more resilient and better equipped to deal with cultural differences and take advantage of them. The importance of this issue would suggest that substantial efforts should be made in overcoming these barriers through recruitment, training, and structured company policies, such as rotation. Nonetheless, a relatively recent study (Saraiva de Magalhães and Da Rocha 2002) shows that among Brazilian firms that have subsidiaries abroad, at least until the beginning of the 2000s, very few had specific recruitment and training policies for international personnel. For marketing areas, many companies preferred to recruit in the target countries to ensure adequate knowledge of the local market, to the detriment of familiarity with the culture of the organization. In finances, because companies often lacked sophisticated control systems, the determinant in recruiting was often trust, and in-house, Brazilian professionals were recruited, often coming from positions not directly related to the subject matter, with less technical training than would have been ideal or with no knowledge of the language in the target country.[8] Within the companies interviewed by Saraiva de Magalhães and Da Rocha, there was seldom formal training for recruited international executives and, when it did exist, it rarely addressed cultural issues. Finally, although the adaptation of executives and their families to life outside their native country did arise as a concern for some companies, there is little in the way of company policy to facilitate adaptation and accumulate know-how on the problems presented by these situations and their possible solutions. The ECLAC Survey did not directly address the issue of human resources policies. One company, however, reported a range of training and other measures, including the integration of foreign personnel in domestic operations in order to expose the organization as a whole to different cultural realities to a much larger extent than is feasible by relocating local personnel.

The difficulty, however, in some cases lies way beyond finding people with linguistic capabilities and multicultural exposure and training. The complexity of foreign operations often require that executives dominate a range of skills, such as commercial, financial, *and* industrial engineering, whereas at headquarters managers are specialists in one of these areas. As one interviewed manager stated, these executives must also have entrepreneurial skills and drive, and must be willing to relocate often to places with less comfortable living conditions. All these conditions make it very hard to find the right person for key positions.

The importance of cultural difficulties in internationalization probably has a lot to do with the fact that many of the internationalization processes of Latin American companies are relatively recent and companies and countries are still only starting to develop a corps of executives with international exposure. Brazilian auto parts manufacturer Weg, for example, seems to have benefitted from the fact that they established a firm export strategy early in their history (as opposed to companies that exported only the surplus not sold on the local market) and by the time they started making substantial direct investments abroad they had accumulated knowledge of the international market (Fundação Dom Cabral/London Business School 2002).

3.6. Conclusions

Beyond the obvious benefits of growth toward foreign markets, OFDI has helped Latin American companies overcome some of the characteristics of developing economies that had been defined by the early literature on transnational firms from developing countries, among which are risky macro-economic and regulatory environments, and markets that are small in scale for activities that are relatively intense in research and development. OFDI has also enabled companies to continue growing despite the limits of competition policy that is increasingly strong within the region, and to take advantage of investment opportunities created by competition policy outside home countries, as well as to grow and defend their positions in domestic markets. Finally, while exports have exposed companies to higher product quality standards, outward Latin American investors have benefitted from exposure to best practices in management, logistics, and technical and technological solutions, contributing to the competitiveness of both domestic and foreign operations.

There is as yet little evidence of strong and intrinsically 'Latin American' advantages when investing abroad. To the extent that these exist, they are largely based on cultural and language proximity or common historical backgrounds, or on know-how on operating in high-risk environments with fluctuating macroeconomic and regulatory conditions, among other uncertainties, or under complex infrastructure situations. There is a small group of truly global players, leaders in their respective markets, that have developed unchallenged competitive advantages. In many cases, a history of state-ownership or support followed by successful privatization and post-privatization management have been key for these players. Besides the immediate challenges of learning how to deal with cultural issues and the idiosyncrasies of host country markets and of finding and retaining competent international professionals, the main challenges are to renew these advantages and avoid their erosion as countries develop and as these companies broaden their investment sites. The other main challenge is to maintain independence as internationalization advances and companies become increasingly attractive for takeovers by global competitors, as a number of relatively recent acquisitions illustrate.

Notes

1. The ECLAC Survey was undertaken as part of the research for the 2005 issue of ECLAC's annual report on *Foreign Direct Investment in Latin America and the Caribbean*, published in March, 2006. This and former issues can be read at http://www.cepal.org
2. Data on FDI is collected by Unctad largely based on national balance of payments statistics. Differences in countries' data collection methodologies, incomplete reportings, exchange rate issues and other factors limit the accuracy of these numbers, that should be read as indicators of orders of magnitude and trends. For a more detailed explanation of the problems with FDI data, please see Unctad 2005, pp. 4–5. However, available data are useful as indicators of trends (Dunning, van Hoesel, and Narula 1996).
3. These numbers should also be read as indicators of orders of magnitude, since data on some of the companies is missing on these lists.
4. This list has been drafted on the basis of qualitative information collected by ECLAC on significant OFDI experiences from the region. It is not exhaustive and the absence of a company from this list should by no means imply the irrelevance of its outward investments. Some companies are subsidiaries of transnational corporations but have been considered either because they undertook relevant investments as independent companies before acquisition or because they have an internationalization logic that is specific to the subsidiary. Not all companies were interviewed for the ECLAC Survey.
5. For a definition and explanation of the Brazil Risk, see ECLAC 2005.

6. A similar argument has been made by Khanna and Palepu (2005) who show that deficient institutions and infrastructure in emerging markets can force companies to generate internal competencies to overcome those voids, that then become competitive advantages in other markets.

7. Barreto and Da Rocha (2003) applied these concepts to experiences of Brazilian firms and confirmed their relevance, although, they argue, there was a reduction of psychic distance in the 1990s (Da Rocha 2003).

8. Finding the balance between local and home country personnel was also a challenge brought up by companies interviewed by ECLAC in 2005.

References

Agência Estado (2002). 'Investimento direto brasileiro da China é pequeno, mas vai crescer', March 27.

Barretto, A. and Angela da Rocha (2003). 'A expansão das fronteiras: brasileiros no exterior', *As novas fronteiras: a multinacionalização das empresas brasileiras*. Rio de Janeiro: COPPEAD/MAUAD.

Cemex (2001). Remarks of Lorenzo Zambrano, Chairman and CEO, to the 'Cemex Americas' global analyst meeting, July 19, 2001, Houston, TX.

Chudnovsky, D. and López, A. (1999). 'Inversión extranjera directa y empresas multinacionales de países en desarrollo. Tendencias y marco conceptual', in Daniel Chudnovsky, Bernardo Kosacoff, Andrés López, and Celso Garrido (eds.), *Las multinacionales latinoamericanas: sus estrategias en un mundo globalizado*. Buenos Aires: Fondo de Cultura Económica.

Corus Group (2003). 'Corus acquires and sells 50 per cent of Lusosider', April 22. At http://www.corusgroup.com

Da Rocha, A. (2003). 'Por que as empresas brasileiras não se internacionalizam', *As novas fronteiras: a multinacionalização das empresas brasileiras*. Rio de Janeiro: COPPEAD/MAUAD.

Dunning, J. H. (1993). 'Introduction: The Nature of Transnational Corporations and their Activities', in John Dunning (ed.), *The Theory of Transnational Corporations*. The United Nations Library on Transnational Corporations, Vol. 1. London and New York: Routledge.

——Roger van Hoesel, and Rajneesh Narula (1996). 'Explaining the "New" Wave of Outward FDI from Developing Countries: the Case of Taiwan and Korea', *Research Memoranda* 009. Maastricht: Maastricht Economic Research Institute on Innovation and Technology.

ECLAC (Economic Commission for Latin America and the Caribbean) (2003). 'Foreign Investment in Latin America and the Caribbean, 2002', (LC/G.2198-P), Santiago, Chile: United Nations publication, Sales No. S.03.II.G.11.

——(2004). 'Foreign Investment in Latin America and the Caribbean, 2003', (LC/G.2226-P), Santiago, Chile: United Nations publication, Sales No. S.04.II.G.54.

——(2005). 'Foreign Investment in Latin America and the Caribbean, 2004', (LC/G.2269-P), Santiago, Chile: United Nations publication, Sales No. E.05.II.G.32.

——(2006). 'Foreign Investment in Latin America and the Caribbean, 2005', (LC/G.2309-P), Santiago, Chile: United Nations publication, Sales No. E.06.II.G.44.

Exame (2005). 'Três problemas ao mesmo tempo', 19 September.

Expansión (2004). 'El juego de Zambrano', 10 November.

——(2005). 'Bimbo: Nueva Dirección', 28 September.

Folha de São Paulo (2005). 'Petrobras sobe no ranking da PIW e é a 14ᵃ empresa de petróleo do mundo', 29 December.

Fundação Dom Cabral (2005). 'A internacionalização da Embraco', unpublished.

——and The London Business School (2002). 'WEG: adaptando o capitalismo familiar ao mercado global', August.

Goldstein, A. and Shaw, T. (2007). *Multinational Companies from Emerging Economies—Composition, Conceptualization and Direction in the Global Economy*. Palgrave Macmillan.

Hymer, S. (1960). Excerpts from 'The International Operations of National Firms', in John Dunning (ed.) (1993), *The Theory of Transnational Corporations*. The United Nations Library on Transnational Corporations, Vol. 1. London and New York: Routledge. First printed by the MIT Press in 1976.

Johanson, J. and Vahlne, J.-E. (1977). 'The Internationalization Process of the Firm—A Model of Knowledge Development and Increasing Foreign Market Commitments', *Journal of International Business Studies*, 8.

————(1990). 'The Mechanisms of Internationalization', *Internatonal Marketing Review* 7(4), 11–29.

Khanna, T. and Palepu, K. (2005). Emerging Giants: Building World-Class Companies in Emerging Markets. Harvard Business School, revised September 15.

Kosacoff, B. (1999). 'Las multinacionales argentinas—una nueva ola en los noventa', *Documento de Trabajo* no. 83ECLAC (Economic Commission for Latin America and the Caribbean). Buenos Aires.

Lall, S. (1983). 'The Theoretical Background', *The New Multinationals: The Spread of Third World Enterprises*, New York: John Wiley and Sons.

Latin Finance (2005). 'Brazil Special Report', September.

Lessard, D. R. (1974). 'International diversification and direct foreign investment', in D. Eitman and A. Stonehill (eds.), *Multinational Business Finance*. Reading, MA: Addison-Wesley. Reproduced in John Dunning (ed.) (1993). *The Theory of Transnational Corporations*. The United Nations Library on Transnational Corporations, Vol. 1. London and New York: Routledge.

López, A. (1999). 'El caso brasileño', in Daniel Chudnovsky, Bernardo Kosacoff, Andrés López, and Celso Garrido (eds.), *Las multinacionales latinoamericanas: sus estrategias en un mundo globalizado*. Buenos Aires: Fondo de Cultura Económica.

Petrobras (2000). *Annual Report, 1999.*

——(2004). *Annual Report, 2003.*

Saraiva de Magalhães, F. and da Rocha, A. (2002). 'A formação de executivos internacionais', *A Internacionalização das Empresas Brasileiras—Estudos de Gestão Internacional*. Rio de Janeiro: COPPEAD/MAUAD.

Stonehill, A. I. and Moffett, M. H. (1993). 'Introduction: International Financial Management', in Stonehill and Moffett (eds.), *The Theory of Transnational Corporations*. The United Nations Library on Transnational Corporations, Vol. 5.

Techint (2004). 'The Techint Group of Companies 2003–2004.'

UNCTAD (United Nations Conference on Trade and Development) (1996). *World Investment Report, 1996: Investment, Trade and International Policy Arrangements.* New York and Geneva: United Nations publication, Sales No. E.96.II.A.14.

——(2001). *World Investment Report, 2001: Promoting Linkages.* New York and Geneva: United Nations publication, Sales No. E.01.II.D.12.

——(2004). *World Investment Report, 2004: The Shift Toward Services.* New York and Geneva: United Nations publication, Sales No. E.04.II.D.33.

——(2005). *World Investment Report, 2005: Transnational Corporations and the Internationalization of R&D.* New York and Geneva: United Nations publication, Sales No. E.05.II.D.10.

—— (2006). *World Investment Report, 2006: TDI from Developing and Transition Economies: Implications for Development.* New York and Geneva: United Nations publication, Sales No. E.06.II.D.11.

Wells, Jr., L. T. (1983). *Third World Multinationals—The Rise of Foreign Investment from Developing Countries.* Cambridge, MA; London, England: The MIT Press.

4

Cycles of Creation and Destruction of Production Capacity and the Development of New Export and Technological Capabilities in Latin America

Jorge Katz

4.1. Introduction

For more than three decades now—at different times and with varying degrees of success—Latin American countries have opened up their economies to foreign competition, deregulated markets, and privatized economic activities. Said actions, which are frequently referred to as market-oriented structural reforms, involved a major departure in policy regime from the 'inward-oriented' 'state-led' regime, which prevailed in the immediate postwar period. The new regime—together with the rapid process of globalization of the world economy that obtained throughout the 1990s—induced a major transformation of the economic, institutional, and technological scenario of each one of the countries in the region. The new model of institutional and socioeconomic functioning of the Latin American economies has significantly affected their growth performance, international competitiveness, equity, and pattern of development of domestic technological capabilities.

New sectors of economic activity have emerged in the economy throughout the 1990s, while many 'old' activities, and forms of production organization, have been gradually phased out (see Table 4.1 below). Labor expulsion both in manufacturing and agricultural activities, and a rapid increase of the informal sector in the economy, obtained in most Latin American countries as a result of that. Different forms of capital intensive computer-based production organization technologies have been introduced by the larger firms in the economy—many of them subsidiaries of multinational corporations (MNCs), or property of nationally owned conglomerates—displacing 'old'—more labor intensive—production organization routines. Said transition introduced a major labor-saving bias in the economy, particularly among 'large' companies. On the other hand, most SMEs have not been able to follow the same path. Thousands of them were forced to leave the market—estimates being that around eight thousand SMEs closed down in Chile and more than twelve thousand did so in Argentina during the 1980s—while the large majority of the ones that remained in business found themselves 'lagging behind' 'large' firms as far as productivity growth and innovation are concerned.

Market-oriented reforms and the process of globalization of the world economy of the past two decades can then be thought of as having triggered off a major episode of 'creation and destruction' in the economy, significantly altering the prevailing production structure and model of social organization. Many sectors of economic activity reduced their participation in the economy, or simply disappeared, while new ones emerged, some firms expanded relative to others, gaining share in total industry output, structural unemployment and informality expanded, and equity in income distribution deteriorated.

Even though the reforms have not delivered what was a priori expected from them in terms of a generalized improvement in economic performance it is nevertheless true that in each and every country in the region a (small) modern sector of economic activity has emerged over the past two decades, involving some 40 percent of GDP in the richest countries in the region, and not much more than, say, 10 percent in the poorest ones. Firms in that segment of the economy have gradually moved into computer-based production organization technologies, attaining much higher than average levels of labor productivity. Said sector includes: (a) natural resource processing activities—such as genetically modified soya beans and vegetable oil in Argentina, salmon farming and wine production in Chile, fresh flowers in Colombia, and many others; (b) high productivity service industries including banks, telecoms, energy, and tourism; and (c) a few technology intensive manufacturing industries, such as airplanes and telecommunication equipment in Brazil.

At variance with the above, however, average labor productivity increased at a much slower pace. As far as labor productivity growth is concerned Latin America has fallen behind more developed industrial nations, or East Asian countries, many of which managed significantly to improve on their long-term performance on these matters during the 1990s, making the 'catchup' process of the Latin American economies all the more difficult. The bottom line is that average labor productivity in Latin America still remains in the range of 20–50 percent of labor productivity in the United States, with Argentina and Chile in the upper part of the range and Ecuador, Paraguay, and Bolivia in the lower one (Katz 2004).

Modern growth theory is not particularly helpful for the understanding of the above mentioned process of structural transformation. Said theory is specified in terms of an aggregate, institutionally free, equilibrium, algorithm, in which changes in the structure of production, macro-to-micro interdependencies, the coevolution of economic, institutional, and technological forces, and the process of creation and destruction of production organization capabilities that obtain during the process of economic development, do not receive adequate treatment. In our view, said aspects are of crucial significance for the understanding of what economic development is all about. In Section 4.2 of the chapter we discuss the role of structural change as a source of economic growth. In Section 4.3 we examine the empirical evidence concerning structural change in various Latin American economies during the course of the past three decades. Section 4.4 turns to various sector-specific scenarios in order to show how important it is to examine micro level economic and institutional issues if we are adequately to understand the ongoing transformation of Latin American production structure and pattern of international competitiveness. Section 4.5 wraps up examining the likely contents of a policy agenda for the future aiming at enhancing the overall growth performance of Latin American economies.

4.2. Structural Change as a Source of Economic Growth

In classical economics structural change constitutes a major source of growth. A growing economy is one that becomes more complex and sophisticated through time as a result of the creation of new sectors of economic activity and the entry of new, technologically more sophisticated, firms. *Pari pasu* with the above new institutions develop and learning processes obtain and diffuse throughout the entire production fabric. It is such a process of economic, technological, and institutional development that induced S. Kuznets and M. Abramovitz to differentiate between the 'immediate' and the 'ultimate' sources of economic growth. An expanding capital labor ratio—resulting from a higher rate of investment—is seen by them as an 'immediate' source of growth in the economy, while learning, the accumulation of domestic technological capabilities, institutional changes, and the improvement of production organization capabilities are regarded as the 'ultimate' determinants of growth. They constitute hidden 'social capabilities' which operate beneath the surface. The fact that we do not normally measure them—in many cases we do not even know how to do it—does not really mean that they are not present and constitute the essence of what development is all about.

Given the above, we believe that the long-term performance of the economy needs to be described not just in terms of macro variables and with reference to the 'immediate' sources of growth—as modern growth theory does—but rather as the outcome of the interaction between macro and micro forces involving the coevolution of economic, institutional, and technological forces that come together in the process of structural change. Said process is centrally associated to the inception of new economic activities in the economy. In our view, development it is not just a matter of adequate macro 'fundamentals' but rather a more complex social phenomena which involves in a very fundamental way changes in institutions, learning processes, and the expansion of production organization capabilities in the economy. Of course macroeconomic stability plays a major role for these results to be attained, but it is certainly not a sufficient condition for it.

Many of the above mentioned changes in the 'ultimate' sources of growth come together in the process of inception of new activities in the economy. As production capacity expands learning processes are triggered off and new institutions—in the sense of long-term habits and patterns of social interaction—develop. The inception of new activities—and the phasing out of 'old' ones—is what explains the long-term process of transformation of society.

Contrary to conventional growth theory which takes the production structure as given and examines its expansion through time—in the late 1990s A. Harberger used an illuminating metaphor of the above considering neoclassical growth as an expanding balloon, in which the relative size of each part of the structure does not change as the size of the balloon increases (Harberger 1998). Rather, we notice that structural change constitutes much of what development is all about. It is the change in the production structure that allows for more division of labor, specialization, and productivity growth, as well as for the gradual expansion of more knowledge intensive production activities, including the production of capital goods and engineering services.

Furthermore, we notice that subsequent to the inception of new sectors of economic activity in the economy gradual changes obtain in the structure and behavior of said sectors, with markets becoming more 'contested' and international competitiveness improving through time as a result of learning and accumulating externalities. New patterns of interaction emerge between firms and other organizations in the economy such as universities, intermediate input suppliers, engineering firms, trade unions, banks, insurance companies, public sector regulatory agencies, and so forth. No universal and unique pattern of economic and institutional development can be used adequately to describe the evolutionary process of different sectors of economic activity. Variety is the essence of complexity. In some cases the dynamic agent motorizing the inception of a new activity in the economy appears to be a multinational firm (or more than one), that plays a major role transferring technology, opening up external markets, training domestic labor and subcontractors and enhancing domestic engineering practices and capabilities. In other cases such a role is played by family-owned SMEs or by large domestic conglomerates, both public and/or private. The industrial organization model that obtains in each case is bound to be different in terms of market structure and performance, as well as in terms of 'clustering' and interactions between 'large' and 'small' firms in the economy, subcontracting practices, access to external markets and so forth.

Looked at from this perspective—the inception of new sectors in the economy as a source of economic growth—we notice that a great deal has happened in Latin America over the past three decades, *pari pasu* with the process of trade liberalization and market deregulations. Chile has gone through a successful process of new industry inceptions in the late 1980s and during the 1990s. The mining sector, the telecom sector, the pulp and paper industry, the salmon farming industry, the transformation of the 'old' wine industry into a new and highly competitive one in international markets, the more recent expansion of the retail industry constitute very vivid expressions of an economy which has experienced a dramatic process of structural and institutional transformation. State-of-the-art plants, professional management, increasingly sophisticated regulatory institutions and growing penetration in world markets gradually resulted from this process. Far from being a 'hands-off' strategy from the point of view of public sector intervention the Chilean process shows an active government behind the wheels. In our opinion this provides a rich micro story of the Chilean successful transformation of the past three decades that a 'conventional' macro interpretation of the Chilean successful transformation simply fails to capture.

In the same vein, Argentina and Colombia have also gone through an important process of structural transformation, involving, for example, the inception of genetically modified soya beans and vegetable oil production in the case of Argentina and of the fresh flower industry in the case of Colombia. Table 4.1 provides preliminary information—at the three digit level of aggregation—of the changing composition of manufacturing production in Argentina, Brazil, Chile, Colombia, and Mexico over the period 1970–2002. It also presents an index of 'structural transformation' of the industrial sector for the above mentioned countries, comparing 1970 with 1996, 2002, and 2002.[1]

Table 4.1 indicates that:

(a) The process of structural transformation has been strongly biased in favor of natural resource processing activities and foodstuff production in Argentina, Chile, Colombia, and Brazil. This is not the pattern of change that prevailed in Mexico.

(b) *Pari pasu* with the above, the share of metalworking industries—which we should regard as engineering intensive sectors—have significantly contracted in Argentina, Chile, and Colombia, but not so in Brazil and Mexico.

Table 4.1. Changes in the structure of industry (1970, 1996, 2000, 2002)

	ARGENTINA				BRAZIL				CHILE				COLOMBIA				MEXICO			
	1970	1996	2000	2002	1970	1996	2000	2002	1970	1996	2000	2002	1970	1996	2000	2002	1970	1996	2000	2002
I	13.2	9.9	8.6	6.7	16.2	25.6	26.0	26.5	11.4	10.4	10.5	10.0	12.3	10.1	8.7	9.0	12.0	14.4	16.4	15.6
II	10.9	7.2	7.4	6.1	6.8	7.3	8.3	8.9	5.5	1.9	2.3	1.9	3.0	6.5	4.9	6.5	8.4	14.6	18.8	18.6
III+IV	47.8	62.1	65.3	71.7	37.8	43.4	41.6	41.5	58.3	59.7	60.7	61.9	46.2	55.4	57.0	57.1	43.2	43.4	39.1	40.8
V	28.1	20.7	18.7	15.6	39.2	23.7	24.0	23.1	24.9	28.0	26.5	26.2	38.5	28.1	29.4	27.3	36.4	27.6	25.8	25.0
Total	100	100	100	100	100	100	100	100	100	100	100	100	100	100	100	100	100	100	100	100
ICE*		14.3	18.0	25.3		18.9	32.3	27.6		40.1	27.3	33.5		19.4	29.9	30.9		17.3	22.1	22.5

Source: PADI.
* Structural change index, vis-à-vis 1970.
I. Engineering intensive industries (excluding automobiles) CIIU 381, 382, 383, 385.
II. Automobiles (CIIU 384).
III+IV. Natural resource intensive industries. Foodstuffs, beverages, and tobacco (CIIU 311, 313, 314); resources processing industries (CIIU, 341, 351, 354, 355, 356, 371, 372).
V. Labor intensive industries (CIIU 321, 322, 323, 324, 331, 332, 342, 352, 361, 362, 369, 390).

(c) The vehicle industry—a clear example of an engineering intensive sector—expanded in Brazil, Colombia—and strongly so—in Mexico.

As far as the index of structural change is concerned—which compares the current industrial structure with that of the 1970s—it indicates that Chile is the country in which the structure has changed the most, particularly in the 1980s and early 1990s. This is of course consistent with our previous argument as to the crucial role the inception of new production activities has played, particularly so in the case of Chile, explaining a successful pattern of structural transformation.

Having thus far shown the global direction in which the industrial sector of Argentina, Brazil, Chile, Colombia, and Mexico changed during the past two decades, we now turn to a more micro examination of the impact such change has had upon sector-specific industrial organization regimes and country-wide international competitiveness. The exploration is intended to show the complex web of coevolving sector-specific technological, institutional, and economic forces that underlie the process in the various national scenarios. A conventional macroeconomic interpretation of what is going on in the region does not provide an adequate description of the issues we want to highlight.

4.3. The Inception of New Industrial Activities in the Economy

We have so far argued that structural change is associated with the inception of new production activities in the economy and that this process is associated with major changes in industrial organization and in international competitiveness. Also, that the inception process involves economic, institutional, and technological forces that coevolve and interact in time. Furthermore, we have argued that the process can not be adequately described in terms of an aggregate algorithm as the one employed by modern growth theory. We now consider three different scenarios that show this to be the case.

(1) genetically modified (genetically modified) soya beans and vegetable oil production in Argentina: The diffusion of transgenic crops started in the world in 1995. By 2002 there were nearly 60 million hectares under cultivation, 14 million of which were located in Argentina. More than 90 percent of current production of soya beans in Argentina corresponds to the genetically modified type, the country being the second largest world producer and exporter of said product, after the United States.[2] Close to 20 percent of current Argentinian exports come from this industry.

The transition from conventional to genetically modified soya beans involved a major transformation in production organization as well as in institutions. 'Cero tillage' (*siembra directa*) and 'contract agriculture' (*agricultura de contratos*)[3] now dominate the scene in Argentina, with the farmer having taken a step back as organizer of the production process, his role having been taken over by large independent subcontractors and financial intermediaries. Soya bean production now constitutes the subject of risk-sharing contracts among farmers, financial intermediaries, and specialized agricultural consulting firms. The technology package—seeds, fertilizers, herbicides—is privately owned by a few large multinational corporations, establishing a clear difference with the situation that prevailed during the 'green revolution'— in the 1960s—when agricultural technology was basically a 'public good' disseminated by public sector agricultural agencies.

Many new institutions have emerged during the process of transition to genetically modified soya beans in Argentina. It is believed, for example, that as much as 40 percent of the genetically modified seeds used in any given agricultural campaign constitute 'retained' seeds from the previous campaigns (the so-called 'bolsa blanca') which are being sold as unauthorized versions, violating intellectual property rights held by Monsanto. This reflects the weak enforcement capacity the company has so far been able to attain in Argentina. Monsanto is now beginning to retaliate as a result of the above, putting pressure on Argentina to strengthen IPR protection.

A similar picture of deep structural transformation can be found as we move from the agricultural sphere to the industrial one, and consider the way in which vegetable oil production is being carried out. A new vintage of automated and highly capital intensive plants came on stream in Argentina during the 1990s for such purpose. These plants are highly sophisticated and they feature a significantly different technology—they are based on catalytic processes—than those that characterized manufacturing vegetable oil production in Argentina in the 1970s.

The above information indicates that the Argentinian transition to genetically-modified soya bean and vegetable oil production has involved major economic, institutional, and technological forces that have coevolved and retrofitted into each other through time, opening up a new 'window of opportunity' for the expansion of Argentinian international competitiveness on the basis of its rich natural resources. It is interesting to observe that a sophisticated biotechnological 'cluster' is presently developing around the genetically modified soya bean seed industry, this appearing as a major externality associated to the process of structural change. (Bisang 2005).

(2) Salmon farming in Chile:[4] The process through which international competitiveness was attained by the Chilean salmon farming industry covers the best part of two decades, a period in which many new firms—national and foreign—entered the market, sector-specific institutions and skills developed, professional management took over an originally quasi-artisan industry significantly altering production organization and international marketing practices. As a result of the cumulative impact of these changes Chile gradually

acquired 'world-class' status as one of the three major salmon farming countries in the world, side by side with Norway and Scotland.

Salmon farming in Chile can be described as having evolved through three quite different 'stages' of development, in which the actors and the problems changed quite significantly. There is first an inception 'stage' in which salmon farming was successfully introduced and adapted to the Chilean environment, almost entirely starting from imported genetic material. This is a stage in which trial and error and learning appear as major factors explaining both individual firm behavior and the starting-up period of a new industry. 'Teething' problems were proverbial during that period, both at the individual firm and industry level. The Chilean government played an important role during this period through the action of both Corfo and Fundacion Chile. There is then a second 'stage' in which the industry rapidly increased in size and complexity with the entry to the market of many intermediate input suppliers, service-firms, and the building up of a strong sector-specific industrial 'cluster'. During those years the industry made a strong inroad into the international market place, becoming the second ranking worldwide exporter of salmon after Norway. The role of the state changed quite significantly during this period, taking a step back as a dynamic agent inducing the inception of a new activity, but strongly concentrating in developing the regulatory environment and surveillance mechanisms in which the industry was due to operate.

The sector finally evolved into a third stage in which a major transformation in industrial structure obtained through M&A, changes in plant ownership, FDI, and a rapid process of internationalization.

In the short period of less than twenty years Chilean salmon exports—almost entirely cultivated salmon—increased from less than US$50 million in 1989 to around US$1,700 million in 2005. Salmon exports now account for close to 5 percent of Chilean total exports. From an almost a negligible participation in the world's production of salmon—2 percent in 1987—Chile's share in world farmed salmon has reached nearly one third in recent years.

Public organizations, foreign companies, and a large number of SMEs participated in the early years of industry inception. Although there was a clear public sector involvement in the industry right from the beginning—through Corfo and Fundacion Chile—it is also clear that right from the start a new vintage of Chilean entrepreneurs entered the industry and became the driving force behind the wheel. Regulatory and sanitary activities—such as fishing and cultivation permits, monitoring environmental impact, controlling salmon egg imports, and so forth—are adequately performed by government agencies such as SAG, Sernapesca, Conama, and others. The required legal infrastructure supporting the above was set up in the late 1970s and during the 1980s and was considerably improved thereafter complying with international standards (*Acuanoticias*, November 1997).

It was in the late 1990s that the Chilean salmon farming sector attained many of its present features as a 'mature' oligopoly.[5] World prices for salmon fell significantly in the second half of the 1990s, unit gross margins contracted, as competition increased and the markets for salmon became more 'contested.' The technological and competitive regime of the industry became more demanding as a result of M&A which, on the one hand, made the average size of firm considerably bigger and technologically more sophisticated and, on the other, increased business concentration and turned the industry into an oligopolistic sector.

It is important to notice, though, that although the above mentioned process of convergence of Chilean salmon farming production to world-class status involved the absorption of 'state-of-the-art' production organization and environmental protection technologies, it did not so far involved a strong commitment to R&D and knowledge generation activities. In-house technological efforts are still frail among Chilean salmon farming firms. Neither have local firms yet developed more sophisticated forms of direct international marketing using Chilean trade marks and building up a case for local geographical denominations.

(3) Fresh flower production in Colombia: Production of fresh flowers for export started in Colombia as a quasi-artisan activity in the mid-1960s. By 2004, exports amounted to nearly US$ 700 million annually. Nearly 400 companies—many of them SMEs—are actively engaged in this activity, providing direct employment to some 90,000 workers and indirect employment to some further 75,000. Close to 10,000 hectares have been brought into cultivation. Colombia accounts for nearly 16 percent of the total world trade in fresh flowers.

The Colombian fresh flower sector is gradually developing into a lively 'cluster' of independent suppliers of hybrid seeds, herbicides, and pesticides, financial and insurance services and so forth. Much remains to be done, though, supporting the development of 'collective action' for the supply of 'public goods' to the industry in terms of genetic research and development activities, the strengthening of international marketing practices, the legal enforcement of local trade marks and geographical denominations, and so forth. A large number of public and private organizations are presently involved in these activities and new institutions and mechanisms of interaction between firms and other organizations in the economy are gradually developing. For example, quite recently Floraverde has been created in order to certify firms for adequate and sustainable use of water resources, herbicides, and the protection of the environment. Some 150 firms already belong in its network and as many as sixty of them have already received certification for 'good manufacturing practices'. Although none of these firms is actually involved in formal R&D activities it is to be noted that many of them have introduced fairly advanced waste management technologies, water consumption reduction routines, and other 'state-of-the-art' practices. The diffusion of information and communication technologies—which is presently a major issue in the technological upgrading path of this industry—will no doubt help achieve network externalities associated with the diffusion of ICTs and its subsequent impact upon the provision of marketing and technological information. The development of sector-specific software for this industry should be encouraged as a major contributing mechanism for further sectoral expansion.

The three cases so far presented show the sector-specific nature of the economic, technological, and institutional forces that are involved in the inception of new production and export activities in the economy. No doubt macroeconomic forces play an important role conditioning microeconomic behavior, but it is the complexity and sector-specific nature of the process that needs to be understood if policymakers are to succeed in enhancing international competitiveness and the development of domestic technological capabilities. Neutral interventions—such as better quality education, energy provision, efficient transport and shipping facilities and so forth—are, no doubt, of major importance, but sector-specific actions are crucially required if countries are to strengthen their domestic technological absorption capabilities and further improve in international competitiveness. The fact that different forms of market failure as well as the lack of public goods negatively affect the functioning of capital and technology markets suggests that public sector interventions are required in order to develop dynamic comparative advantages based on knowledge and innovation. We close with a few policy suggestions in such direction.

4.4. Policies for the Enhancement of Technological Capabilities and International Competitiveness

Technology and capital markets provide canonical examples of different forms of market failure. Improving on their efficiency and efficacy appears as a sine qua non condition for productivity growth and innovation throughout the region.

In order to expand knowledge-generation and diffusion activities Latin American countries have to deal with financial, human capital, and institutional constraints. National Innovation Systems in the region are still highly inefficient pieces of social machinery, whose various parts respond to different spheres of government and are scarcely coordinated and accountable for performance. Public and university R&D labs, public sector regulatory agencies, banks, and engineering firms appear as highly isolated organizations which do not normally think of themselves as being partners of a joint and common mission, that is, that of expanding the rate of innovation in the economy and of enhancing the technological absorption capabilities of domestic enterprises and human resources. Coordination efforts making the above more of a 'collective' goal seem to be needed in the years ahead if Latin American countries are to close the international productivity gap they presently exhibit.

It is of crucial importance to increase the amount of resources countries allocate to R&D activities, but it is also of high priority to induce the private sector in the economy to expand its commitment to R&D and knowledge-generation efforts and to develop a more long-term attitude with respect to resources spent in this field. Strengthening intellectual property rights and providing stronger financial incentives appear to be crucial mechanisms to lure private firms in such a direction. Adequate mechanisms for the legal enforcement of property rights need to be set up, given the weak legal environment most countries in the region presently exhibit in this field. This should be done, however, within the framework of adequate competition and regulatory policies that would keep an eye on the likely exploitation of monopolistic market power from the part of firms whose patent rights are to be strengthened.

Surely the public sector has an important role to play—through its universities and R&D labs—exploring the basic knowledge frontier related to the sustainable exploitation of natural resources. Molecular biology and biotechnologies, genetics and immunology, and human and animal health sciences (including those related to the production of vaccines and pharmaceuticals), should be supported as part of a global strategy further to exploit domestic natural resources on the basis of sound environmental protection principles. Also, the expansion of computer sciences and information technologies, of fundamental importance for the ongoing transition to a learning economy, should be supported with public sector resources. But beyond the above, it is the private sector in the economy that needs to be lured into adopting a more 'hand-on' attitude in the development and adoption of new technology 'down-stream' of the basic sciences, if Latin American countries are to attain a more rapid pace of innovation and technological progress. This appears as a sine qua non for countries to attain, on the one hand, a more rapid expansion of exports featuring higher domestic added value and, on the other, better provision of 'merit' goods and services such as health, water and sanitation services, and housing facilities. All of the above—exports of a higher quality and more access to 'merit' goods as those previously mentioned—is required if Latin American countries are to reduce within a reasonable time the income and productivity gap they presently exhibit vis-à-vis more developed industrial nations.

Other actors of the National Innovation System—such as banks, universities, and municipal authorities, for example—should be called to take a more active participation in domestic technological affairs exploring, for example, new mechanisms through which to develop venture capital markets and human capital upgrading programs. In relation to the financing of R&D efforts new ways of developing venture capital markets should be explored. The role of government acting as a 'second floor' financial intermediary, decentralizing the management of public R&D funds to commercial banks should be examined, inducing the banking system to assume a more active role in the field. Also, large financial firms involved in the provision of social security services should be brought to bear in the development of a more vibrant domestic capital market.

The creation of technological parks and incubators might be explored in fields such as agribusiness, aquaculture, novel ways of using timber in housing and furniture, and others fields 'down-stream' of the rich natural resources now under exploitation in the region. Firms offering computer software and engineering services for SMEs should be encouraged to develop, as engineering companies seem to be presently catering almost exclusively for the needs of 'large' firms in the economy, making digital production organization technologies almost inaccessible for most SMEs.

The strengthening of the production fabric at the local and municipal level demands many new forms of 'collective' action and public sector coordination. The rationale for this comes from the evidence that strong network externalities result when acting at the local level. Inducing the development of industrial 'clusters' organized around the exploitation of natural resources opens up the opportunity for collaborative efforts between municipalities, regional universities, research centers, and small family enterprises, exploring forms of interaction which have so far remained basically untapped in agribusiness, the forestry industry, aquaculture, and many others. The protection of the property rights of the local aboriginal communities should be carefully taken into account when considering policies in this direction, as many of the new natural resource intensive activities might collide with traditional communities which have for many years made their living from these resources.

To trigger off collective action and more coordination efforts at the local level constitutes a complex problem. Market mechanisms, 'subsidies to demand' and 'public brokers' could be used in order to help SMEs developing innovative projects. A rich experience in this direction has recently developed in countries such as Chile, Brazil, Costa Rica, and others indicating that efforts in this direction—though small in terms of their relative impact upon aggregate GDP—might turn out to be quite important at the local and municipal level.

The speeding up of the transition to a knowledge-based economy also appears as a promising area for public/private action. Its impact upon productivity growth and equity improvements is likely to be quite strong in the years ahead. The subject is highly prominent in the current public policy agenda of many countries in the region which are making progress in the expansion of the ICT infrastructure in schools, hospitals, and local municipalities. Such process could be combined with further support for the development of domestic content industries specifically catering for the health and educational needs of regional and local communities. Expanding internet connectivity and closing down both the international and domestic 'digital divide' might become the corner stone of a global productivity improvement program facilitating the transition to a knowledge economy.

It is difficult *ex ante* to say which policies would succeed and which ones would fail in the process of enhancing the rate of innovation and the technological performance of the economy. The process of inducing more knowledge generation and diffusion efforts and of expanding access to the goods and services underlying the transition to a knowledge-based economy should be seen as highly strategic issues under current circumstances. No 'one-size-fits-all' policy is likely to succeed. Trial and error and a highly pragmatic approach to these matters seem hardly avoidable. The experience of the dynamic East Asian economies, as well as of Ireland, New Zealand, and Israel, confirms the fact that this is not a field in which readily available recipes can be found. Capitalist regimes are highly different across the world and it is time enough for Latin American countries to begin searching for their own brand of capitalism, starting experimentation with proactive interventions aiming at the development of a more dynamic national innovation system.

Notes

1. The figures presented in the table have been calculated using ECLAC's PADI program and software. Thanks are due to Mr G. Stumpo and Ms J. Marincovic from the DDPE Division at ECLAC for providing me with access to the data and helping me with the calculations.
2. Brazil is also a large producer of soya beans—together with Argentina and the United States they account for nearly 95 percent of the total world supply of said product— but it has not so far entered into the genetically modified variety. Its large output is basically of 'conventional' soya and it has not so far liberated genetically modified versions of this crop (Trigo et al. 2002).
3. In actual fact both these changes do not necessarily depend on the use of genetically modified seeds, and they were already employed by local farmers before Monsanto started to commercialize Roundup Ready (RR), its registered trade mark.
4. This section is based on a previous paper of the present author written for the World Bank in 2004 (Katz 2004).
5. What a 'mature' industry actually is, and how the notion applies to the case of salmon farming, has been made quite clear in a recent public conference by Mr Torben Petersen, CEO of Fjord Seafood Chile, a subsidiary from the Norwegian company of the same name when he stated that 'The real maturation process begins

when we see that company actions are aimed at the markets and not at production, in other words, when salmon farming growth is determined by its market and not by its production'. See *Acuanoticias* No. 79, 18 May 2004.

References

Ablin, E. and Paz, S. (2000). 'Productos transgenicos y exportaciones agricolas. Reflexiones en torno a un dilema argentino', *Mimeo*, Cancillería Argentina, Direccion de Negociaciones Economicas y Cooperación Internacional. Bs.As.
Amsdem, A. (2001). *The Rise of 'the Rest.' Challenges to the West from Late Industrializing Economies*. Oxford University Press.
Aquanoticias (Journal of the Chilean Salmon Farming Industry). Various numbers.
Benavente, J. M. March 2005. 'OECD Survey, Chilean Innovation Policy', *Mimeo*, Department of Economics, University of Chile.
Bisang, R. (2005). 'La empresas de biotecnología en la Argentina', *Mimeo*, UNGS, Junio.
Goldstein, A. (August, 2007). 'Embraer: From National Champion to Global Player', *Cepal Review*, 77: 97–115.
Goldstein, A. (2005). 'The Political Economy of Industrial Policy in China. The Case of Aircraft Manufacturing', *Mimeo*, OECD, Paris.
Harberger, A. (March 1998). 'A Vision of the Growth Process', *American Economic Review*, Vol. 88.
Katz, J. (2002). 'Efficiency and Equity Aspects of the New Latin American Economic Model', *Economics of Innovation and New Technologies*, Vol. 11.
—— (2003). 'Market-Oriented Reforms, Globalization and the Recent Transformation of Latin American Innovation Systems', *Research Policy*.
—— and Stumpo, G. (2001). 'Regimenes competitivos sectoriales, productividad y competitividad internacional', *Desarrollo Productivo*, 103, ECLAC, Santiago de Chile.
Moguillansky, G. (1999). *La inversion en Chile: el fin de un ciclo en expansion?* Fondo de Cultura Economica—CEPAL, Santiago de Chile.
OECD (2002). *Education at a Glance*. Paris: OECD.
Saviotti, P. and Gaffard, J. L. (November 2004). 'Innovation, Structural Change and Growth', *Revue Economique*, Vol. 55.
Trigo, E. et al. (2002). *Los transgenicos en la agricultura argentina. Una historia con final abierto*. IICA-Libros del Zorzal, Buenso Aires.
Williamson, J. and Kuczynski, P. P. (2003). *After the Washington Consensus. Restating Growth and Reforms in Latin America*. Institute for International Economics, Washington.

5

The Politics of Institutional Renovation and Economic Upgrading: Lessons from the Argentinian Wine Industry

*Gerald A. McDermott**

5.1. Introduction

Scholars of economic development increasingly argue that growth and international competitiveness depend on the ability of a society to upgrade its firms and industries—a shift from lower- to higher-value economic activities by using local innovative capacities to make continuous improvements in processes, products, and functions (Doner, Ritchie, and Slater 2005; Giuliani, Pietrobelli, and Rabellotti 2005*b*). The attendant creation and diffusion of skills and knowledge relies on collective resources and coordination. In turn, innovative capacities depend not simply on the presence of foreign investors but especially on particular local constellations of interfirm networks, institutions, and state capacities.[1] Yet, as is evident in current debates about the origins and change in institutions (Mahoney and Rueschemeyer 2003; Campbell 2004; Greif and Laitin 2004), the developmental state (O'Riain 2004; Doner et al. 2005), clusters (Schmitz 2004*b*; Perez-Aleman 2005), and socioeconomic networks (Ansell 2000; Kogut 2000; Padgett 2001; Adler and Kwon 2002; Powell et al. 2002), it is less clear how public and private actors forge innovative capacities in the first place. This is particularly distressing for regions like Latin America, where the history of failed development and backwardness

* I am indebted to the Mack Center, the Reginald H. Jones Center, and the GE Fund for their generous financial support for this research. I have also benefitted from comments on earlier versions by Ron Burt, Richard Doner, Laszlo Bruszt, Tulia Falleti, Gary Gereffi, Elisa Giuliani, Bruce Kogut, Richard Locke, John Paul MacDuffie, Ben Ross Schneider, Sean Safford, Jordan Siegel, and Sid Winter as well as participants in the Bowman Workshop at Wharton, the Workshop in Organizations and Markets at the University of Chicago, and the HBS International Seminar Series. All errors and omissions are my own.

points to a lack of the requisite social and institutional preconditions (Pack 2000; Haber 2002; Levitsky and Murillo, 2005).

Analysis of the Argentinian wine sector may be especially helpful here. On the one hand, Argentina is typically known for its dysfunctional social capital and political–economic institutions (Ross Schneider 2004; Levitsky and Murillo 2005), and its wine industry has a long history of backwardness and virtually no international presence. On the other hand, the Argentinian wine sector witnessed a turnaround in the 1990s and now accounts for more than 2 percent of the over $12 billion global wine market. In particular, the divergent upgrading paths of the dominant, neighboring winemaking provinces of Mendoza and San Juan offer a unique opportunity to use a longitudinal, subnational comparative analysis to evaluate the determinants of more or less successful attempts to create new innovative capacities (Schmitz and Nadvi 1999; Montero 2001; Snyder 2001). Mendoza has captured the disproportionate share of exports by building in the 1990s a new constellation of institutions and networks that support sustained improvements in processes and products in a wide variety of firms. In contrast, San Juan has been a laggard in upgrading its wine and grapes, despite advancing policies that did usher in large amounts of new investment. Moreover, the institutional model pioneered by Mendoza is being replicated at the national level. In 2004, the Argentinian congress and president signed into law a strategic wine sector policy that is self-financing and is governed by a non-state body composed of representatives from relevant business associations, research institutions, and provincial and federal ministries. This policy and governance structure are arguably without precedent in a country known for the executive imposing protectionist policies that end up draining the budget and benefitting a few elites (Guillen 2001; Ross Schneider 2004).

What types of institutional innovations contributed to the upgrading in Mendoza? How did the policymaking process in Mendoza enable public and private actors to build these new institutions and networks in the 1990s, when they were unable previously and while those in San Juan could not?

This article argues that changes in upgrading and institutions are not wholly determined by preexisting conditions or by the sudden implantation of new rules or incentives. Rather, different political approaches to reform, especially during crises, can facilitate or impede the construction of new public–private institutions that underpin upgrading and the recombination of socioeconomic ties between previously antagonistic groups. Political approaches to reform are prior to and broader than particular policies. They are strategies governments use to construct political power that define the mechanisms linking the functioning and substance of institutions with policymaking coalitions (Jacoby 2000; Thelen 2003). In this view, upgrading and institutional change are incremental processes, in which the relevant firms, associations, and public actors jointly experiment with new roles and rules. In identifying the basic spectrum of political approaches to reform, this article aims to clarify the governance conditions that can help initiate and sustain these experiments.

During crises, governments have the political space to overcome past sociopolitical constraints by formulating a strategy to confront the dual challenge of reconstructing the boundary between the public and private domains and recombining the relative power and social ties among firms and their associations (Snyder 2001; Ross Schneider 2004). On the one hand, a government may choose what I call a 'depoliticization' approach, which aims to insulate centralized policymaking and quickly impose new rules based on high-powered economic incentives. On the other hand, a government may choose what I call a 'participatory restructuring' approach which aims to embed the state and policymaking in society in new ways (Hirst 1994; Sabel 1994; Montero 2001; Evans 2004). This approach rests on two key principles of empowered participatory governance (Fung and Wright 2001): (a) empowering a variety of public agencies and socioeconomic groups to participate in institution-building; and (b) requiring participants to share private information in ways that induce collective problem solving and mutual monitoring. The former approach may initially stimulate investment but will tend to impede upgrading and keep the past disproportionate distribution of resources. The latter approach can bring together previously disparate and even antagonistic groups in new ways so as to foster collective learning and monitoring and thus new public–private institutions supportive of upgrading.

Section 5.2 lays out the theoretical underpinnings of this argument. Section 5.3 reviews upgrading in the Argentinian wine industry. In the 1990s, Mendoza appears to have initiated and sustained coordinated, decentralized product and process experiments across a wide variety of firms, microclimates, and products. Section 5.4 argues that the divergent outcomes in San Juan and Mendoza can not be explained alone by inherited structural variables, such as soils, climates, industrial and social structures, macroeconomic conditions, legal regimes, strength of political executive, and political party affiliation. In particular, the evidence suggests that inherited social and professional ties alone may help initiate new forms of collective learning, but their exclusionary principles can also thwart broad-based upgrading and collective action due to the diversity of interests, historical animosity, and resource inequalities between regions within a province. Section 5.5 analyzes the different political approaches by the governments of the two provinces in confronting the general economic turbulence and growing crisis in wine sector in the late 1980s. It shows how Mendoza's participatory restructuring approach to building new public–private institutions helped overcome these conflicts by recombining the ties among diverse groups and fostering collective problem-solving.[2]

5.2. Linking the Macro and the Micro for Change and Growth

There are two broad views about the social and political forces that shape the development of new interorganizational networks and institutions supporting innovative capacities. The 'top down' view understands change as epochal. During periods of crisis, governments have the political space to insulate a strong, coherent policymaking apparatus from particularistic interests to design and impose rapidly a new set of rules and institutions on society. Whether one emphasizes rapid market liberalization and private property rights or strategic interventions into industries, the new rules are based largely on high-powered economic incentives that will guide domestic and foreign firms to make the necessary investments into new technologies and capabilities (Haggard and Kaufman 1995; Boycko, Shleifer and Vishny 1995; Amsden 1989).

In contrast, the 'bottom up' view emphasizes the continuity of social forces and is suspicious of the interventions and rules suddenly imposed from the commanding heights. Economic activity is mediated by and embedded in networks and associations that embody distinct sets of social ties, norms, reputations, and resources. Scholars may argue about whether the origins and reproduction of these properties are rooted in repeated interactions among individuals facing common externalities (Ostrom 1990), deep traditions of civic mindedness and kinship (Putnam et al. 1993), or past sociopolitical conflicts (Padgett 2001; Schneider 2004). But they share the view that these properties are enduring and that, at the limit, the public rules, policies, and institutions are essentially the formal manifestations of the attendant social norms and structure. Government receives and enforces the game but rarely defines it autonomously.

These literatures have certainly improved our understanding of the conditions for growth and innovation. However, their apparent incompatibilities reveal some common weaknesses. First, to the extent that development in general and institution building in particular relies on the insulation of the executive and a team of technocrats, then the lack of information and knowledge flows between groups of policymakers and recipients not only can breed self-dealing and 'monocropping', but also can destroy social and human capital (Ostrom 1995; McDermott 2002a, 2002b; Evans 2004). Second, many of the received accounts of social structure and institutions tend to reify interests and social groups in such ways as to make them functional, binary, and immutable to change (Granovetter 1985). Third, although a society may contain a plethora of, say, professional associations, the attendant social ties and norms that can ground collaboration and collective learning can also be self-limiting and exclusionary. To the extent that these groups have different needs and resources, are relatively isolated, and are not incorporated into more encompassing institutions, a diverse socioeconomic environment can easily produce a balkanized society that thwarts broad-based innovation, knowledge diffusion, and institutional change (Ostrom 1999; Safford 2004; Schneider 2004).

These criticisms highlight that optimal incentives or the inherited structure of the state, electoral rules, and socioeconomic groups may be indeterminate in clarifying how public and private actors forge new organizational and institutional forms to promote innovative capacities even during crises, particularly when a society has a long history of dysfunctional social structures and political–economic institutions. In order to begin to capture the interaction of continuity and change, one must first clarify the political approaches toward reform that can both redefine the boundary between the public and private domains and recombine the ties and resources of relevant socioeconomic groups. This article aims to specify the spectrum of these approaches and their mechanisms for inducing and sustaining change. These specifications can provide the conceptual links between the broader sociopolitical trends of a society and the upgrading outcomes.

The first insight toward filling this gap comes from research that emphasizes the public–private nature of upgrading institutions and the ways in which they help embed the state and constituent business associations in a constellation of horizontal governance and professional ties (Evans 1995; Perez-Aleman 2005; Montero 2001; Schmitz 2004b). While market failures may require government intervention, uncertainty, and informational asymmetries make unclear just what new rule or initiative is applicable (Ostrom 1999; Jacoby 2000; Evans 2004). For instance, Rodrik (2004) has aptly noted that 'the task of industrial policy is as much about eliciting information from the private sector on significant externalities and their remedies as it is about implementing appropriate policies.' Rodrik's point is based on the understanding that policymaking and institution building are not one time events but rather experimental, demanding continual information and knowledge exchange between the superiors and subordinates, between policymakers and their constituents (Sabel 1994).

But opening up the policymaking process can easily result in capture by the existing privileged groups, which can restrict the diversity of information and interests and sow the seeds of self-dealing. To avoid these outcomes, political approaches to reform would have to include two criteria: economic and political empowerment of a variety of, especially marginalized, groups and rules of governance that sustain collective-problem solving. First, research on Latin American political economy shows that even resource constrained governments can break the status quo by granting a variety of associations and cooperatives new access to public resources and policymaking (Tendler 1997; Snyder 2001; Schneider 2004). In particular, the combination of incentives for firms to channel their demands via their collective organizations and of rules of inclusive participation in the formation of new institutions and programs can create new social and professional ties among previously isolated, even antagonistic socioeconomic groups and the state (Padgett and Ansell 1993; Stark and Bruszt 1998; Burt 2000). Such a process of recombination can allow the relevant public and private actors to access new knowledge, resources, and partners, improve mutual monitoring, and induce a greater variety of firm and policy experiments (Cohen and Rogers 1992; Locke 1995; Ross Schneider 2004; Safford 2004).

Second, in return for membership, participants adhere to governance rules of deliberation and collective problem solving, while non-state participants may gradually increase their material contribution to the institution. Deliberation is the iterative process by which the participants jointly define objectives, evaluate results, and decide on the next measures to be taken by the nascent institutions (Baiocchi 2001; Fung and Wright 2001). As participants attempt to justify their interests and opinions, they increasingly reveal private information to one another. The public and private actors can then better assess one another's actions, the needed changes in services, and the terms under which they may increase their resource contributions. Access to and contributions of resources may act as incentives, but the participatory governance style provides direct feedback loops, increases information flows, and builds confidence. Scholars from Ostrom (1999) to Culpepper (2004) to Sabel (1994, 1996a) have shown how collective problem-solving via deliberation is the substantive occasion in which previously antagonistic groups and individuals can begin to identify points of common interest, compromise, and effectively learn how to monitor one another. Moreover, research on collective problem solving at both firm and policymaking levels has been shown to enhance learning, the exchange of tacit knowledge, and the creation of new strategies and capabilities (MacDuffie 1997; Helper, MacDuffie, and Sabel 2000; Winter 2003; McEvily 2005). As participating associations and their constituent firms see the benefits of collaboration through the institutions, they are likely to build broader strategic considerations on top of their past rent-seeking instincts (Hirst 1994; Stark and Bruszt 1998; Doner 2000; Berk and Schneiberg 2005).

The cumulative term I give to these conditions is 'participatory restructuring'. I argue that one can explain the divergent paths of upgrading in Mendoza and San Juan by whether the governments pursue participatory restructuring or the contrasting depoliticization approaches to reform in the face of common crises. Participatory restructuring approaches enable societies to break out of low equilibrium paths and build new innovative capacities at both public and private levels when relevant services and programs are delivered through public–private institutions. Effective creation of these institutions occurs: (a) when reforms to resolving crises are used to reshape the information and resource asymmetries among relevant firms and their attendant associations and cooperatives; and (b) when participation by relevant public and private actors is guided by rules of inclusive membership and of deliberation that induce collective problem solving. In contrast, depoliticization approaches attempt to insulate policymaking from society and induce change by imposing new rules based on arm's length economic incentives. This approach may foster new capital investment by firms but not upgrading, and indeed the benefits of such an approach will likely accrue to existing privileged elites.

In this view, the structure of prior social, political, and economic resources can constrain upgrading initiatives. Building new innovative capacities for upgrading begins not simply providing public goods. Rather, it begins with the government incorporating a wide variety of relevant socioeconomic groups to develop together new institutional solutions to crises in such ways that focus on recombining the substantive and structural ties among these groups and the state itself (Hirst 1994).

5.3. The Transformation of the Argentinian Wine Industry and the Challenge of Upgrading

'Can Argentina fulfill its potential and produce world-class wines? The answer is an emphatic yes.'

Wine Spectator, March 24, 2003.

Argentina is historically one of the largest volume producers and per capita consumers of wine in the world, but production focussed on low-quality wine and grapes for the domestic market. Throughout the 1980s, the industry suffered under hyperinflation, negative growth, and heavy regulations, such as price controls and output quotas, which led to such perverse strategies as the eradication of potentially high value grapes, like 30 percent of the stock of Malbec (Walters 1999; Giuliani and Bell 2005a). Both Mendoza and San Juan had a few large firms, several hundred small- and medium-size wineries, and thousands of small grape producers, which were often propped up by each province's state owned winery. The old regulations were rapidly eliminated in 1990, as the administration of President Carlos Menem (1989–99) implemented pro-market reforms in Argentina. Price and trade liberalization, privatization, and a currency board supporting an overvalued Peso ushered in a decade of low inflation, a sudden increase in FDI, and volatile growth. Argentinian manufacturing, however, shifted away from higher value-added production as it did not export much or focussed on the less sophisticated Mercosur markets.[3]

In contrast, the Argentinian wine sector, though still very dependent on domestic sales, underwent a profound transformation in the 1990s. Wine exports grew from a few million dollars in 1990 to 1.5 percent of the world

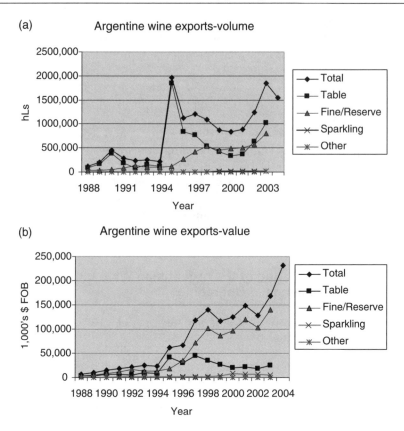

(a)   Argentine wine exports-volume

(b)   Argentine wine exports-value

Figure 5.1a & b. The growth of Argentinian wine exports (by volume and value)
Source: INV.

market even at the height of Peso overvaluation to over 2 percent of the world market (including 3% of the highly competitive UK market) or over $480 million in 2004, growing at an average annual rate of about 23 percent.[4]

These gains came not only from comparative costs, but especially from consistent advancements in product quality and innovation. First, Argentinian vineyards gradually improved the quality of grapes ('70 percent of the wine's value is in the grape'). Varieties of high enological value vastly increased their shares of vine surface area—from about 20 percent in 1990 to about 43 percent in 2001 (Cetrangolo et al. 2002). Second, wine quality improved. As Figures 5.1a and b show, by the mid-1990s the vast majority of export revenues came from fine wines (now 85%), as opposed to cheap table wine. Over 70 percent of Argentinian wine exports are sold in the United States, EU, and Japan, hence sophisticated, competitive markets. By the end of the 1990s, an increased number of Argentinian wines were being rated by such elite

Table 5.1. Scores for Argentinian and Chilean wines by *Wine Spectator*

Year	1993	1994	1995	1996	1997	1998	1999	2000	2001	2002	2003
Argentina Distribution of Ratings Per Year											
Mean	81	81	82	81	81	79	84	84	84	85	84
Median	82	82	83	81	82	78.5	84	84	84	85	85
SD	4.4	4.4	3.9	4.3	4.6	4.7	4.2	4.3	4.5	4.6	4.7
Observations	27	33	33	65	102	60	145	146	137	194	79
Minimum	73	73	74	71	61	64	73	72	71	70	75
Maximum	89	89	91	92	92	87	93	92	92	95	89
Chile Distribution of Ratings Per Year											
Mean	82	83	83	83	82	83	83	83	83	84	84
Median	83	83	84	84	82	83	83	83	83	84	84
SD	5.2	3.7	4.1	3.6	4.3	4	4.3	4.3	4.8	3.9	3.5
Observations	112	146	200	257	269	308	310	340	326	287	155
Minimum	55	71	62	69	55	70	71	69	60	76	76
Maximum	91	90	90	92	91	91	92	94	95	93	91

Note: Wines are rated on 100 point scale. Scores over 90 are considered excellent and over 85 very good.

wine magazines as *Wine Spectator*, and were receiving as a group ever better scores, even when compared to better-known Chilean wines (see Table 5.1 and Figure 5.2). At the same time, average export prices per bottle dramatically increased to just 30 cents less than the Chilean average. Third, with the world market for the standard 'fighting four varietals' (cabernet, merlot, sauvignon blanc, and chardonnay) virtually saturated, the Argentinian firms focussed on producing a greater variety of new products, such as previously undervalued

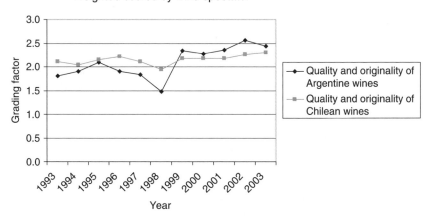

Figure 5.2. Weighted scores for Argentinian and Chilean wines (wine spectator)

Note: Scores were weighted by multiplying the number of wines in a particular range (e.g. 80–4, 85–9, 90–4, etc.) by a grade factor given to the range (1, 2, 3, 4, 5, etc.).

varietals (e.g. Malbec, Torrontes), 'redesigned' varietals from other specialized regions of the world (e.g. Tempranillo, Bonarda), and distinctive blends.[5]

This shift demanded new capabilities in coordinating multiple, continuous process and product experiments across a variety of organizations and microclimates. Increased wine value begins not simply with the adoption of new hard technology and fertilizers or with market and distribution but namely with transforming the middle and upstream segments of the value chain: state-of-the-art quality control and product development running from vine planting to careful vineyard maintenance to flawless harvests to vinification and blending. Enologists work closely with agronomists and growers to introduce and experiment with new modes of growing, pruning, sanitizing, and watering with new and old varietals and clones of grapes. They then test, for instance, different types of indigenous yeasts and enzymes as well as methods of refrigeration, processing, and storage to optimally ferment the wine and elicit the grape's flavors and aromas. Similar to codesign and co-benchmarking processes used in complex manufacturing (Helper et al. 2000; Kogut 2000), these actors develop new systems to carefully document practices and products, share the information, and evaluate the results over time and space. Because of the variation in climates, soils, varietals and clones, experimentation is contextualized, knowledge is often tacit, and dissemination is necessarily social and interactive, often demanding a complex network of vertical and horizontal ties among firms (Walters 1999; Roberts and Ingram 2002; Henderson, Pagani, and Cool 2004; Giuliani et al. 2005a). Moreover, upgrading is highly time-consuming—any new vine takes 2–3 years to yield testable results and any quality and taste modification to grape growing take 18–24 months.

This gradual, multiparty process of upgrading in Argentina has occurred in the 1990s across a wide variety of grape growing conditions, varietals, and firm strategies. Mendoza and San Juan have about 100 microclimates with the potential to support at least twelve red and white varietals of medium and high value (Cetrangolo et al. 2002). Grape production remained rather decentralized across relatively small plots, even after some consolidation and a significant decline in the number of vineyards and in total vineyard surface area in the 1980s and 1990s.[6] By 2001, Mendoza still had over 16,000 vineyards totaling about 140,000 hectares and San Juan had over 6,000 vineyards totaling about 50,000 hectares. According to the agricultural survey of the Mendoza for 2003, the largest eighteen vineyard owners controlled only 5 percent of surface area dedicated to grape growing for wine and about 1,100 owners controlled about 50 percent. Indeed, despite the asset specific nature of grape development, subcontracting has actually increased from about 50 percent of a winery's grape needs in the 1980s to almost 70 percent by 2000 (Cetrangolo et al. 2002). In contrast, in Chile the fighting four varietals historically accounted for about half of the vineyards, and much of the upgrading and exports in the 1980s was dominated by less than a dozen large, vertically integrated firms.[7]

The relatively high variety of firm strategies and organizational forms is further reflected at the level of the winery.[8] During the 1990s, the number of registered and active wineries in Mendoza and San Juan dropped by about 35 percent and since 2000 have gradually risen. Today there are 683 active wineries in Mendoza and 169 in San Juan. As of 2003, there were about 200 firms that exported wine, with the top five firms accounting for about 40 percent of total wine export sales and the top twenty for about 70 percent. No firms are publicly listed, most are small- and medium-sized family firms and partnerships, about 10 percent are cooperatives, and very few are controlled by Argentinian business groups or foreign investors.[9] Indeed, foreign investors control less than half of the thirty top exporters, and though estimates vary greatly, it appears that FDI accounts for about half of the $1–1.5 billion invested in the wine industry in Argentina between 1991 and 2003, with most coming after 1996. The seven companies that account for 80 percent of cheap table wine have also diversified in economically priced fine wine. Two are prominent cooperatives, which have twenty to thirty-five member firms and draw on a few thousand small grape suppliers. The approximately fifty premium wineries that account for about 45 percent of fine wine volume and 70 percent of fine wine exports had previously focussed on cheap table wine but now have products that fetch a US retail price per bottle ranging from $5 to $40. They have their own vineyards but also together depend on about 3,000 grape suppliers. The number of grape suppliers used per winery varies widely, from boutique wineries with about ten specialized suppliers each to the largest diversified wineries with about 200–300 nonexclusive suppliers each.

These advances in wine and grape upgrading have, however, been much more profound and broad-based in Mendoza than in San Juan, despite the similar climatic conditions and soil qualities (Cetrangolo et al. 2002), and even the greater importance of winemaking to the latter's economy. Table 5.2a shows the relevant wine and grape production and export data. For instance, Mendoza accounts for a highly disproportionate share of Argentina's wine exports. As of 2002, 65 percent of the Mendoza harvest and 26 percent of the San Juan harvest were classified as composed of high and medium quality grapes. Moreover, upgrading has spread to large zones of Mendoza, like the *Zona Este* (about 50% of Mendoza's vine surface area), that were historically considered backward and capable of producing only poor quality wines and grapes. The surface area share of high- and medium-enological value gapes/vines in the *Zona Este* vineyards increased to about 26 percent of its total by 1998 and to over 37 percent by 2001. By 2003, about 55 percent of *Zona Este* wineries had modern quality control systems and also accounted for almost a third of those exporting from Mendoza.[10]

Table 5.2a & b. Comparing Mendoza and San Juan

	Year	Mendoza	San Juan
(a) Comparative wine, grape, and industry data			
Winemaking/ind output	1994	21.10%	26.50%
Mfg Industry/GDP	1993	18.96%	24.69%
Agro/GDP	1993	8.47%	11.11%
Province's Share of National Wine Production	1990	66.55%	24.88%
	2000	61.07%	31.06%
Province's Share of Grapevine Area	1990	69.74%	21.94%
	2001	70.08%	22.51%
Province's Share of Wine Exports	Ave. 2000–03	90.62%	6.40%

	Mendoza	San Juan	Argentina
(b) Comparative economic, social, and political data			
Population (2000)	1,607,618	578,504	37,074,032
GDP (Millions USD, 1993)	$6,925	$2,266	236,505
GDP/Capita (1993)	$7,878	$4,571	$7,254
Growth of GDP (1993–00)	1.17%	1.04%	—
Gini Coeff (2000)	0.375	0.378	0.491
Human Development Index (2000)	0.747	0.736	0.854
Impact of Coparticipation (1997)	65.10%	56.50%	—
Deficit/GDP (1999)	3.40	2.30	1.89
Current Account Balance (Ave. 1996–8)	−5%	4%	—
Debt Service/Current Revenues (Ave. 1993–99)	14.54	7.27	20.21
Unemployment Rate (Ave. 1993–99)	5.90%	8.50%	13.93%
No. of 4 yr. Terms Governor Can Serve	One	Two	n/a
Electoral Competition Score* (1991)	2.53	20.64	—
Electoral Competition Score* (1995)	22.54	19.28	n/a
No. of NGOs/1,000 inhabitants**	2.3	2.18	—
No. of Total Cooperatives (1989)	397	333	—
No. of Agricultural Cooperatives (1989)	64	79	—
Crimes against property per 1,000 inhabitants***	42.6	25.8	—

Sources: INV; Consejo Federal de Inversiones, Argentina.

Notes: *Measured as the margin of victory in the gubernatorial elections. See Remmer and Wibbels (2000) and Wibbels (2005). **See Fiel (2003) and GADIS (2004). ***See Fiel (2003).

5.4. Mendoza vs. San Juan—Inherited Resources as Indeterminate to Upgrading

Mendoza appears to have promoted broad-based upgrading often by taking advantage of and not simply being paralyzed by a wide variety of firms, interests, microclimates, and products. But how can one explain its ability to initiate and sustain the attendant coordination and knowledge creation in the 1990s, when it could not previously and while San Juan stalled and became such a laggard? There are three main explanations that focus on the importance of legal and inherited socioeconomic resources. (See also Table 5.2b.)

One could argue that Mendoza had better legal institutions. However, both provinces are subject to the same national system of commercial law and property rights, which are not strong by international standards and which appear to be at times less secure in Mendoza than in San Juan.[11] The wine industry has been subject to largely the same national and regional regulatory laws, including a 1993 agreement by the two provinces on regulating the volatility of grape prices. Contracts are also rarely used among wineries and grape growers in both provinces (Cetrangolo et al. 2002).

A second explanation would be that Mendoza entered the 1990s with a greater stock of human and knowledge resources, such as well trained and connected industry elites (Cohen and Levinthal 1990; Ziegler 1995). Mendoza did not have a relatively large number of licensed enologists, and the one program in the region (Facultad de Enologia Don Bosco in Mendoza) annually graduated no more than five enologists who were employed in both provinces (Walters 1999). But many of the first upgrading initiatives in Mendoza came from firms in the best climatic zone (*Zona Primera*) that were led by Argentinians with foreign education and contacts with well known foreign consultants. While knowledgeable international equipment and chemical suppliers flooded both provinces after liberalization in 1989–90, such firms as the French owned Chandon and the domestically owned Catena, Trapiche, and Arizu began the reorganization of wine production, vineyard maintenance, and bottling in accordance with world standards. Moreover, since relatively few firms in Mendoza had the resources to hire globe-trotting consultants, these elite firms of the *Zona Primera* became sources of knowledge as they developed systems of incentives and personalized technical assistance to extend process and product upgrading to their grape suppliers (Foster 1995; Walters 1999: 111–14).

But the diffusion and application of 'best practices' was hampered not only because of the experimental nature of upgrading but also because of the variation in climates, soils, irrigation, and pests. What may work in one part of the world, or one part of a province, may not be applicable in another place, even for the same varietal or clone. For instance, in the mid and late 1990s, several leading winemakers advised many of their suppliers to incorporate new water reduction grape growing methods from abroad. These had devastating consequences, since the method under local climate conditions 'cooked' the grapes. The growers bore almost all of the losses themselves.[12] Several firms also acquired large amounts of debilitating debt in the 1990s because of overly ambitious technology acquisitions based on advice and cheap financing of the international equipment suppliers (Walters 1999). In turn, diversity combined with uncertainty can impede knowledge diffusion and coordination via markets. As attempts at quick imitation lead to dead-ends and multiple failures, nascent collaboration across firms can easily die on the vine, so to speak (Stark 2001; Evans 2004).

A third set of explanations would argue that Mendoza had already a superior stock and structure of social capital and associationalism that could mediate complex coordination under uncertainty. However, the conventional reasoning falls short. First, the stock argument appears indeterminate, since, as shown in Table 5.2b, both provinces have about the same number per 1,000 inhabitants and indeed San Juan had more cooperatives in agriculture (slightly less in general). Second, it is unclear in these cases whether the presence of a strong encompassing business association necessarily improves policy coordination and coherence (Ross Schneider 2004). San Juan and Mendoza have similar structures of business interests, with several sectoral and peak-level business associations.[13] They also had similar histories through the 1980s, with their winemaker associations and peak-level associations battling for access to their respective provincial governments to play a zero-sum game over price supports and subsidies (Rofman 1999; Paladino and Jauregui 2001).

This is not to say that the social fabric and structure of associations are unimportant variables. Existing social and professional experiences can be the basis of new forms of concerted, collective action (Sabel 1996*b*; Stark 1996; McDermott 2002*a*). For instance, the elite firms of Mendoza's *Primera Zona*, including those mentioned above, began organizing two main voluntary forms of collective learning based on past professional and local ties. First, elite firms created a few learning groups (CREA), each of which included eight to ten firms that shared the cost of a consultant and met regularly to share tacit knowledge and help solve common problems of upgrading vineyards.[14] Second, they also began organizing annual wine and label evaluation competitions, in which wineries presented their products for review and prizes (Walters, 1999; Paladino et al. 2001). The most noteworthy was EVICO, the wine evaluation event created in 1990 by the association for enologists (CLEIF), the association of the most prestigious wineries (Bodegas de Argentina AC), and the Facultad de Enologia Don Bosco. A panel of widely respected enologists benchmarked the year's harvest and the wines as well as provided constructive advice on improving the wines during and after processing. In the late 1990s, winemakers and their associations from the historically more backward and less climatic advantageous zones of Mendoza and San Juan began organizing similar events.[15] These events helped spur debates about the direction of the industry and accelerate the sharing of tacit knowledge, as actors from firms, associations, and educational and public institutions began to see the benefits of gradual collaboration and the suspension of their old institutional identities. As Walters notes (1999: 152), '[They] helped shift the focus of attention of former rent-seeking wine business associations, now far more involved in the discussion of quality and production issues.'

Nonetheless, these experiences also demonstrated their limitations in bridging the social and economic gaps between subregions of Mendoza. Regional discrimination and antagonisms limited the interaction of wineries and grape growers from the different *Zonas*, and thus the creation and diffusion of new knowledge. EVICO and the Grupos CREA were largely limited to the most elite wineries of the *Primera Zona* that viewed the other *Zonas* as incapable of producing fine varietals because of their apparent substandard economic, educational, and climatic conditions. At the same time, winemakers of these *Zonas* saw little to gain from those who always criticized their products and from discussions not focussed on improving the kind of intermediate and low enological quality grapes that composed their wine supply chains (Walters 1999: 151–2). As a result, few took little notice of the efforts of innovators such as La Agricola's Rodolfo Montenegro from the *Zona Este*. Rather than replacing old systems with newly imported ones, he adapted the 'antiquated' high-yield orthogonal vine training systems (*parrales*) to produce high- and intermediate-quality grapes at higher than average yields, in turn innovating in both quality and cost. As Montenegro noted in the mid-1990s, 'Most of the elite firms and their enologists in Mendoza are still focussed too much on the *Primer Zona*, ignoring the productive potential of the areas like Eastern Mendoza. There is still a lot of arrogance' (Walters 1999: 123).

In many ways, this dual nature of social structure—being both facilitating and exclusionary, reflects the research of Locke (1994), Cohen and Rogers (1992), Padgett (2001), Safford (2004), and Schneider (2004) on other regions and industries. The need for ever more specific knowledge and skills, coupled with traditional rivalries, identities, and resource inequalities, can create barriers to the processes of aggregation and joint action that are vital for a broader sustainable base of innovation. If more encompassing structures are not historically or organically given, then government could help create them (Ostrom 1999; Schneider 2004).

5.5. Politics and the Emergence of Public–Private Institutions

Notice that the challenge of coordination and knowledge diffusion becomes a sociopolitical problem beyond simply redirecting public spending. Creating institutional resources that help coordinate decentralized experiments and develop upgrading capabilities is simultaneous to reshaping the relative power and relationships among government agencies and socioeconomic groups or associations. However, it may not be sufficient to rely on inherited political incentives to explain how these institutions emerged in the 1990s in Mendoza and not in San Juan. Some might argue that an executive with greater expectations of political security would invest in building new institutions, as took place in Mendoza. But San Juan's governor can be reelected, whereas Mendoza's can not. Political competition may be indeterminate (Remmer and Wibbels 2000) as San Juan had closer gubernatorial elections than Mendoza. Moreover, the Peronist party dominated the executive and legislative branches of both provinces in the late 1980s and early 1990s.

A more fruitful comparative analysis would focus on how the differences in the political approaches of Mendoza and San Juan to the crises of the late 1980s shaped both the creation and effectiveness of institutions supportive of upgrading. This section briefly shows how San Juan's 'depoliticization' approach induced new investment but impeded upgrading. It then details how Mendoza's 'participatory restructuring' approach resulted in the gradual construction of public–private institutions that helped firms improve their skills and knowledge and aided the government and the relevant associations form new lines of communication and coordination.

5.5.1. *Diverging Political Approaches to Reform in San Juan and Mendoza*

5.5.1.1. SAN JUAN

San Juan's approach toward the wine industry was based largely on the use of arm's length economic incentives implemented by a government with little consultation of major socioeconomic groups. Three major policy areas reveal this pattern. First, by the mid-1980s, the provincial state owned winery, Cavic, which supported thousands of small grape producers, was insolvent. The government quickly elected to sell it to local investors. The resulting company soon collapsed, and the government was forced to take it over and liquidate it.

Second, San Juan utilized a federally supported tax incentive program for small, poorer provinces as the principal policy to improve agribusiness, especially for the wine sector. San Juan joined three other provinces (not including Mendoza) in this program in 1983. By 1990, it had gained about 290 projects in manufacturing and agriculture at a fiscal cost of about $1.2 billion. After the program was revised to focus on agriculture and tourism projects, San Juan again elected to participate actively. In the 1990s, it gained over $1 billion in direct investment from over 400 projects, about half of which were fully or partially dedicated to wine and grape production. Some estimate that these programs cost Mendoza $100–200 million per year in production output from diverted investments.[16] Approximately 193 firms were committed to investing into the industry, including upgrading over 14,000 hectares, about half of which have been for the development of grapes for fine wine (Allub 1996; Borsani 2001).

As argued by both independent researchers (Allub 1996; Rofman 1999) as well as the Ministry of Economy of San Juan itself (Gobierno de San Juan 2004), reliance on this program as the framework for wine sector restructuring brought little upgrading and increasingly antagonized and fragmented the stakeholder groups of the value chain. The main beneficiaries were large firms with rather short-term interests that had limited knowledge or capacities in undertaking the time-consuming experiments for transforming vineyards and developing a broad base of capable grape suppliers. Small grape producers and wineries and their respective trade associations grew increasingly disillusioned with the policy, the government, and the large wineries (Rofman 1999). At the same time, there were no few helpful support programs or institutions.

Third, San Juan failed several times to build new public–private institutions to help regulate and promote the development of the wine sector. Following damaging volatility of grape prices, the San Juan government signed but failed to enact an agreement in 1993–4 with Mendoza to build a new institution to help stabilize grape prizes and to share new policies toward the wine sector. On three different occasions between 1989 and 1999, San Juan also attempted but failed to create a new provincial export agency. On the one hand, the government was reluctant to share policymaking and resources with other actors, be they from Mendoza or provincial sectoral associations. On the other hand, the government was satisfied that the existing regime of tax incentives provided sufficient support for inducing investment.

5.5.1.2. MENDOZA

In contrast, the policy approach of Mendoza was based on empowering a wide variety of public and private actors to actively participate in resolving the crisis at hand and building new institutions for the broader restructuring of the agricultural sectors. The first step came in 1987, when newly elected governor Jose Octavio Bordon and his allies confronted the collapse of the Mendoza state-owned winery, Giol, which was losing over $500,000 per month with a debt of over $35 million. Giol produced over 10 percent of the nation's wine and processed over 15 percent of the provinces grapes from more than 4,000 small- and medium-sized grape suppliers. The Bordon administration was wary of the poor privatization of Cavic in San Juan and was equally concerned about the unrest that restructuring Giol could set off among large business interests, labor unions, and the communities of its thousands of grape suppliers. Hence, the administration aimed to transform Giol into a federation of cooperatives (Fecovita) as a way to initiate broader industry restructuring and forge compromises among the warring factions.

The government and the new Giol director, Eduardo Sancho (the former head of the Association of Wine Cooperatives) led a drive to incorporate stakeholders into the process while improving their organizational resources. The new Giol board included three members appointed by the governor, three elected 'by the people', and one representing labor unions (Paladino and Morales 1994a). The government and Giol organized a large publicity and information dissemination campaign, regularly consulted with the labor unions and the trade associations, and organized over 500 community meetings that included representatives from all sides—the provincial and municipal governments, labor unions, civic associations, and trade associations. At the same time, government and Giol officials encouraged small farmers and winemakers to organize themselves into cooperatives by offering new credit programs, technical and legal advice, the leasing of Giol wineries to coops at special rates, and purchase guarantees as a transition policy. By the end of 1988, nine new cooperative were formed, and within a few years the new Fecovita had twenty-five new cooperatives that incorporated over 1,500 of the original 4,000 grape suppliers of Giol (Juri 1990; Paladino and Morales 1994*a*, 1994*b*).

Upgrading Fecovita and its members has been gradual. Most the initial upgrading, as was typical for most firms, focussed on new technology rather than linking new product standards with new production practices (Walters 1999: 137–9). But through regular review by its members and outside auditors, elected management adopted increasingly stringent operational and product standards as it diversified its product portfolio, modernized systems, and revamped its marketing. Fecovita and its member cooperatives gradually lowered minimum purchase–supply agreements, allowing all parties also to use the market as an additional disciplining device. Upgrading support came from on-time payments at preferential prices and access to Fecovita's pooled resources and services, especially its projects in R&D and training with new institutions that would emerge in the 1990s. Fecovita helped members gain access to credit, markets, inputs, training, and knowledge at low cost through both its combined bargaining power and its alliances with banks, domestic and international distributors, as well as public–private research and extension organizations in Mendoza, such as INTA, the Instituto Desarrollo Rural (IDR), and the agronomy faculty of the Universidad Nacional de Cuyo (Amendola 2003).

The Fecovita experiment had three main impacts on Mendoza. First, Fecovita soon became profitable, as improvements from grape growing to label management led it to expand both domestically and internationally in table and fine wine.[17] Second, the Fecovita experiment enhanced the diversity of wine and grape producers by reviving small producers and cooperatives. During the 1990s, the number of cooperatives in the wine sector grew by about 30 percent to 50, which have over 4,500 grape producers as members or dedicated suppliers. About 35 percent of the output of Mendoza cooperatives is focussed on premium and super-premium wines.[18]

Third, the Fecovita experiment appears to have launched effort by the government to create new policies and institutions with socioeconomic partners. For instance, according to federal documents detailing the programs and institutions related to agriculture in every province, Mendoza developed over seventy-five programs and policies (from credits, to insurance, to R&D, to health standards and pest prevention) in the 1990s that have directly and indirectly assisted firms in the wine sector.[19] Virtually all programs are jointly developed and administered by partnerships between the government and approximately fifty nongovernmental organizations. In contrast, San Juan's relatively few support programs mostly come from the federal government and are managed mainly by a government office alone. This change in policymaking and implementation may also partially explain why, in both absolute and per capita terms, Mendoza has many more civic organizations than in San Juan that have inclusive membership, have both internal and external funding sources, and produce nonexclusive benefits. Scholars have shown that such organizational traits tend to improve information flows, professional ties, and policy responsiveness.[20]

In short, the richness and effectiveness of Mendoza's policy portfolio toward the wine industry is not a product of simply inherited associationalism or state capacities. Rather, it should be seen as part of the gradual construction of a dense public–private network of organizations that are pooling information and resources while improving their collective capacities to problem solve. The Fecovita experience began a political strategy by Bordon and his allies (who led two more successive administrations) to gain the loyalty of small-holders and renovate the relationships among the government and the wide variety business associations. I now turn to a more detailed analysis of how this approach to creating the most prominent public–private institutions in Mendoza in the 1990s provided governance mechanisms that enhanced the upgrading capabilities for both firms and the government.

5.5.2. Experimenting with Public–Private Organizations

Mendoza's approach to reform provided two mechanisms that linked the process of institution-building with the ability of the institutions to help solve the coordination and knowledge diffusion problems discussed earlier. First, in confronting new strategic challenges, the government convened a variety of relevant associations to generate and jointly govern an institutional solution, for which it would provide much of the vital resources. Second, representatives of the participating bodies would supervise institutional over-sight and progressively engage in collective problem solving by regularly and jointly defining key constraints they faced, evaluating the outcomes of proposed solutions, and deciding on corrective measures or the next policy measures. These two mechanisms helped: (*a*) reshape the relationships among the government, the participating associations, their firms; (*b*) the institutions improve knowledge and skills creation; and (*c*) the public and private actors develop and implement new collective strategies.

5.5.2.1. EMBEDDING THE GOVERNMENT AND RECOMBINING PUBLIC–PRIVATE TIES

As Table 5.3 reveals, the most prominent institutions that contributed to upgrading in the wine sector in Mendoza were mainly charged with providing a variety of 'supply-side' services and resources to firms in a variety of sectors. These institutions cut across the public and private domains in their member-ship, governance, funding, and missions. The founding and restructuring of

Table 5.3. Leading upgrading support institutions in Mendoza in the 1990s

Institution	Year of creation or restructuring	Governing Members	Activities	Resources	Legal Form
INTA Cuyo	1991	Govts of S Juan & Mza, 9 Agro Ass'ns, 2 Nat'l Univ's	Regional development plan, oversee budgets & activities of EEAs	National and provincial budgets	1 of 15 semi-autonomous Regional Centers; Federal body in Sec. of Agro.
INTA EEAs	1991	Gov't of Mza, Munis. Agro Ass'ns, Nat'l and Prov'l Institutes and Univ's	R&D (inputs, plants, tech), extension training, consulting	Half—nat'l budget (salaries & overhead); Half—services, alliances, gov't Mza, cooperadoras	Part of INTA Cuyo; 4 in Mza, 1 in SJ; Each has 1–4 AERs
Fondo Vitivinícola	1993–4	Gov't Mza, 11 wine/grape Ass'ns	Oversees new wine regulations, promotes wine industry/marketing	Tax on firms from over produc'n of wine	Public, nonstate, nonprofit entity.
Fondo para la Transformación y el Crecimiento (FTC)	1993–4	Min. of Economy, Regional advisory councils	Subsidizes loans and credit guarantees to SMEs for tech against extreme weather and for grape conversion	Self-financing; initial capital from privatization of gas and oil reserves	Independent legal entity under authority of governor
Instituto Desarrollo Rural (IDR)	1994–5	36 founders—INTA Cuyo, Gov't Mza, ISCAMEN, 2 peak ass'ns, various agro sectoral ass'ns	Technical info collection & dissemination; Database mgmt; R&D, training, consulting	Mza Gov't; services; gradual increase of fees from member ass'ns	Nonprofit Foundation; with oversight by Min of Economy
Pro Mendoza	1995–6	Gov't Mza, 3 peak business associations	Export promotion—organize fairs, delegations, strategic information, training	Gov't Mza; Peak ass'ns; services	Non-profit Foundation

Abbreviations: INTA—Instituto Nacional de Tecnología Agropecuaria; EEA—Estaciones Experimentales (Subregional centers); Mza—Mendoza; ISCAMEN—Instituto de Sanidad y Calidad Agropecuaria Mendoza; Cooperadors—Nonprofit NGOs.

the institutions emerged mainly from the government convening relevant public and private actors to confront a new shock or strategic challenge. In turn, a variety of public entities and sectoral associations jointly became responsible for the governance and resource support of the institutions. For instance, in 1991 the federal government greatly decentralized and reduced the budgets of INTA's regional centers.[21] With the aim of increasing and diversifying its sources of revenues and services, INTA Mendoza gradually expanded its subregional centers and required that the new advisory councils and affiliated NGOs ('cooperadoras') be composed of representatives from relevant government agencies (provincial and municipal), associations, firms, and educational institutions. In 1992–3, Mendoza and San Juan experienced destructive winters that caused great volatility in grape prices and left thousands of SME producers devastated. This crisis resulted in two major initiatives. At the end of 1993, the two provinces signed agreements to help stabilize the wine and grape supplier markets and develop support policies. Only Mendoza implemented the new regulations and institutions. In 1994, the government and the major wine and grape producers associations created the Fondo Vitivinicola to oversee the new regulatory regime and use the proceeds of a new penalty for noncompliance to promote the wine industry and wine consumption.[22] In 1993–4, the Mendoza government also launched a series of policies to help protect farmers from weather damage and aid them in vineyard restructuring. The main institutional vehicle was the Fondo para la Transformacion y el cfecimiento (FTC), which coordinated with provincial banks and had regional advisory councils composed of relevant municipalities. IDR and ProMendoza grew out of a need for services that INTA Mendoza and the federal export agency were not providing. But because of a new federal law restricting provincial budgets, the Mendoza government had the associations take on part of responsibilities and resource demands.

The public–private nature of the formation and organization of these institutions over time allowed each to become more embedded with another and the associations of Mendoza and act as bridges between the public and private domains as well as between the relevant associations. Figures 5.3a and 5.3b depict this process in a simplified form. Figure 5.3a shows the sparseness of ties in 1989 among the government and firms and associations of different parts of the value chain and zones. Figure 5.3b shows how by the end of the 1990s the new institutions tied these different actors together. By comparison, San Juan in 1990 and 2000 would look like the structure in Figure 5.3a. (The appendix shows the resulting public–private network in more complex form, using membership and board data of the institutions and the associations. The bridging role of the new institutions is revealed in their relatively high 'betweenness' scores (Burt 2001). Note also how the creation of the new institutions improves the structural position of several associations.)

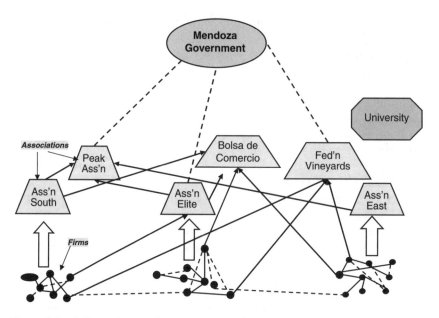

Figure 5.3a. Policymaking and strategic ties in the Mendoza wine industry, 1989

NB. Guide for both Figures 5.3a and 5.3b: Solid black circles represent firms in different regions in Mendoza. Each region has its main wine business association, as shown by a large white arrow. Dashed lines represent weaker links of contracting or communication than solid lines. Solid arrows denote membership or board participation in relevant associations and institutions.

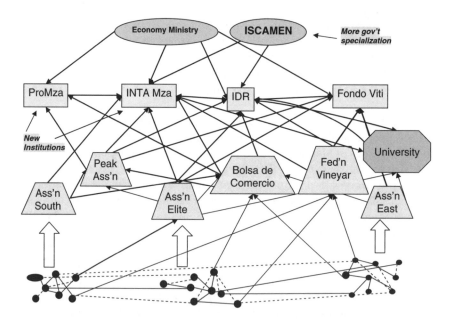

Figure 5.3b. Policymaking and strategic ties in the Mendoza wine industry, 2000

This model of organization was gradually replicated at more micro levels. For instance, the Fondo Vitivinicola, INTA, IDR, and ProMendoza began opening offices in different zones with local partners, sitting on one another's boards, and actively participating in such events as the wine evaluation committees mentioned in Section 5.4. The latter three institutions also began developing joint training and research programs and increasingly used network methods of training and R&D. That is, these institutions provided services to groups of firms, forcing them to undertake joint projects in field experiments and collective problem solving.

The key innovation of these models was not simply providing public goods and services, but changing the sociopolitical landscape that could improve socioeconomic outcomes. First, by bringing in the different associations from inception, the government encouraged a greater sense of ownership for the new initiatives. Second, the multivalent (and often multisectoral) nature of institutions allowed the participants to pool and access new resources and information that each could not have done individually, especially for previously marginalized associations of producers from the more backward zones of Mendoza (Padgett and Ansell 1993). Third, the institutions provided new social ties and channels of communication not only between the government and the associations but also between the associations themselves. Firms and associations from different zones and also different sectors were now meeting regularly with one another.

5.5.2.2. PARTICIPATORY GOVERNANCE FOR INSTITUTIONAL AND FIRM UPGRADING

The new ties and institutions would be void of content without additional triggers. Besides gaining the rights of representation and often of electing executive boards, the participating members of each institution had to provide resources. While the government often supplied the bulk of at least initial resources, the other members were obligated to provide complementary resources, if not financing then personnel, facilities, and information. In turn, as access to new resources attracted, for example, associations, to the table, each increasingly had a stake to ensure its own contributions were being well used. Moreover, participants were charged with regularly defining the institution's objectives and reviewing the results of actions taken. In defining constraints and benchmarks, the participants drew on their own experiences and contacts, from the most advanced to the most backward. In evaluating results, participants used not only benchmarks and comparisons with other relevant institutions, but also the feedback from their own constituents. Participants could voice their proposals and grievances directly through the board and indirectly to the government, which was continually interested in building its new cross-sectoral and cross-regional coalition.

The combination of rules of inclusion and participatory governance brought forth both collective problem solving and mutual monitoring that pushed the institutions to gradually provide a scale and scope of services that no association could do alone and most provinces lacked. For instance, INTA Mendoza and later IDR pioneered new information resources, such as detailed mappings of the microclimates for grapes and other agricultural products. They and ProMendoza also developed databases on best practices (internationally and subregionally), harvests, and product markets, training programs for different sectors, zones, and segments of the value chain, as well as teams of experienced consultants. By the end of the 1990s, Mendoza had amassed an enviable set of upgrading resources. There were seven times more INTA employees working on viticulture issues full time in Mendoza than in San Juan, a figure disproportionate to the differences in the size of the sectors or the number of EEAs. ProMendoza had helped almost 1,000 firms from various sectors participate in international trade fairs, and maintained an annual budget of about $2 million, comparable to the budget of the Argentinian national export promotion agency (ExportAr). The FTC had provided credit supports of over $50 million dollars for about 5,000 firms. In contrast, Argentina historically lacked SME financing programs and did not even have an SME support agency until 1998 (McDermott 2000).

These constellations of resources came in part from the ability of the institutions to access and recombine the contributions of their members. Consulting and R&D contracts with the most elite firms brought revenue streams that could subsidize training and research programs for more backward firms. Standards, practices, and experiences from one zone or one sector could be diffused and reengineered for others. But upgrading through scope, adaptation, and diffusion was also the gradual by-product of the members to monitor one another and push the institutions to take greater concern for their own needs.

For instance, in the early 1990s INTA launched a national program, Cambio Rural (CR), which mimicked the network learning model that the elite firms in the *Primera Zona* had created with their Grupos CREA. CR was subsidized and adapted by INTA for producers from more backward regions. But CR in Mendoza had limited initial success. Drawing on feedback from the CR participants and its council members, INTA Mendoza adapted the program by reorganizing the composition of the learning groups and customizing methods to different regions. Around the same time, when the federal government elected not to renew CR, the Mendoza government stepped in to cover some of the costs. By the end of the 1990s, CR in Mendoza had some of the best participation and cost-benefit rates in the country and far better than in San Juan[23] (Cheppi 2000; Lattuada 2000). INTA Mendoza's dependency on multiple constituencies both forced and enabled it to gradually adapt programs and build new joint projects with firms and other institutions (e.g. FECOVITA, IDR, the universities). Its testing labs were being used with the elite firms as well as cooperatives; it began documenting and teaching practices from the most advanced form of computer monitored drip-watering to Montenegro's innovative use of the orthogonal vine training systems, mentioned in Section 5.4. In turn, INTA in Mendoza was able to overcome the historical criticism of the national INTA system—that its bureaucratic lethargy made its knowledge base and technology too backward for the advanced firms and too advanced for the small, weak producers (Casaburi 1999).

ProMendoza, IDR, the FTC, and the Fondo Vitivinicola also soon became the object of criticism that they were too focussed on the needs of only a few constituents. In response, the government opened a network of regional offices in the late 1990s to house local branches of IDR, ProMendoza, the FTC, ISCAMEN (the phitosanitary agency), and the provincial statistical office. The institutions also worked on expanding their services. ProMendoza built new databases and promotional activities to include over forty foreign markets for both agricultural and manufacturing products. It also organized annual tours for foreign journalists to visit winemakers directly from a variety of zones, not just the better-known firms. IDR began to collaborate with INTA, INV (the national wine regulatory agency), and relevant associations to deliver timely information on international and domestic harvests and market prices. IDR and INTA signed agreements with ISCAMEN for joint projects on data collection in the more backward zones and develop new food safety and pest prevention regulations that better addressed Mendoza's diversity of microclimates and agricultural products. The FTC reorganized itself to work more closely with local banks and relevant associations to reduce approval time, codify new forms of loan security, and help finance a greater number of small firms from more backward zones for grape harvests and vineyard conversion (Salvarredi 2001).

The presence of multiple, related institutions also allowed participants to change alliances and force competition. For instance, in 2001, Bodegas de Argentina, the association of the largest and most refined wineries, withdrew its membership from the Fondo de Vitivinicola after continued complaints with the Fondo's management and promotional campaigns. In turn, Bodegas created its own foundation, Wines of Argentina, to develop and implement international marketing campaigns for Argentinian wine, often in collaboration with ProMendoza. The Fondo has since revamped its domestic marketing campaign.

As the different forms of multiparty governance brought pressure and changes to the institutions, the institutions themselves were forced to bring pressure upon their clients. That is, institutions like ProMendoza, IDR, and INTA began to use international and locally developed standards of products and processes not only to benchmark clients but also to restrict their access to certain programs. For instance, ProMendoza realized that unprepared Mendoza firms were soiling the reputation of commercial delegations as well as wasting limited resources. In turn, ProMendoza developed a system to evaluate whether a firm joining a trade delegation has the capabilities to communicate specific commercial, product, and process information to relevant international buyers and journalists. Before allowing firms to access more sophisticated R&D and extension programs, INTA performs systematic evaluations of a firm's processes and products and then places the firm in its relevant cohort.

This use of standards and diagnostics helps upgrading by exposing the competitive weaknesses in client firms. But when combined with the feedback mechanisms, it also has revealed weaknesses in the support system of the institutions themselves. That is, the institutions and the participating associations began to learn where training was needed to help firms overcome the diagnosed constraints. As a result, IDR and ProMendoza expanded services from data collection to training seminars and benchmarking distinct parts of the firm's value chain. They also amassed information on training resources at other institutions that went beyond their own capacities. INTA as well developed multistage extension services that gradually exposed firms to increasingly complex standards and technologies.

5.5.2.3. OVERLAPPING TIES AND DELIBERATIVE FORUMS FOR IMPROVING PUBLIC POLICY AND COLLECTIVE ACTION

The overlapping ties and participatory governance process in one institutional or policy domain equally led to collective action solutions that gave rise to institutional changes in other domains. On the one hand, improvements in older, more archaic institutions emerged from their participation in new advisory councils and upgrading projects. For instance, by the late 1990s, the two major Mendozan universities, Universidad Nacional de Cuyo (UNC) and Universidad Maza, had new or vastly expanded degree programs in enology and viticulture; UNC was also for the first time undertaking applied agronomy research with firms.[24] These changes in part grew out of responding to specific demands and market information revealed via the universities' participation in and joint research projects with INTA and IDR. ISCAMEN, the Mendozan government's food safety regulator, also sits on the boards of INTA and IDR. It created new crop protection and anti-pest prevention systems from joint data collection and field testing projects with INTA and IDR.

On the other hand, the institutionalization of collective problem solving and evaluation gradually turned project and council meetings into deliberative forums, in which the participants increasingly identified common strategic needs in other functional areas of upgrading. The creation of IDR and ProMendoza emerged in part from ongoing debates in INTA Mendoza and the Fondo Vitvinicola about whether these institutions could handle the increasingly diverse demands from firms and their associations. At the same time, an agreement between the provincial and federal governments on budget reforms restricted the hiring of new public employees. What became IDR was actually first a small team of agronomists and economists financed via a contract between the Mendoza Ministry of Economy and INTA Mendoza. ProMendoza started as a joint project between the Ministry and the Bolsa de Comercio to evaluate export opportunities for provincial firms. As the teams passed their first hurdles, the institutions were formalized and other relevant associations were brought on board. A similar process spawned the creation of ITU, a public–private university offering a three year technical degree in management, and of IDIT, a public–private institution for applied operations research in engineering and manufacturing.[25]

The different governing councils also became repositories of grievances and forums of negotiations among representatives of the government and the diverse interest groups over core, controversial regulatory issues. Laws on the protection of contracting rights for wine and grape suppliers, on the securitization of the grape market, on government subsidized hazard insurance for small producers, and on the aforementioned 1993 penalties to limit volatility in the wholesale wine and grape markets divided firms bitterly, especially those from more backward and more advanced zones. In the 1980s, the government would have either ignored such disputes or delivered patronage to the most powerful and well organized group. But in the 1990s, the participatory restructuring approach had not only improved the balance of power between relevant associations but also had provided them with a greater variety and frequency of deliberative forums. Regular and incremental changes in the above laws were realized (IDR 2001) because the public and private participants were learning how to monitor one another in other areas, had established multiple lines of communication, were increasingly well informed about market trends and one another's positions, and found that compromises in one sphere could lead to rewards in others over time.

The constellation of overlapping ties and forums for structured deliberations would aid the associations and the government to formulate more complex collective actions and policy changes that reached beyond the province. For instance, the Instituto Nacional de Vitivinicola (INV) is the federal agency regulating the wine industry and was historically a symbol of government incompetence and patronage. The Mendozans led negotiations with the federal government in 1995–6 to create a new Interprovincial Consultative Council that included seven representatives of the wine and mosto (a natural sweetener from grapes) value chain and effectively decentralized its decision-making process (Azpiazu and Basualdo 2003). By embedding the INV more deeply into the region (including bringing INV representatives onto other advisory councils) and carefully using its collective political capital, the Mendozan actors were able to secure improvements in the INV's technical capabilities and even expand its mission to include such issues as certifying DOC standards. Similarly, the Mendozan government and ProMendoza have been active in shaping Argentinian trade negotiations with the Mercosur and the EU and has taken the lead to appoint Argentina's representatives on specific international bodies that impact trade in wine, mosto, and grapes.

These experiences in identifying common constraints and formulating joint strategic responses laid the groundwork for the effort to replicate the model on a national scale via the creation of the Ley Pevi and its governing body, COVIAR, which were mentioned at the beginning of this article. As Mendoza gained a foothold in the key world wine markets, the institutional participants increasingly realized that their sustained international competitiveness demanded upgrading and resources that went beyond their own capacities.[26] These discussions converged in 2000 at a series of meetings of the advisory council of the EEA Mendoza that decided to initiate a plan to develop a 20-year strategy. The council formed executive and technical teams composed of members of its representative institutions and associations as well as other key actors not on the council. With the Fondo Vitvinicola covering most of the overhead costs, the technical team benchmarked Argentinian firms, products, and policies against those of such countries as Chile and Australia, and the executive team began a campaign to gain support among political and industry leaders within and outside of Mendoza. Similar to the Fecovita experiment, the teams organized a series of workshops over an 18 month period in the winemaking regions of Argentina to solicit input from, explain their strategy to, and build a broad coalition with relevant political and professional groups.

The Ley Pevi had three fundamental provisions. First, it mapped out a national policy to promote export objectives via an expanded form of the Mendozan model across the relevant provinces—forging a network of public and private institutions to improve the capacity and strategic use of human, material, and knowledge resources. Second, in order to enhance autonomy, avoid backlashes from other interest groups, and increase the incentives of stakeholders, the additional funding would come from a new tax on the sales of wine products. Third, the Ley Pevi and all its components would be governed by a new nonprofit, non-state entity, COVIAR, whose twelve-member executive and advisory boards would be composed, again in the Mendozan style, by representatives of the federal and relevant provincial governments as well as the leading wine and grape producer associations.

5.6. Concluding Remarks

This article has attempted to offer a political constructionist view of the emergence of a society's innovative capacities to upgrade by comparing the evolution of the wine industries in San Juan and Mendoza, namely the latter's ability to pioneer upgrading in the production of fine wine exports during the 1990s. The comparison's cross-sectional and longitudinal dimensions were able to control and thus reveal the limited individual explanatory power of such *a priori* structural factors as natural resource, knowledge, and economic endowments, social capital, commercial law, and provincial electoral institutions. Rather, the article has argued that the different restructuring paths of San Juan and Mendoza is largely a product of the different political approaches to reform the provinces chose to confront a shared economic crisis in the late 1980s. San Juan's weak upgrading in the 1990s is rooted in its 'depoliticization approach' that emphasized the use of arm's length economic incentives designed and imposed on the market by a government relatively insulated from society. In contrast, Mendoza's 'participatory restructuring approach' helped improve upgrading capabilities and reshape the relationships among the government and relevant sectoral associations through the construction of new public–private institutions. This process rested on two key mechanisms: (*a*) in confronting new strategic challenges, the government convened and empowered a variety of relevant associations to generate and jointly govern an institutional solution; (*b*) representatives of the participating bodies would supervise institutional oversight and progressively engage in collective problem solving by regularly and jointly defining the key constraints they faced, evaluating the outcomes of proposed solutions, and deciding on corrective measures or the next policy measures.

As with many complex industries, creating the innovative capacities for the wine industry is a dual problem of breaking old practices as well as getting the government and the diverse, often conflicting groups in the value chain to collaborate in previously unimagined ways. Some Mendoza firms and their attendant business associations did recognize that upgrading cut across firm boundaries, and initially responded with efforts to build new supply networks and new forums for social learning. As much as these efforts helped, they were also self-limiting. The very diversity of skills and experience that can accelerate new knowledge creation can also present barriers to collaboration. Decentralized, voluntaristic attempts at coordination and collaboration can lead to fragmentation of an industry, especially when diversity is coupled with a history of distrust, false starts, regional biases as well as resource and skill inequalities.

The participatory restructuring approach helped Mendoza gradually overcome these barriers and sustain broad base improvements at both the firm and institutional levels in three important ways. First, the inclusionary principles of policymaking and institutional construction provided economic and political incentives for previously dispersed actors to come to the table and potentially forge new social and economic ties. Second, the focus on collective problem solving in governance and services through iterative deliberations about priorities and the evaluation of remedies allowed the public and private participants to begin to share knowledge and resources, to learn how to monitor one another, and collaborate in new ways. Third, the participants were able to learn how to improve both government policy and firm practices as well as identify new areas of common problems for subsequent institutional innovations.

My emphasis on the determining impact of different political approaches is an attempt to contribute to the growing attention scholars of economic development and institutional change are placing on the role of process variables.[27] For instance, the aforementioned rules of inclusion and participatory governance are proposed conditions under which government can experiment with new industrial policies (Rodrik 2004), institutions will be horizontally embedded (Montero 2003), and public–private institutions will facilitate joint action for the creation of new innovative capacities (Schmitz 2004; Giuliani et al. 2005; Perez-Aleman 2005). They are also the mechanisms that help specify how the recombination of existing social and political resources can inform the substance and sustainability of institutional change (Hirst 1994; Thelen 2003).

The proposed framework, in turn, invites further examination about the origins, sustainability, and replication of development institutions in two important ways. First, it suggests researchers pay closer attention to the ways broader sociopolitical struggles promote and inhibit the ability of governments to forge new public–private institutions with a variety of stakeholder groups, particularly during periods of crisis. For instance, the literature on federalism and party systems in developing countries often emphasizes the determining impact of optimal market preserving and financial incentives (Weingast 1995). But this literature also shows how ongoing attempts to manipulate and control the given federalist and party systems creates great variation in policies at the subnational level (Guinazu 2003; Levitsky 2003; Montero and Samuels 2004; Falleti 2005). At the same time, Doner et al. (2005) have proposed a framework of systemic vulnerabilities, in which a particular combination of international and domestic political forces give countries greater incentives to invest in innovative capacities. In turn, by uniting these literatures with a focus on the experimental processes of policy reform and institution building, one can better identify the broader sociopolitical conditions that give rise to politicians adopting depoliticization or participatory restructuring approaches at subnational and national levels.

Second, the evidence here suggests that the principles of participatory restructuring can help overcome common barriers to sustainability and replication of local institutional innovations—large firms, especially MNCs, limiting access to new markets and knowledge (Schmitz and Humphries 2004; Gereffi and Sturgeon 2005) and poor histories of coordination among business associations, and provincial and national governments (Ostrom 1999; Levitsky 2003; Schneider 2004). The creation of multiple public–private institutions as both receptors and promoters of new innovative capacities helps keep any one particular set of firms from becoming the sole 'gatekeepers' of knowledge and resources (Schmitz and Nadvi 1999) and from accumulating the disproportionate economic power that would reverse expansion of innovative networks (Farrell and Knight 2003). At the same time, the rules of inclusion and participatory governance can improve the ability of both public and private actors to monitor and learn from one another. For instance, despite changes in directors, government administrations, and political coalitions, the Mendozan institutions continue to be stable and self-adapting, something rather unusual for Argentina (Levitsky et al. forthcoming). Moreover, San Juan is witnessing significant change in the behavior of its government and relevant wine sector associations through greater coordination with INTA's regional center, their participation in Coviar, and the recent inclusion of some San Juan firms in ProMendoza's export promotional programs. The government has openly criticized the old approach of tax incentives and advocated the creation of new public–private institutional resources for training, R&D, and export promotion (Ministerio de Economia de San Juan 2003). Leading grape producers have also left the old sectoral association to form a new one and actively participate in Coviar.

In sum, economic upgrading is determined not simply on the presence of certain institutions but especially how they are constructed and governed. As researchers on development readdress the roles of industrial policy (Rodrik 2004), clusters (Schmitz 2004), multinationals (Gereffi et al. 2005), and business associations (Schneider 2004), they may be better able to identify the political conditions of development by incorporating the literature on institutional change (Thelen 2003) and participatory governance (Sabel 1994; Fung and Wright 2001).

Appendix

Figures 5A.1 and 5A.2 were generated in 2001 using institutional membership (affiliation) and board data processed with the network program, UCINET. The data set is a matrix of 325 unique associations and institutions (and about twenty firms) linked to the wine and grape sectors. The lines denote a board or membership connection between associations or institutions. To create Figure 5A.1, I simply removed the institutions (INTA Mza, IDR, ProMendoza, etc.) that were nonexistent at the time. This allows one to systematically see the ways the new public–private institutions bridged communities and indeed strengthened the secondary position of sectoral associations.

Table 5.A1. Largest betweeness scores, Mendoza, 2001

	FEM-peak ass'n	IDITS	UCIM-peak ass'n	Fecovita	INTA Mza	IDR	Wines of Arg	INTA Junin (EEA)
Betweenness	20718.12	18107.32	13556.21	12894.66	8431.386719	8041.07	5469.87	4148.68
nBetweenness	39.59	34.6	25.91	24.64	16.11	15.37	10.45	7.93

INTA Rama Caida (EEA)	INTA S. Juan	ProMza	INTA Cuyo	Ctr Agro'ts– South Zone	Fondo Viti	Bod. Arg (elites)	Univ Natl Cuyo	Govt Mza	Assn Vinas Mza
3734.21	3429.17	2962.12	2805.07	2498.73	1363.44	1353.71	1205.5	969.71	943.64
7.14	6.55	5.66	5.36	4.78	2.61	2.59	2.3	1.85	1.8

Figure 5A.1 reveals a few 'ghettos' of some associations; the large majority of associations and institutions are isolates (lined on the left) and not shown by the program. Figure 5A.2 shows Mendoza in 2001. The new institutions are labeled and have box shaped nodes. Table 5A.1 shows the twenty large betweeness statistics from 2001 data. This shows that the new institutions, along with some government agencies, the university, and the two peak associations, play the most important bridging or 'brokering' roles in the industry and province. (See Burt 1992; Safford 2004.)

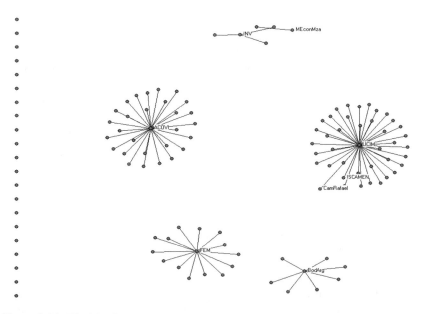

Figure 5.A1. The Mendozan wine industry and policymaking, 1989.

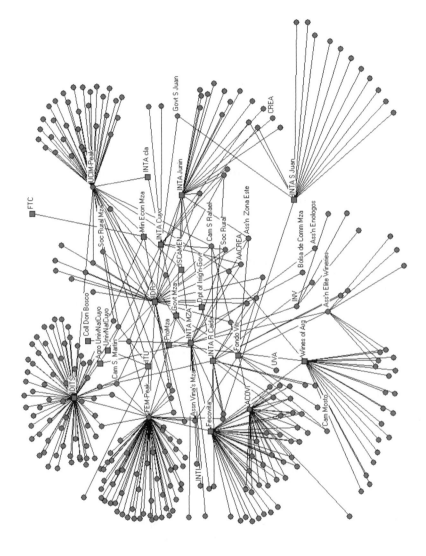

Figure 5.A2. The Mendozan wine industry and policymaking, 2001.

Notes

1. On the indeterminate impact of FDI and export firms on upgrading see (CEPAL 2002; Cornelius and Kogut 2003; Humphrey and Schmitz 2004). See, for instance, on networks (Saxenian 1994; Powell, Koput, and Smith-Doerr 1996), social capital (Putnam, Leonardi, and Nanetti, 1993), property rights (North, 1990; Johnson, McMillan, and Woodruff 2000), state coherence and capacity (Amsden 1989; Evans 1995; Guillen 2001), and on 'industrial districts' or 'clusters' (Piore and Sabel 1984; Locke 1995; Herrigel 1996; Humphrey et al. 2004; Schmitz 2004a, 2004b).

2. This research was based on field work during 2003–5 that utilized over sixty-five open-ended interviews with relevant managers, enologists, agronomists, and policymakers as well as current and historical data bases on relevant provincial and national policies, civic associations, and firms.

3. Through the 1990s, Argentinian exports accounted for only 10 percent of GDP. Most exports were in commodities and low-value added, even in sectors such as leather goods where Argentina historically had comparative advantages and a well-developed processing segment (Lugones 2000; CEPAL 2002; Guillen 2001).

4. Over the past 20 years, there has been a decline in per capita wine consumption, increased consumption in fine wines (especially the four fighting), and intense competition from 'New World' wine producing countries (e.g. United States, Chile, Australia) threatening the traditional producers of Europe. See Henderson et al. (2004) and Bartlett (2001).

5. For more on this strategy and the rise of Argentinian export prices, see Cetrangulo et al. (2002); 'La amenaza a las vinas chilenas', *El Mercurio*, Nov. 2, 2005; and the lengthy annual reviews of Argentinian wines in *Wine Spectator* (November 15, 1995; December 15, 1997; March 24, 2003; November 30, 2004; November 30, 2005).

6. Between 1980 and 1990, the number of vineyards fell by 31 percent and then another 29 percent until 2001; the amount of vineyard surface area fell by about 35 percent in the 1980s and then slightly declined in the 1990s (with eradication of vines being largely offset by new plantings). As of 2001, vineyards with less than 25 has still accounted for 92 percent of the number of vineyards and 60 percent of surface area. The figures are about the same for San Juan.

7. See Walters (1999), Giuliani and Bell (2005), and Bartlett (2001). In Australia, the top three firms account for 50 percent of exports; the top ten firms account for almost 20 percent of vineyard surface area. In Chile, the top six firms account for about 80 percent of exports.

8. I draw here on a few studies which attempt to clarify the terrain of the principal fine wine companies, using different sets of data (Blazquez 2001; Cetrangolo et al. 2002; Vila 2002; Ruiz and Vila 2003).

9. According to a 2003 survey of 400 wineries in Mendoza, only 4 percent have foreign investment and only about 6 percent are associated with or controlled by a diversified Argentinian business group or corporation. FDI estimates come from CEM (1999) and Nimo (2001).

10. The calculations on surface area and high-quality grapes are done by the author using the data provided by the INV. See also Cetrangulo et al. (2002); Bocco (2003); and 'Cosecha 1999–2002', La revista de la Bolsa, N⁰ 441, October 2002. The figures

on capabilities and exports of firms from the *Zona Este* are from a survey of 400 wineries in Mendoza undertaken in 2003 by the Ministry of Economy of the government of Mendoza.

11. Argentina ranks consistently low in measures of rule of law and property rights protection. See: http://www.worldbank.org/wbi/governance/govdata/index.html. In an analysis of provincial business climate, measures of legal efficiency were similar between the two provinces, while Mendoza had a much higher number of crimes against property per 1,000 inhabitants than San Juan. (FIEL 2003)

12. This type of story was repeated to me on ten different occasions.

13. By the 1990s, San Juan had five wine/grape sectoral associations, one economic federation, and one export association; Mendoza had six wine/grape sectoral associations, two economic chambers, and one export association.

14. ACREA (Asociacion de Consrocios de Experimentación Agropecuaria) is an association that began decades earlier coordinating and promoting collective learning among farms in the Pampas regions—the regions of grain, cattle, and dairy. The participants meet monthly at one of the member's vineyards to address a common problem or strategic concern via the 'live' example at the given vineyard. There were no Grupos in San Juan, but between 1990 and 1996 the number of Grupos grew from three to six, falling in the late 1990s back to three in Mendoza.

15. The events in Mendoza, CODEVIN San Rafael (*Zona Sur*) in 1995 and CODEVIN de *Zona Este* in 1997, grew rapidly from a few dozen samples to over 150 each within two to three years. San Juan firms created EVISAN in 1997. It grew from fifty samples by fourteen participating wineries in 1997 to over 102 samples by twenty-nine wineries in 2004.

16. *Promoción industrial* was started in 1973 and included San Juan in 1983 as the fourth beneficiary, in addition to the provinces of Catamarca, La Rioja, and San Luis. This program appeared to have had a significant impact in manufacturing and agriculture expansion in San Juan. Although partially suspended in 1987, President Menem renewed it, first in 1992 by decree and then in 1996 by law (Guinazu 2003); (Heymann and Kosacoff 2000; Zudaire 2001). Its revised form focussed on deferring about 75 percent of income taxes to the investor in agroindustrial and tourism projects. Estimates put the federal fiscal cost at about $7 billion in the 1990s. (Consejo Empresario Mendocino 1999; Borsani 2001)

17. During 1988 and 1989, Bordon would appoint an outside auditing commission, spin-off periphery units (such as in fruit, bottling, distilling), and reduce employment from 3,500 to about 300. Also, seven coops purchased wineries and twelve leased them in the beginning. Leverage was slashed and virtually all the new cooperatives paid back the special loans ahead of maturity. By 2002, Fecovita had sales of over $54 million, 28 percent of which was exports. More recently, it has emphasized improvements in packaging, bottling, and label management and expanding medium-quality fine wine (e.g. Marcus James in the United States). (Amendola, 2003)

18. Fecovita now includes thirty-two cooperatives, commercializes over 80 percent of the wine made by its members, and each cooperative ranges from 20 to 120 members. There was virtually no growth in the number of wine cooperatives in San Juan in the 1990s. See Paladino and Morales (1994) and Juri (1990). By 2000,

over 2,500 grape producers in Mendoza were members of cooperatives, accounting for over 15 percent of total grape production in the province, and another 2,000 producers are estimated to be dedicated suppliers of the cooperatives (Amendola et al. 2003).

19. The PROINDER program is administered by the Secretary of Agriculture of the federal government. Each province had to submit documentation, following a standard format, during 2000–3. Policy areas include programs for the prevention and diminished impact of negative climatic shocks, such as sudden hail storms and freezes (including subsidized credits to SMEs for relevant equipment and a specialized monitoring system), subsidized credits for small and medium farmers for improvements in technology, water management, and grape conversion, programs in the research, tracking, and dissemination of best practices in the management, processes, and technologies of farms by every subregion, continued tracking of the climate, soil qualities, fertilizer uses, and harvests in every subregions, and the expansion of the capabilities of the provinces phitosanitary regulator.

20. See Locke (2001); Cohen and Rogers 1992; and GADIS (2004). According to the data from the UNDP/IDB civil society index in Argentina, by 2000 there were 419 such organizations in Mendoza and only ninety-two in San Juan. As the UNDP notes in its analysis, these types of civic organizations, by virtue of the membership and services, tend to connect individuals from different backgrounds and sectors in new ways, are experimental in service development, and help pool various sources of information and resources for public access. Moreover, chief among organizations in this classification are support organizations, especially those focussed on economic development and social services. Whereas Mendoza has proportionally more organization linked to training, education, sciences, and SMEs, San Juan has many social, neighborhood, and sports clubs.

21. INTA's budget was radically changed, as the federal government eliminated its primary stable source of funding, a 1.5 percent tax on agricultural exports, incorporating INTA's funding into the general government budget (Casaburi 1999). The national Executive Committee includes representatives of the federal government, agricultural educational institutions, and the top agricultural producers' associations. INTA has gone through three reorganizations between 1991 and 2005. For instance, from 1991 to 1997, the Cuyo center concerned only Mendoza and San Juan, and then from 1997 to 2004 this center included the provinces of of La Rioja and San Luis as well. Since 2005, the Center has returned to including Mendoza and San Juan.

22. By law, any firm that uses at least 20 percent of its input grapes for mosto (the natural juice sweetener) does not have to pay an annual, relatively small tariff to the Fondo. The Fondo Vitivinicola is financed from these tariffs and matching funds from the government of Mendoza.

23. Within about 4 years the program boasted nationwide over 1,900 groups of over 21,000 producers and a network of almost 200 full- and part-time field agents and consultants in many agro sectors. CR in Mendoza reached better than expected results. It claimed over 100 learning groups that accounted for about 1,250 producers, while in San Juan it created only nineteen groups of 133 producers. By 1996, about 350 grape growers were participating in CR Mendoza. See Cheppi (2000).

24. According to data from these two universities, the number of students and gradu-ates in agronomy and enology degree programs increased by 50 percent between 1996 and 2001.
25. The Instituto Tecnologico Universitario was founded in 1993 by the Mendoza government, Universidad Nacional de Cuyo, Universidad Tecnológica Nacional and two peak level Mendoza business associations to provide a three year technical degree in management and technology.
26. This is based on interviews and documentation of the minutes of relevant meetings at INTA Cuyo.
27. On Russia, see Woodruff (2000); Herrera (2005); and Johnson (2001); on China, see Huang (2003) and Oi (1992); on Brazil, see Tendler (1997); and Montero (2002); on Germany, see Herrigel (1996); and on Italy, see Locke (1994); and Farrell and Knight (2003).

References

Adler, P. S. and Kwon, S.-W. (2002). 'Social Capital: Prospects for a New Concept', *Academy of Management Review*, 27(1): 17–40.

Allub, L. (1996). 'Globalizacion y modernizacion agroindustrial en la provincia de San Juan', Argentina', *Estudios Sociologicos*, 14(41): 473–92.

Amendola, F. (2003). *Estrategias de las Cooperativas Vitivinicolas de la Provincia de Men-doza, de Argentina*. Centre National d'Etudes Agronomiques des Regions Chaudes, Montpellier, Argentina.

Amsden, A. H. (1989). *Asia's Next Giant: South Korea and Late Industrialization*. New York: Oxford University Press.

Ansell, C. (2000). 'The Networked Polity: Regional Development in Western Europe', *Governance*, 13(3): 303–33.

Azpiazu, D. and Basualdo, E. (2003). 'Industria Vitivinicola', in E. S. E. 1.EG.33.6 (ed.): CEPAL: Argentina.

Berk, G. and Schneiberg, M. (2005). 'Varieties in Capitalism, Varieties of Association: Collaborative Learning in American Industry', *Politics and Society*, 33(1): 46–87.

Borsani, A. (2001). 'Los diferimientos Impositivos Agropecuarios en la Provincia de San Juan', *Apuntes Agroeconomicos*, 2(3).

Boycko, M. Shleifer, A., and Vishny, R. (1995). *Privatizing Russia*. Cambridge, MA: MIT Press.

Burt, R. S. (2000). 'The Network Structure of Social Capital', in R. Sutton and B. Straw (eds.) *Research in Organizational Behavior*, Vol. 22. Greenwich, CT: JAI Press, 345–423.

——(2001). 'Networks and Markets', in J. E. a. A. C. Rauch (ed.), *Networks and Markets*. New York: The Russel Sage Foundation.

Casaburi, G. G. (1999). *Dynamic Agroindustrial Clusters: The Political Economy of Compet-itive Sectors in Argentina and Chile*. New York: St. Martin's Press.

CEPAL. (2002). 'Globalization and Development', in CEPAL (ed.).

Cetrangolo, H. Fernandez, S. Quagliano, J. Zelenay, V. Muratore, N., and Lettier, F. (2002). *El Negocio de los Vinos en la Argentina*. Buenos Aires: FAUBA.

Cheppi, C. (2000). La Nueva Arquitectura de los Programs de Intervencion y su Rol en el Desarrollo Rural: INTA.

Cohen, J. and Rogers, J. (1992). 'Secondary Associations and Democratic Governance', *Politics and Society*, 20(4): 393–472.

Cohen, W. M. and Levinthal, D. A. (1990). 'Absorptive Capacity: A New Perspective on Learning and Innovation', *Administrative Science Quarterly*, 35: 128.

Consejo Empresario Mendocino (1999). Impacto economico de los regimenes de promocion de las provincias San Juan, San Luis, La Rioja y Catamarca: CEM.

Cornelius, P. and Kogut, B. M. (2003). *Corporate Governance and Capital Flows in a Global Economy*. New York: Oxford University Press.

Culpepper, P. D. (2004). Institutional Change in Contemporary Capitalism: Coordination and Politics in Finance during the 1990's.

Doner, R. F., Ritchie, B. K., and Slater, D. (2005). 'Systemic Vulnerability and the Origins of Developmental States: Northeast and Southeast Asia in Comparative Perspective', *International Organization*, 59(2).

Doner, R. F. a. B. R. S. (2000). 'Business Associations and Economic Development: Why Some Associations Contribute More Than Others', *Business and Politics*, 2(3): 261–88.

Evans, P. (2004). 'Development as Institutional Change: The Pitfalls of Monocropping and the Potentials of Deliberation', *Studies in Comparative International Development*, 38(4): 30–52.

Evans, P. B. (1995). *Embedded Autonomy: States and Industrial Transformation*. Princeton, NJ: Princeton University Press.

Falleti, T. (2005). 'A Sequential Theory of Decentralization: Latin American Cases in Comparative Perspective', *American Political Science Review*, 99(3).

Fung, A. and Wright, E. O. (2001). 'Deepening Democracy: Innovation in Empowered Participatory Government', *Politics and Society*, 29(1): 5–41.

Giuliani, E. and Bell, M. (2005*a*). 'The Micro-determinants of Meso-level Learning and Innovation: Evidence from a Chilean Wine Cluster', *Research Policy*, 34(1): 47–68.

—— Pietrobelli, C., and Rabellotti, R. (2005*b*). 'Upgrading in Global Value Chains: Lessons from Latin American Clusters', *World Development*, 33(4): 549–73.

Gobierno de San Juan (2004). Proyecto de Fortalecimiento Institucional Para el Desarrollo Rural: Provincia de San Juan.

Granovetter, M. (1985). 'Economic Action and Social Structure: The Problem of Embeddedness', *American Journal of Sociology*, 91: 481–510.

Greif, A. and Laitin, D. D. (2004). 'A Theory of Endogenous Institutional Change', *American Political Science Review*, 98: 633–52.

Guillen, M. (2001). *The Limits of Convergence: Globalization and Organizational Change in Argentina, South Korea, and Spain*. Princeton, NJ: Princeton University Press.

Guinazu, M. C. (2003). *The Subnational Politics of Structural Adjustment in Argentina: The Case of San Luis*. Massachusetts Institute of Technology.

Haber, S. H. (2002). *Crony Capitalism and Economic Growth in Latin America: Theory and Evidence*. Stanford, CA: Hoover Institution Press.

Haggard, S. and Kaufman, R. R. (1995). *The Political economy of Democratic Transitions*. Princeton, NJ: Princeton University Press.

Helper, S., MacDuffie, J. P., and Sabel, C. (2000). 'Pragmatic Collaborations: Advancing Knowledge While Controlling Opportunism', *Industrial and Corporate Change*, 9(3): 443.

Henderson, J., Pagani, L., and Cool, K. (2004). Collective Resources and Cluster Advantage: An Examination of the Global Wine Industry. Paper presented at the strategic Management Society conference.

Herrigel, G. B. (1996). *Reconceptualizing the Sources of German Industrial Power*. New York: Cambridge University Press.

Heymann, D. and Kosacoff, B. P. (2000). *La Argentina de los noventa: desempeäno econâomico en un contexto de reformas* (1. ed.). Buenos Aires: Eudeba: Naciones Unidas, CEPAL.

Hirst, P. Q. (1994). *Associative Democracy: New Forms of Economic and Social Governance*. Amherst, MA: University of Massachusetts Press.

Humphrey, J. and Schmitz, H. (2004). 'Globalized Localities: Introduction', in H. Schmitz (ed.), *Local Enterprises in the Global Economy*. Cheltenam and Northampton: Edward Elgar.

Jacoby, W. (2000). *Imitation and Politics: Redesigning Germany*. Ithaca, NY: Cornell University Press.

Johnson, S., McMillan, J., and Woodruff, C. (2000). 'Entrepreneurs and the Ordering of Institutional Reform', *Economics of Transition*, 8: 1.

Kogut, B. (2000). 'The Network as Knowldge: Generative Rules and the Emergence of Structure', *Strategic Management Journal*, 21: 405–25.

Lattuada, M. (2000). *Cambio Rural: Politica y Desarrolllo en la Argentina de los '90* (Primera Edition ed.). Rosario, Argentina: CED-Arcasur Editorial.

Levitsky, S. (2003). *Transforming Labor-Based Parties in Latin America: Argentinian Peronism in Comparative Perspective*. Cambridge, UK; New York: Cambridge University Press.

—— and Murillo, M. V. (2005).'Theory Building in a Context of Institutional Instability', in S. Levitsky and M. V. Murillo (eds.), *Argentinian Democracy: The Politics of Institutional Weakness*. Pennsylvania State University Press.

Locke, R. M. (1995). *Remaking the Italian Economy: Local Politics and Industrial Change in Contemporary Italy*. Ithaca, NY: Cornell University Press.

Lugones, G. a. F. P. (2000). La Industrialization del Cuero y Sus Manufacturas en Argentina: Un Cluster en Desarticulacion o un complejo Desarticulado? CEPAL.

MacDuffie, J. P. (1997). 'The road to 'Root Cause',: Shop-floor Problem-solving at Three Auto Assembly Plants', *Management Science*, 43(4): 479.

Mahoney, J. and Rueschemeyer, D. (2003). *Comparative Historical Analysis in the Social Sciences*. Cambridge, UK; New York: Cambridge University Press.

McDermott, G. A. (2002a). *Embedded Politics: Industrial Networks and Institutional Change in Postcommunism*. Ann Arbor, MI: University of Michigan Press.

—— (2002b). 'The Reinvention of Federalism: Governance over Decentralized Institutional Experiments in Latin America', *Desarrollo Economico*, 41(164): 611–42.

McEvily, B. a. A. M. (2005). 'Embedded Ties and the Acquisition of Competitive Capabilities', *Strategic Management Journal*, 26(11): 1033–55.

Montero, A. P. (2001). *Shifting States in Globel Markets: Subnational Industrial Policy in Contemporary Brazil and Spain*. University Park, PA: Pennsylvania State University Press.

Montero, A. P. and Samuels, D. J. (2004). *Decentralization and Democracy in Latin America*. Notre Dame, IN: University of Notre Dame Press.

North, D. C. (1990). *Institutions, Institutional Change, and Economic Performance.* Cambridge; New York: Cambridge University Press.

O'Riain, S. (2004). *The Politics of High Tech Growth: Developmental Network States in the Global Economy.* New York: Cambridge University Press.

Ostrom, E. (1990). *Governing the Commons: The Evolution of Institutions for Collective Action.* Cambridge, England; New York: Cambridge University Press.

Ostrom, E. (1995). 'Self-organization and Social Capital', *Industrial and Corporate Change,* Oxford University Press/UK, p. 131.

—— (1999). 'Coping with Tragedies of the Commons', *Annual Review of Political Science,* 2: 493–535.

Pack, H. (2000). 'Industrial Policy: Growth Elixir or Poison?', *World Bank Research Observer,* 15: 47.

Padgett, J. (2001). 'Organizational Genesis, Identity, and Control: The Transformation of Banking in Renaissance Florence', in J. E. Rauch, and A. Casella (eds.), *Networks and Markets.* New York: The Russell Sage Foundation.

Paladino, M. and Jauregui, J. M. (2001). 'La Transformacion del Sector Vitivinicola Argentino.' Argentina: IAE, Universidad Austral.

Perez-Aleman, P. (2005). 'Cluster Formation, Institutions and Learning: The Emergence of Clusters and Development in Chile', *Industrial and Corporate Change,* 14(4): 651–77.

Piore, M. and Sabel, C. (1984). *The Second Industrial Divide: Possibilities for Prosperity.* New York: Basic Books.

Powell, W., White, D., Koput, K., and Owen Smith, J. (2005). 'Network Dynamics and Field Evolution: The Growth of Interorganizational Collaboration in the Life Sciences.' *American Journal of Sociology* 110: 1132–1205.

Powell, W. W., Koput, K. W., and Smith-Doerr, L. (1996). 'Interorganizational Collaboration and the Locus of Innovation: Networks of Learning in Biotechnology', *Administrative Science Quarterly,* 41: 116.

Putnam, R. D., Leonardi, R., and Nanetti, R. (1993). *Making Democracy Work: Civic Traditions in Modern Italy.* Princeton, NJ: Princeton University Press.

Remmer, K. and Wibbels, E. (2000). 'The Subnational Politics of Economic Adjustment: Provincal Politics and Fiscal Performance in Argentina', *Comparative Political Studies,* 33(4): 419–51.

Roberts, P. and Ingram, P. (2002). 'Vertical Linkages, Knowledge Transfer and Export Performance: The Australian and New Zealand Wine Industry, 1987–99.'

Rodrik, D. (2004). 'Industrial Policy for the Twenty-First Century', *Working Paper prepared for UNIDO.*

Rofman, A. B. (1999). *Desarrollo regional y exclusión social: transformaciones y crisis en la Argentina contemporánea.* Buenos Aires: Amorrortu Editores.

Ross Schneider, B. (2004). *Business Politics and the State in Twentieth-Century Latin America.* Cambridge; New York: Cambridge University Press.

Sabel, C. (1994). 'Learning by Monitoring: The Institutions of Economic Development', in N. J. Smelser and R. Swedberg (eds.), *The Handbook of economic sociology:* Vol. viii, Princeton: Princeton University Press, p. 835.

—— (1996b). 'A Measure of Federalism: Assessing Manufacturing Technology Centers', *Research Policy,* 25: 281–307.

Sabel, C. F. (1996a). *Ireland: Local Partnerships and Social Innovation*. Paris, Washington, DC.: Organisation for Economic Co-operation and Development; OECD Publications and Information Centre, distributor.

Safford, S. (2004). 'Why the Garden Club Couldn't Save Youngstown: Civic Infastructure and Mobilzation in Economic Crises Paper', *MIT Industrial Performance Center Working Paper*.

Salvarredi, G. (2001). 'Reconversion Vitivinicola'. INTA Lujan de Cuyo: Buenos Aires.

Saxenian, A. (1994). *Regional Advantage: Culture and Competition in Silicon Valley and Route 128*. Cambridge: Harvard University Press.

Schmitz, H. (2004a). 'Globalized Localities: Introduction', in H. Schmitz (ed.), *Local Enterprises in the Global Economy*. Cheltenam and Northampton: Edward Elgar.

—— (ed.) (2004b). *Local Enterprises in the Global Economy: Issues of Governance and Upgrading*. Northampton, MA: Edward Elgar.

—— and Nadvi, K. (1999). 'Clustering and Industrialization: Introduction', *World Development* 27, 1503–1733.

Schneider, B. R. (2004). *Business Politics and the State in Twentieth-Century Latin America*. Cambridge; New York: Cambridge University Press.

Snyder, R. (2001). *Politics after Neoliberalism: Reregulation in Mexico*. Cambridge, UK; New York: Cambridge University Press.

Stark, D. (1996). 'Networks of Assets, Chains of Debt: Recombinant Property in Hungary', in R. Frydman, Cheryl Gray, and Andrej Rapaczynski (eds.), *Corporate Governance in Central Europe and Russia*, Vol. II. Insiders and the State. Budapest and London: Central European University Press, pp. 108–50.

—— (2001). 'Ambiguous Assets for Uncertain Environments: Heterarchy in Postsocialist Firms', in P. Di Maggio (ed.), *The Twenty-First-Century Firm: Changing Economic Organization in International Perspective*, Princeton, NJ: Princeton University Press, pp. 69–104.

—— and Bruszt, L. (1998). *Post-Socialist Pathways: Transforming Politics and Property in Eastern Europe*. New York: Cambridge University Press.

Tendler, J. (1997). *Good Government in the Tropics*. Baltimore: Johns Hopkins University Press.

Thelen, K. (2003). 'How Institutions Evolve: Insights from Comparative Historical Analysis', in J. Mahoney, and D. Rueschemeyer (eds.), *Comparative Historical Analysis in the Social Sciences*. New York: Cambridge University Press.

Walters, A. (1999). *Rebuilding Technologically Competitive Industries: Lessons from Chile's and Argentina's Wine Industry Restructuring*. Massachusetts Institutue of Technology.

Winter, S. G. (2003). 'The Satisficing Principle in Capability Learning', in C. E. Helfat (ed.), *The SMS Blackwell Handbook of Organizational Capabilities: Emergence, Development, and Change*: x, 438. Malden, MA: Blackwell Publication.

Ziegler, J. N. (1995). *Governing Ideas: Strategies for Ideas in France and Germany*. Ithaca, NY: Cornell University Press.

Zudaire, H. E. (2001). *Incentivos Tributarios y el Costo Fiscal de la Promocion Industrial*. Buenos Aires: La Ley.

Part II

Micro-Level Strategies of Firms in Specific Sectors

6

Antioquia Entrepreneur Group (GEA)'s Strategies for Facing International Competitors: The Case of the Food Manufacturing Group

Héctor Ochoa[1]

6.1. Introduction

The most outstanding company internationalization cases in Colombia can be divided into two groups. On the one hand, there are those companies that were purchased by foreign investors after a modernization process took place. Some of these acquisitions were followed by expansion within or outside Colombia; and others were the result of a financial crisis. This is what happened to the companies in the consortium owned by the Santodomingo family. Some of the most well-known cases are Avianca, a commercial airline purchased by Brazilian investor G. Efromovich, and Bavaria,[2] a brewery recently purchased by SABMiller. Several public utility companies and banking institutions owned by the Colombian government which were privatized in the 1990s can also be classified in this group.

On the other hand, there are those companies that have gone through a technological modernization, refinancing, and management reengineering process to be able to face and survive international competition, with Colombian investors maintaining ownership of these companies. Most of these companies had previously ventured into the international markets, initially exporting to other countries in the Andean Region and subsequently developing strategies to ensure continuous presence of their products in these markets.

Some established alliances with other companies. Some examples include among others: Noel, a cookie and confectionery manufacturing company (this case is further discussed below), partnered with Danone, a French company; Almacenes Exito, a supermarket chain partnered with Casino, another French company; Colcafé partnered with Japanese Mitsubishi; and Corona, a sanitary porcelain manufacturer, partnered with Chilean Sodimac at the Homecenter stores. Others made the decision to purchase production facilities in some of the countries in which they positioned their companies, thus maintaining their independent nature, such as Pintuco,[3] a paint manufacturer; Leonisa,[4] a women's lingerie manufacturer; Carvajal, S. A,[5] a company engaged in the book printing, telephone directory, and school notebook business; Argos, a cement manufacturer that purchased 'Southern Star Concrete' and 'Concrete Express' in the United States; and Corona, which purchased Mansfield Plumbing in the United States. A few others such as Colombina, a confectionery company, decided to follow a more conventional strategy using distributors to service its customers abroad.

Last, but not least, are those companies engaged in the manufacture of goods that cannot be traded in the international market, because of the high costs of transportation of products composed mainly of water and sugar. These companies ran the highest risk of losing their market share to foreign competitors who could establish in the country in order to place their products in the market. This was the well-known case of the traditional soft drink companies owned by the Ardila Lule consortium, which strengthened its position in the market by purchasing its competitors' businesses, thereby achieving a company size that guaranteed their survival. In order to have access to low-cost supplies and services (sugar, containers, and advertising in the media), these companies underwent a vertical integration process. In order to have access to low sugar prices, the group is one of the largest sugar producers in Colombia; besides that, it owns a television channel and a container factory, among other investments, as a strategy to access low price services and components for its production of soft drinks.

The above mentioned cases are different from each other in many ways. In each case, a study could be conducted to identify the strategies and behavior of businessmen and then compare the results with international experience. We decided to study the case of the GEA, Antioquia Entrepreneur Group, taking into account that it has certain characteristics and encompasses a wide range of goods and services in the finance, insurance, security brokerage, food, and cement industries. GEA has also managed to keep a public partnership structure in all of its businesses, the shares of which are tradable in the stock market. It has followed a wide range of strategic approaches to the internationalization process, including strategic alliances with foreign investors, mergers within the same business group to size their businesses properly, acquisition of companies abroad, and financial integration through Bancolombia, the largest bank in Colombia, thus ensuring access to liquid funds. From the companies owned by GEA, we selected the group of food manufacturing companies which is probably the group with the most innovative internationalization strategies.

6.2. GEA: Antioquia Entrepeneur Group (*Grupo Empresarial Antioqueño*)

In order to understand the behavior of the managers who run the GEA-owned companies, it is necessary to know something about the background that has characterized these companies from the time in which they were established in the early 1920s to the present. Several economic events that occurred in Colombia set a landmark in their business evolution. First of all, it is worth noting that GEA is an unincorporated business and is not exactly a business holding unit. It does not have a board of directors, a chairperson, or a similar entity. Its companies engage in different businesses that do not compete with each other. The fact that they are rather complementary to each other has enabled them to take advantage of synergies and reach agreements that do not hinder operations in the markets. They have maintained a commitment to refrain from duplicating businesses in any given sector.

Not long ago this consortium was known as the Antioquia Union (*Sindicato Antioqueño*). People spontaneously came up with this name as the result of the events that took place in the late 1970s when companies from Antioquia, Colombia, were under the serious threat of a hostile takeover if their shares were purchased in the stock market by economic groups located outside the Department of Antioquia in Colombia.

This situation encouraged businessmen in this Colombian region to secure ownership of their companies by engaging in stock market transactions to discourage potential buyers. Using a chess term, this gave rise to some sort of castling to protect the king from the contender's attacks. Nevertheless, as a consequence of internationalization strategies, business managers recently decided that they would be much better off if they changed their business name to one that had no political connotations involved. Therefore, they changed the business name from 'union' to Antioquia Entrepreneurs Group, their current name. In short, this group reflects the collective willingness of the companies to achieve common internationalization goals.

Most of the GEA-owned groups were established in the 1920s as the result of investments made by businessmen, mine owners, and coffee producers from Antioquia who wanted to secure a local supply of the consumer goods that they had been importing. This could be considered the precursor of the import substitution approach that was later adopted in Latin America under the sponsorship of CEPAL. They opted for a public corporation structure that enabled them to add their own wealth from their trade, gold mining, and coffee growing activities to additional public resources and investments between companies engaged in supplementary activities (Alvarez Morales 2003).[6] This kind of approach was unique in Colombia where closed family-owned businesses were typically established in other regions. In spite of failed attempts made by family-owned groups outside Antioquia to take possession of these companies in the stock market in the 1970s and 1980s, this approach continues to be the most common in Antioquia, where publicly-traded corporations continue to rule.

Strategic alliances between companies within GEA began to emerge in the 1920s and remained solid throughout the rest of the twentieth century. Noel, a cookie and confectionery company, was the result of an alliance between businessmen and *Compañía Nacional de Chocolates*. A detailed review of these two companies is provided below. Then, in the troubled 1930s, sellers of products from both companies decided to merge into a single marketing unit. In the 1940s both companies made a commitment to not compete with similar products. One of the companies was to engage exclusively in the production of cookies and confectionery products, while the other one would only manufacture chocolate. Alvarez Morales says: *'around 1940 business decisions were based on intertwined relationships built in the course of 2 decades. These intertwined relationships entailed sharing risks and benefits, and having a unified willingness and a feeling of belonging to a group.'*[7] Therefore, it is no surprise that the current organizational culture of the GEA companies is clearly marked by an alliance-based approach that facilitates the adoption of strategies for internationalization.

Today GEA has 141 companies engaged in the food, banking, security brokerage, insurance, cement, self-service stores, and pension fund businesses. Because its products and services have been positioned in foreign markets, the group recently achieved higher levels of competitiveness. In preparing for a possible free-trade agreement with the United States, they have adopted strategies to consolidate businesses through internal mergers. Their strategy is aimed at consolidating the organizational structure and getting rid of redundant production, marketing, and logistics processes related to products that use the same distribution channels. It also plans to strengthen access to short-term and long-term financing sources, taking advantage of the overall solvency of the group, and to offer a more transparent response to its shareholders. Some of the group's core businesses have undergone a merging process in the past three years, thus leading to changes in its organizational structure. Each of its business divisions is now more focussed and more specialized than ever before.

The following is a brief review of the above mentioned mergers. In the banking industry, mortgage, investment, and consumer credit businesses merged into Bancolombia, thus leading to the establishment of the largest all-purpose banking institution in Colombia. Its total net worth (US$1.6 billion) and 630 branches all over the country make it the largest bank in Colombia. The

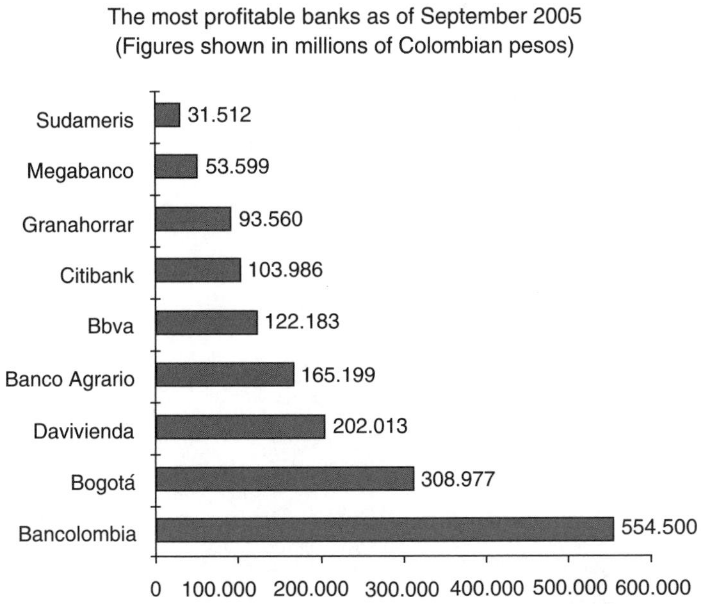

The most profitable banks as of September 2005
(Figures shown in millions of Colombian pesos)

Sudameris	31.512
Megabanco	53.599
Granahorrar	93.560
Citibank	103.986
Bbva	122.183
Banco Agrario	165.199
Davivienda	202.013
Bogotá	308.977
Bancolombia	554.500

0   100.000   200.000   300.000   400.000   500.000   600.000

Figure 6.1. Profits of Colombian banks from January 1, 2005 to September 30, 2005[8]
Source: Bank Superintendence: Chart supplied by EL PAIS

group recently registered with the New York stock market for selling its shares publicly in the international market.

As a result of its strategy for growth, the group's profits from January to September of 2005 were US$2.5 billion, which represents the largest profitability in the Colombian banking industry. They reflect a growth of 73 percent over the same 9-month period in 2004. Figure 6.1 shows a comparison of the group's profits with those of its competitors.

In the cement industry,[9] sixty-four facilities located in Colombia and abroad (United States, Venezuela, Panama, Haiti, and the Dominican Republic), which used to operate as regional independent businesses, merged into Cementos Argos, the parent company. After merging, the new company now has a net worth of US$4.17 billion and a cement production capacity of 8.68 million cubic meters per year. Since 2005, 58 percent of the company's revenue has come from international activities. Figure 6.2 below shows the recent expansion of the cement group.

In the food industry, thirty-three companies engaged in the cookie, meat, confectionery, pasta, and chocolate business merged into *Compañía de Inversiones Nacional de Chocolates* last September. These companies rely on leading brands and have their own distribution networks both in Colombia and in

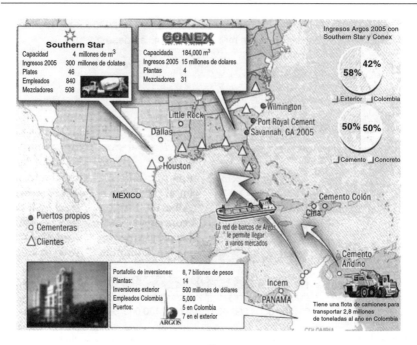

Figure 6.2. Expansion of the cement group[7]

those countries where the group conducts operations. It has an overall net worth of US$1.08 billion.[10]

In the insurance business, *Compañía Suramericana de Seguros* (*South American Insurance Company*) demerged into an investment and an insurance division in 1997 as part of its internationalization process. The investment division is called INVERSURA, which is a well-known investor in the insurance business. German 'Munich—Re' holds 19.5 percent ownership of this investment company. The other division is *Compañía Suramericana de Seguros* (*South American Insurance Company*) which takes care of the pension, life, general, and medical insurance business. This division has established alliances with 'Positiva' in Peru, 'Alianza' in Bolivia, 'Equinoccial' in Ecuador, 'Interoceánica' in Panama, and 'Seguros América' and 'Pellas Group' in Central America. Nevertheless, the most important step in this internationalization strategy is the current transaction being negotiated with the Chilean Construction Chamber and 'La Positiva' to establish a Latin American insurance holding company with mutual interest in the entire continent.[11]

Yet all these new companies, which are the result of mergers, continue to be publicly traded corporations. GEA has been distinguished in Colombia as one of the most honorable groups with respect to the treatment it gives to its minority shareholders. It is ruled by corporate governance bylaws, which provide confidence to its shareholders.[12]

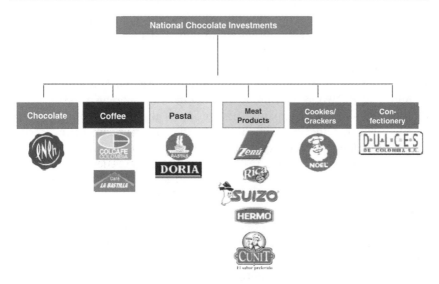

Figure 6.3. Businesses and brands in GEA's food group
Source: Inversiones Nacional de Chocolates

The positive expectations resulting from its internationalization strategies have translated into an increase in the demand for the group's shares in the stock market. As a result, the value of shares of all the GEA companies registered in the stock market so far this year has had an approximate growth of 130 percent.

6.3. The GEA's Food Group (INCH)

We decided to select GEA's food group because we believe it will enable us not only to delve into the analysis of strategies for internationalizing and improving the competitive ability of Latin American companies, but also to provide an answer to the question that gave rise to this study in Colombia which is sponsored by the Thunderbird Business School.

The food group consists of thirty-three companies engaged in the manufacture of crackers and cookies, chocolate bars, and powdered chocolate; delicatessen items such as sausages, hams, meat spreads, and fresh meat for homes and restaurants, and integration with slaughter houses and cold storage facilities; all kinds of confectionery products such as chewing gum, as well as instant coffee, ground coffee, and Italian-type pasta. The groups' companies and brand names are shown in Figure 6.3.

Carlos Enrique Piedrahita,[13] INCH's CEO, defines the main product portfolio of this conglomerate as one consisting of consumer goods that are popular among Latin Americans. Accessible to all consumers regardless of their income level, these products account for 88 percent of the group's total sales. In a separate category, gourmet products are aimed at high income consumers in foreign countries such as the United States, Japan, Canada, China, and some European countries. These products are dark chocolate bars of origin, which are produced from cocoa of the Santander variety. This kind of cocoa is unique in the world. It is produced only in one Colombian region under direct guidance of the company. These products also include gourmet coffee of origin which comes from small organic crops in the main coffee growing region of Colombia. Production of gourmet coffee is conducted under the guidance of the company and the Colombian National Federation of Coffee Growers. The coffee group is now present in the markets of forty countries. Production will most likely continue to grow as more and more people from industrialized countries are turning back to high-quality coffee drinks.

The group possesses the necessary knowledge to innovate with new brands of a high added value. It can make use of the technological development that coffee growers have achieved in Colombia to produce coffee of superior quality. This gourmet product portfolio accounts for 12 percent of the group's total sales.

As mentioned earlier, thirty-three companies merged into *Inversiones Nacional de Chocolates or INCH*, the leading parent company, which is responsible for managing 100 percent of the shares of the six business divisions that rely on solid leading brands, production facilities, and distribution networks in Colombia and abroad. 'In spite of the merger, these companies will continue to run autonomously, having their own administrative and business structures', said CEO Piedrahita. 'INCH, the parent company, does not run the business. Each division is autonomous and has its own financial and human talent resources to manage and operate its business. The merger is going to generate synergies and enable the group to have more transparent relations with its shareholders.'

Carlos Mario Giraldo, CEO at Noel (Cookies, Crackers, and Confectionery) and Executive Vice President of the conglomerate, says: 'We expect the merger to generate value to the shareholders. Investments will have a greater potential and the group will be more competitive with respect to other global companies in the food industry. It should open the doors to national and international expansion of several companies. Since all operations will focus on one single investing company, the shareholders will see things more clearly.' The merger resulted in a conglomerate with a net worth of US\$1.08 billion and 15,000 employees. It expects to achieve annual sales for US\$2.47 billion. The group's shareholders view the merger as a transaction in which one share of the cookie, cracker, confectionery, meat product, and pasta manufacturing company called *Inveralimentos* was traded for 3.10 shares of the newly incorporated company called *Compañia Inversiones Nacional de Chocolates* (INCH).

Figure 6.4. Evolution in the price of shares since last year for. Inversiones Nacional De Chocolates (INCH) vs. IGBC Index (Colombian Stock Exchange overall Index).
Source: Colombian stock market

Figure 6.4 shows the change in the value of INCH's shares in the Colombian stock market, before and after the merger, compared to the IGBC index in the Colombian stock market. The price of these shares began to rise in September 2004, and in February 2005, it reached 175 percent. In October, a few days after the merger, the shares reached their highest price of US$4.04, in comparison with the price it had in June the previous year, that is, US$2.56. *Nacional de Chocolates* shares have been one of the best investment alternatives in Colombia since 1995. On average, these shares have had an effective nominal profitability of 25.5 percent, which is higher than the 17.2 percent of other Colombian company shares.

6.4. International Expansion of the Food Group

The INCH conglomerate is now present in seventy countries. The countries with the largest sales volumes are located in the Andean Community, Central America, and the Caribbean, and the Latino population living in the United States and Spain. Products sold include cookies, crackers, confectionery products, coffee, chocolates, and Italian-type pasta. Meat products, however, are only distributed in Colombia through production facilities located in the four largest cities in Colombia and Venezuela, where Hermo was recently purchased. These products are not traded in other Latin American countries because of the high tariff and sanitary restrictions imposed on these kinds of products in most countries.

CEO Piedrahita defines the success of the internationalization strategy as the result of two efficient networks: a production and a distribution network. Both of these networks rely on the value that the conglomerate has added to its own brands. With regard to production, he affirms that the company is now in similar competitive conditions as its competitors worldwide. Because it has the necessary financial resources, it has been able to acquire the best technology and gather the most talented human resources to design new products. Since some products (such as confectionery products specially aimed at children and youths) have a very short life cycle, new products need to be launched constantly.

For five years, the company had a strategic alliance with Danone, the leading French cookie manufacturer, and through it Danone purchased 30 percent of the shares of Noel, the cookie, cracker, and confectionery manufacturer. The purpose of this alliance was to gather experience in the production of cookies and new products which would allow the company to compete with Nabisco, Kraft, and other similar companies in the category of diet and whole-grain crackers.

In spite of the success of this alliance, the company recently made the decision to terminate it, repurchasing the shares from Danone. Because of its production strengths, the group was convinced that it could move forward alone. To complement the production network and seize free-market opportunities in Central America, the Caribbean, and Mexico (CARICOM), the company purchased Nestlé's manufacturing plants in Costa Rica and Nestlé's exclusive cookie, chocolate, and confectionery brands for the region. It is now looking into the possibility of purchasing other manufacturing plants which would enable the company to be closer to the markets it serves and save in transportation costs.

With respect to the distribution network, CEO Piedrahita states that the key strategy that has differentiated his company from other multinationals and enabled it to secure a successful penetration in the target international markets is the system that the company devised in Colombia in the 1940s. In his own words, he defines this system as 'capillary'.

In explaining this strategy, he starts from the fact that, as mentioned above, this conglomerate's portfolio consists of consumer goods that are popular and typical of Latin American countries. These products are available in bins at self-service store chains where, on average, they account for 40 percent of the market share, but the remaining bulk (i.e. approximately 60 percent) of the market sales are made at traditional points of purchase, close to the households where a large number of low income families live in Latin America where the company's products are important.

The conglomerate established several *Cordialsas* (*Corporación Distribuidora de Alimentos S.A.*), food distribution companies, which constitute its most important international distribution strategy for this target population. These companies reflect more than sixty years of experience in trading mass consumer goods in Latin American countries. They are composed of a large number of small independent businessmen who own at least one distribution vehicle. Each of these distributors is assigned to serve a territory under supervision of one of the conglomerate's employees or specialized sales leaders, who have been trained in the corporate culture. These leaders work as agents who convey this culture and coach others.

Right now there are eleven *Cordialsas* in each of the countries where the conglomerate conducts operations in Latin America and two in the United States; one in the southwest and the other one in the southeast of the United States. A new distribution company will soon start operations in the area of influence in Chicago to reach the locations where the largest communities of Latinos are concentrated.

Cordialsas are incorporated as national companies according to the laws of the country where they are located. They are run by Colombian immigrants who have been trained not only in the organizational culture, but also in the culture, business practices, and laws of the host country.

They are responsible for recruiting distributors, providing counseling in the establishment of their small distribution companies, training them on product management, and accompanying them on their distribution routes on a regular basis. They are also responsible for promoting the brands and investing in advertising in the media to ensure that knowledge of these brands is widely spread on the market.

Cordialsas are in charge of the distribution of all the product portfolios of the five business divisions of the conglomerate outside Colombia, but they are also distributors of meat products in this country. Except for coffee, the entire above-mentioned gourmet class products are traded in industrialized countries through specialized representatives. A significant portion of gourmet coffee production is traded through a strategic alliance with Japanese Mitsubishi.

The operation of the networks described above depends on the existence of the conglomerate's exclusive brands used for trading its products in different countries, except in CARICOM, where it also uses brandnames purchased from Nestlé. CEO Piedrahita emphasizes the huge investments made by the conglomerate not only in advertising in the media to position its brands in each country, but also in providing support to traders in the different distribution channels (wholesalers, large distributors, and small distributors) to create a name for the brands.

He defines the marketing strategy of the group in his own words as: '*A set of actions aimed at building a brandname. This involves positioning our products at all the points of purchase and having a good knowledge of the consumer's tastes to produce a greater added value that is perceived by the customer. This calls for 2 different strategies: a 'light' distribution strategy that addresses all the channels permanently and communicates with the customers, and another one with an adequate budget for advertising to keep the brands active'.*

6.5. Competitive Strategies of the Food Group in the Colombian Market

Though Section 6.4 focussed on a discussion of strategies to be competitive in foreign markets, we still have to analyze the question of the ability to protect the local market against potential competitors that may come from abroad. What are the strategies of the GEA's Food Group in Colombia in this regard?

Juan Pablo Nicholls, the Group's International Vice President, conducted a review of the strategies of each of the six business divisions within the group. These strategies are consistent with strategies on an international level. First of all, the group has been strengthening its position since the 1980s when it was under the threat of a hostile takeover by a financial group outside the Antioquia region. As a result, the group realized that it needed to grow in order to secure a larger market coverage by both expanding its product portfolio and enhancing its distribution network.

They consolidated as companies specialized in mass consumer goods in a wide range of product categories; products of well-known quality at a fair price. This entailed having extremely efficient production facilities with state-of-the-art technology. Built from the late 1980s to the early 1990s, these facilities replaced old facilities that had been in operation since the 1950s when the import substitution process started out in Colombia.

Vice President Nicholls describes the production, branding, marketing, and distribution strategies for each of the six business divisions of the group. In the early 1990s after establishing an economic opening policy in Colombia, there was a trend toward the introduction of cookies, crackers and confectionery products from abroad. The group, however, managed to neutralize this trend by developing new products (i.e. cookies and whole-grain crackers) and continuously renewing its snack portfolio, but particularly those products aimed at children and youths. It also achieved substantial improvements of its product appearance and reduced the cost of raw materials and supplies such as imported wheat by developing better negotiating skills.

Direct distribution has been used for all the companies in the group since the 1950s even before the merger took place. It was undoubtedly the most important strategy to deal with the competition. Distribution to small stores close to the homes of the bulk of the population in mid-low and low social income neighborhoods (which accounts for nearly 70% of the demand for mass consumer goods) became the main barrier and source of high costs to multinational competitors who tried to introduce their products in the market.

The capillary system that CEO Piedrahita mentioned in Section 6.4 of this chapter was the fundamental strategy that differentiated the group from its international competitors. This difference became more evident because, according to surveys conducted periodically by the *Dinero* magazine,[14] Noel is one of the brands of cookies and confectionery products most easily recalled by general consumers in Colombia. The outstanding presence of the brand at the points of purchase in supermarket chains that serve high- and middle-income consumers and stores in mid-low and low income neighborhoods in large cities and small towns has contributed to the strong positioning of the brand.

In the meat product category, during the past twenty years, the company bought the main cold competitors' production plants and brands in the most important regional markets in Colombia. It also followed a vertical integration approach to add slaughter houses and cold storage facilities to its production network, which would enable the group to include livestock, beef and pork meat, in order to guarantee raw materials of standard quality, and avoid the volatile costs in the carcass meat market.

By the late 1990s, the company had consolidated a leading position as a meat processing company in Colombia. It had its own facilities and well-known regional brands, which were purchased in Cali, Bogota, and Barranquilla in addition to the initial plant located in Medellín. Similarly to the cookie business, distribution is done using a 'capillary' distribution system. At present, the group serves 80 percent of the demand for this product category in Colombia.

In the coffee product category, the group owns two coffee brands in Colombia: a soluble coffee brand, which competes against multinational Nestlé, with an approximate 60 percent market share, and a ground coffee brand that faces extensive competition from mid-size and small businesses in all market niches. As with other products, its major strength lies in the distribution network and in the fact that its brands are easily recognized. As mentioned earlier, however, the strongest capabilities of its production facilities are focussed on exporting goods.

In the chocolate industry the group is the leader in Colombia. Since colonial times, hot chocolate has been a traditional drink in Colombia. Families drink chocolate at breakfast every day or as a special refreshment in the mid-afternoon. The group's strategy was to purchase most of these chocolate brands in the course of the past century. These brands have a high emotional content involved and are used for trading products in each particular region. The company developed 'Jet', a chocolate bar brand that has become the star product that leads the market in the chocolate candy category. The group's significant strategy for investment on advertising in the media and the different product sizes, which range from sizes that cost a few cents to more sophisticated expensive presentations, for which consumers believe they are paying a fair price, have allowed the brand to be easily recognized.

It was with the chocolate products that the group started implementing its capillary distribution strategy in the 1950s. The food group has approximately a 60 percent share of this market. The second best company has approximately 30 percent of the market share, and the remaining 10 percent is in the hands of small local businesses. Colombia is a self-sufficient country with regard to the production of top quality raw materials such as cocoa, which is sold at competitive prices in the international market.

Notwithstanding, it faces a major production issue because of the high cost of sugar compared to international prices, particularly if compared with Brazil. This sugar pricing issue undermines its competitiveness in the international area. In spite of an economic opening policy, this artificial fixed-price situation in Colombia restrains the ability to purchase sugar from foreign suppliers and forces the group and other confectionery manufacturers to adopt strategies to offset this surcharge on other production fronts. As CEO Piedrahita says: *'sugar producers will only be happy when they are done eating the goose that lays the golden eggs.'*

Finally, the recent merger of the food group is one of the group's most powerful strategies to face potential foreign competitors, particularly from the United States, who could introduce their products into the market if a successful free-trade agreement is reached with the United States. CEO Piedrahita affirms that the merger is going to allow the group to simplify its organizational structure and to be more profitable from synergies, especially in the areas of distribution and logistics. The merger should also translate into an improved cash flow management, generation of its own resources for financing long-term investments, and the attraction of new investors because it avoids conflicts of interest among shareholders, who used to be shareholders of the different companies that now comprise the group. *'This is going to allow us to have more transparent relations with our minority shareholders and with the rest of our partners, employees, and suppliers'*, says CEO Piedrahita.

Vice president Nicholls believes that thanks to a combination of leadership skills (which the group has built in the market) and strategies for efficient and quality production, the group has been able to stand on solid ground to face the risk of competitors introducing their products in some of its businesses. The group has constantly renewed its product portfolio in response to the short life cycle of the products. Because of its proper management of production and transaction costs, it is able to manufacture goods at fair, affordable prices to serve different population groups. It has added value to its brands, and improved its experience with its own distribution network to enable the group to reach all points of purchase and be constantly in touch with customers.

Today the group ranks among the top eight food manufacturing companies in Latin America. In less than ten years from now, its internationalization strategies, to which all its business divisions are committed, should enable the group to position itself as one the top three Latin American multinationals in the food industry, being present not only on the entire American continent, but also in Europe and Asia.

Lastly, CEO Piedrahita also stated that: *'La Nacional de Chocolates' is a company that has undergone a continuous renewal process. It is an 85-year old company that continues to be vital, young, and innovative.'*[15] In another interview, he reiterated *'We are not available for sale, we're here to purchase. We're building an original model of regional competition. This company is still made with Colombian capital. We're not for sale and we're not looking for strategic deals either.'*[16]

6.6. Is INCH's Globalization Approach Consistent with the Core Competence Model?

In order to answer the question: how can Latin American companies compete in a globalized market?, one can turn to the model developed by Prahalad and Hamel (April 2001),[17] which provides an explanation of the characteristics of the core competences that are typical of companies that succeed in going global. The model suggests that long-term competitiveness is the result of the ability to develop core competences at a lower price and faster pace than the competition. These core competencies can lead to the development of products that are not expected by the competitors and are difficult to imitate in the short term.

The true source of advantages lies in the management skills to consolidate technology and production capabilities in competences that enable a company to adjust to changes rapidly. A successful corporation needs to be built upon these core competences. Developing and identifying core competences is a process that involves an analysis of each of the competencies identified in order to determine whether they: (*a*) provide potential access to a wide variety of markets; (*b*) make a significant contribution to the product benefits perceived by consumers; and (*c*) are difficult for competitors to imitate.

A competence can be considered a core competence provided that it meets the aforementioned conditions. Therefore, building these competences is only possible based on continuous improvement processes, which must be the focus of corporate strategies because they are defined as the intrinsic characteristics of a business group.

According to the above mentioned authors, companies now face the challenge of defining the operational tools that enable them to acquire new

Table 6.1. Key competitive advantages over domestic competitors

Comparative Advantage	Description
Being a member of an economic group	INCH is part of the Antioquia Entrepreneur Group (*Grupo Empresarial Antioqueño*), which is a consortium of companies engaged in different complementary activities that do not compete with each other
Establishing a business consortium in the same industry	INCH consists of thirty-three companies that manufacture different kinds of foods
Access to distribution channels	The shared use of distribution channels allows for a reduction of costs to the companies in the group
Availability of financial resources	Availability of resources from the GEA and the capital market through the issuance of shares
Top quality products	Different kinds of food products that are well positioned in the domestic market because of their excellent quality, variety, and price. The products meet the needs of different market segments
Technological development and access to efficient production processes	Edge-technology that enables the company to adjust easily to the changing demand conditions of domestic and international markets

competitive advantages. Thus, the directors' role is to channel and focus their efforts to accomplish the company's goals. To this end, directors need to be aware and knowledgeable of the size of the issues at hand and need to be prepared to face the diversity of the changing aspects that organizations have to deal with in a globalized market. Starting from this assumption, INCH was able to identify and develop a number of core competences that have enabled it to structure a much more solid company. This has also enabled it to be successful both in the domestic and international markets in the past few years.

Tables 6.1 and 6.2 below provide a detailed description of INCH's competitive advantages that have become the core competences of the company. These advantages are the outcome of its ability to turn its technological resources and production capabilities into tools that have enabled the company to easily adjust to the changing and increasingly competitive environment of both domestic and international markets.

Table 6.2 below lists the core competences that have enabled INCH to position itself in the globalized market.

The first of these competences, that is, being a member of an economic group such as the GEA, has enabled INCH to have access to a large number of activities which provide an advantage over domestic competitors. This strengthens and consolidates its organizational structure and, in turn, eliminates duplication of production and trading processes for products that use the same distribution channels. Having access to financing sources within the group not only decreases costs associated with cash flow management and long-term project financing, but also allows sharing risks and benefits.

Table 6.2. Key competitive advantages over international competitors

Comparative Advantage	Description
Being a member of an economic group	Ability to apply economies of scope
Access to distribution channels	Establishing *CORDIALSAS* in order to have access to efficient distribution channels
Top quality products affordable by people of all income levels	Offering a wide variety of products with a good quality-price ratio, adjustable to the characteristics of foreign markets
Availability of financial resources	Use of resources from INCH, GEA, and the capital market based on good tradability
Availability of efficient technology and production processes	Ability to adjust to the changing and increasingly competitive environment both on a national and an international level, supported by the purchase of facilities abroad

Being a member of a business group also represents significant advantages for competing in international markets. This is due to the possibility of applying economies of scope based on the ability of companies to follow their consumers when they move to other countries and to sell high-quality products that can be adjusted to the characteristics of new markets.

The second competitive advantage that constitutes a core competence is associated with the fact that INCH is also a conglomerate of thirty-three food manufacturing companies specialized in products that are complementary to each other. These companies are classified into the following six categories: chocolate, coffee, noodles, meat, cookies, and confectionery and dairy products. This wide range of products enables INCH to secure extensive market coverage thanks to the production of different families of consumer goods that can be adjusted to the needs of different market segments.

The third core competence is access to an extensive local and international distribution networks. In the first case, the wide range of companies that are part of INCH and their autonomous management of operations allows them to share the same distribution channels, thus reducing costs and achieving wide market coverage. As far as international distribution is concerned, the extension of the system of *CORDIALSAS* has enabled INCH to have access to efficient distribution channels at a lower cost than those of the competitors. Today INCH owns eleven distribution companies. It is able to trade its products easily, securing wide coverage, strong presence, and a significant cost reduction in the markets. All this ultimately reflects on the possibility of setting different prices that are competitive and appealing to the consumers.

The next two core competencies are supplementary to each other. The first is the ability to produce excellent quality products at affordable prices to

the different market segments, and the other is the availability of financial resources from: (*a*) the consolidation of the thirty-three companies
into a financial conglomerate; (*b*) access to resources within the GEA, of
which it is part; and (*c*) the high tradability of its shares on the stock
market.

It is thanks to the aforementioned competences that the companies that
now comprise INCH have been able not only to focus major efforts on
permanent product innovation and promotional strategies in Colombia and
other countries, but also to improve their production processes, thereby developing new technologies. This has allowed INCH to position its products and
adjust them to the characteristics of the various markets which it has been
able to enter. It has also developed its own production capabilities based
on the acquisition of manufacturing facilities from other companies abroad,
thus reducing costs, improving efficiency, and offering better prices to the
market.

Having ethnic relations also plays an important role in international competition. Taking advantage of the existing Hispanic market, but particularly
the Colombian community, in the markets in which INCH is present, has
become a competitive advantage because of the brand recognition and the
link with the country or region of origin of consumers in this market which
makes products attractive to the consumers. Lastly, independence of each
business that comprises INCH is a significant advantage that has enabled
INCH to strengthen and expand operations. It has allowed each business to
have autonomous business management and, because of centralized operations, INCH has also simplified relations with the shareholders, thus facilitating access to financial resources and reducing risks associated with the
operation of these companies. If any of the companies has poor results,
then the good results of the other companies will make up for any such
deficiencies.

Figure 6.5 below shows the core competences developed by INCH and the
correlation thereof. These competences have enabled INCH to have a solid
ground for conducting business and leading competition in different national
and international markets.

6.7. Conclusions

The following is a discussion of conceptual considerations to complete the
review of strategies of GEA's food group and to provide an answer to the
question raised by this study: *how can Latin American companies compete with
domestic and foreign rivals in the twenty-first century?*

Several authors have studied the dynamics of investments by Latin
American companies in foreign countries in the past ten years (Garrido

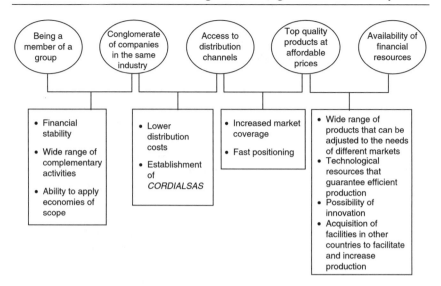

Figure 6.5. Relationship of INCH's core competences

and Peres[18] 1998; López[19] 1999; Ramírez[20] 2003, 2005). These studies have revealed that a company internationalization process had already begun even before the economic opening policy in the 1980s. This process was encouraged by incipient integration agreements between some governments in Latin America.

A study conducted by UNCTAD (1998)[21] showed that this number was still limited. Out of fifty major investments made by multinationals from developing countries, thirty came from Asia, fifteen from Latin America, and five from other regions. While Asian companies generally engaged in advanced technology investments, Latin American multinationals primarily engaged in the production and trade of mass consumer goods. This finding is consistent with the characteristics of GEA's food group. A study conducted by Whitmore, Lall, and Hyun (1989)[22] regarding the motivation of companies that ventured into international investments in the 1980s revealed that Colombian and other Latin American companies that traded their products, particularly in neighboring countries (Colombia, for example, exported to Venezuela and Ecuador) were driven by the need to avoid the costs of customs duties considering the inconsistent application of the Andean Pact rules. In general, these deals were conducted in the form of joint-venture businesses with locals in the importing country.

Investments made by GEA in the 1980s, at a time when the Andean Pact was going through permanent changes at the discretion of the governments, clearly fit in with these characteristics. Dunning (1988)[23] developed the theory of the eclectic paradigm to explain how companies adopt investment strategies when they have tangible or intangible assets that enable them to secure a competitive position in other markets. These assets include, among others, brands, management talent, and distribution technologies.

In this case study, GEA's assets were its brands, management talent, production differentiation, and the capillary distribution system. The group was convinced it had the necessary strengths to venture into foreign markets so, instead of simply having distributors, it settled in the target markets of these foreign countries.

In a further study, Dunning (1994)[24] employs two different criteria to define the motivation of companies that decide to invest abroad. In a first stage he calls 'initiation' stage, companies seek either critical strategic resources to conduct their activities or new markets.

The first choice deals with the company's strategy to guarantee access to natural resources, and low-cost raw materials and supplies for the benefit of not only production in a foreign country, but also in their country of origin, or access to intangible assets to facilitate their entry to the market. The second choice has to do with the need to have access to new markets as a critical factor of survival. Along these lines, Chudnovsky and López (1999)[25] discuss the companies' need to look for foreign markets when the domestic market is reaching a saturation point. Thus, venturing abroad turns into a need for companies to ensure their continuous growth.

This is what happened to GEA, but particularly to the food and cement groups. Both of these markets have reached a high saturation level in Colombia. This is due to increasingly worse poverty conditions, deterioration of income per capita, and relative stagnation of the GDP.

The GEA has ensured its long-term presence in host countries because it has acquired strategic assets that enable it to have competitive abilities including access to distribution channels, exclusive brands, like the ones purchased in the host countries, and production facilities such as those in Venezuela and Costa Rica. These assets have allowed the group to start a regional business network in Central America and the Caribbean in a more mature internationalization stage. UNCTAD (1994)[26] contends that after completing the initial internationalization stage, companies that have succeeded at exporting from their own countries to markets in foreign countries can easily develop the dynamics that allow them to move on to a new phase based on their knowledge of the market. In the new phase, companies look for strategic assets that facilitate production in the host countries. Once they ensure continuous presence of their own managers, these companies adopt distribution strategies that reflect their experience in their countries of origin, especially if there are similarities in the cultures of both countries.

Later on, companies that succeed in several host countries move on to a complex integration stage, in which they transform their exclusively local activities into integrated regional production and distribution networks. This seems to be the first step toward the beginning of a process to turn these companies into global multinationals.

Company restructuring processes such as the mergers that have recently taken place in GEA's business divisions, but particularly the Food Group, are a fundamental part of the process to internationalize Latin American companies. These processes enable the companies to sustain a productive positioning in their countries of origin as well as in the host countries, in spite of the threats associated with an increasingly hostile environment as a result of globalization.

According to Grosse (2001),[27] the relatively small size of Latin American companies poses a risk of losing ownership to multinationals from the United States, Europe, and Asia. Therefore, if shareholders of Latin American companies intend to maintain ownership of these companies and prevent hostile or voluntary takeovers when they no longer have control over their businesses, they will need to adopt suitable strategies for growing and sizing their companies to overcome technological and financial limitations.

According to a study conducted by Barham (2005),[28] internationalization focusses primarily on building strategies in the markets by developing and building global brands. Customers need to recognize and associate these brands with differentiated high added-value products. As countries achieve economic development and generate more income and well-being, people turn to the demand for recognized brands that guarantee higher added value and product differentiation. Latin American economies, but particularly a large number of Central American and Caribbean countries where the Food Group conducts most operations, are now in an intermediate stage, in which low income levels continue to keep the markets from achieving a higher degree of sophistication.

The custom of buying at the 'store on the corner' still prevails. Consequently, the group's strategy of having a distribution force run by *CORDIALSAS* that goes to the 'stores' seems to be adequate at this stage of the internationalization process. However, as it moves forward to another more advanced internationalization stage (such as the one mentioned by UNCTAD), the group's distribution strategy will need to evolve. The group will also need to create brandnames and products that differ to a greater extent from its currently traded products.

Additionally, the group will have to achieve production capabilities at nodes of the regional network, especially in the United States, in the same way it did with the cement group. Merging into *Inversiones Nacional de Chocolates* is going to facilitate the process because the group will be able to channel its own financial resources or raise financing funds in capital markets because it can use its size, performance, and corporate governance practices as collaterals.

Lastly, while GEA's Food Group (like other competitors in Latin America) has followed a successful path toward internationalization during the past twenty-five years and has overcome the preliminary stages to the regional internationalization of its operations, it still has a long way to go before achieving the status of a global company.

In our opinion, however, in consideration of the review conducted in this study, one could answer the question that prompted this study by saying that the group is moving in the right direction toward globalization. It is certainly prepared to continue to successfully face local and international competitors in this century.

Notes

1. Héctor Ochoa Díaz, Ph.D., Dean at the School of Economics and Administrative Sciences at Icesi University, Cali, Colombia, hochoa@icesi.edu.co. The author acknowledges the assistance provided by students Valentina Echeverry P., Liliana Fernández O., Tatiana Quintero R., and Pilar del Socorro Wilches P.
2. Ramírez, C. E., Jiménez, A., and Garrido, J., 'Inversión Colombiana en el exterior: Bavaria y su estrategia internacional con las cervezas', Estudios Gerenciales, No. 86, Enero — Marzo, 2003, Universidad Icesi, Colombia.
3. Ramírez, C. E. y Rodríguez, J., 'Pintuco se internacionaliza en el mercado Andino', Estudios Gerenciales, No. 152, Octubre-Diciembre, 2004, Universidad Icesi, Colombia.
4. http://www.leonisa.com
5. http://www.carvajal.com.co
6. Alvarez Morales Víctor, 'De las sociedades de negocios al "Sindicato Antioqueño". Un camino centenario', en Dávila L. de Guevara, Carlos, compilador, *Empresas y Empresarios en la Historia de Colombia. Siglos xix–xx.* Editorial Norma, Bogotá, 2003.
7. Ibidem, p. 237.
8. '*El País*, newspaper issue from October 27, 2005, Cali, Colombia.
9. 'Huracán Argos', *Semana*, October 10, 2005, p. 70.
10. http://www.benchamark.com
11. http://www.suramericana.com
12. http://www.supersociedades.gov.co
13. The author would like to thank Dr Carlos Enrique Piedrahita, CEO at INCH, and Juan Pablo Nicholls, International Vice President at INCH, for the thorough interviews they gave in connection with this study on October 27, 2005.
14. http://www.dinero.com.co
15. *El Colombiano*, Abril, 21 de 2005, Medellín, Colombia.
16. *El Colombiano*, Marzo 31, 2005, Medellín, Colombia.
17. Prahalad, C. K., y Hamel, G., 'The core competence of the corporation', HBR OnPoint Enhanced Edition, Boston, April, 2001.
18. Garrido, C. y W. Peres, 'Las grandes empresas y grupos industriales latinoamericanos en los años noventa', en W. Peres (coord.), Grandes empresas y grupos industriales latinoamericanos, Siglo xxi, CEPAL, México.

19. López, A., 'El caso Chileno', 'el caso Brasileño', en Chudnovsky, D., et al., Las multinacionales latinoamericanas. Sus estrategias en un mundo globalizado, Fondo de Cultura Económica, Buenos Aires.
20. Ramírez, C. E., Op. Cit.
21. UNCTAD, 'World investment report', 1998, Trends and determinants, Geneva.
22. Whitmore, K., S., Lall y J., Hyun, 'Foreign direct investment from the newly industrialized economies', Industry and Energy Department, Working Paper, No. 22, 1989, The World Bank, Nueva York.
23. Dunning, J., 'Explaining international production', 1988, Unwin Hyman, London.
24. Dunning, J., 'Re-evaluating the benefits of foreign direct investment', Transnational Corporations, Vol. 3 No. 1, 1994.
25. Chudnovsky, D. and A., López, 'Las empresas multinacionales de América Latina. Características, evolución y perspectivas', Boletín Techint, Abril–June, 1999, Buenos Aires, Argentina.
26. UNCTAD, 'World investment report 1994', Transnational corporations and competitiveness, Ginebra.
27. Grosse, R., 'International business in Latin America', Cap 23, in: Alan Rugman and Thomas Brewer (comp.), Oxford Handbook of International Business, Oxford: Oxford University Press, 2001, pp. 652–80.
28. Barham, J., 'Rewiring corporate Latin America', Latin Finance, No. 167, June, 2005, pp. 12–20.

References

Achi, Z., Boulas, C., Buchanan, I., Fortaleza, J., and Zappei, L. (1998). 'Conglomerates in Emerging Markets: Tigers or Dinosaurs?', Strategy and Business, 11.

Alvarez, V. (2003). 'De las sociedades de negocios al Sindicato Antioqueño. Un camino centenario', in C. Dávila, (ed.), Empresas y empresrios en la hstoria de Colombia. Siglos xix y xx, Editorial Norma, Bogotá.

Amsden, A. and Hikino, T. (1994). 'Project Execution Capability, Organizational Know-How and Conglomerate Growth in Late Industrialization', Industrial and Corporate Change, 3.

Aulakh, P., Koabe, M., and Teegen, H., (2000). 'Export Strategies and Performance of Firms from Emerging Economies: Evidence from Brazil, Chile and Mexico', Academy of Management Journal, 3.

Barham, J. (2005). 'Rewiring Corporate Latin America', Latin Finance, 167.

CEPAL (2004). 'Balance preliminar de las economías de América Latina y el Caribe'.

Chudnovsky, D. and Lopez, A. (Abril–Junio, 1999). 'Las empresas multinacionales de América Latina. Características, evolución, y perspectivas', Boletín Techint.

Dawar, N. and Frost, T. (March, 1999). 'Competing with Giants: Survival Strategies for Local Firms in Emerging Markets', Harvard Business Review.

Dunning, J. (1988). 'The Eclectic Paradigm of International Production: A Restatement and Some Possible Extensions', Journal of International Business Studies, 19.

—— (1988). 'Explaining International Production', Unwin Hyman, London.

—— (1994). 'Re-evaluating the Benefits of Foreign Direct Investment', Transnational Corporations, 3.

Economist (2004). 'Cement: One Giant Leap for Mexico', *The Economist*.
—— (2005). 'Chinese companies abroad: the dragon tucks in', *The Economist*.
Eisenhardt, K. (1989). 'Building Theories from Case Study Research', *Academy of Managemenet Review*, 14.
Garrido, C. and Peres, W. (1998). 'Las grandes empresas y grupos Latinoamericanos en los años noventa', W. en Peres (ed.), *Grandes empresa y grupos industriales Latinoamericanos*, Siglo Veintiuno Editores, Mexico.
Ghemawat, P. and Kennedy, R. (1999). 'Competitive Shocks and Industrial Structure: The Case of Polish Manufacturing', *International Journal of Industrial Organization*, 17.
Granovetter, M. (2000). 'Coase Revisited: Business Groups in the Modern Economy', *Industrial and Corporate Change*, 43.
Grosse, R. (2004). 'The Challenges of Globalization for Emerging Market Firms', *Latin American Business Review*, 4.
—— (2001). 'International Business in Latin America', in A. Rugman and T. Brewer, (eds.), *Oxford Handbook of International Business*, Chapter 23, Oxford University Press.
Guillen, M. (2000). 'Businees Groups in Emerging Economies: A Resource Based View', *Academy of Management Journal*, 43.
Hoskinsson, R., Eden, L., Lau, C., and Wright, M. (2000). 'Strategy in Emerging Economies', *Academy of Management Journal*, 43.
Khanna, T. and Papelepu, K. (2002). 'The Right Way to Restructure Conglomerates in Emerging Markets', *Harvard Business Review*, 77.
—— and Papelepu, K. (1999). 'Policy Shocks, Market Intermediaries, and Corporate Strategy: The Evolution of Busissness Groups in Chile and India', *Journal of Economics and Management Strategy*, 8.
—— and Papelu, K. (2002). 'Emerging Markets Giants: Building World Class Companies in Emerging Markets', Harvard Business School case No. 703-431.
—— and Papelepu, K. (2000). 'The Future of Business Groups in Emerging Markets: Long Run Evidence from Chile', *Academy of Management Journal*, 43.
Kock, C. and Guillen, M. (2001). 'Strategy and Structure in Developing Countries: Business Groups As an Evolutionary Response to Opportunities for Unrelated Diversification', *Industrial and Corporate*, 10.
La Porta, R., Lopes de silanes, F., and Schleifer, A. (April, 1999). 'Corporate Ownership Around the World', *Journal of Finance*.
Leff, N. (1978). 'Industrial Organization and Entrepreneurship in the Developing Countries: The Economics Groups', *Economic Development and Cultural Change*.
Lieberthal, K. and Lieberthal, G. (2003). 'The Great Transformation', *Harvard Business Review*, 10.
López, A. 'El caso Chileno', 'El caso Brasileño', D. en Chudnovsky (ed.) (1999). 'Las multinacionales latinoamericas. Sus estrategias en un mundo globalizado', Fondo de Cultura Económica, Buenos Aires.
Ochoa, H. and Collazos, J. (2004). 'La evaluación del desempeño de las empresas privatizadas en Colombia: ¿Coincide con la experiencia internacional?', Estudios Gerenciales, Universidad Icesi, 152.
Peres, W. (ed.) (1998). 'Las grandes empresas y grupos industrials latinoamericanos. Expansión y desafíos en la era de la apertura y la globalización', Siglo Veintiuno editores, Mexico.

——(ed.) (1998). 'Grandes empresas y grupos industriales latinoamericanos', Siglo Veintiuno Editores, Mexico.

Ramírez, C. E., Jiménez, A., and Garrido, J. (2003). 'Inversión Colombiana en el exterior: Bavaria y su estrategia internacional con las cervezas', Estudios Gerenciales, Universidad Icesi, 86.

Revista Semana (Octubre, 2005). 'Huracán Argos', Bogotá, Colombia.

Ruelas, A. Febrero, (2004). 'Innovar en mercados emergentes: el paradigma de la T grande', *Harvard Business Review*, América Latina.

Salas, A. (1998). 'Estrategias de las empresas mexicanas en sus procesos de internacionalización', Revista de la CEPAL, 65.

Suárez, F. and Oliva, R. (2003). 'Learning to Compete: Transforming Firms in the Face of Radical Environment Change', *Business Strategy Review*, 3.

Toulan, O. (1997). 'Internationalization Reonsidered: The Case of Siderar', *Sloan Working Papers*, 3938.

——(2002). 'The Impact of Market Liberalization on Vertical Scope: The Case of Argentina', *Strategic Management Journal*, 6.

UNCTAD (1998). *World Investment Report*, Geneva.

——(2005). *World Investment Report*, Geneva.

Whitmore, K., Lall, S., and Hyun, J. (1998). 'Foreign Direct Investment from the Newly Industrialized Economies', Industry and Energy Department, The World Bank, Working Paper 22.

7

Competing Under Stress: The Shrimp Cluster in Venezuela

Michael Penfold

7.1. Introduction

As a consequence of the great economic and institutional volatility experienced during the past two decades, Venezuela has registered low economic growth rates that have blocked the creation of a competitive nonoil export sector. In spite of many efforts to diversify the country's production, especially during the early nineties when policies were adopted to open the economy and promote free trade agreements, the nonoil sector has not responded by creating a robust, competitive export sector. Quite the opposite has occurred since the end of the nineties, private investment has fallen to about 6 percent of GDP and in the industrial sector more than 6,000 companies closed their doors and only a very small group of firms have entered international markets (Conindustria 2004).

In the case of Venezuela, direct foreign investment has been attracted fundamentally to capital intensive sectors such as oil and telecommunications; few foreign investors have ventured into the country in areas like agro-industry or manufacturing as an export platform for their products.[1] Local companies have not responded either to the incentives to diversify risk by internationalizing their activities. Some have even decided to close shop, and others have deepened their relationship with the oil sector and with the State. The result is an increasingly oil-dependent economy.

The outlook for the country's economic diversification appears more and more unlikely since 2003 when foreign exchange controls as well as price

I would like to thank Rafael Díaz and José Gómez Pablo who helped as research assistants for the field research of this chapter. Patricia Márquez, Johanna López, Virginia López Glass, and Pavel Gómez have provided useful comments while writing this chapter. Finally, I would like to acknowledge the detailed suggestions made by Robert Grosse, and Luiz Mesquita to improve the final version of this chapter.

controls were introduced to mask structural problems such as high fiscal deficits, rigid labor regulations, lack of access to new markets, and institutional weakness. Given the current high oil prices that characterize the world economy since the beginning of the millennium and which have favored Venezuela, it is difficult to suppose that the current administration controlled by a populist president such as Hugo Chávez will address these structural problems during the next years. By contrast, it is expected that the government will decide to continue implementing the protectionist policies which limit the capacity for international competitiveness of local and foreign firms in the country.

One of the few exceptions, not well studied, is the emergence and growth of the shrimp industry dominated by both national and international firms. In spite of institutional difficulties and the lack of economic growth during the nineties, the industry was able to concentrate its activities in the export sector. By focussing on the growth of international markets, the shrimp industry was able to successfully become competitive. The industry was born at the end of the eighties, growing exponentially to represent by 2004 more than 0.5 percent of GDP with annual sales above US$350 million. The Venezuelan shrimp production has not attained the same importance as its counterparts in countries like China, Vietnam, and Thailand but is among the most important regional players in Latin America, following countries such as Brazil, Ecuador, and Colombia. The sector's productivity is among the highest in the region and the profit margins before taxes are relatively high (close to 40% according to different firms). More than 95 percent of their production is exported to markets such as the United States and the European Union.

There are many reasons for the success of the shrimp industry, but they are not necessarily those which will guarantee their future growth. One of the most important causes to explain their success was the ability of local firms, which initiated the development of the sector, to concentrate the sale of their products to the export market. This lead to two direct effects: the contact with the higher standards required by international consumers induced early additional investments in the industry in order to ensure the quality and productivity needed to compete internationally; second, the ability to separate the export operations from constant institutional changes in the national market served as an insulation mechanism from the country's inherent instability. Once these national companies were able to demonstrate that it was possible to produce and export from Venezuela, multinational firms decided to invest in the industry creating a more compact industry. This, then, permitted improvements in productivity through the leakage of technology transfers to the other producers. In other words, the need to remain apart from the local business environment and beyond the sphere of government influence, strengthened their ability to concentrate on the export sector. Nevertheless, the possibility of future growth will also depend on the capability of the government to provide those support institutions needed by these companies to continue investing. The achievement of this goal seems difficult, given the high levels of political and social polarization which currently characterizes the country.

This chapter attempts to analyze the foundations of the shrimp industry by researching the cluster as a nascent concentration of firms; and based on this analysis the future challenges that producers need to confront to increase their levels of productivity and competitiveness will be identified. The analysis defines clusters as a compact geographical complex of companies and related institutions that interact in the production of a specific product or service (Porter 1998). This geographic concentration of firms should be seen as a dynamic process in which the firms will be influenced by the different kinds of industries that interact within the cluster, their maturity, as well as their competitive and cooperative strategies, leading to increasing levels of innovation. The evidence shows that clusters permit the increase of innovative initiatives for increasing competitiveness and productivity by improving economies of scale, promoting joint action, and creating opportunities for knowledge-sharing externalities (Audrestesch and Feldman 1995; Schimtz and Nadvi 1999). Overall, clusters develop through different stages: nascent, growth, mature, and a decline or renewal phase.

In Venezuela, the shrimp cluster is in the transition process from a nascent to a growth stage. Although firms have been able to concentrate in specific geographical regions, they lack a constant interaction among themselves and with interconnecting industries. As we see, an important conclusion of this chapter is that the existing evidence indicates that the shrimp cluster in Venezuela is lacking in the tools for cooperation between its producers and the support institutions which would guarantee its long-term consolidation. The firms level of competitiveness are very dependent on inherited factors, and their ability to continue expanding will be related to their ability to innovate and to enhance their productivity. For this to happen, firms and support institutions, such as public agencies and universities, will have to start interacting on a permanent basis with the firms to build the export platform required to boost productivity through innovation. This type of outcome cannot be provided by a sole producer but will require some cooperation between the affected companies and perhaps the government. However, given the institutional characteristics of Venezuela (high economic volatility and low administrative capabilities) a complex process requiring strong leadership from within the shrimp cluster will be needed to promote the desired results.

This chapter is structured as follows: Section 7.2 describes the basic characteristics of the business climate in Venezuela and the impact of transaction costs which lessen the ability of the companies to effectively compete at the international level. Sections 7.3 and 7.4 relate the development of the shrimp industry in Venezuela; the formation of the cluster, the description of its current structure, and the identification of its most important strengths and vulnerabilities. Section 7.5 describes the problem of lack of cooperation among firms and public agencies that the shrimp cluster has had to face which have limited its competitiveness. Specifically, this section illustrates this problem by analyzing the introduction of the 'taura', a disease imported from Ecuador that temporarily lowered the level of productivity of the Venezuelan firms. The 'taura' could have been avoided if there had been greater cooperation within the shrimp cluster. Section 7.6 presents some conclusions and lessons about the conditions that promoted the internationalization of the Venezuelan firms and the challenges that they will have to face in the near future.

7.2. The Business Climate in Venezuela: Bias against Exporters

During the past years, Venezuela has experienced one of the most adverse business climates; not only in Latin America but also in the developing world. During both the 1980s and 1990s, the growth rates have been so low that the past two decades from an economic standpoint have been considered almost lost. The GDP per capita in 2003 was the same in real terms as in 1953. In comparison with other countries of the region, the deepening of structural reforms has been negligible, and along with Argentina, Venezuela is one of the few Latin American countries where market reforms have been totally reversed. According to Lora and Panizza (2002), structural reform index, in 2002, Venezuela was in last place in areas related to fiscal, privatization, financial, and labor market reforms. In 2003, this situation continued to deteriorate in a significant manner due to the introduction of foreign exchange controls, price controls, and the adoption of policies to protect certain industrial sectors.

The institutional environment in Venezuela since 1989 has been characterized by political and social polarization. This situation has had a negative impact on the business climate and the country's ability to attract national or foreign investment in the nonoil sector. The country's low economic achievement can be explained by the high levels of volatility, both electoral and institutional, and the long-term decline in oil fiscal revenues experienced until the late 1990s. This outcome influenced citizens to vote for different options in order to promote a radical political change. In 1998, Hugo Chávez was elected president of Venezuela with 56 percent of the vote and without the support of the traditional political parties such as AD and COPEI. Chávez won the elections promising institutional reforms through a Constituent Assembly, which was elected in 1999, in order to transform the political system which the electorate perceived as corrupt and inefficient. This process of political change has increased nonetheless the level of social and political polarization helping to further deteriorate the relationship between the public and private sector.

Therefore, the competitiveness of Venezuelan firms has been negatively affected by the political changes and the economic measures cited. According to the competitive growth index of the World Economic Forum in 2003, Venezuela was in 68th place among 80 countries, relating to its future growth potential. This same year, using the same index, Venezuela's public institutions were classified among the worst worldwide. According to the World Bank governance indicators, in relation to the rule of law, Venezuela occupied the lowest percentile (12.6%) of the Latin American region and in relation to the quality of the regulatory environment it was also placed among the lowest (9.9%). Regarding corruption, Venezuela was in the last position at the continental level and reaching the 14.3 percentile at the world level. Generally speaking, in the words of a business leader: 'To do business in Venezuela not only is a difficult art but also a real miracle'.[2]

A more detailed study of transaction costs facing the private sector was carried out in 2003; this study describes the most severe problems which business encounters in order to successfully compete internationally (Penfold 2003). Venezuelan firms face growing transaction costs due to public security, red tape, public infrastructure, tax law instability, judicial insecurity and labor costs. Citing as an example, tax law instability, the companies have had to face more than seven changes in tax regulations and export incentives, such as the drawback, which are not easily available. A start-up company can spend more than 179 working days in order to register and operate legally in the country. Firms report that on average they lose seventy-five operating days due to electric power outages and thirty-four days due to the shut down of water supplies. Regarding the cost of public security, in order to be protected from organized crime for every unit spent by the State, the private sector would spend an additional 75 percent of that same unit. As a result of these factors, the investment climate has worsened, also affecting their ability to compete in international markets.

This business climate has had a negative impact on the nonoil sector. Venezuela continues to concentrate its export sector in oil products, petrochemicals, and other natural resources such as iron, ore, and aluminum. The private sector's ability to initiate and innovate in other activities, with higher value added, is limited. Several studies have demonstrated that the fall in GDP per capita has resulted from the long-term decline in oil income and the lack of private investment in the nonoil sector during the 1990s (Hausmann 2003; Penfold 2003). Even though in real terms, the oil income fell in comparison to the 1970s (even considering the positive shock that Venezuela now experiences), the exchange rates and the foreign exchange policies have been extremely volatile. The real exchange rate has registered different levels of appreciation especially during those times that oil prices permitted the government to anchor the nominal exchange rate as a mechanism to control inflation (Rodriguez 2004). Historically, during two previous periods (1994–6 and 2003), exchange controls were introduced in Venezuela creating significant distortions in the economy. This reality along with the rising transaction costs, resulting from institutional weaknesses, has not created the appropriate climate where new export sectors could emerge.

Among the few exceptions was the shrimp sector. Starting in 1990, a new sector emerged that proved to be highly competitive. How did this sector overcome the institutional volatility that affected other sectors? What were the competitive bases that allowed the Venezuelan shrimpers to sustain their growth in the international markets? The CEO of one of the most important shrimp farms sums up this paradox with the following words:

In the beginning we had a stroke of luck. But I don't know how long it will last as we are very afraid that the government will begin to regulate aggressively. The key to success was that we were regulated by international markets where we export our products; these markets demand very high standards of quality, and the government ignored us as we were very small, almost unseen. The government did not even know we existed and we did not ask for help. We were an island. This absence of the government explains why we were successful as does the fact that the destination of almost all our production was the international markets.[3]

In order to understand the competitive foundations and the future challenges of the shrimp sector, it is necessary to analyze the structure of the cluster and the characteristics of its internal relationship.

7.3. The Origin and Development of the Shrimp Cluster

7.3.1. *The Importance of Clusters*

The development of clusters in distinct economies is an important resource for understanding the nature of competition within a complex set of interrelated industries and the foundation that supports its competitiveness. Underlying the study of clusters, the most important assumption as cited by Michael Porter is 'that the presence of clusters suggests that much of the competitive advantage lies outside a given company or even outside its industry, residing instead in the location of its business units' (Porter 1998: 198). Firms develop their processes of innovation and productivity improvement not only because of the existing rivalry within an industry, but also because they can promote cooperative practices within their localities that will improve the competitive foundations of all the interconnected firms and industries. Therefore, clusters are defined as a complex set of companies and institutions interrelated because of their common and complementary factors (Porter 1998: 199). This definition emphasizes not only firms but also public and private institutions, usually not-for-profit, that promote cooperative practices between companies in order to stimulate technological adjustments, training, changes in regulations in order to improve competition and therefore promote higher levels of productivity.

Clusters usually develop through differentiated stages. In a first phase, clusters are nascent and characterized by the success of few firms that (although located in a similar region) rarely interact or exclusively perceive themselves as rivals. In a second stage, the success of individual firms attracts further investment helping the cluster to start growing. During this growth stage, the cluster starts facing important challenges that emerge from a competitive environment. In this stage, firms start to perceive the potential benefits of cooperation to sustain high growth rates. In a third phase, the cluster matures thanks to the development of support institutions and the interaction of the cluster with other industries. Finally, the cluster enters a decline stage that usually forces firms to explore individually or collectively alternative development paths that can lead to a death, renewal, or the creation of a different cluster.

The literature on clusters has identified several mechanisms that help individual firms to improve their productivity levels. By locating their business within existing clusters, companies are able to reduce costs by improving economies of scale. In addition, clusters promote improvements in best practices since it facilitates learning processes by suppliers and competing firms. As a result, due to this process of imitation, leading firms are induced to innovate in order to differentiate themselves and continue enhancing their productivity. This process generates positive externalities that benefit all the firms located within the cluster. Finally, clusters usually develop support institutions that promote cooperation among existing firms and industries in order to improve standards, share risks in technological developments and diffusion, as well as provide services for management training and help the cluster to rapidly identify future challenges. Therefore, this cooperation can serve as an important factor to help firms sustain and improve their competitiveness.

As it is discussed below, the shrimp cluster in Venezuela is in a transition period between a nascent and a growth stage. Two distinct areas in the country (east and west) have successfully attracted investments in the shrimp cluster, which has allowed companies to imitate each other and learn from their failures and success stories. However, these two clusters have developed very different production processes and technologies due to the lack of cooperation within and across each cluster. Finally, the lack of support institutions in Venezuela that promote cooperative strategies among firms has reduced the ability of existing companies to continue improving their productivity and consolidate the shrimp cluster. Hence, the ability of the shrimp cluster to sustain its growth rates will be contingent on the ability of the firms to collectively overcome some of these challenges.

7.3.2. *The Origins of the Shrimp Cluster*

Venezuela, given its geography, is an appropriate site for the growth of the shrimping activity having 2,850 km of coastline on the Caribbean Sea. In spite of these favorable geographic conditions, the shrimp cluster only began to emerge in Venezuela in the early 1990s with domestic capital investment that attempted to industrialize the traditional fishing methods and drag net fishing for shrimp (with the resulting environmental costs) by introducing a more efficient and environmentally sustainable technology. The technology consisted of shrimp farming which duplicates the life cycle of shrimp in their natural habitat by building laboratories and water pools that acted as ponds. Before this period, the shrimping activity was dominated by traditional fisherman in the states of Nueva Esparta and Anzoategui (located in the north east parts of the country) and Falcón (located far apart from these other states in the west). Various elements delayed the emergence of the cluster: the high investments required for this type of shrimp farming, the availability of the technology required, and the complicated administrative steps to obtain the necessary permits. Also there was doubt among the scientific community about the farming of exotic species (non-native) and a legislative climate that questioned the environmental impact of this industry due to the experiences in other producing countries (Inapesca 2003: 5).

Overall, the growth of the shrimp farming industry in Venezuela during the past few decades has been exponential. In 1995, 7 Venezuelan companies produced close to 3,088 metric tons of shrimp on 1,065 hectares. In 2004, 27 companies produced 22,266 metric tons of shrimp on 7,000 hectares. During the same time period, the productivity greatly increased from 2.9 metric tons per hectare to 3.7 metric tons per hectare (Figure 7.1). The relative importance of the shrimp industry within Venezuela's economy has also increased; for example, it grew from 0.25 percent of GDP in 2002 to 0.5 percent of GDP in 2004. Lastly, the 2004 export sales exceeded US\$350 million to markets in the United States, Europe, and Mexico. In fact, 95 percent of the total production was exported to international markets.

The interest in the shrimp industry by some businessmen was linked to the success of the tuna exports in the late eighties. At the beginning of the nineties, Venezuela had become a relevant exporter of tuna to the United States. Nevertheless, American environmental groups, many financed by business groups seeking market protection, were able to convince the US government to close temporarily their markets to this product. Large Venezuelan firms, like Mavesa, attempted to transfer their knowledge of the tuna export markets to other sea products such as shrimp. Mavesa decided to invest for the first time in shrimp farms in the state of Anzoátegui using water tanks. Unfortunately, due to the lack of specific knowledge about shrimp farming, the investment encountered many problems related to the weight of the water

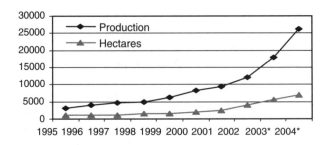

Figure 7.1. Growth of shrimp production in Venezuela
Source: INAPESCA (2003); *FAO (2004) y Padrón (2004).[11] Production is in metric tons.

tanks located on land platforms near the ocean. As a result of the heavy weight, the land platforms collapsed. Mavesa, although it had contracted various specialists with international expertise, abandoned the project. The same specialists were contracted by other Venezuelan firms, which designed their investments so as to avoid Mavesa's mistakes; the shrimp farms were located in areas in the east in Island of Coche, Uchire, and Araya (states of Nueva Esparta and Anzoátegui, respectively) and in the west mainly in the Lake of Maracaibo (state of Zulia) and Punto Fijo (state of Falcón). That is why two distinct geographic clusters were created, one in the east and the other in western Venezuela. See Figure 7.2 to observe the location of the two clusters in a map of Venezuela.

The western region provides more than 80 percent of the national production and has the highest growth rate. The explanation for its greater growth was related to the quality of the nutrient rich water coming from the Lake of Maracaibo. Another factor refers to the regional business community in Zulia which was able to complement the shrimp industry with their other agro-industries, specifically cattle farming by obtaining more access to the land and capital markets needed to develop the shrimp farming industry. This complementarity created significant economies of scale that helped to boost production. In the eastern region, although it was the original site of the industry, the shrimp farm has not grown at the same speed. Nevertheless, a relevant characteristic of the zone is the rapid spread of technological improvements among local producers due to the interaction with the research centers of the Eastern University (*Universidad de Oriente*); this has contributed to important recent increases in both productivity and quality of the products.

Once local firms showed some level of success in their export activity, foreign investors started locating new shrimp farms in both the east and west regions of the country. In Coche Island (east), foreign investors started new farms with their own laboratories for reproduction. In the Lake of Maracaibo (west) and Paraguaná (west), foreign investors acquired large extensions of land to start shrimp farms on a larger scale. In addition, multilateral

Figure 7.2. Location of the shrimp clusters in Venezuela

organizations, like the World Bank, started to finance some of the new investment projects inducing producers to upgrade their environmental practices.
Most of these foreign investors have decided to manage directly their investment and operations rather than creating joint ventures with existing local
companies (Table 7.1).

By analyzing the competitiveness benchmarks for the shrimp cluster, several strengths are identified, specifically in comparison with the indicators
of other shrimp-producing countries like Colombia, Brazil, Ecuador, China,
Vietnam, and Thailand. Venezuela has a shorter farming cycle (115 days),
placing it in a more favorable position to all other countries except Colombia.
The survival rates (70%) are among the highest together with Brazil. The
productivity rates, measured in metric tons per hectare, are not yet comparable to Colombia and Brazil but are similar to Asian producers. The same

159

Table 7.1. International indicators for shrimp production

Indicators	Venezuela*	Colombia	Brazil	Ecuador	China	Vietnam	Tailand
Life cycle (days)	115	115.4	150.7	146	150	150	150
Harvest density (larvae/ha)		23.5	45.5	15	23.6	23.6	23.6
Food conversion (kg food/kg shrimp)	1.8–2	1.66	1.51	1.3	2.01	2.01	2.01
Survival rates (number of shrimps/ larvae cultivated in farm)	70%	65%	70%	30%	65%	ND	49%
Productivity (MT/ha)	3,500–6,000	4,100	6,000	1,352	3,000	3,100	3,500

* Inapesca (2005);[8] Manrique (2005);[9] Cabrera (2005).[10]
* Data was gathered through statistics collected at INAPESCA and AGROCADENAS and validated through interviews with shrimp experts.
Source: Inapesca (2005) and Agrocadenas (2005).

can be said regarding the density of the seeding. As long as Venezuelan producers incorporate technology improvements, they will be able to improve their efficiency and given the advantage of the shorter farming cycles and the high survival rates, the cluster will be able to ensure its international competitiveness. The producers have also been trying to increase the value added of the product which is being increasingly classified as a commodity. As a consequence, improvements have been made in the freezing method, shape, size, and flavor of the shrimp. Lastly, some producers have begun to adopt stricter environmental practices so as to obtain certifications that will allow them to obtain a better price and classification of their products.

7.4. Structure of the Cluster

The value chain of shrimp harvest has four distinct stages: (*a*) the laboratories, (*b*) the harvest farms, (*c*) the processing plants, and (*d*) distribution and marketing. The laboratories' main activity is to contribute in the imitation of the environmental conditions the shrimp needs to mate and reproduce.[4] The farms, in turn, have to imitate the conditions that are required in order for the shrimp to grow and fatten.[5] The third link to the chain of shrimp harvest is the shrimp processing plants. This stage includes the handling of the shrimp according to the market's demands: beheaded, deveined, cleaned, selected, weighed, packaged, and/or frozen. Additionally, it is during this stage that other added-value processes may be added such as butterfly cut, breaded and with flavors.

The last link in the chain belongs to the distribution and marketing of the products. This stage is controlled by intermediaries between the destination market and the producers. The intermediaries usually control the distribution channels and manage the brand for which the farmers produce. Additionally, they also serve as intermediaries between the methods of production and the regulatory demands of the markets. Several examples of these can be found among the European countries, and particularly northern Europe, where strict regulations require the shrimps to be certified as not having been fed with genetically modified supplies, not having been harvested by forced labor and the exclusion of sardines as the base for manufacturing shrimp feed. This last requirement has been introduced in order not to use proteins to feed people of the developed countries instead of using them to feed people in the developing nations.

In general terms, it is possible to graphically describe the shrimp clusters in Venezuela in the manner shown in Figure 7.3.

The shrimp cluster has a series of characteristics that need to be highlighted in order to understand the challenges it faces in the future, particularly managing the transition from a nascent to a growth stage. Most of these characteristics were identified in interviews with the most relevant actors within the cluster. As we see, the kind of problems the cluster currently confronts reveals that it is still in a transition period (from nascent to growth) that requires a great effort of coordination between the public and the private sector to achieve its consolidation.

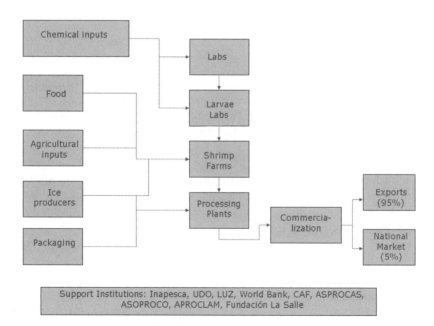

Figure 7.3. Structure of Shrimp clusters

7.4.1. *Lack of Integration*

One of the most outstanding elements of the Venezuelan shrimp cluster is that few companies have been able to arrive at a vertical integration, particularly, at the commercialization level. The companies, especially the Venezuelan ones, tend to concentrate their activities in the production phase and have left the brand development and the creation of distribution channels into the markets in the hands of other firms. It is only the multinational firms that have been able to lean on their processes of forward integration in order to gain access with greater ease to international markets.

7.4.2. *Scarce Cooperation among Companies*

Another very interesting characteristic of the Venezuelan shrimp cluster is the great rivalry and little collaboration between the producers. As defined by the executive director of one of the associations of shrimp companies (curiously enough they are organized according to their geographic location) 'the mistrust among us is a common ground'. Although the companies are competing in an environment of global growth for shrimp products, the concerted initiatives to improve the conditions and the factors that could positively affect the development of the cluster as a whole are rare. The example from Taura, to be described below, reflects the vulnerabilities to which the cluster is subject as a consequence of this kind of behavior from the companies.

7.4.3. *Absence of Support Institutions*

The shrimp companies have developed without the support of any organizations, be it public or private, that traditionally could help them to overcome different obstacles and improve the cluster's levels of productivity. Only the Eastern University (Universidad de Oriente) has produced a series of programs focussed around the shrimp cluster in eastern Venezuela to support R&D programs. This initiative has been an isolated effort that does not count with enough support from the private sector nor was it reproduced in the western part of the country where the greater number of producers are located. Similarly, the regulatory agency, Inapesca, has not fulfilled its role of promoting the strategies for the sector. Instead, this public agency has limited itself to the regulation and approval of permissions without addressing the long range problems that guarantee the growth of the cluster in the future.

7.4.4. *Lack of Knowledge of Their Competitive Advantages*

Another outstanding characteristic of this cluster is the lack of knowledge of the international markets and of its competitive position by the producers.

This is the consequence of the lack of integration of the companies with the commercialization stage of the process. One of the risks that this situation carries with itself is that the Venezuelan producers are fairly oblivious of their position within the cost structure of other countries in the region or in Asia. This lack of information could undermine the adoption of better practices at the international level, the difussion of technological innovations and thus affect the improvement of the levels of productivity.

7.4.5. Lack of Access to Capital

The lack of access to capital from the private banking sector is closely linked to a vicious circle that needs to be broken. On the one hand, the banking sector considers the harvest of shrimp to be a high-risk enterprise because it deals with live animals and because of previous negative experiences in this industry in Venezuela. All of these limitations make it impossible for the industry to show its potential for growth as a sector that generates income for Venezuela. It was only in 2004 that some international financial institutions such as the International Finance Corporation (IFC) began reversing this trend when they approved a loan to a rather large project (Sea Farms Venezuela) in the Lake of Maracaibo. The project has high social and environmental standards that guarantee a sustainable development of the investment project.

7.5. The Threat from Taura

In January 2005, there were high mortality rates among shrimps in some Venezuelan farms. During the following month, several other farms in Zulia, Falcon, Nueva Esparta, and Sucre had been affected as well. Production was frozen in 22 of the farms, roughly 80 percent of the shrimp production in the country. Later on, Inapesca, as the main regulatory agency, revealed that the laboratory tests that had been run confirmed the presence of the Taura virus in Venezuela. This virus represented the obstacle of greatest risk that the cluster has had to experience since its creation. The news surprised many of the producers because of the environmental and sanitary demands to which they are subjected by both the international markets and the Venezuelan law. These regulations allowed many of the producers to think, as one of them put it, 'that they are not immune to these kinds of shocks'.[6]

The virus was first identified in Ecuador in 1994 in a shrimp farm near to a town called Taura. This virus does not affect human health. It does, however, affect shrimps that are less than 5 cm in length. Its effect has been felt in shrimp farms all over Central and South America. One of the reasons Taura was allowed an entry into Venezuela was the import of shrimps by one of the companies without the appropriate supervision. This jeopardized the production of all the shrimp cluster. One of the members of the association of producers has said: 'this problem was easily avoidable. But it happened because we do not cooperate among us and we did not take into account the risks that were involved with unsupervised imports. It was something that had already happened in other countries and we did not want to reduce the risk and confront it collectively. It was an announced tragedy'.[7]

One of the solutions put forth was the import of reproducers that were resistant to this virus from labs abroad. In this sense, the regulating association comments:

In Venezuela, INAPESCA handled the shrimp sector diligently propitiating and facilitating several meetings with the producers, the technicians, the scientists and the administrators. Between Feb. 9 and March 23 of 2005, more than 10 meetings or workshops were held and on April 4 the producers were informed about the legal dispositions that establish measures for biosafety so that no illnesses will proliferate and the dispositions that will allow the import of reproducing shrimps that are free of illnesses, as well as quarantines that they need to comply with after they are imported from specialized labs abroad.[8]

For the first time since the beginning of the shrimp cluster in the early 1990s, regulators, producers, and research facilities showed a certain degree of cooperation. As a whole, these three groups traveled abroad to verify that the reproducing shrimps to be bought did comply with the guidelines established in Venezuela and to initiate the shipments of healthy shrimps. In April 2005, 8,000 reproducing shrimps arrived and after a rigorous and supervised quarantine period they were certified free of any disease. According to Inapesca, they expect levels of production to return to the same levels as in 2004 in a twelve-month period. This joint effort of producers, scientists, and regulators (i.e. Inapesca) made the partial reactivation of this industry possible in what could be considered a brief period of time. Since the appearance of Taura the actors within this cluster started to realize that the competitive advantages of their companies not only depended on internal factors but also on external conditions that must be worked at collectively.

7.6. Lessons and Conclusion

The successful experience of the shrimp cluster in Venezuela can help us understand several of the conditions that allow firms to internationalize in Latin America even under an adverse business environment. The shrimp cluster experience can also illustrate some of the challenges that firms face within a cluster to sustain the transition from a nascent to a growth period. Many of these lessons are intuitive and require further research.

(1) Firms can internationalize their activities even under adverse institutional conditions. Despite the negative business environment that firms experienced in Venezuela, companies within the shrimp cluster were able to internationalize by focussing their activities almost exclusively on the export of their products. High growth rates in the shrimp cluster were linked to the fact that most of their production was oriented toward international markets, helping to access more sophisticated consumers and adopting higher standards. This factor allowed firms to isolate themselves temporarily from the inherent risks and the transactional costs of doing business in Venezuela while benefiting from more competitive markets. In fact, certain comparative advantages, such as the geographical location and the quality of the water, enabled them to compensate the costs associated to a complex and volatile business climate.

(2) The factors that allow the internationalization of an individual firm do not depend exclusively on its productivity levels and strategic capabilities but are also closely tied to the strengths and weaknesses developed by the cluster in which they interact. The shrimp cluster in Venezuela shows how vulnerable firms are to external shocks that are difficult to compensate for if the cluster is not adequately integrated through cooperative strategies among the different firms competing in that sector. Therefore, the ability to compete at the international level is a function both of competitive and cooperative strategies developed by the firm in a specific cluster. In other words, the possibility of the shrimp cluster to improve in the near future its competitiveness and surpass many of the obstacles created by the business climate in Venezuela will depend on the capacity of the firms to deepen the level of trust among the different actors involved and develop cooperative strategies that will allow them to continue upgrading their industry.

(3) The business climate in which firms operate is fundamental to guarantee the long-term sustainability and consolidation of the internationalization effort. As a result, the factors that allowed for the internationalization of a set of firms are not necessarily the same reasons that will explain its sustainability over time. The shrimp firms in Venezuela were capable of internationalizing their activities, though they confronted an adverse business climate; however, their capacity to sustain their future growth will be contingent on substantial improvements in that same business environment. Access to new markets, increase in investments, technological transfers, and the reduction of transaction costs are factors that depend on the public sector willingness to improve microeconomic and macroeconomic conditions under which Venezuelan companies compete.

165

Table 7.A.1 Shrimp Farming Companies in Venezuela, 2006

Name	State	Capital
Aquamarina de la Costa	Anzoátegui	Venezuelan
Siembramar (Siembras Marinas)	Anzoátegui	Not available
Agromarina Sea Land	Falcón	Not available
Agromarina Terra Azul	Falcón	Not available
Grucasa	Falcón	Not available
Acualpaca (Acualarvas Paraguaná)	Falcón	Not available
Agrocamsa (Agropecuaria Camaronera San Sebastián, CA)	Falcón	Not available
Ecocultivos Larvarios	Falcón	Not available
Sinerita (Invermar)	Falcón	Not available
Ricoa Agromarina, CA	Falcón	Venezuelan
Atlantic Lab. CA	NE/Zulia	Venezuelan
	NE/Zulia	Venezuelan
Agropecuaria Isla de Coche	Nueva Esparta	Venezuelan
	Nueva Esparta	Venezuelan
Cooperativa Sol, Mar y Río 22	Nueva Esparta	Not available
D.P. Tecnología CA	Nueva Esparta	Venezuelan
Naturamar CA	Nueva Esparta	Venezuelan
Agropecuaria Los Cocos	Nueva Esparta	Foreign
Aqua-Tec	Nueva Esparta	Extranjero
Nauplios	Nueva Esparta	Extranjero
Demaca (Desarrollos Marinos)	Sucre	Not available
Laboratorio Las Brisas	Sucre	Venezuelan
Inversiones Punta Escarceo	Sucre	Not available
Agrícola Arapuey	Trujillo	Not available
Agrícola La Esperanza	Zulia	Not available
Agrícola Monte Alto	Zulia	Not available
Agropecuaria Camaronera El Majagual	Zulia	Not available
Pecuaria Nuevo Mangle	Zulia	Not available
Gutierrez Sandoval	Zulia	Not available
Agrícola Las Brisas	Zulia	Not available
Aquamar (Ex–Rincon del Lago)	Zulia	Not available
Inmarlaca	Zulia	Not available
Agricola San Jose	Zulia	Not available
Agrícola Tomoporo	Zulia	Not available
Agroboca (Agropecuaria La Bogotana)	Zulia	Not available
Agropecuaria La Feltrina	Zulia	Not available
Inbufonca (Inversiones Baez, Urdaneta y Fonseca)	Zulia	Not available
Inter Sea Farms De Venezuela	Zulia	Extranjero
Agromarina Costa Sur	Zulia	**Not available**
A Quacam Ca		Not available
Acuicultura Peninsula de Araya	Sucre	Venezuelan
Agropesca		Not available
Enmar Cultivos y Asociados	Oriente	Not available
Frigus Venezolana Ca		Not available
Ingopesca SA		Not available
Inter Sifal De Venezuela		Extranjero
Megasupply	Oriente	Extranjero
Nutrishrimp CA	Oriente	Not available
Representaciones PSG		Not available
Stelca		Not available

Notes

1. There are very few export-oriented sectors beyond oil, iron, and aluminum. Some interesting exemptions are biruqettes, engineering services, chocolates, rum, and autoparts (Frances and Garcia 1998).
2. This was a phrase used by Lope Mendoza, president of Conindustria, after meeting with President Chávez in Miraflores. El Nacional, 02/07/2005.
3. Interview with Felipe Brillembourg who is the owner of one of the largest shrimp farms in Venezuela. The interview was conducted in Caracas, April 17, 2005.
4. Labs produce two lines of products; naplios and postlarvae. Naplios are the small larvae recently hatched (first stage as larvae) which are sold by the million. Postlarvae are those larvae that have been through three stages as such and are sold by the thousands. The lab cycle begins with the copulation of the shrimp at the end of the afternoon and the birth of between 50,000 and 300,000 eggs by the next day's dawn. A day later, these eggs will become a *naplios* and later on *zoeas*, which is the second stage as larvae. Three to five days later and using a diet that includes algae and artemia, the *zoeas* go on to the third and last stage as larva, the *mysis* when you can observe several characterisitics of the grown shrimp such as the body and the tail.
5. The shrimp farms have, as their main infrastructure, pools that imitate the conditions of the statuaries; these are classified according to the density of animals per unit of the area (generally per hectare); extensive, semi-intensive, and intensive. These classifications go from smaller to larger according to the density of metric tons of shrimp per unit of land.
6. Interview with Anaydee Morales, Maracaibo, 03/04/2005.
7. Ibidem.
8. www. INAPESCA.gov.ve, 2005.
9. Interview with Ramón Manrique, General Manager of Granja Aguamarina de La Costa; June 2005.
10. Interview with Tomás Cabrera, Professor, Eastern University, (UDO), Unit Nueva Esparta; April 2005.
11. Interview with Max Padrón, Consultant for INAPESCA; May 2005.

References

AGROCADENAS (2005). www.agrocadenas.com.Las Camaroneras en Venezuela.june.

Audretsch, D. and Feldman, M. (1995). *Innovative Clusters and the Industry Life Cycle*. London: Centre for Economic Policy Research.

Audretsch, D. B. and Feldman, M. P. (1996). 'R&D spillovers and the Geography of Innovation and Production', *American Economic Review*, 86(3): 630–40.

Brandenburger, A. M. and Nalebuf, B. J. (1996). *Co-Opetition*. New York: Doubleday Books.

Chamberlain, G. (2003). *World Shrimp Farming*. Salvador de Bahias: World Aquaculture.

CIS-Madera (2000). El *Cluster* de la Madera de Galicia como Instrumento de Integración y Cooperación para la Mejora Competitiva.

Conindustmia (National Confederation of Chambers of Industry) (2004). *El Cievre de Empresas Industriales en Venezuela*. Caracas: coninceel.

Dumais, G., Ellison, G., and Glaeser, E. (1997). *Geographic Concentration as a Dynamic Process*. Cambridge, MA: National Bureau of Economic Research.

Eduardo, L. and Panizza, U. (2002). 'Structural Reforms in Latin America Under Scrutiny', Working Paper 1012, Inter-American Development Bank, Washington DC.

Enright, M., Frances, A., and Saavedra, S. (1996). *Venezuela: The Challenge of Competitiveness*. New York: St Martin's Press.

Fairbanks, M. and Lindsay, S. (1997). *Arando en el Mar*. Boston, MA: Harvard Business School Press.

Haussman, R. (2003). 'Venezuela's Growth Implosion: A Neoclassical Story', in Dani Rodrik (ed.), *In Search of Prosperity*. Princeton, NJ: Princeton University Press.

INAPESCA (2005). Base Estadística. Características de Empresas Cultivadoras de Camaríon Marítimo. ministerio de Agricultura Y Tierras. Caracas.

——(National Fishing Institute) (2003). *La Industria Camaronera*. Mimisterio de Agricultura y Tierras. Report. Cavacas.

Ketels, C. (2003). *The Development of the* Clusters *Concept—Present Experiences and Further Developments*. Duisburg: Institute for Strategy and Competitiveness.

Munn-Venn, T. and Voyer, R. (2004). Clusters *of Opportunity,* Clusters *of Risk*. Ottawa: The Conference Board of Canada.

Padrón, M. (2003). *Diagnostico Actual de la Camaronicultura en Venezuela*. Caracas: INAPESCA.

Penfold, M. (2003). *El Costo Venezuela: Opciones de Política para Mejorar la Competitividad*. Caracas: CAF.

Porter, M. (1998). *On Competition*. Boston, MA: The Harvard Business Review Book Series.

—— (1990). *The Competitive Advantage of Nations*. New York: Free Press.

Rodriguez, F. (2004). 'The Anarchy of Numbers: Understanding the Evidence of Venezuelan Economic Growth', Working Paper, Wesleyan University.

Roldan, D. and Salazar, M. (2003). *La Cadena de Camarón de Cultivo en Colombia*. Bogota: Ministerio de Agricultura y Desarrollo Social Colombia.

Sánchez, R. and Alvarez, S. (2004). *Cultivo de Camarón con Carácter Social*. Punto Fijo, Venezuela: Universidad Nacional Experimental Francisco de Miranda.

Schmitz, H. and Nadvi, K. (1999). 'Clustering and industrialization: Introduction', *World Development*, 27(9): 1503–14.

Tobey, J., Clay, J., and Vergne, P. (1998). *Impactos Económicos, Ambientales y Sociales del Cultivo de Camarón en Latinoamérica*. Kingston: Universidad de Rhode Island.

www.agrocadenas.com, Junio 2005.

www.fao.org, Junio 2005.

www.greenpeace.org/espana/news/greenpeace-pide-a-los-consumid-2, Julio 2005.

www.greenpeace.org/espana/news/greenpeace-pide-a-los-consumid-3, Julio 2005.

www.shrimpnews.com/About.html, Junio 2005, Bob Rosenberry.

8

Can Argentinian Companies Survive? A Study of the Determinants of Organizational Flexibility

Andrés Hatum* and Andrew Pettigrew

8.1. Introduction

Many writers have characterized today's business environment as 'high velocity' (Eisenhardt 1989) and 'hypercompetitive' (D'Aveni 1994). Behind such claims lies an interest in understanding the different ways organizations adapt to fast-changing environments.

From a social science point of view, organizational adaptability is *'the ability of an organisation to change itself, or the way in which it behaves, in order to survive in the face of external changes which were not predicted in any precise way when the organisation was designed'* (Tomlinson 1976: 533). This definition confirms March's assertion that adaptation is essential to survival. Those companies that do not adapt *'seem destined to expire'* (March 1995: 431).

However, adaptation views of organization development have been contested. In an attempt to distinguish the different debates within organizational theories, Astley and Van de Ven (1983) argue that one of these debates is about the adaptation/selection dichotomy. Even though the adaptation approach is widely accepted in strategy and organization theory (Lewin and Volberda 1999), some theories emphasize the idea of selection, retention, or inertia (Hannan and Freeman 1977, 1984; Di Maggio and Powell 1983).

However, Lewin and Volberda (1999) and Lewin et al. (1999), call for an end to viewing the adaptation-selection phenomena as discrete themes. They argue that adaptation and selection should be seen as interrelated forces. In so doing, it is possible to link the processes of firm-level adaptation and the population-level selection pressures thus avoiding single and acontextual

* Correspondent author.

perspectives and taking into account multilevel analysis and embeddedness (Pettigrew 1985, 1990).

Viewing adaptation as a dynamic process—the point of view of this chapter—reveals that for any given organization, elements or variables related to managerial choice and environmental influence coexist (Child 1972, 1997). Change, then, is the outcome of environmental context and managerial action (Pettigrew and Whittington 2003).

So, how is it possible to adapt to environmental changes? This chapter uses the language of organizational flexibility to pose a number of important questions about the adaptation process of companies in an emerging and turbulent market. While existing studies have delved into the problems firms have to confront to adapt in developed countries, there is a dearth of studies tackling the issue in developing economies. We, therefore, aim to understand organizational flexibility and adaptation in emerging economies and answer the following questions:

— What determines a firm to be flexible in an emerging economy and adapt to the fast changing environment?
— What are the managerial and organizational capabilities needed in order to adapt in rapid changing contexts?

It is well recognized that there is a dearth of studies on organizational adaptation in emerging economies and there is a corresponding need for explorative and longitudinal studies in the field (Hoskisson et al. 2000). Chakravarthy (1997) also highlights the fact that environmental turbulence affects many industries. However, studies have been carried out in sectors characterized by short life cycle products such as technology-driven sectors (e.g. information technology) (Eisenhardt and Tabrizi 1995), but there is scant research into industries in which the product cycles are not so short (such as food industries and the pharmaceutical industry).

The empirical focus of the chapter is on the determinants of organizational flexibility over the period 1989–99 in two companies considered highly flexible in the two different industries: pharmaceuticals and edible oils in Argentina, a country that has been characterized by frequent periods of economic, social, and political turmoil. Brief remarks on the behavior of less flexible firms are also highlighted. The period 1989–99 saw the country transform and opening up toward FDI increasing the levels of competitiveness in the internal market.

Our analysis draws upon a combination of primary and secondary material and utilizes qualitative and quantitative data. By means of a combination of deductive and inductive analysis we identify the existence of a set of determinants of organizational flexibility. These findings are discussed and interpreted from the literature on organizational flexibility and innovativeness and from institutional theory.

This chapter is divided into five sections. Following this introductory section, Section 8.2 explores the literature on determinants of organizational flexibility, organizational innovativeness, and institutional theory. We describe how these three alternative literatures can be used to build a more precise approach toward adaptation under circumstances of environmental turmoil. Patterns of adaptation and researchable questions are derived from the literature review. Section 8.3 describes the research design and Section 8.4 discusses and interprets the main findings of this research. Finally, Section 8.5 provides a summary of the chapter and some concluding remarks.

8.2. Key Concepts and Literature

8.2.1. Research on Determinants of Organizational Flexibility

The literature has tended to use the concept of dynamic capabilities to refer to flexibility (Teece et al. 1997; Rosembloom 2000; Tushman and Smith 2001). In their theoretical framework, which is based on dynamic capabilities as enablers of adaptation and change in a rapidly changing environment, Teece et al. (1997: 516) define dynamic capabilities as *'the firm's ability to integrate, build, and reconfigure internal and external competences to address rapidly changing environments.'* More concretely, Teece et al. (1997) indicate that dynamic capabilities should be able to enhance technological, organizational, and managerial processes inside the firm to enable it to organize more effectively. Teece et al. (1997: 521) also state that firms that have honed and perfected these capabilities are referred to as *'high-flex'*. We consider organizational flexibility as a combination of a repertoire of organizational and managerial capabilities that allow organizations to adapt quickly under environmental change.

Flexible structural design means attaining a structure that allows the flexible organization to succeed under environmental pressure and unpredictability. Krijnen (1979) and Overholt (1997) point out that a flexible structure requires decentralization in decision-making, and a high degree of permeability of boundaries and collaborative partnerships. Thus, organic (Volberda 1999), multipolar (Bahrami 1992), or innovative (Krijnen 1979) types of organizational design have been highlighted as possible means of achieving flexibility.

Volberda (1999) refers to the necessity for a broad knowledge base and a variety of managerial expertise. Heterogeneity and broad managerial mindsets foster the ability to create and support ideas. Bahrami (1992) points out the crucial role of the cosmopolitan mindset as a way of incorporating different cultural assumptions and premises. He also states that as a consequence of this, organizations enjoy openness thanks to versatile managers.

8.2.2. Research on Determinants of Organizational Innovativeness

In this article, we adopt a broad approach to understanding innovation, considering product, processes, and services among all the innovative activities companies could exercise (Van de Ven and Poole 1995).

So, what are the factors that make an organization more or less innovative?

The most frequently investigated organizational determinants of innovativeness include the degree of centralization and formalization of decision-making process. There is a general consensus among theorists in the field of organizational innovativeness that higher degrees of centralization and formalization influence innovation in a negative way because they concentrate decision-making, hindering the ability of the members of the organization to participate in and be committed to organizational aims (Damanpour 1991; Webb and Pettigrew 1999).

The process view of innovativeness (Van de Ven et al. 1999) stresses that at any time an organization is likely to be in the process of adopting several innovations, each at a different stage of generation and implementation. The innovativeness of an organization, therefore, will depend on its ability to address the different requirements of each phase of adoption simultaneously. Hence, while low levels of formalization and centralization of decision-making may increase innovativeness in the creation phase, there will be a point at which the relaxation of control will disrupt implementation (Damanpour 1992).

Much of the innovation literature argues for the impact of the characteristics or traits of the top management team on organizational innovativeness. This view of innovation assumes that certain individuals have personal qualities that predispose them to innovative behavior (Slappender 1996).

Diversity of backgrounds and experience (Hage and Dewar 1973) and different mental models—a *'cosmopolitan mindset'* (Robertson and Wind 1983)—among the management team are both key factors in achieving a high level of innovativeness. These concepts of diversity of backgrounds and cosmopolitanism highlight the importance of the internal heterogeneity of the management team. This heterogeneity might boost the setting up of networks outside the organization (Hage and Dewar 1973), the possibility of transferring ideas into the organization (Pettigrew 1972), and the creation or diffusion of both technical and/or administrative innovations (Daft 1978).

The literature on organizational innovativeness thus raises a number of possible issues related to the adaptiveness of a firm. Innovativeness of a firm will be determined by a variety of organizational and individual factors, which include the characteristics and diversity of the firm's top management team and the degree of centralization and formalization of decision-making.

However, institutional influence comes into play when levels of uncertainty and unpredictability increase. There is a need to understand how companies in volatile contexts—such as in the Argentinian case—can adapt fast without being caught by inertial forces (Di Maggio and Powell 1983; Webb and Pettigrew 1999). In the face of uncertainty, mimetic behavior and institutional embeddedness would protect companies from turmoil (Di Maggio and Powell 1983; Abrahamson and Formbrun 1994).

8.2.3. *Institutional Embeddedness*

Institutional theory explains adaptation as a homogenization process through which firms within a sector will become increasingly alike overtime. The process of homogenization that firms undergo in a sector is called isomorphism by Di Maggio and Powell (1983: 149): *'Isomorphism is a constraining process that forces one unit in a population to resemble other units that face the same set of environmental conditions.'*

Therefore, in assessing the adaptation process of an organization in an industry it is important to address the issue of what determines the threshold level at which institutional pressures are overcome and the company can adopt new initiatives or strategies that differ from the rest of the actors in the industry in which it is embedded. The threshold level will be determined by the degree of embeddedness in the dominant macroculture or institutional field operating in an organization's environment (Abrahamson and Fombrun 1994; Webb and Pettigrew 1999).

Passivity and acceptance, rather than activeness, define the perspective so far described. However, more recent literature in this area has taken a different approach toward embeddedness and has given emphasis to the organization's ability to overcome institutional pressures. Oliver (1991, 1992) and Greenwood and Hinings (1996) introduce a less deterministic perspective to the institutional literature by recognizing the critical role of managerial action.

The neo-institutional perspective adopted by Oliver (1991, 1992) and Greenwood and Hinings (1996) provides some insight into the understanding of adaptation processes. This new approach in institutional theory opens up the discussion of a firm's capacity for action that is *'the ability to manage the transition process from one template to another'* (Greenwood and Hinings 1996: 1039). This capacity for action means that change, adaptation, and innovative behavior are possible and avoids the rather passive and deterministic perspective stated by earlier approaches in institutional theory in which organizations were passive recipients of environmental pressure (Di Maggio and Powell 1983). Thus, organizations can challenge the environments in which they are embedded by introducing new practices and strategies.

Table 8.1. Patterns of adaptiveness in the literature on organizational flexibility, organizational innovativeness, and institutional theory

Patterns of adaptiveness	Sources in the literature
At the Sectoral/Industry Level #Low degree of embeddedness in dominant macroculture	*Institutional Theory Literature*: Di Maggio and Powell 1983; Oliver 1991, 1992; Abrahamson and Fombrun 1994; Greenwood and Hinings 1996; Webb and Pettigrew 1999
At the Organizational Level #Decentralization of decision-making (through autonomy of decision-making a flexible organizational design) #Low level of formalization of decision-making	*Literature on Organizational Flexibility*: Krijnen 1979; Overholt 1997; Bahrami 1992 *Literature on Organizational Innovativeness*: Damanpour 1992; Webb and Pettigrew 1999
At the Top Managerial Level of the Firm #Heterogeneity of the dominant coalition (e.g. diversity of backgrounds and experience and cosmopolitan mindset)	*Literature on Organizational Flexibility*: Bahrami 1992; Volberda 1996, 1999 *Literature on Organizational Innovativeness*: Daft 1978; Hage and Dewar 1973; Robertson and Wind 1983

8.2.4. *Patterns of Adaptiveness and Researchable Questions Derived from the Literature Review*

Hitherto, this chapter has been analyzing three distinct bodies of literature: the literature on a firm's flexibility, that on its organizational innovativeness and, finally, institutional theory. These three bodies of literature overlap and complement each other and offered us a more accurate approach toward adaptation under circumstances of environmental shifts. Table 8.1 is a composite table that shows patterns of adaptiveness derived from the literature review.

The common patterns inform the choice of determinants of organizational flexibility in this study. Our literature review and empirical evidence have identified five determinants of organizational flexibility. Three of them are drawn deductively from the literature on organizational flexibility, innovativeness, and institutional theory (see Table 8.1). These determinants are: low macroculture embeddedness; a low level of centralization and formalization of decision-making; and heterogeneity of the dominant coalition. In addition, we are going to explore two further determinants that have emerged inductively from our empirical findings. These determinants are: environmental scanning and a strong organizational identity.

By drawing on and developing theoretical ideas from the three bodies of literature that were historically unrelated, this study lays the foundation for a more inclusive understanding of the determinants of organizational flexibility.

In the section of the chapter which follows, we now consider the research design used to seek answers to our study questions on the determinants of organizational flexibility.

8.3. Research Design

8.3.1. *Sample Selection*

To undertake this investigation of determinants of organizational flexibility, a research design was employed that involved clarifying a set of indicators so as to reveal highly flexible firms and less flexible firms and also a related series of methods to analyze the determinants of organizational flexibility.

In the wider study that forms the basis of this chapter[1] the analysis focusses on four cases from a population of large indigenous family-owned businesses in two industries: pharmaceuticals and edible oils. The cases—two in each sector—are polar types: one a highly flexible firm, the other a less flexible firm. This chapter, however, focusses on the most flexible firms: AGD and Sidus. The decision of analyzing the flexible firms has one main reason that is grasping what determines a firm to be able to be flexible and, therefore, to adapt to the rapid changes of the environment. In studying the flexible firms, and the different ways they were able to adapt, we will be able to explain why and how Argentinian firms survived.

We, however, will briefly summarize some ideas of what happened with the less flexible firms and we will be able to point out the main differences with the flexible firms. This description can be found at the end of Section 8.4.

Both the pharmaceutical and edible oil industries were chosen as sites of this research into organizational flexibility primarily as a result of the strong competitive pressures these industries underwent during the 1990s. The level of competition they faced during this period is indicated by the general level of FDI and the degree of the regulation (CEP 1998).

The Argentinian economy received substantial levels of foreign investment which changed the internal dynamic of the sectors in terms of the entrance of new players and the levels of competition and efficiency (Dunning 1993). Since the 1990s, Argentina has been the second largest destination of FDI in Latin America after Mexico (Toulan and Guillén 1997). The Food and Pharmaceutical sectors are among those that received most FDI in the country (see Table 8.2). Other sectors which received more FDI—such as communication (whose inward investments were more than a quarter of the total FDI during the period 1990–8) banking and television—were rejected because survival rates of indigenous business were too low, thus making comparison very difficult if not impossible (see Table 8.2).

The level of regulation of the industries, on the other hand, illustrates how regulatory agencies act to mediate competitive pressures, thereby protecting the firms from market and competitive forces. Thus, the level of regulation in an industry can shape the demands for organizational flexibility in a firm (Grabowsky et al. 1978; Smith and Grimm 1987). With this in mind, two industries, one regulated but in transition toward deregulation

Table 8.2. Ranking of inward investment per sector 1990–98

Industry	Percentage Inward Investment[a]
Communication*	25.62
Banking and Financial Services**	16.60
Food and Beverage	12.03
TV*	11.58
Chemistry and Pharmaceuticals	11.06
Telephone*	10.82
Commerce	7.37
Petrol***	5.31
Cellulose and Paper	3.70
Automotive	3.50

* No indigenous businesses among the first 20 largest companies.

** Only one indigenous bank among the first 20 largest companies.

*** It does not include the acquisition of Repsol of YPF, the Argentinian Petrol Company that happened in year 2000.

[a] The percentage takes into account the process of merger undertaken by Multinational companies. However, the inflow of foreign investment coming from the privatization process was not taken into consideration because it was mainly directed toward state owned businesses.

Source of information: CEP, 1998.

(pharmaceuticals) and one deregulated (edible oils—within the food sector) were selected.

A list of the first twenty companies in the pharmaceutical and edible oil industries was compiled and ranked so as to reflect their organizational flexibility according to the indicators shown in Table 8.3. The indicators revealing organizational flexibility—product innovation, collaboration and partnerships, and internationalization and diversification—were measured as high, medium, and low and the companies were ranked accordingly.

In the ranking, Sidus and AGD emerged as the most flexible companies in their respective industries (pharmaceuticals and edible oils). Similarly, Dersa and St Martin emerged as the less flexible firms in their own industry (pharmaceuticals and edible oils respectively). Table 8.4 shows the companies' profile.

8.3.2. Data Collection

We collected longitudinal data about the transformation process covering the firms' activities over the period 1989–99. Understanding how organizations transform their core activities can help to shed light on the determinants of organizational flexibility (Volberda 1999). The sources of data in the firms were threefold: in-depth interviews; documentary and archival material; and quantitative and statistical data.

Fifteen semi-structured interviews were held in each company. Pluralism in the selection of the interviewees was considered important because people from different levels in the hierarchy in the organization can offer

Table 8.3. Indicators of organisational flexibility in the pharmaceutical and edible oil industries

General indicator	Customized indicators used in the pharmaceutical industry	Customized indicators used in the edible oil industry	Sources
Product Innovation	• Product innovation in traditional pharmaceutical products • Product innovation in nontraditional pharmaceutical products	• Product innovation (branding)	Eisenhard and Tabrizi 1995; Jonsson 2000
Collaboration and partnerships	• Collaboration and partnerships with local competitors or foreign players	• Collaboration and partnerships with local competitors or foreign players	Regner 2000; Birkinshaw 2000
Internationalization diversification	• Internationalization • Diversification	• Internationalization • Diversification	Aaker and Mascarenhas 1984; Webb and Pettigrew 1999

accounts of the transformation in their companies from alternative perspectives (Pettigrew 1990). A pro-forma interview was used to provide a set of trigger questions to guide the process.

The collection of archive material from the companies complemented the interview process. The archive data ranged from histories of the company, internal documents, institutional information, and external reports. In the

Table 8.4. Companies' profile

Company	Industry	Related businesses	Employees (1999)	Turnover (1999) in US$ millions
AGD	Edible oils	Farming Crushing Transport (Railways/Port) Branding Distribution	1,500	1,042
Sidus	Pharmaceuticals	Biotechnology Pharmaceutical products Retail (Pharmacies) Intermediary companies Distribution	950	232

Source of information: Company's data

Table 8.5. Determinants and methods of analysis used

Determinant	Data sources and method/s	Sources
Heterogeneity of the dominant coalition	• Demographic analysis (quantitative variables and qualitative indicators) • Significance test • Use of qualitative data obtained from the fieldwork	Hambrick and Mason 1984; Wiersema and Bantel 1992; Hambrick 1989
Low centralization and formalization of decision-making	• Coding analysis • Significance test • Use of qualitative data obtained from the fieldwork	Webb and Pettigrew 1999
Low macroculture embeddedness	• Coding analysis • Tracking strategic initiatives • Use of qualitative data obtained from the fieldwork	Webb and Pettigrew 1999; Damanpour 1991
Environmental scanning	• Coding analysis • Use of qualitative data obtained from the fieldwork	Daft et al. 1988; Beal 2000; Pettigrew and Whipp 1991
A strong organizational identity	• Analysis of speeches, discourses, and letters	Collins and Porras 2000; Webb et al. 1966; Hardy 2001

Argentinian context, the fact that these companies are privately owned meant that they had no need to produce public information such as annual reports.

8.3.3. *Data Analysis*

The data were firstly stored using a database designed specifically for the task, to avoid what Pettigrew (1990: 281) calls 'death through data asphyxiation'. Writing down analytical chronologies, as suggested by Pettigrew (1990), was the way chosen to display the data and to start shaping possible determinants of organizational flexibility. In the analytical chronologies, both the story and the story across levels of analysis are told. The analytical chronologies contain the seeds of the analysis itself (Pettigrew 1990; Naumes and Naumes 1999).

To analyze the determinants of organizational flexibility, different methods of analysis were selected based on the empirical tradition in the literatures used in this research. This is the case of the following methods used in analyzing determinants of organizational flexibility: demographic analysis (for heterogeneity of the dominant coalition); coding analysis (for centralization and formalization of decision-making; low macroculture embeddedness, environmental scanning, and strong organizational identity); and discourse analysis (for a strong organizational identity).

Table 8.5 briefly shows the different methods used in analyzing the determinants of flexibility and their sources.

8.4. Main Findings

8.4.1. *Determinants of Organizational Flexibility*

A number of themes were apparent in our data which highlighted a range of managerial, organizational and contextual factors related to the ability of the firms to adapt quickly under environmental pressure. These themes included the effect of new managers coming in from outside the industry, the firms' relationship with its industry peers, the nature of the decision-making process and the early adoption of strategies and organizational changes in the flexible firms.

Furthermore, our review and synthesis of the literatures on organizational flexibility, organizational innovativeness, and institutional theory provides an insight into the explanation of patterns or mechanism of adaptation.

The neo-institutional approach developed by Greenwood and Hinings (1996) and Oliver (1991, 1992) allows us to see the low macroculture embeddedness needed to avoid mimetic and inertial forces exerted by the institutional domain. Organizations that are more peripheral and thus less embedded in an institutional context are less committed to prevailing practices and more ready to develop new ones (Greenwood and Hinings 1996).

The literature on organizational flexibility and innovation offer two predictions: firstly, that only those firms with a heterogeneous dominant coalition are likely to adapt successfully in conditions of environmental turmoil (Bahrami 1992; Volberda 1996; Webb and Pettigrew 1999); and secondly, that fast adaptation requires both low degree of centralization and formalization of decision-making (Damanpour 1991, 1992; Volberda 1999).

From our inductive analysis of the case studies two other determinants of organizational flexibility emerged: environmental scanning and a strong organizational identity. These two determinants and the literature that underpins them are operationalized and analyzed later in this section.

Therefore, how did the family firms in this study build up the flexible capabilities needed to succeed under environmental pressure? Why were AGD and Sidus able to achieve flexibility? The analysis of the determinants of organizational flexibility will seek to answer the foregoing questions.

8.4.1.1. HETEROGENEITY OF THE DOMINANT COALITION

This study uses a broad definition of the dominant coalition as the individuals responsible for determining a firm's direction (Wiersema and Bantel 1992; see also Cyert and March 1963 for organizational coalition). This means that Directors of the companies and the top management team are included in the definition of dominant coalition used in this research.

The study of this determinant is operationalized through the demographic studies tradition that analyzes demographic variables to understand the characteristics of the management team (Hambrick and Mason 1984; Pitcher and Smith 2001 among others). To have a holistic view of the features of the dominant coalition this chapter uses different variables such as age, tenure in the company, tenure in the role, experience in the industry, experience in the industry and other related industries, and finally, experience in other industries (see Figure 8.1).

Pettigrew (1992) criticizes the narrow demographic approach favored in such studies. Pettigrew's main criticism (1992: 176) stems from the *'enormous interpretative leaps'* that are made from *'distant'* demographic data about the managerial team characteristics. In his view this approach leads to a loss of perspective of important issues such as process, structure, and performance of top teams. Consequently, in this study the quantitative results of the demographic analysis are combined with qualitative data drawn from the interviews.

Our interviews show that in the 1980s both AGD and Sidus recruited, for the top managerial positions, people with background experience in the industry in which both companies were participating, that is, edible oils and pharmaceuticals. The dominant coalition of AGD in 1989 consisted of people with long tenures in related industries such as edible oil, food, cereals, and agriculture. In the case of Sidus, managers with background experience in pharmaceuticals, biochemistry, and health industry were recruited for top managerial posts in 1989.

The 1990s, however, show a different pattern. The new strategic initiatives AGD and Sidus undertook needed managerial skills the companies lacked, thus managers with different backgrounds such as marketing, consultancy, auditing, and logistics were recruited.

Figure 8.1 shows the demographic analysis of both AGD and Sidus. In both companies the average age of the management team, tenure (in the company and in the current role), and experience (in the industry and related industries) dropped over the ten-year span of the analysis. The drop in the different variables in Figure 8.1 indicates the renewal of the management team of both companies.

Moreover, new expertise was brought into the management team of the companies mainly by outsiders and, to a lesser extent, from internal promotions of the younger generation of managers. These changes in managerial expertise are illustrated in Figure 8.1 in the increase over the period 1989–99 of the variable 'experience in other industries'.

The need AGD and Sidus had for new skills gave the new managers an important role in the organization. New mental models and ideas were brought into the companies at the higher levels. Competing mental models began to emerge.

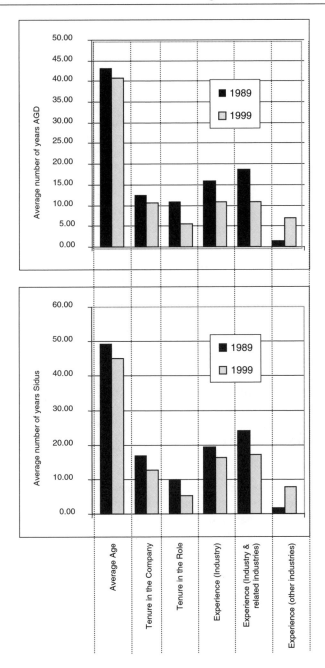

Figure 8.1. Dominant coalition demographics in AGD and Sidus 1989–99 (in average years)

'*The new professionals were thought-provoking. The professionals that entered the company in this decade were different in that they were not afraid of changing the status quo, in fact they were very happy to change it.*'[2]

'*They* [new generation of managers] *brought more ideas into the company and they were less worried about trying to innovate and less wary as well.*'[3]

Briefly, changes in the demographics of the dominant coalition stem from the companies' need for more skills to undertake their strategic initiatives successfully. The new managers brought into the organization not only creativity, skills, and new ideas thereby allowing the companies to move forward in their strategy of diversification, but also new competing mental models that challenged the culture of both AGD and Sidus.

8.4.1.2. LOW CENTRALIZATION AND HIGH FORMALIZATION LEVELS OF DECISION-MAKING

From our review of the literature on organizational flexibility and innovation (Damanpour 1991; Volberda 1999; among others), we would expect that the more formalized and centralized decision-making is, the less flexible an organization will be. However, high degrees of autonomy and laxity in control might constrain the implementation of innovation (Damanpour 1992) and strategies (Fredrickson 1986).

Formalization reflects the emphasis in rules, procedures, and control when carrying out organizational activities. Formalization is frequently measured by the presence of manuals, job description, procedures, and mechanism of control (Damanpour 1991).

Centralization, on the other hand, reflects the extent to which decision-making autonomy is dispersed or concentrated. It is generally measured by the degree of participation of organizational members in decision-making (Damanpour 1991).

To avoid misinterpretation, the interviewees were consistently informed how these concepts of centralization and formalization of decision-making were defined in this research. In the light of these definitions, the interviewees were questioned about their perception of the levels of strategic and operational centralization and formalization in AGD and Sidus throughout the period 1989–99. For example, was strategic decision formalized? (i.e. strategic planning, strategic meetings); were strategic decisions taken mainly by the CEO or the Board (i.e. strategic decisions such as investments, new strategic initiatives)?

The interviewees were also asked to assess the questions on a scale ranging from: low, medium-low, medium, medium-high, to high. The answers were coded on an ordinal scale ranging from 1 (low) to 5 (high). An independent inter-coder reliability check gave a score of 88.2 percent.[4] Figures 8.2 and 8.3 demonstrate the evolution of each company between 1989 and 99.

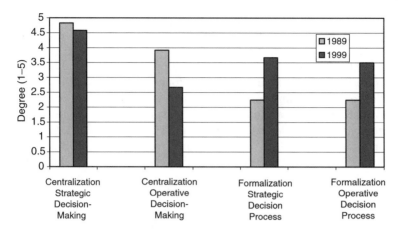

Figure 8.2. Centralization and formalization at AGD: average 1989–99

A common pattern in both AGD and Sidus was a highly centralized process of strategic decision-making and a decentralized operational decision-making process. Our interviews confirmed this trend and highlighted the importance of structural changes throughout the 1990s in boosting operational autonomy while the Board of AGD and Sidus reshaped their role from being an operative and executive Board to having a more strategic role.

However, strategic decisions were still highly centralized in the Board: *'The Directors were very clever; while they stood apart from the operation, they concentrated on strategic issues. They still have a strong grip on these issues.'*[5] Sidus

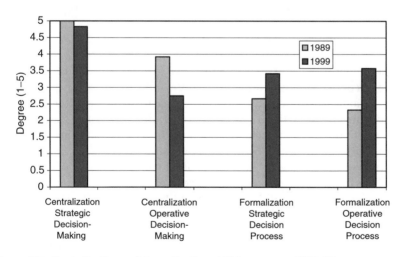

Figure 8.3. Centralization and formalization at Sidus: average 1989–99

is a similar case: *'The Board is reluctant to delegate those aspects that they consider strategic. They think about this, they make their own decisions and we acknowledge this after the decisions have been taken.'[6]*

The levels of formalization—strategic and operational—found at AGD and Sidus surprisingly went against the results found in the literature on organizational innovativeness and flexibility that state that low levels of centralization and formalization of decision-making are required to boost innovativeness and creativity in an organization (Damanpour 1991; Overholt 1997).

Formalization was perceived as increasing over the period 1989–99 in both companies. The 1990s, on the other hand, brought economic stability but difficult times for the companies in terms of competitiveness. More formal procedures and a less relaxed attitude were needed. Long-term thinking replaced the attitude of rushing into short-term matters. More control and planning appeared to be the way to achieve cost-efficiencies. IT systems, budget control, productivity, and indicators of performance appeared in different areas as ways of *'integrating and being more efficient and not with the idea of adding bureaucracy.'[7]* Changes in the structure helped AGD and Sidus mitigate the possible harmful consequences of the upsurge of formalization. The business units at AGD and the new companies or divisions at Sidus had fewer layers, thus facilitating communication and fast responsiveness.

8.4.1.3. LOW MACROCULTURE EMBEDDEDNESS

Another factor identified by this study as a determinant of organizational flexibility is the extent to which AGD and Sidus are embedded in their sector macroculture. This factor reflects the institutional pressures exerted upon the organization and the speed with which it can adopt new strategies (Abrahamson and Fombrun 1994; Dacin et al. 1999, 2002; Webb and Pettigrew 1999).

From our inductive analysis, two factors emerged that indicated the low degree of embeddedness of AGD and Sidus in their macroculture: the perceived similarity and dissimilarity to other firms in the industry and the degree of connectedness to other firms in the industry.

Institutional theory describes how these factors influence the degree of embeddedness within the industry macroculture. The higher the perceived similarity to others in the industry, the more likely it is that firms will accept the prevailing norms and become more institutionalized in that industry (Greenwood and Hinings 1996). On the other hand, the degree of connectedness refers to interpersonal contacts between executives in the same industry (Di Maggio and Powell 1983; Gnyawali and Madhavan 2001). Frequent contacts promote the awareness of practices and values of an industry (Webb and Pettigrew 1999).

The interviewees in both AGD and Sidus were consistent in their description of the extent to which these two factors were present in their companies.

Table 8.6. Level of similarity/dissimilarity within the industry: benchmarking at Sidus

Percentage	1989	1999
With whom is the company benchmarking?		
Benchmarking with indigenous pharmaceutical companies	87%	9%
Benchmarking with multinational pharmaceutical companies	20%	39%
Benchmarking with biotechnology companies	7%	52%

Table 8.7. Level of similarity/dissimilarity within the industry: benchmarking at AGD

Percentage	1989	1999
With whom is the company benchmarking?		
Benchmarking with indigenous edible oil companies	61%	7%
Benchmarking with multinational edible oil companies	44%	27%
Benchmarking with food-processing companies	0%	67%

To shed light on the two factors mentioned as influencing the low embeddedness within the industry macroculture—perceived similarity and degree of connectedness—the interviewees were asked to answer a set of questions. To understand the perceived similarity/dissimilarity in their macroculture, interviewees were asked about which company or companies were used by AGD/Sidus for benchmarking. Similarly, to understand the level of connectedness, the interviewees were asked whether their company supported any professional association in the industry and, if so, which professional association they supported. Questions were asked regarding two periods of time: 1989 and 1999.

Answers for each question were displayed in a table and different percentage scores calculated as shown in Tables 8.6 to 8.9. An inter-coder reliability check gave a reliability score between 85 and 90 percent.[8]

The way AGD and Sidus benchmark illustrates the low level of similarity of the companies in their industries. Both companies set their benchmark beyond sectoral boundaries. For example, the interviewees at AGD mentioned indigenous edible oil companies such as Moreno and Bunge as benchmarks in

Table 8.8. Degree of connectedness in the industry: support of Sidus in participating in professional associations

Percentage	1989	1999
Participation support in professional associations		
YES. Participation in professional associations is actively supported by the company	40%	27%
NO. Participation in professional associations is not actively supported by the company	60%	73%

Table 8.9. Degree of connectedness in the industry: support of AGD in participating in professional associations

Percentage	1989	1999
Participation support in professional associations		
YES. Participation in professional associations is actively supported by the company	80%	47%
NO. Participation in professional associations is not actively supported by the company	20%	53%

the 1980s. Today its benchmarks are Bestfood, an American food company, and Arcor, a regional food company (based in Argentina).

In contrast with the benchmarks that Sidus had in the 1980s, which were with indigenous companies such as Roemmers and Bagó, its current benchmark lies outside the Argentinian market. In 1999, Sidus targeted health companies in the biotechnological market—such as Genetech and Amgen (both American companies)—as the focus of its benchmarking activities.

AGD's and Sidus' low level of connectedness to other firms in the industry can be seen in their participation in the professional associations in their respective industries. While AGD maintains passive participation in CIARA, Sidus no longer supports the most important professional association in the pharmaceutical industry—CILFA—but has instead joined a low profile one—Cooperala: *'We are part of Cooperala because we have to be in one professional association.'*[9]

One consequence of AGD's and Sidus's low level of embeddeness in their macroculture that becomes clear in this research is that it has provided the companies with the freedom to make strategic moves which were innovative for both the edible oil and pharmaceutical industries. Institutional theory states that over time firms tend to adopt a particular strategy that will become increasingly institutionalized within the framework of the industry (Abrahamson and Fombrun 1994). To be able to be early movers or first adopters of strategies, firms must try to avoid the pressures exerted by the environment (Oliver 1991). Therefore, those firms which are less embedded in their macroculture will succeed in their attempt to adopt new strategies more rapidly (Greenwood and Hinings 1996).

The most flexible companies—AGD and Sidus—brought competence-disrupting discontinuities (Anderson and Tushman 1990) into their industries by using strategic initiatives previously unknown to those industries. Examples of such disruptive activities and the weak ties with its macroculture can be seen in Sidus' investments in biotechnology and the integration of its businesses far beyond the wholesaler channel by acquiring a pharmaceutical retail chain. None of the company's competitors was using similar strategies. Sidus was also a first mover in strategies that were later followed by its competitors such as the acquisition of pharmaceutical companies and investments in the OTC market.

AGD disrupted the edible oil industry by integrating all its activities, from farming to selling products in supermarkets. None of its competitors followed this strategy, a fact which demonstrates that AGD operates outside institutional norms. In many cases—such as the investments in brands, transport, farming, and storage capacity—AGD was a first mover in the edible oil industry and its competitors later followers.

The increasing distancing of AGD and Sidus from other competitors in their industries meant that the pressures exerted by the edible oil and pharmaceutical industries were weak. Consequently, institutional pressure had little influence on AGD's and Sidus' strategic responses.

8.4.1.4. ANTICIPATING CHANGES IN THE INDUSTRY: ENVIRONMENTAL SCANNING

Organizations must be able to cope with the instability and turmoil posed by the environment in which they function. To compete successfully, policymakers have to obtain superior information about the environment where their company is participating. Environmental scanning is the means by which managers can perceive and cope with external events and trends (Pfeffer and Salancik 1978; Pettigrew and Whipp 1991; Miller and Toulouse 1998).

From the inductive analysis, two indicators emerged as factors illustrating the importance of environmental scanning in AGD and Sidus. Firstly, both AGD and Sidus sought new sources of information over the period 1989–99 and; secondly, both AGD and Sidus set up formal structures as well as informal ones to scan the environment.

The environmental scanning literature describes the extent to which the two indicators found as shaping the scanning behavior of AGD and Sidus helped them to interpret and anticipate market changes. Daft et al. (1988) emphasized the importance of using different sources of information to prevent managers from forming their impressions on the basis of narrow environment data. They state the importance of scanning both the task or operational environment (customers, suppliers, competitors) and the general environment (government, economy, politics, social, and cultural matters).

Pettigrew and Whipp (1991) on the other hand, recognize that environmental scanning happens across the organization. They also point out that assuming that a single specialist can by himself achieve an adequate interpretation of the outer context is highly dangerous. Therefore, formal structures for scanning the environment are not only not enough, but also dangerous as they can lead the organization to inadequate interpretations. Informal ways of scanning are also necessary.

AGD and Sidus sought new sources of information throughout the 1990s. In 1989, AGD stressed the scanning of the general environment—mainly macroeconomic information—and in the operational environment only gathered data from the crushing industry and '*somehow*' found information about the edible oil industry. Throughout the 1990s this situation changed: *'We are not only aware of what is happening in the edible oil industry, but also in the food industry, and we have stronger relationships with customers and suppliers. They are also key elements in sensing the environment.'*[10]

In the 1980s the most important scanning activity in Sidus sought to understand the national economy and competitors' moves in the pharmaceutical industry. However, by the 1990s new scanning interests in customers, suppliers, and new areas of business such as retail and biotechnology emerged. The transformation of the company from a simple national laboratory in the 1980s to a health company in the 1990s was considered as having an impact in the assessment of the environment: *'Over this period* [from the 1980s to the 1990s] *you could imagine that we went through stages in which more information was needed from different sectors as biotechnology and new relationships were built.'*[11]

The emergence of formal and informal mechanisms of scanning also reveal the ways in which the companies supported the scanning behavior they wanted from its managers and employees. AGD set up an economic studies unit as a means of channelling macroeconomic and sectoral information to the Board and Managers. In Sidus, three areas were created: the legal and regulatory analysis, the sectoral and macroeconomic analysis to keep the Board and Managers abreast of the latest changes in the national economy, and competitors' strategic changes. The information produced by the legal and regulatory area, on the other hand, was widespread throughout the company to keep employees informed of recent changes in the legal and regulatory systems.

The importance of scanning the environment was reinforced by informal mechanisms at different levels of the organization. At AGD, the Board supported different levels of contacts with colleagues from other companies in different industries; trips abroad to visit other companies and institutions; and internal meetings between different levels of employees and experts in different fields as a way to achieve awareness of different topics significant for the company. At Sidus, on the other hand, internal workshops were a widespread practice at different levels of the company in which relevant aspects of the national economy or sectoral trends were discussed. Also employees from different levels of the structure had access to a wide variety of publications ranging from retail reports, sectoral, and macroeconomic reports among others.

8.4.1.5. A STRONG ORGANIZATIONAL IDENTITY

Why does the concept of organizational identity emerge as an important one in understanding how flexible firms adapt? And, what are the main features of this concept of organizational identity?

Albert and Whetten (1985) characterize organizational identity as a concept with three dimensions: firstly, what is considered central to the organization; secondly, what makes the organization distinctive; and finally, what is perceived by members to be an enduring or continuing feature linking the present organization with its past. At the heart of this definition are core values that make organizations act or react in a particular way and are the lenses through which managers interpret organization-level-issues (Gioia and Thomas 1996; Collins and Porras 2000).

The questions that emerge from the previous analysis are: What type of organizational identity do AGD and Sidus have? And how were AGD's and Sidus' organizational identities—through their set of core values—an enabler of their organizational flexibility?

Due to the critical role of the core values within the concept of organizational identity, the analysis of the evolution of AGD's and Sidus's values over successive generations seems more appropriate when seeking to determine whether or not AGD and Sidus were conservative about their values and how this influenced their organizational identity (Collins and Porras 2000); and whether those values acted as enablers of organizational flexibility or constraining factors.

The analysis of values of the firms has methodologically relied on previous works such as Webb et al. (1966) and Campbell et al. (1990). These authors have used discourses, speeches, and mission statements to analyze changes in organizational values over time.

In order to be able to understand how the identity of the company was forged and how values evolved during the tenures of successive generations, quotations that best illustrated the sharing of a particular value throughout time or the incorporation of new values into the companies were selected and coded. An intercoder reliability check with an independent coder gave a score of 81.8 percent.[12]

For each company, a set of values was revealed. At AGD, values such as customer orientation, constant benchmarking, keeping ahead of competitors, continuous learning, and agile decision-making processes were identified as values that had been rooted in the company since the first generation tenure of family members. Efficiency is a new value that was brought into the company in the 1990s.

At Sidus, on the other hand, values such as ethical behavior, innovation, the quality of products, fast decision-making, and differentiation from competitors in order to succeed were found to be ingrained throughout the two generations of family members. Efficiency and professionalism appeared as new values incorporated in the 1990s.

AGD and Sidus have been very conservative when it comes to their values. This is demonstrated by the fact that their values did not change throughout successive generations. However deeply rooted, the strong identities of both AGD and Sidus did not trap them in the rigidity of inertial forces. On the contrary, both companies were able to change quickly and smoothly without affecting their organizational core values. Therefore, how were AGD and Sidus able to cope with the relationship between strong identity and change?

Both companies incorporated values related to innovation and change (in AGD values such as agile decision-making, keeping ahead of competitors; in Sidus values such as innovation, and fast decision-making and differentiation from competitors in order to succeed). The incorporation of these values enabled them to undertake huge transformations without damaging their core identities and avoiding resistance to change.

On the other hand, the strong sense of identity gave the companies the organizational anchor they needed to be able to move forward and change (Gustafson and Reger 1995; Calori et al. 2000). By maintaining core values but changing their strategies, products, and processes, AGD and Sidus managed to transform themselves without creating internal turmoil. The interviews are revealing in this aspect: *'Over the 1990s the company has changed a lot. However, if you ask an employee whether they have felt the changes, they would say that they did not notice internal turmoil. They did not feel threatened by the changes. [. . .] However, if you compare our business now and ten years ago, you would think we were a different company.'*[13]

At Sidus, they stated, *'One amazing aspect of this company is that over the last decade or over the last thirteen years, Sidus has shifted its strategy completely but we still have the spirit of the old times, even similar traditions and stories. We did not lose the thread that links us with our past, although we look to the future—a wise combination that was fostered by the founders and their children.'*[14]

We therefore underlined the critical role of identity and the process of change in explaining organizational flexibility. The strong identity found at Sidus and AGD did not imply an inertial force against change and transformation. On the contrary, their strong organizational identity enhanced their organizational flexibility by providing the anchor they needed to change, try new things and take risks.

8.4.1.6. A BRIEF REMARK ON THE PATTERNS FOUND IN THE LESS-FLEXIBLE FIRMS

So far, we have aimed to highlight the different capabilities, either organizational or managerial, some firms such as AGD and Sidus, had built over time to be flexible and survive a highly uncertain context such as the Argentinian one. We cannot, however, forget the less flexible firms and understand why and how those firms were not able to achieve flexibility. Therefore, we will describe briefly some patterns found in the less flexible firms of this study.

The less flexible firms were not as heterogeneous as the flexible firms. On the contrary, those firms had a homogeneous management team both as regards its backgrounds and the way they saw the company and its environment. That homogeneity increased the degree to which the companies were embedded in the industry macroculture. Similarly, both Dersa and St Martin had higher levels of centralization and formalization of decision-making than their flexible counterparts. The board at both firms (mainly at St Martin) were centralizing strategic and operational decisions. The high level of centralization in the firms, as Fredrickson (1986: 284) highlights increases the probability that cognitive limitations of the top management will constrain the 'comprehensiveness of the strategic process'. Our interviewees have been clear about the lack of fresh ideas of strategic orientation in both Dersa and St Martin.

Regarding the levels of macroculture embeddedness, both companies demonstrated high levels of perceived similarity and connectedness over time. Benchmark was done against indigenous firms within their own industry. Besides, 79 percent of the interviewees at St Martin and 73 percent at Dersa pointed out that throughout time both companies were more connected in the sector by participating in professional associations. The consequence of the high levels of embeddedness found was that the strategic initiatives adopted by the companies were isomorphic with the predominant strategies in the sector.

Neither Dersa nor St Martin got formal structure for scanning nor had they developed the informal mechanisms of the flexible firms. The outcome of this lack of scanning behavior was that while flexible firms anticipated changes and seized opportunities, the less flexible firms simply could not.

The organizational identity of the less flexible firms was different from the flexible ones. At Dersa and St Martin identity was not a strong concept and values have been changing over time. Both companies, for example, rejected values from a previous generation that emphasized change and transformation.

These briefs comments on the less flexible firms let us know the main differences compared with their flexible counterparts. The less flexible firms had a highly homogeneous top team and therefore a low level of cognitive diversity that impeded them to be open to what the context had to say. They also were isomorphic to their own industry because of the high level of macroculture embeddedness. This level made the companies strategize in a similar fashion to other firms in the industry. The lack of mechanisms for scanning, on the other hand, made the firms miss opportunities in the market. The high level of centralization and formalization made the companies stifle decision-making and it was impossible for them to adapt their organization to what the market needed. Finally, the weak identity in both Dersa and St Martin did not help the companies find the anchor the organizations needed in times of rapid change and turmoil.

8.5. Conclusions

This chapter reports empirical findings into the determinants of organizational flexibility in two organizations in Argentina: one, Sidus, from the pharmaceutical industry, the other, AGD, from the edible oil industry, over the period 1989–99.

The combination of three related and relevant theories of organizational flexibility, innovativeness, and institutional theory raised a number of questions regarding patterns of adaptiveness. For example: How did flexible firms cope with institutional pressures? What are the new managerial capabilities needed in order to adapt? What organizational structural conditions better suit rapid adaptive responses?

The literature on environmental scanning and organizational identity were also incorporated because of the importance of these two issues in our data.

The questions raised highlighted two important methodological issues. Firstly, longitudinal data collection was necessary to explain the process of transformation of the firms. Secondly, a wide range of qualitative and quantitative methods—specified in the different literature analyzed—was necessary in order to study the determinants of organizational flexibility.

The results of the analysis of determinants of organizational flexibility are revealing in two aspects. Firstly, they give an insight into the process of adaptation in emerging countries; and, secondly, they reveal some of the characteristics of the content and process of being flexible.

The analysis of the determinants of organizational flexibility highlights firstly the way that companies in emerging countries and under environmental turmoil adapt. What stands out in this analysis are the differences between the empirical findings of this research and what is stated in the literature review. The main contrast with the literature review is the high level of formalization of decision-making found in the flexible firms in this study whereas the literature on organizational innovativeness and flexibility stresses the importance of low levels of formalization (Damanpour 1991; Webb and Pettigrew 1999). We have indicated that the difference in the formalization level emerged as a consequence of the economic stability and competitive pressures of the 1990s that made the companies under study formalize more those aspects that it was impossible to under the economic volatility of the 1980s.

The flexible firms analyzed in this study also had strong identities—whereas many researchers contend that firms with heterogeneous identities and sets of beliefs are able to develop flexible capabilities (Volberda 1999: 169).

However, the findings of this research should be considered to complement the literature rather than contradict it. Taking into consideration the fact that the empirical findings of the literature on organizational innovativeness and flexibility are based on cases or companies in developed countries, the outcome of this research fills a gap in the research into adaptive processes in emerging countries. Differences arise because Sidus and AGD are companies embedded in a particular national business environment different from a developed country such as the United States or the United Kingdom (Clark 2000; Whitley 2000).

Finally, the analysis of determinants of organizational flexibility also shows features of the process and content of being flexible. Achieving organizational flexibility is a long-term process.

The determinants of organizational flexibility did not emerge randomly but were triggered by different stimuli such as contextual pressure (which provoked awareness of the need to scan the environment or the low macroculture embeddedness) as a product of consciously planned and anticipatory action (in the case of the low degree of centralization and high degree of formalization of decision-making and the heterogeneity of the dominant coalition), or were unconsciously driven and the product of the internal dynamic of the family-business (as was the case with the sense of strong organizational identity).

There are some obvious limitations to the findings presented in this chapter. Firstly, we have used a particular set of indicators to select flexible firms. Further research needs to show whether a selection of other indicators would produce similar results regarding the sample of companies to be analyzed. Secondly, the social reality may vary significantly across other firms and industries, thus more case studies and analysis in other industries are needed. Studies comparing highly flexible and less flexible firms within and between sectors will give more insight into the determinants of organizational flexibility.

Notes

1. This refers to the successful doctoral dissertation, 'Determinants of Organisational Flexibility', by Andrés Hatum, September, 2002, Warwick Business School.
2. Interview with HR Manager in Sidus.
3. Interview with Finance Manager AGD.
4. The reliability score was calculated by the independent recoding of four interviews in each company (eight in total) of the set of questions related to the centralization and formalization process in AGD and Sidus. The recoding was then compared with the original coding and the percentage score calculated according to Huberman and Miles (1994) formulae: reliability = number of agreements/total number of agreements + disagreements.
5. Interview with HR Manager AGD.
6. Interview with Finance Manager Sidus.
7. Interview with HR Manager Sidus.
8. The question regarding the perceived similarity/dissimilarity was an open question, that means that the interviewees were free to answer with examples of companies

that they believed AGD/Sidus were using for benchmarking. The answers were coded into three categories of benchmarking for each company as shown in Tables 8.6 and 8.7. In the question regarding the level of connectedness, only two responses were allowed: yes or no.

The reliability score was calculated by the independent recoding of six interview transcripts in each company for the two questions the interviewees were asked.

9. Interview with HR Manager of Sidus.
10. Interview with Director of AGD.
11. Interview with President and CEO of Sidus.
12. The reliability score was calculated by an independent recoding of three speeches from each company (a total of six). The intercoder went through the different speeches and highlighted the quotations that it considered matched values of the coding.
13. Interview with AGD Director.
14. Interview with HR Manager Sidus.

References

Aaker, D. A. and Mascarenhas, B. (1984). 'The Need for Strategic Flexibility', *The Journal of Business Strategy*, 5(2): 74–82.

Abrahamson, E. and Fombrun, C. J. (1994). 'Macrocultures: Determinants and Consequences', *Academy of Management Review*, 19(4): 728–55.

Albert, S. and Whetten, D. A. (1985). 'Organizational identity', in L. L. Cummings and B. M. Staw (eds.), *Research in Organizational Behaviour*. Greenwich, CT: JAI Press Inc., Vol. 7, pp. 263–95.

Anderson, P. and Tushman, M. L. (1990). 'Technological Discontinuities and Dominant Designs: A Cyclical Model of Technological Change', *Administrative Science Quarterly*, 35: 604–33.

Astley, G. W. and Van de Ven, A. (1983). 'Central Perspectives and Debates in Organization Theory', *Administrative Science Quarterly*, 28: 245–73.

Bahrami, H. (1992). 'The Emerging Flexible Organization: Perspectives from Silicon Valley', *California Management Review*, 34(4): 33.

Beal, R. M. (2000). 'Competing Effectively: Environmental Scanning, Competitive Strategy, and Organizational Performance in Small Manufacturing Firms', *Journal of Small Business Management*, 38(1): 24–47.

Birkinshaw, J. (2000). 'Network Relationship Inside and Outside the Firm, and the Development of Capabilities', in J. Birkinshaw and J. Hagedoorn (eds.), *The Flexible Firm*. Oxford, UK: Oxford University Press, pp. 4–17.

Calori, R., Baden-Fuller, C., and Hunt, B. (2000). 'Managing Change at Novotel: Back to the Future', *Long Range Planning*, 33: 779–804.

Campbell, A., Devine, M., and Young, D. (1990). *A Sense of Mission*. London: Hutchinson Business Books Limited.

CEP (Centro de Estudios para la Produccion) (1998). Secretaria de Industria, Comercio y Mineria. Ministerio de Economia y Obras y Servicios Publicos. 'La inversion extranjera en la Argentina de los años 90. Tendencia y perspectivas.' Buenos Aires: CEP.

Chakravarthy, B. (1997). 'A New Strategic Framework for Coping with Turbulence', *Sloan Management Review*, 38(2): 69–82.

Child, J. (1972). 'Organizational Structure, Environment and Performance: The Role of Strategic Choice', *Sociology*, 6: 1–22.

—— (1997). 'Strategic Choice in the Analysis of Action, Structure, Organizations and Environment: Retrospect and Prospect', *Organization Studies*, 18(1): 43–76.

Clark, P. (2000). *Organisations in Action: Competition between Contexts*. London, UK: Routledge.

Collins, J. C. and Porras, J. I. (2000). *Built to Last*. Great Britain: Random House Business Books.

Cyert, R. M. and March, J. G. (1963). *A Behavioral Theory of the Firm*, Englewood Cliffs, NJ: Prentice-Hall.

D'Aveni, R. A. (1994). *Hyper-Competition*. New York: The Free Press.

Dacin, T. M., Goodstein, J., and Scott, R. W. (2002). 'Institutional Theory and Institutional Change: Introduction to the Special Research Forum', *Academy of Management Journal*, 45(1): 45–56.

—— Ventresca, M. J., and Beal, B. D. (1999). 'The Embeddedness or Organizations: Dialogue & Directions', *Journal of Management*, 25(3): 317–56.

Daft, R. (1978). 'A Dual-Core Model of Organizational Innovation', *Academy of Management Journal*, 21(2): 193–210.

—— Sormunen, J., and Parks, D. (1988). 'Chief Executive Scanning, Environmental Characteristics, and Company Performance: An Empirical Study', *Strategic Management Journal* 9: 123–39.

Damanpour, F. (1991). 'Organizational Innovation: A Meta-Analysis of Effects of Determinants and Moderators', *Academy of Management Journal*, 34(3): 555–613.

—— (1992). 'Organizational Size and Innovation', *Organization Studies*, 13(3): 375.

Di Maggio, P. J. and Powell, W. W. (1983). 'The Iron Cage Revisited: Institutional Isomorphism and Collective Rationality in Organizational Fields', *American Sociological Review*, 48: 147–60.

Dunning, J. H. (1993). *Multinational Enterprises and the Global Economy*. USA: Adison-Wesley Publishers Ltd.

Eisenhardt, K. M. (1989). 'Building Theories from Case Study Research', *Academy of Management Review* 14(4): 532–50.

—— and Tabrizi, B. N. (1995). 'Accelerating Adaptive Processes: Product Innovation in the Global Computer Industry', *Administrative Science Quarterly*, 40: 84–110.

Fredrickson, J. (1986). 'The Strategic Decision Process and Organizational Structure', *Academy of Management Review*, 11(2): 280–97.

Gioia, D. A. and Thomas, J. B. (1996). 'Identity, Image, and Issue Interpretation: Sensemaking during Strategic Change in Academia', *Administrative Science Quarterly*, 41: 370–403.

Gnyawali, D. R. and Madhavan, R. (2001). 'Cooperative Networks and Competitive Dynamics: A Structural Embeddedness Perspective', *Academy of Management Review*, 26(3): 431–45.

Grabowsky, H. G., Vernon, J. M., and Thomas, L. G. (1978). 'Estimating the Effects of Regulation on Innovation: An Hypercompetitive Comparative Analysis of the Pharmaceutical Industry', *The Journal of Law and Economics*, 21: 133–63.

Greenwood, R. and Hinings, C. R. (1996). 'Understanding Radical Organizational Change: Bringing Together the Old and the New Institutionalism', *Academy of Management Review*, 21: 1022–54.

Gustafson, L. T. and Reger, R. K. (1995). 'Using Organizational Identity to Achieve Stability and Change in High Velocity Environments', *Best Papers Proceedings*, Academy of Management Journal.

Hage, J. and Dewar, R. (1973). 'Elite Values versus Organizational Structure in Predicting Innovation', *Administrative Science Quarterly*, 18: 279–90.

Hambrick, D. C. (1989). 'Putting Top Managers Back in the Strategy Picture', *Strategic Management Journal*, 10: 5–15.

——and Mason, P. A. (1984). 'Upper Echelons: The Organization As a Reflection of Its Top Managers', *Academy of Management Review*, 9(2): 193–206.

Hannan, M. T. and Freeman, J. (1977). 'The Population Ecology of Organizations', *American Journal of Sociology*, 82(5): 929–64.

——(1984). 'Structural Inertia and Organizational Change', *American Sociological Review*, 49: 149–64.

Hardy, C. (2001). 'Researching Organizational Discourse', *International Studies of Management & Organization*, 31(5): 929–64.

Hoskisson, R. E., Eden, L., Lau, C. M., and Wright, M. (2000). 'Strategy in Emerging Economies', *Academy of Management Journal*, 43(3): 249–67.

Huberman, A. M. and Miles, M. B. (1994). 'Data Management and Analysis Methods', in N. K. Denzin and Y. Lincoln (eds.), *Handbook of Qualitative Research*. Great Britain: Sage Publisher Ltd, pp. 428–44.

Jonsson, S. (2000). 'Innovation in the Networked Firm: The Need to Develop New Types of Interface Competence', in J. Birkinshaw and P. Hagstrom (eds.), *The Flexible Firm*. Oxford, UK: Oxford University Press, 106–25.

Krijnen, H. C. (1979). 'The Flexible Firm', *Long Range Planning*, 12: 63–75.

Lewin, A. Y., Long, C. P. and Carrol, T. N. (1999). 'The Coevolution of New Organizational Forms', *Organization Science*, 10(5): 535–50.

——and Volberda, H. W. (1999). 'Prolegomena on Coevolution: A Framework for Research on Strategy and New Organizational Forms', *Organization Science*, 10(5): 519–34.

March, J. G. (1995). 'The Future, Disposable Organizations and the Rigidities of Imagination', *Organization*, 2(3/4): 427–40.

Miller, D. and Toulouse, J. M. (1998). 'Quasi-Rational Organizational Responses: Functional and Cognitive Sources of Strategic Simplicity', *Revue Canadienne De Sciences De L'Administration*, 15(3): 230–44.

Naumes, W. and Naumes, M. J. (1999). *The Art and Craft of Case Writing*. USA: Sage Publications Inc.

Oliver, C. (1991). 'Strategic Responses to Institutional Processes', *Academy of Management Review*, 16(1): 145–79.

——(1992). 'The Antecedents of Deinstitutionalization', *Organization Studies*, 13(4): 563–88.

Overholt, M. H. (1997). 'Flexible Organizations: Using Organizational Design As a Competitive Advantage', *Human Resources Planning*, 20(1): 22–32.

Pettigrew, A. M. (1972). 'Information Control As a Power Resource', *Sociology*, 187–92.

—— (1985). *The Awakening Giant*. Great Britain: Basil Blackwell Ltd.

—— (1990). 'Longitudinal Field Research on Change: Theory and Practice', *Organization Science*, 1(3): 267–92.

—— (1992). 'On Studying Managerial Elites', *Strategic Management Journal*, 13: 163–82.

—— and Whipp, R. (1991). *Managing Change for Competitive Success*. Great Britain: Blackwell Oxford.

—— and Whittington R. (2003). 'Complementarities in Action: Organizational Change and Performance in BP and Uniliver 1985–2002', in A. M. Pettigrew et al. (eds.), Chapter 8 in *Innovative forms of Organizing*. London: Sage Publications, pp. 173–207.

Pfeffer, J. and Salancik, G. R. (1978). *The External Control of Organizations*. New York: Harper & Row.

Pitcher, P. and Smith, A. D. (2001). 'Top Management Team Heterogeneity: Personality, Power and Proxies', *Organization Science*, 12(1): 1–18.

Regner, P. (2000). 'Strategy in the Periphery: The Role of External Linkages in Strategy Creation', in J. Birkinshaw and J. Hagedoorn (eds.), *The Flexible Firm*. Oxford: Oxford University Press, pp. 82–106.

Robertson, T. S. and Wind, Y. (1983). 'Organizational Cosmopolitanism and Innovativeness', *Academy of Management Journal*, 26(2): 332–38.

Rosembloom, R. S. (2000). 'Leadership, Capabilities, and Technological Change: The Transformation of NCR in the Electronic Era', *Strategic Management Journal*, 21 (Special Issue): 1083–1103.

Slappender, C. (1996). 'Perspectives on Innovation in Organizations', *Organization Studies*, 17(1): 107–29.

Smith, K. G. and Grimm, C. M. (1987). 'Environmental Variation, Strategic Change and Firm Performance: A Study of Railroad Deregulation', *Strategic Management Journal*, 8: 363–76.

Teece, D., Pisano, G., and Shuen, A. (1997). 'Dynamic Capabilities and Strategic Management', *Strategic Management Journal*, 18(7): 509–33.

Tushman, M. L. and Smith, W. (2001). 'Technological Change, Ambidextrous Organizations and Organizational Evolution', *Companion to Organizations*, Baum, J.A.C.—USA: Blackwell Publishers.

Tomlinson, R. C. (1976). 'OR, Organisational Design and Adaptivity', *OMEGA*, 4(5): 527–37.

Toulan, O. N. and Guillen, M. F. (1997). 'Beneath the Surface: The Impact of Radical Economic Reforms on the Outward Orientation of Argentinian and Mendozan Firms, 1989–1995', *Journal of Latin American Studies*, 29: 395–418.

Van de Ven, A. (1986). 'Central Problems in the Management of Innovation', *Management Science*, 32(5): 590–607.

—— and Poole, M. S. (1995). 'Explaining Development and Change in Hypercompetit', *Academy of Management Review*, 20(3): 510–40.

—— Polley, D. E., Garud, R., and Venkataraman, S. (1999). *The Innovation Journey*, Oxford, UK: Oxford University Press.

Volberda, H. W. (1996). 'Toward the Flexible Form: How to Remain Vital in Hypercompetitive Environments', *Organization Science*, 7(4): 359–74.

Volberda, H. W. (1999). *Building the Flexible Firm*. Oxford, UK: Oxford University Press.

Webb, D. L. and Pettigrew, A. M. (1999). 'The Temporal Development of Strategy: Patterns in the U.K. Insurance Industry', *Organization Science*, 10(5).

Webb, E., Campbell, D. T., Schwartz, R. D., and Sechrest, L. (1966). *Unobstrusive Measures*. Chicago, IL: Rand McNally & Company.

Whitley, R. (2000). *Divergent Capitalism: The Social Structuring and Change of Business Systems*. Oxford, UK: Oxford University Press.

Wiersema, M. F. and Bantel, K. A. (1992). 'Top Management Team Demography and Corporate Strategic Change', *Academy of Management Journal*, 35(1): 91–121.

Part III

Competitiveness of Firms from Selected Countries

9

Corporate Strategies of Business Groups in the Wake of Competitive Shocks: Lessons from Argentina

*Eduardo Fracchia and Luiz F. Mesquita**

A growing body of literature has been concerned with the behavior and performance of business groups—that is conglomerates of legally independent companies operating in multiple markets but bound by financial and informal ties (Khanna and Rivkin 2001)—in the wake of 'market liberalization policy reforms' (e.g. Ghemawat and Kennedy 1999; Khanna and Palepu 1999, 2000*a*; Toulan 2002; Carrera et al. 2003). Such reforms—also known as *competitive shocks* (Ghemawat and Kennedy 1999: 847)—occurred across many emerging economies around the world as of the late 1980s, and most especially across Latin American countries, such as Argentina, Brazil, Chile, Colombia, Mexico, and Peru (Sachs and Warner 1995; Toulan 2002: 552); such shocks involved both 'external' reforms, such as liberalization of foreign trade and Foreign Domestic Investments, as well as 'internal' reforms, such as liberalization of financial, inputs, and commodities markets (Ghemawat and Kennedy 1999).

As these reforms caused shifts in microeconomic conditions, they enhanced competition among firms (Ghemawat and Kennedy 1999), and as a result, both the performance and behavior of business groups have been observed to change (e.g. Khanna and Palepu 1999; Carrera et al. 2003). For example,

* Corresponding author

The authors are thankful for comments and suggestions by Patricia Friedrich, Robert Grosse, and seminar participants at the 'Can Latin American Firms Compete' conference, at the Thunderbird, Garvin School of International Management, Glendale, AZ. We are also grateful for the suggestions by Management Research editor Prof. Isabel Gutierrez and two generous reviewers of Management Research. (From Management Research: the *Journal of the IberoAmerican Academy of Management* 4(2): 81–98. Copyright © 2006 by M.E. Sharpe, Inc. Reprinted with permission). The authors also thankfully acknowledge support from the IAE School of Business of Austral University, Argentina.

Khanna and Palepu (2000*a*) found an association between greater levels of firm diversification and decreases in firm performance in Chile. They found that firms above a high threshold of diversification still had higher performance, but observed that as the business landscape became more competitive this threshold increased leading fewer and fewer firms to find it advantageous to pursue greater levels of diversification. Studies relating competitive shocks to business behavior and performance in India (Khanna and Palepu 2000*b*), Poland (Ghemawat and Kennedy 1999), and Latin America (Gonçalves 1991; Bisang 1996; Kosacoff and Porta 1997; Peres 1998) seem to validate these precepts. In Argentina, market liberalization reforms seem to have impelled firms to decrease corporate portfolios. The logic is that these firms would focus resources on competition within fewer business domains (Carrera et al. 2003), increase internationalization levels to increase the scale efficiencies of remaining businesses (Toulan 2002; Carrera et al. 2003), and reduce levels of vertical integration, given their access to more scale efficient operations and supply in a foreign trade-liberated environment (Toulan 2002).

Despite the scholarly advances mentioned above, we still seem to lack a full understanding of the effects of such competitive shocks on business groups. For example, Carrera et al. (2003) point out that not all business groups respond similarly to such competitive shocks: while many business groups do seem to be inclined to decrease their levels of product diversification and concomitantly increase their levels of internationalization in such conditions, several others seem to delay strategy changes significantly, whereas still others even behave in strikingly opposite ways, such as increasing their corporate scope and/or ignoring foreign market opportunities. In light of this paradox, we ask: if competitive shocks create the conditions for business groups to reduce corporate scope and increase their levels of internationalization, what factors are associated with firms *adopting or not* such strategy changes?

We believe responding to this question is an important scholarly endeavor for at least three reasons. First, conspicuous business groups from emerging economies across the globe have grown to become fierce competitors in global markets.[1] Thus, understanding their specific indigenous management practices used to overcome specific emerging market difficulties is an important step to our understanding of how they grow to compete globally. Second, business groups represent a large portion of GDPs of many Latin American countries (Bisang 1996), and their existence as well as their strategic behavior must be understood, if we are to more thoroughly grasp economic and business patterns of development in these environments. Third, current 'western' management literature seems to theoretically explain well why groups could reduce their corporate portfolios and increase internationalization in the wake of competitive shocks, but largely overlooks why some of these firms strategically take diverse approaches to corporate strategy; in this regard, our study enables us to refine such theories and expand our scholarly knowledge of the business group phenomenon.

Thus, to respond to the question above, we contrast the predictions established in the literature with the observed strategic response by business groups in Argentina (henceforth ABGs) in the period of 1991 through 2001, that is, the decade following this country's reforms. As such, we validate some of the existing theories, but most importantly, *induct* new theories so as to explain why some of the firms behave in ways which seem to defy established hypotheses. Specifically, we find that, on the average, ABGs did change their strategies in the aftermath of the competitive shock of the early 1990s according to established literature (i.e. they reduced product/market diversification levels and increased internationalization levels). We find from our observations, however, that such 'averages' hide more detailed nuances which enable us to enrich existing theory. Specifically, we find that specific market factors, resource path dependency as well as management decision-making styles are also likely to moderate the likelihood that firms will behave or not as hypothesized. Together, the variances in these three sets of factors affect corporate behavior, and the resulting pattern of corporate responses turns out to be a much richer pattern of varying grays as opposed to being a monotonous black and white picture.

In the following sections, we review conventional theoretical precepts and environmental conditions that help explain the appearance and growth of business groups in twentieth-century Argentina; we follow with an empirical analysis and then review findings. We conclude by exploring implications for theory and practice.

9.1. Theoretical Background

9.1.1. *The Appearance and Growth of Business Groups in Argentina*

The appearance and growth of large Argentinian groups seem to follow closely two waves of developmental policy reforms implemented in that country: 'import substitution' and the 'Washington consensus'. 'Import substitution' represents an industrialization movement—common across most of the developing world in the twentieth-century—trying to counter the effects of mass poverty. The motivation was that less developed countries believed they would be unable to benefit from international trade with their richer counterparts because their economies relied primarily on commodity agricultural and mineral activities. As such, they would not be subject to the same potential for technological shifts and increases in productivity and income *per capta* as the industrialized economies of their richer counterparts (Bruton 1998).[2] Thus, governments centralized developmental efforts, as opposed to letting market forces take their course; they also encouraged industrialization by sponsoring imports of capital goods through exchange rate manipulations and direct subsidies (Hirschman 1967), as well as by squeezing investment capital away from agriculture. To protect the nascent consumer goods industry from foreign competition, governments also closed the country for trade by implementing a series of tariffs, import licenses, quotas, and exchange controls (Bruton 1998: 908).

In Argentina, import substitution was especially significant during Juan Peron's presidency in the 1950s (Carrera et al. 2003: 34). Peron's government controlled and even owned large sectors of the economy, leading investments in areas such as roads, energy, telecommunications, and even real estate; such investments were escorted by a lax monetary policy with heavily financed social benefits (Carrera et al. 2003: 32). Peron also retracted Argentina from foreign-trade, with populist slogans of national sovereignty (Lewis 1992; Kosacoff 1993).

Such policies favored the rise of several large and powerful business groups (Acevedo, Basualdo, and Khavisse 1990; Guillen 2000; Carrera et al. 2003), especially where the protection of some of the economic sectors allowed local firms to seek more stable cash flows into unrelated markets with favored government supply contracts (Lewis 1992) and market monopolies (Bisang 1996).[3] Favored contracting schema were offered to selected firms in sectors such as construction, services, aluminum, and petrochemicals (Carrera et al. 2003).

Although 'import substitution' was believed to 'jump start' the economy, it on the other hand distorted relative prices and resulted in greater uncertainty for private investments as a whole. This situation was exacerbated by the lack of solid market institutions and intermediaries as well as functional judicial systems. For example, without an independent audit industry, Argentinian investors did not have access to appropriate disclosure of corporate investment information (Carrera et al. 2003: 34). Moreover, with weak or inexistent market intermediaries—such as analysts, investment bankers, securities agencies, and skilled-labor procurement—capital and skilled labor were difficult to find (Acevedo et al. 1990; Carrera et al. 2003). Also, Argentina's characteristically slow judicial system, often suspicious of favored political connections (Salvadores 2002; Mesquita 2003)[4] created investment uncertainties as investors become wary of transacting parties holding up their end of the bargain (Carrera et al. 2003). As a result, investment capital, skilled-labor, and secured supply contracts were at a premium.

These distortions created even more fertile ground for business groups to flourish. As Khanna and Palepu (1997) explain, in economies characterized by failures in products, capital and labor markets, and absence of market intermediaries, business groups are said to have a competitive advantage (see also Kock and Guillen 2001). Specifically, as buyers and sellers in these markets are members of the same group, they have superior information and executive decision-making capabilities (Leff 1976; Hoskisson et al. 2000). Thus they are able to more quickly agree on transfer price matters related to the relocation of tangible resources such as capital (Myers and Majluf 1984; la Porta et al. 1997), and intangible resources such as seasoned labor skills (Khanna and Palepu 1997), and as a result, more quickly cease upon entrepreneurial opportunities (Hoshi 1994; Chang and Hong 2000). Sluggish judicial systems also helped business groups, as these firms had stronger business connections and political ties (Khanna and Palepu 1999, 2000a), which gave individual group members advantages over stand-alone competitors in events involving judicial disputes (Acevedo et al. 1990; Carrera et al. 2003). Foreign trade-related distortions too helped the growth of business groups. Specifically, as import substitution policies favored local firms, foreigners needed to partner with business groups to market their goods locally (Lewis 1992; Guillen 2000). Even where foreigners were permitted direct entry, partnering with locals provided access to seasoned managers who were able to navigate through the maze of economic and business uncertainties, build the required relationships, and deal with government bureaucracies. As business groups were in a unique position to match market-access permissions and local managerial expertise with foreign capital and technology, they diversified even further to exploit new entry opportunities in a genuine rent-seeking mode.

Import substitution policies did not ease problems of poverty, however. In fact, they created major distortions, resulted in the misuse of country resources and concentrated wealth in the hands of a few. Investment rates and growth in imports-substitution in Argentina lagged behind those of most other countries (Bruton 1998: 915). The disappointment, similar to that felt across Latin American countries following similar policies, along with the success of countries such as Taiwan and South Korea, which otherwise structured economies based on minimal government and export orientations, veered the attention of Argentinians toward the so-called 'Washington Consensus' (Kucynski and Williamson 2003). The 'consensus' encapsulated the received wisdom of the time on the most urgent reforms that Latin America needed to adopt to promote economic growth. Such reforms, summarized in a ten-item list of market-oriented recommendations, included liberalization of trade, foreign investment, interest rates, and financial markets, as well as the promotion of privatization, market deregulation, and security in property rights. This new political economy led to a different competitive landscape, with minimum government, trade-open market forces, and subsidy-free investments and exports.

Argentina embraced the consensus wholeheartedly (Mussa 2002). Its government enacted the reforms based on three main drivers: financial stability, freer foreign trade, and minimal government. In regard to the first, with the newly independent central bank, Argentina finally launched a stable monetary policy, one that was independent of political bickering and interventions; the local currency was anchored at par to the US dollar, ending decades of money printing irresponsibility. Without the muddling of inflation, information on financial markets improved substantially, attracting venture capitalists and foreign investors. Firms could finally have more abundant access to cash, foresee the long run, and devise product-market oriented strategies (Bisang 1996; Kosacoff and Porta 1997). Second, Argentina opened its market for freer trade by reducing some of its import tariffs for selected goods and also joining the *Mercosur*, a customs union with neighboring Brazil, Paraguay, and Uruguay. The massive inflow of imported goods meant stiffer competition, making product markets more transparent (Kosacoff 1999). Third, the Argentinian government backed off from its business ventures (Carrera et al. 2003) by privatizing and or deregulating state monopolies such as oil, telecommunications, electricity, gas, water, subways, and ports, as well as ridding itself of money losing companies, such as Aerolineas Argentinas, two television channels, steel and petrochemical firms, hotels, and even race tracks. Reregulating the economy for its own sake was exchanged for the invisible hand of market friendly rules.

Such competitive shock resulted in incentives for ABGs to change their old approach to doing business. Specifically, business groups had incentives to both decrease the scope of their business portfolios (i.e. decrease their levels of product/market diversification) and increase their levels of internationalization (i.e. increase the number of international markets they operate in). The rationales are as follows. First, with internal market liberalization reforms, and the resulting enhancement of competitive conditions, business groups observe both a decrease in the marginal gains of each business unit as well as an increase in the related costs to assigning more resources to compete in each business (Khanna and Palepu 1999, 2000*a*; Carrera et al. 2003). Also, as Carrera et al. (2003) and Ghemawat and Kennedy (1999) point out, with the resulting increase in the transparency in market regulation, business groups would observe a decrease in the potential value they create as largely integrated conglomerates.

Second, with 'external liberalization' policy shifts, the government established a more transparent set of rules that allowed not only foreign firms to increase direct investments and to control resources in the local market, but also local firms to make investments abroad (Sachs and Warner 1995; Guillen 2000). Thus, with such policy shifts, business groups had at least two strong reasons to expand internationally. First, by entering foreign markets they would be better equipped to establish a multi-market contact with foreign firms that are now able to compete in the local market. As multi-market contact scholars point out, by competing across several geographical markets firms reduce the level of competitive intensity in individual markets by inducing competitors to refrain from attacking each other, an effect known as 'mutual forbearance' (Barnett 1993; Gimeno and Woo 1996; Gimeno and Jeong 2001). Second, as Toulan (2002) and Sachs and Warner (1995) explain, in more competitive market conditions, several firms may decide to expand the scale efficiencies of selected business units by expanding internationally. With greater scale efficiency, they would be able to more efficiently compete against multinationals entering the local market.

In sum, with internal and external liberalization policies, one would expect business groups to both decrease product/market scope, and increase internationalization levels. However, it does not appear that all business groups in Argentina behaved as such. Indeed Carrera et al. (2003) point out that, although there existed a trend for such strategy changes in Argentina, many business groups either ignored such market changes or even behaved in strikingly opposite ways, increasing their portfolios while maintaining a focus on domestic markets. To investigate the factors behind such corporate strategy behavior, we implemented an empirical analysis to experiment with possible factors associated with this 'altered' behavior, as well as to help better refine such existing theoretical expectations in regard to business group corporate strategies in the wake of competitive shocks. In the following section, we lay out our study in detail.

9.1.2. Theory Building Process—An Inductive Approach

Our investigative initiative on the behavior of business groups in the wake of competitive shocks follows an inductive approach. Specifically, we extend previously revised theory frameworks by exploring the overtime effect of various factors on the behavior of sets of business groups that follow particular types of corporate strategies. As such, our approach has several advantages. First, based on our longitudinal analysis, we can observe the overtime effect of the adoption vis-à-vis non-adoption of expected strategies by business groups and consequently theorize about the factors that influence (i.e. speed, delay, or even impede) the adoption of new corporate strategies. Thus, we are sensitive to distortions and lags observed in the shift of corporate strategies, as opposed to simply observing parametric changes in corporate strategies (Eisenhardt 1989). A similar approach was adopted by Ghemawat and Kennedy (1999). Moreover, by further evaluating lags for or even abstinence from the adoption of new strategies with motives pointed out by managers in a survey (which we explain below), we are able to further refine the theories above. Theory building based on case analysis is a common resource used by scholars, (e.g. Miles and Huberman 1984; Strauss 1987; Eisenhardt 1989; Yin 1995). Finally, several similarities and differences can be identified across the conduct of different business groups. In sum, by clustering firms following similar corporate strategies and comparing the factors and conditions affecting these firms' behaviors across these clusters, we are able to refine a new theoretical framework for the behavior of business groups.

Our following an inductive process does not mean our study is a-theoretical to begin with. As shown in Figure 9.1, the main effects of policy changes on corporate strategies of business groups—illustrated in the arrow from 'B' to 'C'—is moderated by three sets of factors which are known to affect strategic decision making in most modern corporations: industry structure, resources and capabilities, and firm-specific decision-making processes (see factors 'D', 'E', and 'F' respectively, in Figure 9.1). The first set of these factors relates to the evolution of market structure for particular sectors of the economy (Caves and Porter 1978; Gerosky 1995); these factors include aspects such as governmental policies and privatization, size and conditions of the demand, as well as entry by foreigners (Johanson and Vahlne 1977; Dunning 1988; Hill, Hwang, and Kim 1990). We expect these factors are unlikely to uniformly affect all sectors of the economy; we expect instead these effects to vary in terms of degree and speed. Thus, the increase in market forces shaping competitive behavior is at least likely to take longer in some sectors vis-à-vis others (Caves and Porter 1978), and consequently, business groups are likely to be more sensitive to redefining their corporate objectives in accordance to the conditions under which such changes occur. For example, some business groups may decide to increase their corporate scope (as opposed to focussing it) to benefitted from government sell out of companies at bargain prices (Achi et al. 1998; Kock and Guillen 2001).

The second set of factors relates to how resources and capabilities being developed by business groups influence their strategic response. We specifically look at the path dependency of capabilities (Dierickx and Cool 1989; Teece, Pisano, and Shuen 1997; Eisenhardt and Martin 2000) and firm characteristics, such as experience (Johanson and Vahlne 1977), capabilities which impact production costs (Dunning 1988) and other intangible resources such as brand names, processes, and reputation (Barney 1991) and abilities to conduct 'political strategies' and 'government relationships' (Baron 1995; Hillman and Hitt 1999; Henisz 2003). We believe these sets of factors affect decisions to change corporate strategies because resource investments are subject to noteworthy path dependency, which means that some business groups may be subject to a larger degree of corporate inertia than others. We expect that those firms working on a more focussed business portfolio centered on a given set of core competencies will be less likely to pursue highly diversified portfolios.

The third component in our framework relates to the mission and vision of top management teams, especially as it relates to decision-making style and attitude in regard to perception of risks (Johanson and Vahlne 1977), strategic goals, and hierarchical promotion based on technical competence versus heritage (Hill et al. 1990). As Harris, Martinez and Ward (1994) explain,

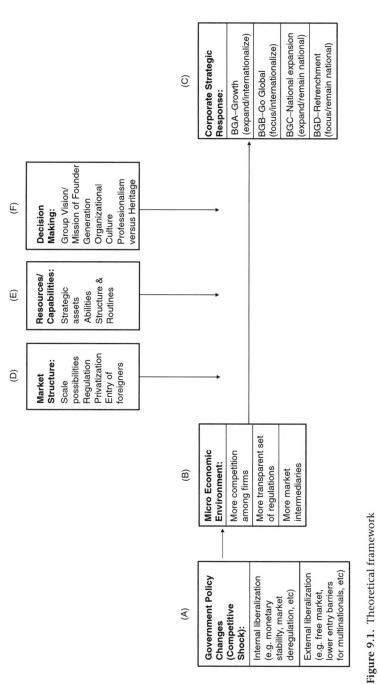

Figure 9.1. Theoretical framework

The figure contains the following boxes:

(A) **Government Policy Changes (Competitive Shock):**
Internal liberalization (e.g. monetary stability, market deregulation, etc)
External liberalization (e.g. free market, lower entry barriers for multinationals, etc)

(B) **Micro Economic Environment:**
More competition among firms
More transparent set of regulations
More market intermediaries

(D) **Market Structure:**
Scale possibilities
Regulation
Privatization
Entry of foreigners

(E) **Resources/ Capabilities:**
Strategic assets
Abilities
Structure & Routines

(F) **Decision Making:**
Group Vision/ Mission of Founder Generation
Organizational Culture
Professionalism versus Heritage

(C) **Corporate Strategic Response:**
BGA–Growth (expand/internationalize)
BGB–Go Global (focus/internationalize)
BGC–National expansion (expand/remain national)
BGD–Retrenchment (focus/remain national)

family firms' decision-making styles may include more conservative decisions, aimed at protecting family equity and tradition. Because ABGs usually evolve around the family (Carrera et al. 2003), we included this highly important perspective for understanding their decisions.

Despite our reliance on the above intuitively logical theoretical elements to explain alternative firm behaviors, our study remains intrinsically explorative in nature, where we rely upon a strong empirical study to refine well received theoretical frameworks on business groups.

9.2. Research Methods

9.2.1. *Sampling and Data Collection Method*

Our analysis was carried out on a sample of Argentinian business groups in the decade of 1991 through 2001. This setting offers an ideal opportunity for our analysis; specifically, the speed and breadth of the reforms implemented in Argentina provide a 'quasi-experimental setting' for a study of this magnitude (see Toulan 2002: 552). Moreover, in Argentina, early policy shifts began in the late 1980s, but gained significant momentum in the presidency of Menem, especially in 1990/1991, making this decade ideal for the study (see Carrera et al. 2003). In 1991, the government enacted the *Plan de Convertibilidad* (which pegged the local currency to the US dollar), and is thus considered by many as a symbolic year, representing a large process of change. We avoided including data for 2002 and beyond so as to exclude the business restructurings resulting from the Argentinian financial crash of that year.

We rely on several sources of information: we collected primary data through a survey with top managers of business groups and personal interviews with each of these managers. We also collected secondary data from the ministry of economy, company reports, and business press. As far as our survey is concerned, Figure 9.1 includes a list of the items in each of the three sets of factors that we believe are likely to influence the behavior of business groups (measured through a Likert scale of 1 to 7). The items on this list as well as our secondary database were used to guide our unstructured interviews. Our goal was to try and associate the corporate behavior of business groups in relation to the factors explored in the survey and interviews.

As far as the selection of business groups is concerned, we chose firms with an operational base in Argentina, a conglomerate-type organizational structure, and firms which were not founded nor acquired during the period of our study. Based on secondary data, and our own definition of groups above, we considered the firms listed in Table 9.1 to be business groups operating in Argentina in 1990, the year prior to our period of analysis.

Table 9.1. Argentinian business groups (1991–2001)

Argentine business groups (1991–12001)	Revenues, 1997 (source: CEPAL)
1 Aceitera General Dehza (A.G.D.)	n/a
2 Acindar	$601
3 Alpargatas	$422
4 Aluar	$655
5 Antelo	n/a
6 Arcor	$1,070
7 Astra	n/a
8 Avila*	n/a
9 Bago	$400
10 Bemberg (Quinsa)	$892
11 Bulgheroni	n/a
12 Bunge & Born	$1,340
13 Cartellone	$560
14 Clarin	$1,651
15 Eurnekian	n/a
16 Fortabat	$384
17 Galicia	n/a
18 Garovaglio & Zorraquin	$204
19 IRSA—Inversiones y Representaciones SA*	n/a
20 Isaura**	n/a
21 Karatex*	$134
22 La Nacion*	$179
23 Ledesma	$250
24 Mastellone Hermanos*	$681
25 Minetti***	n/a
26 Perez Companc	$1,621
27 Pescarmona	$658
28 Roberts	n/a
29 Roemmers*	$211
30 Roggio	$508
31 Roman	$120
32 Sancor Cooperativas Ltda.	$720
33 Sava—Gancia*	$200
34 Sidus	$200
35 Sociedad Comercial del Plata (SCP)	$360
36 SOCMA Americana SA	$2,170
37 Techint	$7,000
38 Velox/Disco	n/a

* We were unable to find sufficient secondary data on these groups—they were not interviewed

** These groups had been acquired by multinationals by 2001

After selecting the business groups, we identified our target respondents within each firm. We surveyed and interviewed twenty-five top managers who agreed to concede us conferences. Where the past CEO had been 'promoted' to chairman—a characteristic of succession in family-owned Argentinian business groups—we also interviewed this person. This approach enabled us to access historical information on the behavior of each firm within the decade under study. We contacted each respondent individually and personally;

Table 9.2. Sectors in which Argentinian business groups operated during the 1991–2001 period. Analysis includes only surveyed business groups

The table is a matrix listing, for each business group (rows), the sectors in which it operated (marked cells), together with product- and international-diversification indicators.

Business groups (rows): Astra, Acindar, AGD, Alpargatas, Aluar, Antelo, Arcor, Bagó, Bemberg, Bulgheroni, Bunge, Cartellone, Clarín, Eurnekian, Fortabat, Galicia, Garovaglio & Zorraquín, Ledesma, Perez Companc, Pescarmona, Roberts, Roggio, Román, Sancor, SCP, Sidus, Socma, Techint, Velox.

Sectors (columns) and column Total:

Sector	Total
Media and entertainment	4
Garbage disposal	4
Social and medicare services	4
Financial intermediation and services	9
Mail services	1
Transport related services (***)	4
Tellecomunication	4
Transportation and storage	10
Hotels and restaurants	1
Non-specialized retail sales	1
Construction	8
Drinking water	2
Electricity Utilities	7
Automotive & autoparts	2
Electronics and Information Technology	3
Domestic goods	1
Machinery	2
Iron and steel	2
Non-metal mineral products	2
Plastics / Glass	1
Petrochemicals	3
Chemicals (**)	2
Publishing and printing	1
Paper and paper products	5
Footwear	1
Textile	2
Beverages	3
Food	9
Oil and gas (*)	5
Mining and quarries	2
Fishing	2
Agriculture, cattle, hunting and forestry	16

Product Diversification and International Diversification indicators:

Group	Sectors 1991	Sectors 1996	Sectors 2001	Countries 1991	Countries 1996	Countries 2001
Astra	4	(x)	(x)	2	(x)	(x)
Acindar	2	2	2	2	2	3
AGD	2	3	4	9	18	21
Alpargatas	6	4	1	2	3	3
Aluar	3	3	3	5	11	13
Antelo	1	(x)	(x)	1	(x)	(x)
Arcor	5	5	4	11	20	29
Bagó	2	2	2	4	11	14
Bemberg	3	3	3	6	12	13
Bulgheroni	2	3	3	2	3	3
Bunge	6	4	4	7	14	16
Cartellone	3	5	4	5	7	4
Clarín	2	1	1	1	2	3
Eurnekian	2	5	4	3	3	2
Fortabat	1	1	1	3	6	4
Galicia	6	6	4	3	4	3
Garovaglio & Zorraquín	3	4	6	3	5	4
Ledesma	7	9	5	8	17	19
Perez Companc	5	8	7	5	12	15
Pescarmona	2	(x)	(x)	1	(x)	(x)
Roberts	3	7	4	2	4	4
Roggio	2	2	2	2	3	3
Román	4	2	4	4	6	5
Sancor	3	9	2	2	5	6
SCP	2	2	8	9	19	25
Sidus	3	9	7	3	13	16
Socma	6	8	4	9	19	27
Techint	3	7	6	3	9	12
Velox	3	4	4	3	9	12
Total (average)	3.379	4.346	3.615	4.31	8.96	10.4

Table 9.3. Business groups clustered upon their conduct during period 1990–2001

Internationalization	Diversification	
	'Related-constrained'/'unrelated'	'Focussed'/'related-linked'
Foreign markets	BGA (growth)—business groups following a related-linked or unrelated diversification strategy, coupled with an international expansion strategy. Business groups which clearly followed such a strategy include Perez Companc, Pescarmona, Socma, Techint, Velox	BGB (go global)—firms following a focussed or related-constrained diversification strategy, coupled with an international expansion strategy. Business groups which clearly followed such a strategy include AGD, Aluar, Arcor, Bago, Bemberg, Bunge, Sidus
Domestic markets	BGC (national expansion)—firms following a related-linked or unrelated diversification strategy coupled with a national market strategy (i.e. retrenchment from international market opportunities). Business groups which clearly followed such a strategy include Bulgheroni, Cartellone, Garovaglio and Zorraquin, Ledesma, Roggio, Sociedad Commercial del Plata	BGD (retrenchment)—firms following a focussed or related-constrained diversification strategy, coupled with an national market strategy (i.e. retrenchment from international market opportunities) include Alpargatas, Clarin, Eurnekian, Fortabat, Galicia, Sancor, Roman

each of them completed the questionnaire during our interview. The firms we succeeded finding sufficient secondary information about are marked in Table 9.1, and listed in Table 9.2. The groups we interviewed are listed in Table 9.3. As shown in Table 9.2, some groups are more focussed and often have satellite interests evolving around this core. For example, Clarin, with a core business on news media, also had interests in paper products (used to supply its newspaper), as well as radio and television interests. Similarly, Galicia, with a corporate focus on 'banking' had interests in traditional banking services, as well as management of pension funds.

9.2.2. Analysis

In our analysis, we first performed a one way ANOVA to investigate the average behaviors of business groups, vis-à-vis our reviewed literature; we then clustered business groups to perform case analyses and explore alternative patterns of corporate strategy behavior. In the ANOVA statistical analysis (Neter et al. 1996), we perform an F-test to evaluate whether the group means on the dependent variable (i.e. both the number of sectors and the number of foreign markets in which business groups competed) differed across time (i.e. we considered firms in 1991 as one sample and firms in 2001 as another sample).

As far as the clustering of business groups is concerned, related case analyses, and theory induction are concerned, we adhered to the more strict procedures prescribed in Eisenhardt (1989), involving theoretical sampling techniques as well as within and cross cluster comparisons. Thus, to cluster business groups into sub-samples of 'cases', we used theoretical sampling, as opposed to statistical sampling. Theoretical sampling is based on theoretical reasoning, as opposed to statistical reasoning (Gleiser and Strauss 1967). Our goal is to replicate reality and exceptions to existing theory so as to allow for fine grained analysis and enable emergent theory. Moreover, theoretical sampling enables the selection of polar types (e.g. firms going international versus firms focussing on national markets). In such cases, random selection is less of a concern, and rather extreme cases are often preferred (Pettigrew 1988; Eisenhardt 1989). Further, we also selected multiple cases within each category to allow findings to be replicated within the category and substantiate our theorizing (Gleiser and Strauss 1967; Eisenhardt and Bourgeois 1988; Gersick 1988; Eisenhardt 1989).

Based on these methodological perspectives, and interviews with CEOs, we clustered the twenty-five interviewed *grupos* into four sets, based on their corporate strategies in the aftermath of the competitive shock (i.e. the type of product/market as well geographical diversification). We then related each cluster to the survey responses managers provided, in regard to market structure, resources and capabilities, and decision-making style. More specifically, we classified business groups following Rumelt's classification (1974) of product/market diversification. In this classification, firms followed either one of the following strategies: 'focussed' (at least 95% of revenues from main business), 'related-constrained' (at least 70% of revenues from main business, where business units were interrelated), 'related-linked' (less than 70% of revenues from main business, where business units not necessarily related), and 'unrelated' (revenues dispersed across several, often unrelated, business units). Based on this, we gathered business groups following focussed or related-constrained strategies in one group, and related-linked or unrelated product in another. Additionally, we also classified firms on whether they had expanded internationally or retrenched into national markets throughout the 1991–2001 period. The resulting four clusters of business groups and their respective strategies (clusters A, B, C, and D) are summarized in Table 9.3. CEOs interviewed confirmed our classification.

Based on this classification, we then associated these corporate strategies with factors which managers considered influential in their decision making for choosing such strategies throughout the 1990s. In such theory induction process, we followed guidelines from Eisenhardt (1989) and Eisenhardt and Bourgouis (1988) in performing within cluster and across cluster comparisons. Within cluster comparisons allow us to identify common patterns of behavior.

However, analyses limited to within group often lead to biases due to limited data (Gilovich, Griffin, and Kahneman 2002); at the same time, we seen the risk of disconfirming evidence, due to statistical powerlessness (Nisbett and Ross 1980; Gilovich et al. 2002). Thus, by also highlighting the differences across clusters, we are more likely to look for more striking differences and similarities (Eisenhardt and Bourgeois 1988; Eisenhardt 1989), break simplistic frames and go beyond initial impressions, thus improving the likelihood of accurate and reliable theory development, that is, theory which has a closer fit to reality. Moreover, cross cluster analyses can enhance the probability that we capture the novel findings which may be indicated by the data (Eisenhardt and Bourgeois 1988; Eisenhardt 1989).

The final goal was to arrive at a systematization of the process of responses to the competitive shocks, distinguishing common patterns among each of the four groups which enable us to theorize about some of the characteristics of the phenomenon and more useful aspects for the analysis of the strategic response patterns. We believe our findings do not allow us to generalize the strategic response patterns for all circumstances, but enable us to gather useful elements for analysis in equivalent circumstances occurring in other countries.

9.3. Results and Discussion

9.3.1. *Average Levels of Diversification*

As indicated in Table 9.2, on a general level, the degree of product/market diversification observed in 2001 for all business groups was statistically similar to that observed in 1991. The average number of product/markets in which business groups operated was 3.4 in 1991 and 3.6 in 2001. Our observation of Bonferroni adjustment for alpha 0.05 (Gill 2001) resulted insignificant. Based on these findings, we proceeded with a more detailed analysis. Specifically, we compared product/market diversification levels from 1991 through 1996 and from 1996 through 2001. We observed that on average business groups first increased their portfolio sizes substantially early in the decade (1991–6), and only then decreased such portfolios. Specifically, business groups increased their average portfolio to 4.3 sectors in 1996. This analysis indicates that, initially, on average, business groups took advantage of the privatization process through which the government sold out its businesses; based on our analysis of secondary data, the observed focus was on sectors such as telecommunications, utilities, oil transportation, and garbage disposal services. The retraction of corporate portfolios, later in the decade (1996–2001) is consistent with the theoretical perspectives explored in our review.

9.3.2. *Average Levels of Internationalization*

Throughout the 1990s, numerous business groups expanded internationally (see Table 9.2). The average number of foreign markets per business group increased 142 percent in the period, going from 4.3 markets in 1990 to 10.4 in 2001. We found that this increase was consistent throughout the period 1991–2001. This process included exports, alliances, and direct investments. We also observed through interviews that business groups with no prior international experience had a tendency to focus on regional neighboring markets with similar cultural environments. The business groups with previous international (mostly regional) experience expanded beyond Latin America, on the other hand.

Results from our interviews indicate that the prevailing factor leading business groups to expand geographically was the new competitive landscape in the home market, as well as their need to expand scale efficiencies for given business lines. The first of these factors, the entry of multinationals into Argentina, had been especially motivated as part of a larger scale integrated entry into the wider Free Trade area shared with neighboring Brazil, Paraguay, and Uruguay. Moreover, such entry of multinationals into the local market was also fueled by the prospects of a rapidly growing consumer market, that is, the combination of scale and market growth enabled foreign multinationals to rapidly move down the learning curve. In our survey, 80 percent of the business groups indicated they perceived their businesses had been affected directly or indirectly by the entry of multinationals one way or another. Given this aggressive entry of foreigners, a few business groups (e.g. Isaura and Minetti) disappeared, as their response choice to the competitive shock was to 'merge' with (i.e. be acquired by) such multinationals. This threat of takeover was considerably large at the time, given the new competitive landscape and the lack of financial resources necessary for sustainable growth.

The second of these factors, the increase in scale efficiencies, was highlighted by interviewees as a key factor for international expansion. Particularly, managers pointed out that their firms set sail to foreign markets as a bold response to the saturation of their domestic market. They also pointed out that such expansion was seen as a favorable action related to the seeking of reputation for their companies within the region, of learning new business practices through the alliances forged with regional partners, as well as risk diversification.

In sum, we initially find that on average business groups behaved more or less according to expectations set out in the extant literature. Particularly, as the competitive intensity increased, later in the decade, the corporate portfolios of business groups tended to decrease (albeit they had increased early in the decade, as a result of government sell outs). We also observed that business groups increased their internationalization levels, according to expectations. As shown in Table 9.3, however, these changes are not uniform across the sample; in fact such average changes hide important details which are crucial for a complete picture of corporate behavior under scenarios of competitive shocks, a fact which we will explore next.

9.3.3. *Clusters of Strategic Responses to the Argentinian Competitive Shock*

In order to understand the factors leading to different strategic responses, we proceed with 'case analyses', that is analyses of clusters of ABGs that present similar strategic behavior, using an inductive approach to refine our theoretical model. We summarize survey responses in Table 9.4, and analyze the resulting implications in the section below.

9.3.4. *Cluster BGA: Greater Importance to Market Forces As Well As Tangible Resources*

9.3.4.1. MARKETS

These firms adopted a very aggressive and proactive response to the shock by diversifying their business portfolios even further (i.e. across several economic sectors), and by expanding internationally, on a regional and even global scale. The sectors these firms expanded into were mostly government-related; that is, their entry spanned out of their taking advantage of the privatization process in sectors where they had been key government suppliers. For example, the group Perez Companc had been a key supplier for government firms in areas such as telecommunications and energy. During the privatization process, the group moved in to acquire firms in these sectors. They also expected their rent-seeking behavior would result in success due to more favorable regulatory measures. Moreover, these firms also expanded abroad in search of minimum efficient scales, as well as their establishing a 'mutual forbearance' approach to geographical diversification (i.e. their domestic markets were attacked by multinationals, leading them to expand abroad).

9.3.4.2. RESOURCES AND CAPABILITIES

These firms had a considerable amount of financial slack which proved to be extremely flexible and crucial during the process of government privatization. These firms also attempted to include services in their businesses, aiming at improving value added, which was further enhanced by their reputation in the local market and other valuable intangible resources such as strong brand names. These firms also leveraged some flexibility and speediness in assembling work groups for managing new entrepreneurial projects across markets. They also benefitted from their capabilities to extract synergies

Table 9.4. Importance of selected factors on corporate strategies of Argentinian business groups

Our corporate strategy choices (i.e. choice of product / market and geographical diversification) were mostly influenced by the following factors …	BGA	BGB	BGC	BGD
1. Markets:				
Our need for Minimum Efficient Scale				
Our desire to concentrate in our traditional sectors/domestic market				
The increasing rivalry in domestic market				
The entry of multinationals in domestic market				
The deflation of retail prices in domestic market				
The favorable regulatory environment in particular sectors we chose to enter				
The privatization of 'government owned companies' in sectors we chose to enter				
2. Resources & Capabilities				
a. Resources				
Our financial slack				
Our reputation (e.g. reputable name)				
The strategic investments we made previous to the competitive shock				
Our strategic slack of human resources				
b. Capabilities				
Our ability to set up new teams and replicate local experience in other markets				
Our ability to coordinate and transfer know how to subsidiaries				
Our competencies for managing quality and service across businesses				
Our overall cost advantage (further ahead in experience curve)				
Our technological know-how				
Our flexibility for spinning off unwanted business units				
Our ability to create synergies among seemingly unrelated businesses				
c. 'External' capabilities				
Our abilities to scan the environment to find new product/market opportunities				
Our dense relationships with governments				
Our ability to negotiate and take advantage of privatization				
Our abilities to set up and maintain long term alliances				
3. Overall decision-making approach				
Based on our long term vision, we acted in anticipation to market changes				
Our decision making is often based on intensive international benchmarking				
a. Family characteristics				
Promotion in our company is based on competence as opposed to heritage				
Decisions always promote 'unity'—we strive for 'no-conflict' among family members				
Decisions strongly rely on parentage figure of CEO				
Decisions are based on commitment to founding mission				
b. Organizational history				
We consider acquisitions more of a 'market opportunity' than 'access to intangibles'				
Decisions always consider deep relationships with government				

■ Extremely important — on Likert scale from 1 to 7, average response was between 5 and 7
▨ Reasonably important — on Likert scale from 1 to 7, average response was between 3 and 5
☐ Not so important — on Likert scale from 1 to 7, average response was between 1 and 3

among seemingly unrelated businesses (parenting advantage), a long history of strong and close relationship with the government, and the history of irreversible resource commitments prior to the competitive shock.

9.3.4.3. DECISION-MAKING APPROACH

These firms had developed long-term vision for their businesses, aiming at fast growth, as well as acting in anticipation of market changes. They were mostly proactive in professionalizing the firm, avoiding, for example, staffing top managerial positions simply based on family affiliation.

In sum, the key component behind the strategic response of BGA firms to the competitive shock related to its vast amounts of financial slack, which as an easily transferable resource, could be used in alternative businesses as well as in their international expansion. Moreover, their intangible resources were also deemed to be transferable across product and geographical markets, as they had developed a keen sense of entrepreneurship and abilities to create relationships among businesses. Given their abundance of financial slack, these firms took advantage of the general government sell out. Because this group had grown out of closer relationships with the government in past decades, they took advantage given their experience in the sectors where they had contracts. Thus, their corporate behavior emerged out of the favorable conditions in the sell out. Those firms who entered once government dominated market domains were successful, given that they met with favorable legislation as well as unmet demand for those types of services. Such groups amassed a larger amount of assets which enabled them to face market adversities in the new future. Their entry into these sectors seemed driven by their rent-seeking motives, that is profitable acquisition opportunities in seemingly unrelated markets.

9.3.5. *Cluster BGB: Greater Importance to Tangible and Intangible Resources*

9.3.5.1. MARKETS

These firms sought to position themselves in economic sectors subject to major economies of scale, especially in international markets. Their emphasis relied on sectors related to natural resources. The fact that foreign multinationals had entered their domestic market was also an important factor for them to expand abroad. Based on our interviews, we found that the fiercest competition occurred with opponents from the Mercosur area, that is, the regional free market trade agreement Argentina shares with neighboring Brazil, Paraguay, and Uruguay.

9.3.5.2. RESOURCES AND CAPABILITIES

These firms watched their processes and capabilities very closely, aiming at improving efficiencies. This process also relied heavily on their strategically managing their slack of qualified human resources so as to enable their long-term resource-dependence growth strategies. They also relied on strong brand names, like the BGAs, but were much more eager to aggressively pursue inter-subsidiary knowledge-transfer. Differently from the BGAs, they also had historically been away from government relationships. Their resources were also less flexible than those of BGAs (i.e. not so much financial slack, but considerably stronger competencies to manage quality and services across subsidiaries and technological know-how), while their production processes were capital intensive. These firms aggressively transformed engineering and technological resources into marketable products, based on a commitment to grow and gain scale economies. Firms had made major and irreversible resource commitments prior to the competitive shock, and their sense of path dependency represented a major factor for their keeping the course.

9.3.5.3. DECISION-MAKING APPROACH

Aggressive benchmarking against international competitors, especially in Marketing. Families characterized by strong unity, with strong technological and cultural inheritance from founder. Strong commitment to historical businesses.

In sum, the major component behind the strategic response of BGB to the competitive shock was its historical commitment to development of core competencies through process improvement. This central component relates to their overall cost advantage, especially with their decision to focus their businesses. In competing against multinationals, BGB firms strove to concentrate within sectors, making sure their expansion was always into related businesses and products that could benefit from corporate core competencies. For firms in this group, scale economies were obtained not only in physical assets but also in functional activities, such as advertising, sales, distribution, and research and development. These firms always had a keen sense of synergies across business units, seeking positions across complementary businesses. These firms based their flexible competitiveness on their own organizational capabilities and flexible human resources practices.

9.3.6. *Cluster BGC: Greater Importance to Market Forces and Family-Based Decision-Making Style*

9.3.6.1. MARKETS

These firms sought to expand product diversification, benefiting from bargain government privatization of firms. They positioned new businesses in economic sectors that were less sensible to major macroeconomic cycles and less attractive to multinationals, facts which gave them a quasi-monopoly. Their diversification was also driven by their need to expand away from sectors which were subject to increasing levels of rivalry, and also the consequent deflation of retail prices in the domestic market.

9.3.6.2. RESOURCES AND CAPABILITIES

These firms usually were smaller in size, and did not depend as heavily on scale economies. They managed their relationships with the government with strong zeal, and had a keen attraction to government sell outs; coupled with these relationships, these groups had developed a refined sense of environmental scanning, which enabled them to perceive profitable opportunities ahead of others. They were known for being skilled in implementing quality and service processes. Its main abilities were related to their flexibility and negotiation skills. Such capabilities were generic in the sense that they could be applied across businesses in seemingly unrelated sectors, and thus enabled more diversified approaches to corporate strategies.

9.3.6.3. DECISION-MAKING APPROACH

These firms were marked by a strong paternalistic influence from the founder, who was seen as a strong leadership figure. Family was united by strong paternalistic leadership. The history of the firms in this cluster are characterized by a strong sense of opportunity when dealing with acquisitions; such business sense often times led these groups to buying and selling businesses, often shuffling its business portfolio.

In sum, these firms diversified business portfolios, especially given their choice of sectors highly subjected to strong swings of economic cycles. Their relationship with the government was usually associated with the management of public services as well as infrastructure investments, such as roads and bridges. The investments by the government have mainly explained the direction business groups within cluster C took in regard to their diversification and scope. Such an intrinsic relationship between business and government is akin to those existing in many other Latin American countries; it works as a key factor behind the strategic response by these firms. Their decision to diversify does not run against efficient resource management.

9.3.7. *Cluster BGD: Greater Importance to Family-Based Decision-Making Style*

9.3.7.1. MARKETS

These firms sought to position themselves in economic sectors subject to economic cycles, mainly in the domestic market, where they had historically had a quasi-monopolistic presence. Unlike the situation faced by BGCs, often times the sectors where BGDs operated were the target of entry of multinationals, who brought in a wealth of capital and technologies. Before the entry of multinationals, these business groups represented leadership and growth in their main sectors, where they had grown a respectable amount of reputation with local clients. Their historical association with given sectors gave them a deeper understanding of possible gaps of efficiencies and regulatory issues, a knowledge which they believed gave them an advantage over new entrants from abroad. All in all, these firms relied mostly on what they refer to as 'market power', that is, the upholding of assets considered by the founder to be in 'strategic' sectors.

9.3.7.2. RESOURCES AND CAPABILITIES

Similarly to BGA and BGC firms, BGD firms maintained a good relationship with the government, although they lacked other resources that could be leveraged as sources of competitive advantage against incoming foreigners. Their main resources were physical assets, reputation, and experience in operating in regulated sectors.

9.3.7.3. DECISION-MAKING APPROACH

The key characteristic of this group was its strong, hands-on leadership by the CEO, with the technical expertise of human resources being less important than family unity and heritage in regard to staffing businesses leadership positions. Guided by strong top leadership and commitment to the mission of the founding father, these firms often perceived organizational change not to be a favorable process.

In sum, the main characteristic of these ABGs, based upon our survey and interviewing, is that they had a strong influence of paternalistic style of decision-making. They associated 'going international' with 'high risk', and retrenched into traditional ways of doing business.

9.3.8. *Why Business Groups Pursue Distinct Corporate Strategies under Competitive Shocks*

The above analysis of clusters of similar corporate behavior allows us to refine the often simplistic expectation that business groups would reduce corporate scope and increase internationalization levels in the wake of competitive shocks. Specifically, based on our analysis, we observe that groups BGB and BGD pursued a focussed or related-constrained corporate strategy, consistent with previous theoretical predictions. However, this was not true of groups BGA and BGC. These groups increased their corporate portfolios, as opposed to decreasing them. Based on our surveying and interviewing we find that these groups pursued such a strategy because of two main reasons. Primarily, these groups took advantage of major government sell out opportunities. The speed and depth of change was strong in these particular sectors, but these changes did not lead firms to refocus their corporate scope, as conventional theory would have us expect. Second, it was not clear to them that market intermediaries had materialized over the course of the decade. In fact, it seems that market deregulation would take longer to affect the appearance of such intermediaries. Thus, our evidence indicates that business groups redefine their strategic objectives in accordance with the developmental stage of the microeconomic conditions surrounding their business across particular sectors, that is, albeit one may assume macroeconomic conditions to affect all sectors more or less the same, it seems that this is not concomitant with reality. In a competitive shock, firms may take advantage of new rent-seeking opportunities and diversify, as opposed to spin-off businesses and focus their corporate scope. We conclude that business group reactions to competitive shocks actually depend on variances across sectors in (a) the extent and speed of changes in microeconomic and competitive conditions, (b) the characteristics of the reform agenda imposed by the government, and (c) the consequences of the competitive shocks to the particular microeconomic environments, such as the emergence of market intermediaries.

As far as international expansion is concerned, based on the above, we observe that groups BGA and BGB pursued a corporate strategy which included international diversification, an approach which is consistent with previous theoretical predictions. However, this was not true of groups BGC and BGD. These groups refrained from going international. In the wake of a competitive shock, the expected reaction would be for firms to be involved in international ventures, especially as they focus their corporate portfolios (i.e. as they reduce the number of businesses they are in); their going international would enable them to achieve greater scale efficiencies as well as establish a multipoint competitive position vis-à-vis incoming foreign competitors. Based on our surveying and interviewing we find that the BGC and BGD groups pursued such a 'nationally focussed' strategy because of three main reasons. First, many of these groups (especially those in the BGC cluster) focussed in sectors which were less attractive to multinationals, and less subject to macroeconomic ups and downs, a condition which gave them a quasi-monopoly in the sector. Thus, we observe that such firms were not as enthused by multipoint competition prospects as were BGAs and BGBs. Second, firms in the BGC cluster also invested their tangible resources such as capital in increasing diversification levels, taking advantage of major government sell outs; thus, the opportunity that presented itself in the form of bargain acquisitions played a major role in their decisions. Third, the decision-making style of these groups, especially those in the BGD cluster, had a strong influence of paternalistic style of decision-making, and many of the groups retrenched in traditional ways of doing business. They saw going international as a high risk, and retrenched into traditional ways of doing business.

In sum, based on our analyses of clusters of business groups pursuing similar corporate strategies, we conclude that the conditions created by competitive shocks that would lead such firms to reduce corporate portfolios and increase internationalization, are moderated by (a) the speed and depth with which microeconomic conditions change across particular economic sectors, (b) the path dependency of core competencies tying business units of particular groups, as well as (c) the influence of paternalistic decision-making styles in the strategic future of given firms. Thus, rent-seeking behavior related to buying and selling firms that governments put for sale, during the competitive shock, arising from market deregulation (e.g. utilities), as well as delays in the appearance of market intermediaries help explain why some groups refrain from corporate reductions (e.g. BGAs). Additionally, the drive of given groups (e.g. BGBs) to tie individual business units with common core resources and capabilities give these groups a more focussed approach to corporate portfolios. Also, the drive of given families to pursue parentage reasons for strategic decision-making explain why given firms, such as BGDs, retrenched into their traditional niches, without bothering to change corporate strategies at all. When it comes to the international dimension, the speed and breadth of entry of international firms, as well as the search for greater scale economies, a key success factor in particular segments, also affected business groups differently. These facts help explain why some firms pursued international ventures (i.e. BGAs and BGBs) while others did not (i.e. BGCs and BGDs).

From what we could observe in our study, relationships with the government continue to play a major role in the success of certain business groups. Particularly in the more domestic clusters (i.e. BGC and BGD), firms often rely on access to privileged information, licenses, or any other form of preferential treatment. Thus, business groups often build and maintain a web of relationships which substitute for the absence of a more formal institutional structure. This would allow us to predict that until the pro-market economic reforms do not consolidate into a more stable and predictable situation, local business groups will continue to thrive. They have a privileged position, given their more protected situation vis-à-vis new entrants.

Although these strategic responses to the Argentinian competitive shock, as discussed above, seem to follow a well-knit theoretical logic, not all strategy approaches resulted 'successful'. While some groups acted as 'paragons' (Khanna and Yafeh 2005) of economic efficiency, by adapting to the new competitive landscape, others continued their 'parasite' behavior, with an exclusive focus on siphoning value from the economy in a typical 'rent-seeking' behavior. For example, firms in the BGD and BGC clusters suffered considerably with the competitive shock, especially those which were in sectors targeted by multinationals (e.g. Alpargatas and Galicia). Their greater focus on paternalistic styles of management, made them insensible to changes in their sectors. By 2001, Galicia, Alpargatas, Cartellone, Garrovaglio and Zorraquin, Ledesma, Roggio, Bulgheroni, and Roman had either disappeared or were under severe financial strain.

9.4. Concluding Remarks

In this chapter we have investigated the corporate strategies of business groups in the wake of competitive shocks, that is, the market-liberalization policy changes that heighten the importance of market forces in microeconomic competitive conditions. Conventional theory has it that these changes would create incentives for business groups to reduce the scope of their corporate portfolios as well as increase their internationalization levels (e.g. Khanna and Palepu 1999, 2000a; Guillen 2000; Chang and Choi 2001; Kock and Guillen 2001; Carrera et al. 2003). However, we observe that firms have not always behaved in such ways; in fact, many of them have behaved in exactly opposite ways. Thus, we further our analyses to specific clusters of strategic behavior and induct new theoretical refinements that more logically help explain such paradoxes. Specifically, we propose that strategic behavior is a function of not only the varying speed and breadth of changes in microeconomic conditions set out by competitive shocks across different segments, but also by the path dependency of resources and capabilities as well as management decision-making style, such as paternalistic patterns of decision-making as well as aversion to risks involved in unknown ventures, such as internationalization.

Our study brings significant implications for theory and practice. Earlier studies had also investigated Business Groups in Latin America (e.g. Khanna and Palepu 1999, 2000a; Toulan 2002; Carrera et al. 2003). We help supplement this literature. Specifically, Carrera et al. (2003) concluded that the pattern of strategic behavior depended upon the previous diversification policy companies were pursuing. In this article, we expand their analysis and propose that not all groups will respond equally to competitive shocks. Their different responses are a function of at least three moderating factors. First, competitive shocks do not systematically affect all economic sectors and industries on an equal basis. Thus, groups will respond to competitive shocks depending on how extensive the impact of such shocks is in their sector. Specifically, we claim that in addition to corporate inertia, the central argument in Carrera et al. (2003), we expect to observe different patterns of business group strategic responses to competitive shocks depending on the environmental characteristics surrounding the businesses in which the group is positioned.

We also supplement traditional business group literature (e.g. Leff 1976; Hoshi, Kashyap, and Scharfstein 1991; Granovetter 1995; Guillen 2000;

Khanna and Palepu 2000a; Chang and Choi 2001; Kock and Guillen 2001) by responding to calls by Khanna and Yafeh (2005) for multi-theory perspectives on the phenomenon that help highlight both the 'paragon' and 'parasite' sides of business groups. Particularly, we find that looking at business groups as a bundle of path dependent resources and capabilities, as well as a place for family feuds to thrive important theory perspectives that help explain the business group phenomenon. Particularly, our case analyses unveil that the theory elements from these perspectives help moderate the influence of microeconomic conditions in the shaping of corporate strategies.

In general, we also understand from previous literature that product/market and geographical diversification are often seen as concomitant initiatives by the firms. The motives used for such diversification often have common elements. One would speculate whether such decisions are complementary or substitutes, sequential or simultaneous. Our study also sheds light on this issue. We corroborate predictions by Caves (1996) that 'studies that compare product-market and geographic international diversification across firms of varying sizes and maturities usually find positive correlations: given time and resources, a firm can exploit opportunities for diversifying in both directions, and the sorts of proprietary assets that support foreign investment are the same ones associated with related diversification. Thus, existing theory explains mostly the behavior of firms in the BGB cluster (i.e. product portfolio reduction and international expansion), whereas, based on interviews and our more segmented analysis in the 1991–2001 time period, we see that the tendency of business groups in the BGA and BGC clusters would be to possibly migrate to the BGB condition.

Responses by business groups are also a function of these firms' resource investment patterns and endowments. For example, business groups clustered as BGBs had been following a related-constrained or even focussed corporate strategy. They had been developing intangible resources in the period anteceding the competitive shock. In the wake of the policy shifts, they did not decrease their corporate portfolios, as their portfolios were already focussed. The same can be said of business groups Sancor and Clarin (clustered in the BGD category). Moreover, decision-making styles also interfere with how a business group will react. For example, those firms clustered in the BGD group had 'paternalistic' structure as a major factor under consideration when establishing their corporate strategy. Therefore, it is no surprise these groups did not change their strategies nor behavior in the wake of the competitive shocks. Naturally, these were the groups that suffered the most with the new competitive environment (with the notable exception of Sancor and Clarin).

Our study also contributes to our understanding of the future of business groups, as emerging markets evolve. Particularly, the study of competitive shocks and the change of corporate strategy of business groups provide an opportunity to study disequilibrium adjustment processes. Very little work has been done, however, on the effects of competitive shocks on corporate strategies. In this chapter, we make a start at such analysis by examining the effects of Argentina's competitive shock on the corporate strategy of ABGs. As more data becomes available, the use of longer time series and more narrowly defined groups will allow finer grained analyses of post shock strategies. Such panel data would provide a major research opportunity for researchers of organization theory not only in Argentina, but also in other larger number of countries going through such competitive shocks.

The most important conclusion for practitioners and students is that although the competitive landscape may change substantially, motivated by new policies, the business groups adjust their strategies to adapt to the new environment in very distinct ways. In other words, growth in such environments is not just a stroke of luck but the result of careful deliberation and reasoning about how specific economic forces evolve in each sector, the right local and foreign contacts as well as resources and capabilities, which enable groups to navigate through the maze of conflicting policies. Business groups can be seen as strong and robust organizational forms devised by savvy entrepreneurs to cope with strong, dynamically changing forces. As a result, foreign firms are likely to succeed locally by maintaining local ties with government officials as well as potential alliance partners, especially as Argentina rebuilds its financial, democratic, and judicial institutions after its 2002 financial crisis; foreigners are also more likely to succeed if they pay attention to local market forces as well as indigenous management styles, especially when forecasting competitive behavior by local opponents.

As for limitations, our study ignores the independent effect of cultural variables such as kinship structures, inheritance customs, and work ethics (Fields 1995). Future research should explore whether the same cultural institutions could have different effects depending on the nature of inward and outward flows. Another perspective that merits attention is the exploration of whether the connection between development strategies and diversified business groups holds in the emerging markets in other important geographical places around the world, such as Eastern Europe, East Asia, and African countries.

Notes

1. A few recent examples from the popular press include Hyundai, the Korean automaker who has aggressively expanded into global markets and recently announced billion dollar investments in a new manufacturing plant in the United States (Economist 2005); AmBev (Companhia de Bebidas das Americas), a Brazilian company, who merged with Belgium's Interbrew, to form the world's largest brewer (Economist 2004a); and Cemex, a Mexican cement giant, who recently took over its main

American competitor, Southdown, and became the largest US cement producer (Economist 2004b).
2. Lewis (1955) and Bruton (1998) indicate that most ignored the potential for agricultural development and exports.
3. See also Amsden (1989) and Amsden and Hikino (1994).
4. Khanna and Yafeh (2005) point to Argentina with historical low ranking in matters of contract enforcement.

References

Acevedo, M., Basualdo, E. M., and Khavisse, M. (1990). *Quien es quien?: los duenos del poder economico (Argentina 1973–87)*. Buenos Aires.

Achi, Z., Boulas, C., Buchanan, I., Forteza, J., and Zappei, L. (1998). 'Conglomerates in Emerging Markets: Tigers or Dinosaurs?', *Strategy and business*, 11.

Amsden, A. H. (1989). *Asia's Next Giant: South Korea and Late Industrialization*. New York: Oxford University Press.

—— and Hikino, T. (1994). 'Project Execution Capability, Organizational Know-How and Conglomerate Growth in Late Industrialization', *Industrial and Corporate Change*, 3: 111–47.

Barnett, W. P. (1993). 'Strategic Deterrence Among Multipoint Competition', *Industrial and Corporate Change*, 2: 249–78.

Barney, J. B. (1991). 'Firm Resources and Sustained Competitive Advantage', *Journal of Management*, 17: 99–120.

Baron, D. P. (1995). 'Integrated Strategies: Market and Nonmarket Components', *California Management Review*, 37(2): 47–65.

Bisang, R. (1996). 'Perfil tecno-productivo de los grupos economicos en la industria Argentina', in J. Katz (ed.), *Los cambios de la organizacion industrial Argentina*. Buenos Aires: Editora Alianza.

Bruton, H. J. (1998). 'A Reconsideration of Import Substitution', *Journal of Economic Literature*, 36(June): 903–36.

Carrera, A., Mesquita, L., Perkins, G., and Vassolo, R. (2003). 'Business Groups and Their Corporate Strategies in the Argentinian Roller Coaster of Competitive and Anti-Competitive Shocks', *Academy of Management Executive*, 17(3): 32–44.

Caves, R. E. and Porter, M. (1978). 'Market Structure, Oligopoly, and Stability of Market Shares', *Journal of Industrial Economics*, 26: 289–313.

Chang, S. J. and Hong, J. (2000). 'Economic Performance of Group-Affiliated Companies in Korea: Intragroup Resource Sharing and Internal Business Transactions', *Academy of Management Journal*, 43: 429–48.

—— and Choi, U. (2001). 'Strategy, Structure and Performance of Korean Business Groups', *Journal of Industrial Economics*, 37: 141–58.

Dierickx, I. and Cool, K. (1989). 'Asset Stock Accumulation and Sustainability of Competitive Advantage', *Management Science*, 35: 554–71.

Dunning, J. H. (1988). 'The Eclectic Paradigm of International Production: A Restatement and Some Possible Extensions', *Journal of International Business Studies*, 19(1): 1–32.

Economist (2004a). 'Beer: An Awful Lot of Brewing in Brazil', *The Economist*.

—— (2004b). 'Cement: One Giant Leap for Mexico', *The Economist*.

—— (2005). 'Hyundai Motor: A Better Drive', *The Economist.*

Eisenhardt, K. M. and Bourgeois, L. J. (1988). 'Politics of Strategic Decision Making in High Velocity Environments: Toward a Mid-Range Theory', *Academy of Management Journal*, 31: 737–70.

—— (1989). 'Building Theories from Case Study Research', *Academy of Management Review*, 14(4): 532–50.

—— and Martin, J. A. (2000). 'Dynamic Capabilities: What Are They?', *Strategic Management Journal*, 21: 1105–21.

Fields, K. J. (1995). *Enterprise and the State in Korea and Taiwan.* Ithaca, NY: Cornell University Press.

Gerosky, P. A. (1995). 'What do we know about entry', *International Journal of Industrial Organization*, 13: 421–40.

Gersick, C. (1988). 'Time and Transition in Work Teams: Towards a New Model of Group Development', *Academy of Management Journal*, 31: 9–41.

Ghemawat, P. and Kennedy, R. E. (1999). 'Competitive Shocks and Industrial Structure: The Case of Polish Manufacturing', *International Journal of Industrial Organization*, 17(6): 847–67.

Gill, J. (2001). *Generalized Linear Models: A Unified Approach.* Thousand Oaks, CA: Sage.

Gilovich, T., Griffin, D., and Kahneman, D. (eds.) (2002). *Heuristics and Biases: The Psychology of Intuitive Judgement.* Cambridge, MA: Cambridge University Press.

Gimeno, J. and Woo, C. Y. (1996). 'Hypercompetition in a Multi-Market Environment: The Role of Strategic Similarity and Multi-Market Contact in Competitive De-Escalation', *Organization Science*, 7: 32–341.

—— and Jeong, E. (2001). 'Multimarket Contact: Meaning and Measurement at Multiple Levels of Analysis', in J. A. C. Baum and H. R. Greve (eds.), *Multiunit Organization and Multimarket Strategy: Advances in Strategic Management*, Vol. 18. Oxford, UK: JAI Press.

Gleiser, B. and Strauss, A. (1967). *The Discovery of Grounded Theory: Strategies of Qualitative Research.* London: Wiedenfeld and Nicholson.

Gonçalves, R. (1991). 'Grupos economicos: uma analise conceitual e teorica', *Revista brasileira de economia, FGV*, 45(Out–Dez): 491–518.

Granovetter, M. S. (1995). 'Coase Revisited: Business Groups in the Modern Economy', *Industrial and Corporate Change*, 4: 93–130.

Guillen, M. F. (2000). 'Business Groups in Emerging Economies: A Resource-Based View', *Academy of Management Journal*, 43(3).

Harris, D. J., Martinez, I., and Ward, J. L. (1994). 'Is Strategy Different for the Family-Owned Business?', *Family Business Review*, 7(2).

Henisz, W. J. (2003). 'The Power of the Buckely and Casson Thesis: The Ability to Manage Institutional Idiosyncrasies', *Journal of International Business Studies*, 34: 173–84.

Hill, C. W. L., Hwang, P., and Kim, W. C. (1990). 'An Ecletic Theory of the Choices of International Entry Mode', *Strategic Management Journal*, 11: 117–28.

Hillman, A. J. and Hitt, M. A. (1999). 'Corporate Political Strategy Formulation: A Model of Approach, Participation, and Strategy Decisions', *Academy of Management Review*, 24(4): 825–42.

Hirschman, A. (1967). *Development Projects Observed*. Washington, DC: Brookings Institution.

Hoshi, T. (1994). 'The Economic Role of Corporate Grouping and the Main Bank System', in M. Aoki and H. Patrick (eds.), *The Japanese Main Bank System*, pp. 285–309. New York: Oxford University Press.

—— Kashyap, A., and Scharfstein, D. (1991). 'Corporate Structure, Liquidity, and Investment: Evidence from Japanese Industrial Groups', *Quarterly Journal of Economics*, 106: 33–60.

Hoskisson, R. E., Eden, L., Lau, C. M., and Wright, M. (2000). 'Strategy in Emerging Economies', *Academy of Management Journal*, 43(3): 249–67.

Johanson, J. and Vahlne, J.-E. (1977). 'The Internationalization Process of the Firm: A Model of Knowledge Development and Increasing Foreign Market Commitments', *Journal of International Business Studies*, 8(1): 23–32.

Khanna, T. and Palepu, K. (1997). 'Why Focussed Strategies May Be Wrong for Emerging Markets', *Harvard Business Review*, 75(4): 41–50.

Khanna, T. and Palepu, K. (1999). 'Policy Shocks, Market Intermediaries and Corporate Strategy: The Evolution of Business Groups in Chile and India', *Journal of Economies and Management Strategy*, 8: 271–310.

—— —— (2000a). 'The Future of Business Groups in Emerging Markets: Long Run Evidence from Chile', *Academy of Management Journal*, 43(3): 268–85.

—— —— (2000b). 'Is Group Membership Profitable in Emerging Markets?', An Analysis of Diversified Indian Business Groups', *Journal of Finance*, 55: 867–91.

—— and Rivkin, J. (2001). 'Estimating the Performance Effects of Business Groups in Emerging Markets', *Strategic Management Journal*, 22: 45–74.

—— and Yafeh, Y. (2005). 'Business Groups in Emerging Markets: Paragons or Parasites?', *Center for Economic Policy Research*, Discussion paper No. 5208 (September).

Kock, C. J. and Guillen, M. F. (2001). 'Strategy and Structure in Developing Countries: Business Groups As an Evolutionary Response to Opportunities for Unrelated Diversification', *Industrial and Corporate Change*, 10: 77–113.

Kosacoff, B. (1993). *La industria Argentina: un proceso de reestructuracion desarticulada*. Buenos Aires: Alianza.

—— (1999). 'El caso argentino', in D. Chudnovsky, B. Kosacoff, and A. Lopez (eds.), *Las multinacionales latinoamericanas: sus estrategias en el mundo globalizado*. Buenos Aires: Fondo de Cultura Economica.

—— and Porta, F. (1997). *La inversion extranjera directa en la industria manufacturera Argentina: tendencias y estrategias recientes*. Buenos Aires: Alianza.

Kucynski, P.-P. and Williamson, J. (2003). *After the Washington Consensus*. Washington, DC: Institute of International Economics.

la Porta, R., Lopez de Silanes, F., Schleifer, A., and Vishny, A. (1997). 'Legal Determinants of External Finance', *Journal of Finance*, 52: 1131–50.

Leff, N. (1976). 'Capital Markets in Less Developed Countries: The Group Principal', in R. McKinnon (ed.), *Money and Finance in Economic Growth and Development*. New York: Marcel Dekker.

Lewis, P. H. (1992). *The Crisis of Argentinian Capitalism*. Chapel Hill, NC: University of North Carolina Press.

Lewis, W. A. (1955). *The Theory of Economic Growth*. London: George Allen and Unwin.

Mesquita, L. (2003). Rationality As The Basis for a New Institutional Environment: Argentina's Former Presidential Candidate Ricardo Lopez Murphy', *Academy of Management Executive*, 17(3): 44–50.

Miles, M. and Huberman, A. M. (1984). *Qualitative Data Analysis*. Beverly Hills, CA: Sage.

Mussa, M. (2002). *Argentina and the Fund: From Triumph to Tragedy*. Washington, DC: Institute for International Economics.

Myers, S. C. and Majluf, N. S. (1984). 'Corporate Financing and Investment Decisions When Firms Have Information that Investors Do Not Have', *Journal of Financial Economics*, 13: 187–221.

Neter, J., Kutner, M. H., Nachtschiem, C. J., and Wasserman, W. (1996). *Applied Linear Statistical Models*. Chicago, IL: Irwin.

Nisbett, R. and Ross, L. (1980). *Human Inference: Strategies and Shortcomings of Social Judgement*. Englewood Cliffs, NJ: Prentice Hall.

Peres, W. (ed.) (1998). Las grandes empresas y grupos industriales latinoamericanos. Expansion y desafios en la era de la apertura y la globalizacion: Siglo Veintiuno Editores.

Pettigrew, A. M. (1988). *Longitudinal Field Research on Change: Theory and Practice*. Paper presented at the National Science Foundation Conference on Longitudinal Research Methods in Organizations, Austin, TX.

Rumelt, R. P. (1974). *Strategy, Structure and Economic Performance*. Boston, MA: Harvard Business School Press.

Sachs, J. and Warner, A. (1995). *Economic Reform and the Process of Global Integration*.

Salvadores, O. F. (2002). *Lopez Murphy: razon o demagogia*. Buenos Aires: Planeta.

Strauss, A. (1987). *Qualitative Analysis of Social Scientists*. Cambridge, England: Cambridge University Press.

Teece, D., Pisano, G., and Shuen, A. (1997). 'Dynamic Capabilities and Strategic Management', *Strategic Management Journal*, 18(7): 509–33.

Toulan, O. N. (2002). 'The Impact of Market Liberalization on Vertical Scope: The Case of Argentina', *Strategic Management Journal*, 23(6): 551–60.

Yin, R. C. (1995). *Case Study Research: Design and Methods*. Sage publications, Inc.

10

Brazilian Firms and the Challenge of Competitiveness

Thomaz Wood Jr and Miguel P. Caldas

10.1. Introduction

Brazil is the fifth largest country in the world in terms of territory and population, the 13th economy in GDP and the ninth based on purchasing power parity (The Economist 2005). However, its commercial ranking is disappointing: Brazil is in 31st place among the world's exporters, a position considered to be far beneath its economy's size and diversity.

Foreign investment always had a strong presence in Brazil. However, the great advance in economic internationalization, in terms of both foreign presence in the country and the presence of Brazilian firms abroad, took place after the 'Plano Real', a comprehensive plan for inflation reduction and economic stabilization, implemented in the first half of the 1990s.

In terms of foreign presence in the country, both the privatization process and the acquisition and consolidation frenzy of the 1990s changed the Brazilian corporate landscape. On the other hand, as it concerns the outbound internationalization, few Brazilian firms set out on international ventures. Most of them, when faced with the threat of reduced trade barriers, seem to have been content to react and adapt to the new competitive context, focussing their efforts on being competitive enough to keep their position in the domestic market.

Lussieu da Silva (2003), in a broad study of the internationalization of Brazilian firms, summarized the landscape that followed the changes in the economy: firstly, a few industries concentrate the majority of the country's exports, which tend to be focussed on agricultural and industrial commodities

The authors would like to thank Sergio Goldbaum for his invaluable indications as to the macroeconomic dimension of competitiveness, as well as Luiz Mesquita and Robert Grosse for their support and assistance through earlier versions of this article.

(based on natural resources and capital-intensive industries); secondly, the internationalization of Brazilian firms is still chiefly commercial, with an early trend toward internationalized production; thirdly, several Brazilian firms that went international seem to have sought culturally and geographically close environments, with development levels similar to or lower than that of Brazil (see López 1999); and finally, only a very small group of firms of assorted size is at more advanced internationalization stages.

As a result, the presence of Brazilian transnational firms at an internationalization stage is still modest. Indeed, several rankings reflect this condition. The Financial Times 2005 listing of the 500 largest companies in the world includes only five Brazilian firms. In the UNCTAD—United Nations Conference on Trade and Development—ranking of developing countries' transnational companies, published in 2000, only five of fifty firms were Brazilian (UNCTAD 2000: 82–83). At AmericaEconomia magazine's ranking of multinational firms operating in Latin America, only one Brazilian firm is listed among the top thirty (AmericaEconomia 2005: 121).

Several authors (e.g. Porter 1990; Austin 2002; Coutinho and Ferraz 2002) have discussed Brazil's difficulties to compete internationally at the country level or at industry level, but the firm level has been little explored.[1] In this analysis, we seek to fill this gap. Our objective is to depict the current situation and explore how Brazilian firms could compete in the global market.

In order to accomplish this objective the chapter is organized as follows: in Section 10.2, after this introduction, we define competitiveness and present a portrait of competitiveness in Brazil; in Section 10.3 we speculate whether and how Brazilian firms may be able to compete internationally; and in Section 10.4 we summarize our arguments and present our concluding comments.

10.2. Competitiveness: Theory and Reality

10.2.1. *The Concept of Competitiveness*

Competitiveness may be defined as the ability of a system—country, industry, group of firms, or a specific firm—to operate successfully in a given business context (Coutinho and Ferraz 2002). Therefore, competitiveness at the country level comprehends its ability to compete internationally, obtaining sustainably superior performance as compared to other nations or regions. In turn, industry competitiveness has to do with the relative ability of a field of activities to be competitive on at least two dimensions: as compared to its peers in other countries, or as compared to other industries in the same geographic area. Finally, firm competitiveness may be defined as a firm's ability to operate successfully, in a continued and sustainable manner, as compared to its peers.

Coutinho and Ferraz (2002: 19–21) suggest that a system's competitive performance is conditioned by three sets of factors: systemic factors, structural factors, and firm-specific factors. Systemic factors are external to the firm's environment, but may have a direct bearing on the configuration of structural factors and on a firm's competitive strategy. They include macroeconomic, political and institutional, regulatory, infrastructural, social, regional, and international factors. Structural factors pertain to the industry in which a firm operates and are those factors it can partly influence. They include the general features of consumer markets, the general industrial configuration in which the firm operates, and the competition model. Firm-specific factors comprehend traits and conditions under the decision jurisdiction of businessmen or executives. They include, mainly, competences and resources the firm accumulates over time and which may be a source of some sort of competitive or comparative advantage as compared to its competitors.

Similarly, Austin's well-known model (2002) proposes a general framework to forecast the possible competitive conditions for enterprises in developing countries, based on the depiction of context factors (at the international, national, and industrial levels), and firm-specific factors and operating conditions. The framework may be used to determine what organizations must do to take advantage of local competitive conditions.

Austin's framework includes several factors divided into analysis levels. The first level contains outside forces that affect the firm, with four groups of environmental factors: economic, political, cultural, and demographic. Austin's second level of analysis is defined by international relations and its effects on a firm and its industry. The third level is made up of the domestic environment, involving essentially the country's trade strategy and the governmental actions and policies that support it. The fourth level is the industrial environment, which includes the usual elements—for instance, customers and suppliers—that immediately surround the firm, including firm–government relationships. Finally, the fifth level is the environment of the firm, including its strategies and operations, and comprehending its structural conditions—technology, logistics, and marketing—and its management. Each of these levels is influenced by external factors and derives several elements that may boost or constrain a firm's competitiveness and, therefore, should drive its adaptive actions.

10.2.2. *Competitiveness at the Country Level*

In cross-country competitiveness comparisons, rankings became very popular in the last decade. Accordingly, several international and local institutions came up with their own rankings, each one based on a different set of criteria.

The **global competitiveness** index has Brazil in 44th place. This index comprehends 259 criteria, including economic openness, the government's role, financial market development, infrastructure quality, technology, business management quality, political and legal institutions, and labor market flexibility (The Economist 2005: 58).

The World Economic Forum's 2005 **competitiveness growth** ranking has Brazil in 65th place among 117 countries. This index tries to reflect productivity, and it is strongly influenced by a perception-based survey of a sample of local executives and entrepreneurs. Regarding selected components of the index, Brazil is 32nd in business operating practices and strategies, 50th in technology, 70th in public institutions and 79th in macroeconomic environment. Its worst positions are found in government-related topics.

A similar index, called **national competitiveness** index, was created by FIESP, one of Brazil's main business representation bodies. In its 2003 edition, Brazil was 39th among 43 countries (Coelho 2005). The publication report observes that despite the country's good performance in exports (including some high value-added products) and technology (with increased investment in research and development, and an increasing number of patents), competitiveness growth continues to face the barriers posed by two factors, capital and government, with particular note for interest rates, bank spreads and the tax burden.

Other indices, directly related to business and competitiveness, are equally unfavorable. In the **business environment index**, Brazil is 36th (The Economist 2005: 58). It is the 29th in terms of research and development expenditures as percentage of GDP, and an incipient patents generator, even compared with its research and development expenditures (see Brito Cruz 2003). In turn, the **innovation capacity index** by UNCTAD has Brazil in 64th place among 117 countries. The index essentially reflects schooling and knowledge development levels in the country (UNCTAD 2005: 113–114).

Taken together, these indices place the country in an intermediate group of nations, at a significant distance from developed countries and with a sizable gap as compared to more successful developing countries.

10.2.3. *Competitiveness at the Industry Level*

We will now discuss an industry-level indicator, using a study of labor productivity (Instituto McKinsey 2000). In the second half of the 1990s, the McKinsey Institute carried out a study on workforce productivity in several Brazilian industries. Each industry was compared to its counterpart in the United States. Based on the general average of the industries surveyed, Brazilian labor productivity is only 27 percent of that in the United States. The study also found that labor productivity indices varied widely among industries, and that there was great intra-industrial variation as well.

The study included an investigation into local management practices. The results show that, despite the great distance between labor productivity in

Brazil and in the United States, evolution could be achieved with the adoption of more modern management practices (p. 18). Another significant portion of the gap could be indirectly dealt with by firms (p. 236). For instance, according to the authors' estimates, productivity at automakers could double with layout changes, reduced inventories, better quality control, and increased automation. In home construction, a productivity leap could come out of reformulated value chains and massive use of prefabricated structures. In retail banks, significant gains could be obtained by inducing customers to change their payment habits and developing credit services.

Significantly, the study observed that many Brazilian firms have already achieved high productivity standards. For example, one of the banks surveyed by the study had productivity 20 percent over the United States average. The same happened with companies in the processed foods industry. In sum, many local firms have showed that high productivity indices are possible, despite unfavorable situational and structural conditions.

Six years after the publication of the study, we may speculate that there has been progress, but in a heterogeneous manner. In the first half of the 2000s, efforts to modernize management models were remarkable. Out of the industries originally surveyed, the automotive chain and the banking system, for instance, have made large investments in products and process automation. Other industries, by their turn, failed to boast similar modernization levels.

10.2.4. *Competitiveness at the Firm Level*

We have emphasized already how Brazil and its industries, in general, do not present high levels of competitiveness. Once its less-than-ideal context is quite pervasive to most of its economy, from a limited perspective, this would imply that contextual limitations would explain and limit Brazilian firms' competitiveness. However, there seems to be room for agency within this inhibited context, because it is clear that a few Brazilian firms have managed to compete successfully internationally.

Sull and Escobari (2004), for example, conducted a multiple case study with ten Brazilian firms. They started with a list of 700 firms, public and private. In successive triage stages, they considered financial performance in the course of a decade, expert appointments and a detailed analysis of operations, as compared to local and foreign competitors. Another selection criterion was the firms' competitiveness in the global market, assessed through their ability to export or to outperform multinational firms present in Brazil. The ten selected firms were then the subject of an in-depth inquiry. For the breadth of industries and characteristics, these firms can be seen as a representative selection of the best Brazil can do in terms of competitiveness (see Table 10.1).

The main conclusion reached in the study is that these successful Brazilian firms have become particularly competent in dealing with environmental

Table 10.1. Successful Brazilian firms

Firm	Business	Sales (US$ million)	Compared firm	Summary description
AmBev	Beer and sodas	2,508	Antarctica	In 1989, investment bank Garantia acquired control of Brahma breweries. In the 1990s, the operation was modernized and sales increased sevenfold. The firm expanded throughout South America and acquired Antarctica, Brahma's long-time rival, whose performance was lagging. It once had the largest EBITDA margin of all the large global firms in its industry
Embraer	Aircraft	2,653	Fairchild Dornier and Bombardier	Embraer arose as a state-owned company in a high-tech center in the city of São José dos Campos. It was privatized in 1994, after a period marked by losses and unsuccessful designs. In subsequent years, it concentrated on the production of new regional jet families and attained a 40% market share, advancing on its direct competition
Votorantin	Conglomerate—basic industry	3,614	Grupo João Santos (cement and derivatives)	Votorantin is a family-owned conglomerate with a strong entrepreneurial culture. With the lowering of trade barriers in the 1990s, the firm underwent massive operations restructuring, attaining world-class performance standards. Its cement division maintained is share of the domestic market when foreign competitors entered or expanded
Itaú	Bank	2,459	Unibanco	The Brazilian financial industry experienced severe shocks in 1986, 1994, and 1999. Banco Itaú overcame these events and came out stronger for it, implementing an organic and acquisitions-based growth strategy. It became the most profitable of all Brazilian banks
Natura	Cosmetics	548	L'Oreal Brasil	In the 1990s, the firm professionalized and consolidated its business model, based on a massive array of trade representatives and the development of products associated with nature. It became the leading Brazilian cosmetics manufacturer, surpassing several multinationals

(Cont.)

Table 10.1. (Continued)

Firm	Business	Sales (US$ million)	Compared firm	Summary description
Promon	Construction and engineering projects management	218	Engevix	After a severe crisis in the 1980s as a result of reduced State-financed infrastructure works, it changed its business model and became a systems integrator specializing in telecommunications, power, and manufacturing. Its workforce dropped from 4,000 to 1,500 workers, but revenues increased tenfold. Many competitors did not survive the industry's crisis
Latin America Logistics	Railroads	215	Ferroban	Became the only privatized company in its industry to post consistently positive results. It modernized management, reduced the workforce from 12,000 to 2,000 workers and managed to achieve 270% sales growth in 5 years. Business expanded into Argentina and highway transportation
Aracruz	Paper and pulp	696	Klabin	Excess capacity and recession caused pulp prices to plunge in the early 1990s. Aracruz suffered losses and accumulated US$ 1 billion in debt. It then restructured, entered to stock market and emerged as a sound, well-managed firm, with 90% of sales to the international market
Pão de Açúcar	Food retail	3,237	Paes Mendonça	Suffered with the assets-freeze implemented by the government in 1990. In later years, it revised its business model and strategy, eliminated unprofitable businesses and restructured its divisions. Successfully faced international competitors, while many Brazilian firms in this industry floundered
Sabó	Auto parts	274	Cofap, Nakata, Metal Leve	Lower duties caused the entire automotive chain to restructure. Practically all Brazilian auto parts makers either were sold or shut down. Sabó, with a sound technology base, restructured and expanded with the purchase of units in South America and Europe. It established ties with automakers' development centers and established itself as a world-class company in its industry

Source: Adapted from Sull and Escobari 2004

turbulence and capable of creating value even under unfavorable conditions. Note that, in the case of Brazil, turbulences are not due to competitor moves and technological breakthroughs, as is often the case in the global market for high-tech products, for example. In Brazil, as for other emerging countries, turbulence is due mostly to macroeconomic instability and to the cyclic crises that impact business activities. Such conditions leave executives to face difficult situations and choices. Faced with trouble projecting the future, many firms were resigned to live for today and concentrate efforts on surviving until the subsequent crisis.

Turbulent environments pose a challenge to firms' resources or situational advantages. They also create risks and opportunities. Sull and Escobari imply that not all Brazilian firms had a fatalistic reaction to this context. Some firms—precisely those that were the most successful—tried to take advantage of the context for its favorable aspects. According to the authors, these firms were able to identify and take advantage of opportunities and to deal proactively with threats. To sustain and allow such moves, they built flexible organizations and learned how to allocate financial and human resources according to immediate conditions.

Besides, to Sull and Escobari, they seem to have learned how to respond to the pace of changes and to use the lulls in between crises to prepare, even though they could not predict exactly when another change or crisis might happen, or even what kind of crisis it would be. According to these authors, such firms learned three ways to create value: first, by rising to and maintaining advantageous positions, as did Votorantim, which managed to prevail over the cement market in the State of São Paulo, Brazil's richest and most developed; second, by building and growing valuable resources, as did Aracruz with its access to more beneficial regrowth forests than its international competitors; and third, by taking advantage of opportunities more quickly than their rivals, as did Natura (a local cosmetics company and one of the most admired firms in the country) with its line of environment-friendly products.

10.2.5. *Internal Competitiveness through 'Ideal Internal Configurations'*

Adopting an agency perspective, and expanding on the work of Sull and Escobari, we propose that Brazilian competitiveness at the firm level has depended mostly on the production of unique firm-level reactions to the hindering external elements local firms faced (see Figure 10.1).

Firstly, as it is portrayed in Figure 10.1, we believe that most of the contextual elements surrounding Brazilian firms converge to produce four basic threats at the firm level: first, high cost and scarcity of capital, second, cost disadvantage, third, insufficient growth of demand; and fourth, weak innovation and excellence standards. These conditions tend to impact negatively

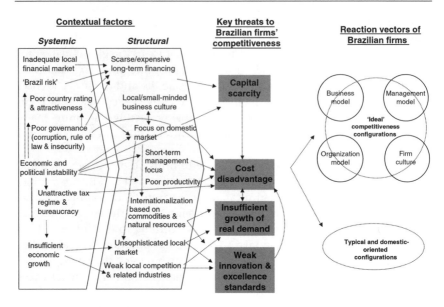

Figure 10.1. Competitive threats to Brazilian firms' international competitiveness and reaction vectors of competitive Brazilian firms

all of Brazilian firms' potential for competitiveness. Such proposition largely agrees with previous studies, particularly with Nakano's (2005). According to this author, Brazilian firm's competitiveness faces five main obstacles: insufficient real demand growth, tax regime, 'Brazil risk' (higher interest rates paid by Brazilian firms due to the country's risk rating), local financial market's inefficiency, and economic instability.

Secondly, drawing on Sull and Escobari's analysis, we point out that Brazil's hindering context does not have a uniform effect on every firm. Ideal external conditions may not be echoed by the alignment of internal central dimensions, which would imply loss of chances to compete. By the same token, poor external conditions can also be compensated for by exceptional configurations of central dimensions at the firm level. Hence, as the figure depicts, two types of reaction seem to have occurred at the Brazilian real: first, typical of the majority of firms, was to protect typical internal arrangements, usually by attempting to protect a domestic position and to safeguard previous configurations; and second, more common among the few internationally competitive Brazilian firms, was characterized by the production of 'ideal internal configurations', created via unique rearrangements of key internal vectors or dimensions, in a way that neutralized, or took advantage of, the key threats of their surroundings.

While Sull and Escobari's work listed mostly individual feats by their panel of firms, we hope to contribute precisely by pointing out what exceptional configurations, or unique internal rearrangements, seem to discriminate internationally competitive Brazilian firms from the vast majority of more domestically oriented firms, using mostly the same panel of firms. More specifically, we will try to point out which key internal variables seem to have been typically rearranged by internationally competitive Brazilian firms, and what type of 'ideal arrangements' seem to have been behind the success of these cases.

Our motivation to expand on Sull and Escobari's work is that, as implied in their work, many of the successful models conceived, although unique and potentially impossible to replicate, can be a source of inspiration and insight to other firms with similar contextual difficulties. In our point of view, and drawing from such generic conclusions, in this article we propose that the careful analysis of the internal rearrangements used by such successful firms may have yielded 'ideal configurations' for each internal dimension that appears to have driven successful internal adjustments to the negative contextual factors that most local firms have equally experienced. In Section 10.3, we attempt to draw out these configurations.

10.3. How Can Brazilian Firms Be Competitive?

In this study, we assume that less-than-ideal context conditions can be offset or mitigated by certain configurations of the central dimensions at the firm level. In this section, we attempt to identify what differentiated behaviors, practices and processes may be successful in facing an adverse context (Wood 2000; Wood and Caldas 2002; Sull and Escobari 2004).

As depicted in Figure 10.1, here we believe that exceptional internal configurations have ultimately enabled the emergence of internationally competitive Brazilian firms. Moreover, we propose that such exceptional configurations are a function of intentional or emerging rearrangements of four interrelated internal vectors or dimensions: first, the business model, including firm direction and all strategic process components; second, the organization model, which comprehends organizational architecture and how the firm assigns roles; third, the management model, which comprehends the main practices and processes that determine how the organization truly works; and fourth, firm culture, comprehending the main traits of management style and the organization's 'way of being'.

Naturally, each rearrangement was unique to its own industry or microcompetitive realm. That is, we assume that the exceptional internal configurations that the internationally competitive Brazilian firms have produced vary immensely in breadth and depth, to a point that it may be hard to thoroughly compare them. Nevertheless, by the same token, given that many of the external threats were common to all Brazilian firms and boiled down

Table 10.2. Success factors for Brazilian firms

Business model	Organizational model	Management model	Enterprise culture
Competitive intelligence and environment monitoring	Lean structure	Balance between centralization and flexibility	Professionalism
Opportunity capture	Structural flexibility	Operational excellence	Entrepreneurship and innovation
Prompt threat response	Large use of networks and strategic alliances	Financial protection	Low power distance
Main focus	Flexibility in the value chain	Risk management	Trust and cooperation in the value chain

to the same sorts of potential competitive disadvantages (see Figure 10.1), we believe that, in a cross-sectional perspective, several commonalities do exist among these configurations, to the point that one may be able to refer to 'ideal internal configurations' for such less than ideal external environments. Table 10.2 summarizes our proposition of some of the 'ideal internal configurations' for the Brazilian context.

As shown in Table 10.2, it seems evident that most—if not all—of internationally competitive Brazilian firms have managed to reinvent their **business model**, and from there rearrange their internal configuration. None of these firms seem to have succeeded based on previously valid models. Of particular relevance in many of these cases was a combination of **environmental monitoring** and the election of a main competitive focus. It is true that watching the markets as they evolve and keeping an eye on competitors' actions has become a common-sense practice for any firm, anywhere. Judging by these firms, it may be even more important, however, in turbulent environments. These firms seem to have particularly succeeded in tracking political and economic trends, and used such monitoring to quickly react and create countermeasures to overcome potential threats, which seemed crucial in an environment like Brazil. An example of a successful combined application of environmental monitoring and quick focussed reaction is the one of Embraer, a Brazilian regional jets manufacturer, currently the 4th largest aircraft manufacturer in the world. The firm based its long-term survival on its total concentration on the regional jet market, an industry marked by a globalized uncertain competitive context, by serial failures by firms from other stronger economies, and by extremely high stakes. Embraer perceived a breach in the market, mostly in the American downturn of the larger jet market, and quickly reacted by adapting a previously unsuccessful aircraft project into a design that made its way into such a market in record time; from such rapid and increased US presence, it constantly increased its market-share worldwide.

The most successful of the Brazilian cases also seem to have in common an acute and distinct (from their local peers) sense of **strategic opportunism**.

Turbulence generates threats, but, at the same time, creates business opportunities. Banco Itaú, a large local family-owned bank, is an example of the ability to identify and take advantage of opportunities. In the 1990s, the bank decisively took advantage of the privatization process to acquire state-owned banks and expand its operations. Another relevant characteristic is the concept of **active waiting**, which consists of keeping the organization in a constant state of alert to anticipate or change or react quickly to it. This must be supplemented by the definition of a **main focus**. Defining a main focus creates a sense of direction and catalyzes resources for action. An instance of main focus was again Embraer, when it gave total priority to the development of its EJR 145 regional jet over several other seemingly lucrative shorter-termed projects.

At the ***organizational model*** domain, internationally competitive Brazilian firms seem to have in common the combination of operational excellence with **structural flexibility**, which translates into the ability to allocate resources as required by the moment. At the projects firm Promon, for example, the adoption of a networked organization model that minimized staff and relied on partners and strategic alliances, enabled them to adapt more easily to drastic environmental fluctuations in their industry. Most similar firms, which seemed to have flourished during the infrastructure boom of the early 1970s, were either unable to reinvent themselves, preserving structures that later demonstrated to be unsalvageable, or insisted on successive structural retrenchments that preserved the same model, and merely attempted to compete by simply reducing size, while keeping the unviable previous organizational models. Most of these firms are now only shadows of the giants they promised to be, while Promon managed to stay afloat by creatively reinventing itself into a networked design.

From the perspective of their ***management model***, the most internationally competitive Brazilian firms seem to have reached a differential from their peers in their internal practices and processes, and most significantly, in **operational excellence** and in **risk management**, counteracting some of their context's major threats.

In terms of the former (operational excellence), which implies the attainment of a more competitive cost base, and enhances a firm's ability to respond to shocks, the most successful Brazilian firms seem to have sought the quest for world-class excellence standards, despite their under-performing immediate (local) environment, and used such unusual high standards to shield them against the negative impacts of turbulence. For example, in the years that preceded the takeover of Antarctica brewery by Brahma (and the formation of the internationally successful AmBev), Brahma systematically implemented steps to optimize and rationalize its operations base. Antarctica tried to emulate its rival, but with a lag and modest results, increasing the gap between the two firm's performance profiles.

243

As it comes to the latter differential of these more successful firms in terms of management model, it seems evident that the most competitive Brazilian firms have attained an unusually high (for local criteria) standard in risk management. Economic turmoil can suddenly change customers' ability to make payments and raise default rates. The environment's inherent high level of risk also favors the presence of conglomerates. Regarded with suspicion in most of the world, due to their trouble establishing strategic focus and coherent actions, some conglomerates have been extremely successful in Brazil. Votorantim, for example, has managed its business portfolio in such a manner as to mitigate risks that may eventually strike its activities. Grupo Camargo Correa, whose roots lie in heavy construction with a main focus on major infrastructure projects, typically Government-driven and highly risky, both altered its focus on private construction projects, procurement and project management, as well as expanded its overall portfolio outside the construction business, and is now active in the fields of highway concessions, garments, footwear, and energy distribution, hence significantly diluting risk.

A turbulent environment also requires maintaining a certain level of **financial protection**, that is, on the firm's preventive use of financial instruments for protection against contingencies such as exchange rate volatility, sudden variation in demand, or abrupt commodity price changes. In developed countries, the cost and availability of capital are predictable. Not so in Brazil and other emerging markets. In several situations, firms that had some inactive capital in stock were able to navigate crises while their competitors faced insolvency or bankruptcy. During the crisis that came in the wake of the 9/11 attacks, for example, Embraer's orders dropped abruptly. If the firm hadn't had financial resources available or hadn't made drastic changes to what previously appeared to be a bullet-proof business model, it would probably have had trouble surviving.

Finally, as it relates to **business culture**, a primary trait among Brazilian most competitive firms seems to be their superior (again, for local standards) **ability to react to change**. In environments that are often in turmoil, one must be able to quickly react and overcome inertia when unexpected changes occur. When Plano Real managed to drastically reduced inflation, many firms that made more money on financial investments than on operations, and banks in particular, suddenly watched their sources of profits dry out. Many of them accumulated losses and took a long time to recover. Others were agile and leaped ahead of their competitors. The promotion of foreign competition in the domestic market also brought about significant discrepancies in how a firm's culture either hindered or promoted change and adaptation. A typical example is that of Sabó. When the introduction of lower duties forced the entire automotive chain to restructure, hundreds of local parts manufactures went broke, disappeared, or were taken over by foreigners.

From 1990 to 1998, practically the entire Brazilian auto-parts manufacturing industry, which comprised more than 3,000 firms at its peak, was either sold out or shut down. Sabó, a traditional and third-generation family-owned firm, managed not only to survive, but to reinvent itself, and established its brand as a world-class company in its industry. The transformation of the company, a mere mid-range local player competitor before the advent of foreign competition and lowered import duties, was leveraged on an innovation-driven and cooperation-prone culture, both internally and at its supply chain: with a sound technology base, Sabó restructured and expanded with the purchase of units in South America and Europe, as well as through the establishment of close cooperation ties with both technology providers, and with global automakers' international development centers.

10.3.1. *Discussion*

Two final considerations should be made about our propositions here on the commonalities and 'ideal' or 'exceptional' configurations discussed above.

The first final consideration refers to the seemingly common-sense nature of some of the configurations we here have called 'exceptional'.

Indeed, some characteristics depicted in such 'ideal configurations' seem to be quite unique to this specific environment, while others may in fact sound like 'common sense'. However, one should note that the adoption of processes and practices that have been consolidated in developed countries may not be 'business as usual' for an emerging country firm. For example: a 'lean structure' may be common practice in traditionally competitive environments, but for many emerging economies, they tend to be rare: structures tend to be overpopulated by subjective and relatively tolerant to sub par performance, fueled by collectivist and paternalist cultural traits, which tend to favor the retention of people based more on factors such as perceived loyalty or longevity than for merit. Multiple layers of authority tend to be more frequent than horizontal structures, due to the strong power distance that is typical of less developed environments. Risk aversion and formalist traits, also frequent in less developed countries, would drive the abundance of detailed rules and procedures, which complicate and increase operational costs, while particularist cultural grounds would simultaneously diminish the actual compliance of such a regulated firm environment and also most of the potential benefit that such regulation might have promoted. And so on. Thus, whereas 'lean' may be common sense and not a particularly differentiating firm attribute in more developed countries, it may be a rare, and indeed a discriminating factor, in emerging contexts such as the Brazilian one. The second final consideration regards other senses by which internationally competitive Brazilian firms may differ, in terms of internal (re-)configuration, from more domestically driven firms.

In our analysis, all internationally competitive Brazilian companies managed not only to rearrange these four elements, but they may be discriminated from the remaining firms by having managed to do so in two senses: (*a*) their rearrangements were driven to overcome or to take advantage of, rather than to simply isolate or protect themselves from, the contextual threats brought in by increased competition in the domestic arena; and (*b*) rather than being isolated rearrangements (such as retrenchments to deal with cost disadvantages, that may not have been convergent with the promotion of innovation which depended on retrenched memory or personnel), their realignments seem to have been done in a way that either by design or by emerging concurrence, turned out to be harmonious and mutually reinforcing.

10.4. Conclusion

In this final section of this chapter, we must address a fundamental question: can Brazilian firms be competitive in the global markets? We believe that the answer is a 'yes, but moderately'. 'Yes', because there are a significant number of Brazilian firms that have, for several years, competed successfully with firms in the local market and, in some cases, in the international market as well. These firms have been able to take advantage of location advantages, develop good business models and learn how to compete in open environments. 'Moderately', because objective data show sizable gaps in the country's conditions for competitiveness, and a significant difference between the size of Brazilian MNCs and that of MNCs based in developed countries, or some MNCs based in Asian developing countries.

Out of all these cases, the most exceptional is probably Embraer, whose success in a high-tech global industry can be understood as the fruit of a long-term effort, seated on a sound organizational culture, near-fatal mistakes and vital 'hits' in the development of new products, and a providential push given by fate (see Avrichir and Caldas 2005). Embraer was able to navigate many internal barriers and build a case that has been exemplary so far.

In fact, the challenges in terms of systemic, structural and business factors, to use terms coined by Coutinho and Ferraz (2002), are significant. The prevalent macroeconomic conditions in the mid-2000s are more stable and favorable than those experienced in recent earlier periods. Still, elements like capital availability and cost, tax system and fragile industrial, trade and technology policies still pose locational disadvantages. The available literature on these topics is rich in diagnoses and suggestions. But only now are paths to implementation being started on. And, even so, in a tentative way and subject to political interference.

At the deepest analysis level, where individual firms lie, the main challenge is to find internal configurations that not only assure domestic survival (which appears to be the model behavior), but provide exceptional arrangements capable of overcoming or mitigating environmental limitations, or even taking advantage of them in the international context. Of course, all this is much easier said than done, and is deeply tied to the quality of individual firms' management.

Some critics have argued that 'Brazil is a poorly managed country', in reference not only to the public sector, but also to the private sector. We might speculate that management in Brazil is still in its infancy. In the past 15 years, the rhetoric underwent a new round of modernization. But significant gaps remain in terms of strategy, operating excellence, and competences development. Even among the exemplary firms mentioned earlier, there are still significant gains to accomplish.

'Brazil is not for beginners', goes the popular saying. Whether those who learned to move across this peculiar environment truly developed a differentiating competence capable of acting as a source of competitive advantage, or developed a negative 'conditioning' that will inhibit adopting modern management approaches is still in the air.

Note

1. It is worth noting the exception presented by the Aircraft industry, and Embraer in particular, which has consolidated itself as a globally competitive maker of regional jets since the 1990s (Avrichir and Caldas 2005).

References

AmericaEconomia (2005). Ranking Multinacionais, N. 303–4, Edição Brasil, p. 121.

Austin, J. E. (2002). *Managing in Developing Countries: Strategic Analysis and Operating Techniques*. New York: Free Press.

Avrichir, I. and Caldas, M. P. (2005). 'Competitividade nas Alturas', *GV-executivo*, 4(3): 46–51.

Calás, M. B. and Arias, M. E. (1997). 'Compreendendo as organizações latino-americanas: transformação ou hibridização?', in F. C. P. Motta and M. P. Caldas (ed.), *Cultura organizacional e cultura brasileira*. São Paulo: Atlas.

Caldas, M. P. (2000). *Demissão: Causas, efeitos e alternativas para empresa e indivíduo*. São Paulo: Atlas.

Coelho, J. R. R. (2005). *Índice FIESP de Competitividade das Nações*. (IC–FIESP). Available online on September 24, 2005 at <http://www.fiesp.com.br/download/competitividade/ICFiesp2005_apres.pdf>.

Coutinho, L. and Ferraz, J. C. (eds.) (2002). *Estudo da Competitividade da Indústria Brasileira*, 4th Ed. Campinas, Brasil: Papinus Editora.

Cruz, C. H. B. (2003). 'A Pesquisa que o País Precisa', *RAE-executivo*, 2(1): 16–26.

de Negri, J. A. (2005). 'Padrões Tecnológicos e de Comércio Exterior das Firmas Brasileiras Inovações, Padrões Tecnológicos e Desempenho das Firmas Industriais Brasileiras', in: de Negri J. A. and M. S. Salerno (eds.), *Inovações, Padrões Tecnológicos e Desempenho das Firmas Industriais Brasileiras*. Brasília: IPEA.

——Salerno, M. S. and Castro, A. B. (2005). 'Inovações, Padrões Tecnológicos e Desempenho das Firmas Industriais Brasileiras', in J. A. de Negri, and M. S. Salerno (eds.), *Inovações, Padrões Tecnológicos e Desempenho das Firmas Industriais Brasileiras*. Brasília: IPEA.

Dunning, J. H. (1993). *Multinational Enterprises and the Global Economy*. England: Addison-Wesley.

Fishlow, A. (2000). 'Brazil and Economic Realities', *Daedalus*, 129(2): 339–58.

Flynn, P. (1996). 'Brazil: The Politics of the "Plano Real"', *Third World Quarterly*, 17: 401–26.

Franco, G. H. B. (2000). *The Real Plan and the Exchange Rate (Essays in International Economics)*. Princeton, NJ: Princeton University International Economics.

Instituto McKinsey (2000). *Produtividade no Brasil: A Chave do Desenvolvimento Acelerado*. Rio de Janeiro: Editora Campus.

López, A. (1999). 'El Caso Brasileño', in D. Chudnovisky et al. (eds.), *Las Multinacionales Latinoamericanas: Sus Estrategias en un Mundo Globalizado*. Buenos Aires: Fondo de Cultura Económica.

Lopez-Claros, A., Porter, M. E., and Schwab, K. (2005). The Global Competitiveness Report 2005–2006: Policies Underpinning Competitiveness. World Economic Forum/Palgrave Macmillan.

Lussieu da Silva, M. (2003). 'A Inserção Internacional das Grandes Empresas Nacionais', in M. Laplane, L. Coutinho, and C. Hiratuka (org.) (eds.), *Internacionalização e Desenvolvimento da Indústria no Brasil*. São Paulo: Editora Unesp.

Nakano, Y. (2005). 'As Multinacionais Brasileiras e o Desenvolvimento Sustentável', *Conjuntura Econômica*, 59(1): 11–12.

Nelson, R. E. and Gopalan, S. (2003). 'Do Organizational Cultures Replicate National Cultures? Isomorphism, Rejection and Reciprocal Opposition in the Corporate Values of Three Countries', *Organization Studies*, 24(7): 1115–51.

Porter, M. E. (1990). *The Competitive Advantage of Nations*. New York: Free Press.

Sachs, J. and Zini, A. A. (1996). 'Brazilian Inflation and the Plano Real', *World Economy*, 19(1): 13–37.

Sachs, J. D., Porter, M. E., and Shwab, K. (2002). The Global Competitiveness Report 2001–2002. World Economic Forum/Oxford University Press.

Schwab, K., Porter, M., and Lopez-Claros, A. (2004). The Global Competitiveness Report 2004–2005. Houndmills: Palgrave.

Sull, D. N. and Escobari, M. E. (2004). *Sucesso Made in Brazil: Os Segredos das Empresas Brasileiras que Dão Certo*. Rio de Janeiro: Editora Campus.

The Economist (2005). *Pocket World in Figures—2005 Edition*. London: The Economist/Profile Books.

Unctad (2000). *World Investment Report 2000: Cross-border Mergers and Acquisitions and Development*. New York and Geneva: United Nations.

—— (2005). *World Investment Report United Nations. 2005 Transnational Corporations and the Internationalization of R&D*. New York and Geneva: United Nations.

Unctad (2006). Unctad's FDI statistics: www.unctad.org/fdistatistics, accessed in January, 2006.

Wood Jr., T. (2000). Configuraciones Organizacionales en Brasil: Transiciones, Rupturas e Hibridismo. Trabajo presentado en el Coloquio 'El Análisis de las Organizaciones y la Gestión Estratégica—Perspectivas Latinas', Zacatecas, México.

——(2004). Gestión de recursos humanos en Brasil: tensiones e hibridismo', *Revista Latinoamericana de Administración*, 33: 68–80.

——and Caldas, M. P. (2002). 'Adopting Imported Managerial Expertise in Developing Countries: The Brazilian Experience', *The Academy of Management Executive*, 16(2): 18–32.

11

Sources of Competitiveness of Large Mexican Groups

Robert Grosse and Douglas Thomas

11.1. Introduction

How can emerging market firms compete in the international marketplace of the twenty-first century? What features may allow them to overcome the traditional weaknesses of small size, limited technological sophistication, and lack of knowledge of foreign markets? These challenges threaten the continued existence of many emerging market firms—especially those trying to compete in globalized business activities, from agriculture to production of clothing to provision of many services.

We have discussed this issue with executives in more than a dozen of the largest 'grupos' (economic groups, which are large firms that are typically diversified into more than one business sector) in Mexico. In pursuing the question of competitiveness with these managers, we discovered that their strategic intent is not very different from goals of US-based medium-sized firms or those from other industrial countries. The question, as for mid-sized US and European firms, is: how can one succeed at home and abroad in an open market against the likes of Nestlé, Levi's, McDonald's, and Citibank?

And just as with medium-sized US firms, the general answer to this last question is: specialize. The Mexican firms are not likely to become global competitors in broad market segments such as production of personal computers or provision of telecommunications services. But they can serve market niches such as the assembly of electronics products that are branded by non-Mexican multinationals, and the provision of services such as media and telecommunications in the Spanish-speaking market worldwide. So then, how can a firm choose the appropriate segment(s), and how can it establish competitive advantages to defend itself against rivals? Based on the information gathered from more than a dozen large Mexican groups, we try to answer these questions.

Table 11.1. Sources of competitive advantage in Mexican firms

Competitive advantage	Description	Examples	Sources
Key advantages in domestic competition			
Access to local distribution channels	Preferential access to local physical distribution or promotional vehicles	Elektra, FEMSA, Kaltex	Our survey; Grosse 2004
Membership in an economic group	Conglomerate spread of activities	Carso; Salinas; Luksic; Cisneros	Our survey; Peres
Superior product or service quality	Better phone service; higher-quality shows; superior parts	Unefon; Televisa, TV Azteca; Desc	Our survey
Internal capital market	Internal financing availability	None in our survey	Khanna & Palepu
Government protection	Tariffs against imports; subsidies; 'buy local' policies; local ownership rules	None in our survey	Our survey found no examples
Key advantages in overseas competition			
Low-cost production	Based on small-scale manufacturing or low wages	Gigante, FEMSA	Our survey; Wells 1983; Peres 1998
Superior product or service quality	Better phone service; higher-quality shows; superior parts	Televisa, TV Azteca, Desc	Our survey
Ties to existing clients	Suppliers to MNEs	Desc	Our survey; Wells
Ethnic connections		Televisa, Gigante	Our survey; Lall
Technology		Cemex	1984; Thomas & Grosse 2005
Membership in economic group	Ability to realize economies of scope	Multivision; Carso; Salinas	Our survey; Khanna & Palepu 2000

Sources: Interviews at 15 Mexican firms in 2004–5; articles/books as cited.

11.2. Mexican Firms Compete Based on What Advantages?

Our initial expectation was that the firms would demonstrate an ability to compete locally in Mexico based on traditional strengths such as possession of a superior distribution network in the country, or protection of some kind from the government. And at the international level, we expected to see market niches served that would correspond to some explicit link to the firm's home-country advantages, such as serving a Spanish-speaking clientele overseas, or serving an existing client overseas. These initial thoughts were not completely off the mark, but additional, sometimes more subtle, features also played an important role in competitiveness.

The capabilities that were identified by these firms are shown in Table 11.1.

It is important to note that most of the competitive advantages identified by our respondents were for competing with foreign and domestic rivals in Mexico, rather than against firms in foreign markets. We can look in more detail at each context separately to better identify the conditions under which the Mexican firms are succeeding.

11.3. Competitiveness in Mexico

Within the domestic market, the Mexican groups have the greatest ability to compete successfully. In this traditionally restrictive environment, firms were previously able to stake out positions as monopoly suppliers to government organizations, or as SOE themselves (e.g. Telmex; Ferrocarriles Nacionales; TMM; Mexicana de Aviacion). Since the economic opening that began in Mexico in the mid-1980s,[1] the local environment has become much more open, and competitive advantages are now based more on strengths such as *superior product quality* or *better access to customers* through proprietary distribution channels. In fact, the most frequently cited advantages were these two, in comparison not only with domestic rivals but also with the multinational firms that have entered Mexico in large numbers during the past decade.

Most of the firms compete primarily in Mexico, with over 80 percent of their sales in the domestic market. The exception may be Grupo Carso, which operates the America Movil cell phone service throughout Latin America, and the Sanborns department store chain in several countries, along with CompUSA in the United States. Even in this case, more than two-thirds of the group's business is based in Mexico. The structure of Carso is fairly similar to many of the other groups, in combining several quite different sectoral activities. Figure 11.1 depicts this group.

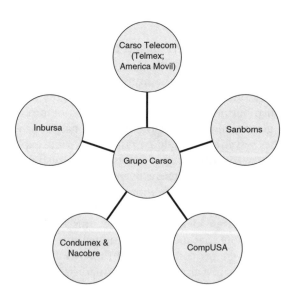

Figure 11.1. Grupo Carso

Note that Carso is comprised of five industrial segments, each of which is a billion dollar company in annual sales. The actual legal structure of the group is somewhat different, with the various commercial enterprises reporting to the Carso holding company, while the telecoms companies and Inbursa report to different boards, also controlled by the Carlos Slim family. Nevertheless, the overall organization is quite similar to FEMSA or Grupo Salinas.

The self-defined strategy of Carso is perhaps not surprisingly to 'keep costs down; get close to customers; and be leaders in every segment we enter'. While almost all the segments originated in the domestic market, both the telecom and the CompUSA activities are clearly multinational, and the copper division as well has expanded into several countries outside of Mexico. In short, Carso sounds more like a US-based multinational than a Latin American firm—except for its decision to operate in half a dozen unrelated business sectors.

The Carso diversification strategy follows a similar line in comparison with other major Latin American groups such as Luksic in Chile, Cisneros in Venezuela, and the Sindicato Antioqueño (Grupo Empresarial Antioqueño) in Colombia. Carso has moved into and out of businesses as conditions change and as competitive advantages shift. The huge move into telecommunications, for example, was only possible with the privatization of the telephone system in 1990. Telmex was aquired in a joint venture with Southwestern Bell at that time; America Movil was spun off from Telmex in 2000 as cellular phone service became important in Latin America. Over the course of the past decade, the Carso group has moved into some new industries and out of some old ones, but the degree of diversification in unrelated businesses remains largely unchanged.

These shifts parallel ones by leading groups elsewhere in the region, producing not the same kind of narrow sectoral focus that typifies the United States, but rather a more opportunistic strategy that is typical in most of the rest of the world.[2] As technological and regulatory conditions change, so also does the portfolio of businesses operated by the large groups. This is not an obvious winning strategy, since many groups have failed in Latin America over the past decade, just as large US firms rise and fall over time. However, the persistently large and successful groups in Mexico (and elsewhere in Latin America) do tend to follow the portfolio strategy in their businesses.

Grupo Salinas is another example of a diversified economic group, though in this instance the businesses mostly relate to retail stores, telecommunications, and financial services. Ricardo Salinas built this group from the original Elektra retail store business founded by his grandfather, Hugo Salinas Rocha, in 1950. He built up the retail stores, which sell mainly electronics, large home appliances, and furniture, adding a credit business that

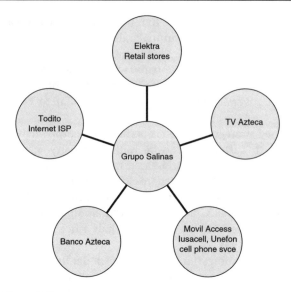

Figure 11.2. Grupo Salinas

ultimately became Banco Azteca in 2002. TV Azteca was launched in 1994, and it developed into a television service, programming, and telecommunications business by the early 2000s. The overall group is described in Figure 11.2.

Grupo Salinas has maintained a focus on the mass-market consumer, rather than the high-end segment. Unefon is a clear example of this, with the lowest cell phone service charges in Mexico, thus attracting the low-end customers to its user base. Likewise, TV Azteca has an explicit focus on mass-market customers, and a large market share in lower-income segments, where rival Televisa dominates the high-end programming. This group has successfully fended off multinational challenges in the retailing sector, even with the arrival of Wal-Mart, Carrefour, and others. Elektra has been able to differentiate itself relative to these others with a mass-market, low-price emphasis— even relative to Wal-Mart.

Similar to Carso, the Salinas group has expanded the portfolio of industries in which it competes during the past decade. In 1994, the Salinas group was focussed on retail stores and some financial services, largely credit offered to purchasers of its large home appliances. By the end of that year, the group had taken its first step into television, with the acquisition of government-owned TV Azteca. Further forays into telecommunications and television content followed, even during the Tequila Crisis of 1994–5.[3]

11.4. Overseas Competitiveness of Mexican Groups

The leading Mexican groups have not been particularly successful in their overseas expansion. With the exceptions of Cemex, FEMSA, and Carso, the groups are much more successful in their domestic markets, and have found that competition in other countries, particularly in the United States, has been daunting. Cemex is a global competitor, among the four largest cement companies in the world and with operations in all major regions of the world. Even Cemex has found its competitiveness to be greater in emerging markets than in the industrial countries (though this may relate to the fact that cement demand is growing faster in the emerging markets than in the traditional Triad countries of North America, Europe, and Japan).

FEMSA, as the main partner of Coca-Cola in Latin America, has found that that alliance enables it to be a market leader in several Latin American countries. Clearly, the ability of FEMSA to compete throughout Latin America in selling Coca-Cola products comes from the Coca-Cola brand name. This competitiveness also derives from FEMSA's ability to build distribution channels in Latin American countries and to manage the affiliate network.

Carso has succeeded most extensively (in the geographic sense) through its operation of the cellular phone network, America Movil. This service is offered throughout Latin America, and is second in the region only to the Telefonica (Spain) network called Telcel. The reasons for this success include such factors as economies of regional scale, that enable America Movil to economize on technical and managerial services, while still needing the signal transmission capabilities that any wireless telecom company must offer. America Movil does not achieve lower costs or greater scale economies than rivals in carrying telephone signals, but rather in its ability to pool human resource usage across countries in the region and its ability to deal successfully with governments in the region when negotiating rates, tax treatment, and other regulatory treatment.

DESC has been a supplier to auto companies operating in Mexico, so it has found the ability to supply those same companies in the US market. DESC has not developed new distribution channels nor projected its image overseas, but rather has pursued existing clients to the US market, when those clients previously had purchased from DESC in Mexico. This firm has been able to compete based on its high-quality production of auto parts for the original equipment manufacturers and its relatively low-cost production capability in Mexico (relative to the United States or Japan).

Overall, the large Mexican groups appear to be able to compete overseas not on the basis of technological superiority or economies of scale, but due to their ability to build distribution channels in Latin America, to follow existing customers to other countries, and to sell high-quality products and services, often to the Hispanic market, in the United States or in Latin America.

11.5. Another View of Mexican Companies' Competitiveness

Some useful insights can be gained into the effectiveness of various strategies of the Mexican groups if we compare them along several dimensions:

1. Low diversification versus high diversification of business activities across sectors,
2. Low diversification into international markets versus high diversification of sales out of Mexico,
3. Low-cost versus high-quality strategy,[4]
4. Performance before and during the Tequila Crisis, and
5. Performance before and during the large-scale economic opening (deregulation) of the 1990s.

This section explores the relations between strategies in points 1 and 2 above and performance in periods 4 and 5 above.

It stands to reason that some firms would have performed better during the Tequila Crisis than others, and perhaps that the firms with greater foreign sales would outperform those concentrated more heavily on the (depressed) domestic market, that would have suffered more. Did greater business diversification help or hurt? Did internationalization strategies work better than focus on the domestic market? Tables 11.2a and 11.2b provide some answers to these questions, based on our set of large Mexican groups.

The table is divided into two subparts, showing the performance of firms with lower or higher business sector diversification in Table 11.2a, and the performance of firms with greater or lesser international diversification in Table 11.2b. Sectoral diversification was identified simply as whether the firm had more than 20 percent of its sales in two or more industry sectors. Only Carso and Desc fell into this category, though Grupo Salinas has been diversified since the early 2000s. International diversification was defined as whether the firm had more than 5 percent of its overall sales outside of Mexico.

Table 11.2a shows that the more highly diversified firms did indeed encounter a generally less-damaging outcome from the Tequila Crisis than their more narrowly focussed comparison group. Return on assets remained at approximately 8 percent for the diversified firms, while it dropped from 6 to 4 percent for the focussed firms. Return on sales increased from 13 to 14 percent for the diversified firms, while it declined from 8 to 6 percent for the focussed firms. Although the number of firms in the diversified group is small, the available evidence does point to superior performance (or less negative impact) during the Tequila Crisis for those firms that had businesses spread across several industrial categories. This is consistent with the logic that diversification allows the firm to compensate downturns in one sectoral

Table 11.2a. Product diversification and performance during the Tequila Crisis

	Low diversification		High diversification	
Low impact of Tequila Crisis	Cemex; Comercial Mexicana; Televisa; Elektra		Carso, DESC (using operating profits)	
High impact of Tequila Crisis	ICA; Bimbo; Casa Saba, Herdez; Gigante, Dina; Iusacell; FEMSA			
Factors that explain performance	Profitability 1992–3 (ROA)		Profitability 1994–5 (ROA)	
Greater diversification across businesses	*Diverse (Carso and DESC)* 0.084	*Narrow* 0.060	*Diverse* 0.076	*Narrow* 0.039
Factors that explain performance	Profitability 1993 (ROS)		Profitability 1994–5 (ROS)	
Greater diversification across businesses	*Diverse* 0.127	*Narrow* 0.082	*Diverse* 0.138	*Narrow* 0.058

business with better outcomes in another, and with the general principle of diversification to reduce risks.

Table 11.2b reports on results of greater international diversification on group performance during the Tequila Crisis. These results are more mixed than for the issue of business sector diversification. It appears that the firms with greater overseas market concentration (>5% of total sales outside of Mexico) suffered somewhat less impact from the crisis than the more domestically focussed firms. Return on assets dropped from 8 to 3 percent for the diversified firms, while it dropped from 7 to 4 percent for the more domestically focussed firms—a fairly similar outcome. Return on sales dropped from 13 to 9 percent for the more-international firms, while it declined from 8 to 2 percent for the focussed firms—showing less dramatic impact for the more international firms. Thus, the effect of greater internationalization appears to be moderately positive in defusing the impact of the Tequila Crisis in Mexico.

These statistical measures give a limited amount of insight into the strategies of large Mexican groups in the turbulent 1990s. Additional understanding

Table 11.2b. International diversification and performance during the Tequila Crisis

	<5% international sales		>5% international sales	
Low impact of Tequila Crisis	Comercial Mexicana; Elektra		Cemex[5] Carso; DESC (using operating profits), Televisa	
High impact of Tequila Crisis	ICA; Bimbo; Casa Saba, Herdez; Gigante, Iusacell; FEMSA		DINA;	
Factors that explain performance	Profitability 1992–3 (ROA)		Profitability 1994–5 (ROA)	
Greater internationalization of sales	*<5% intl* 0.070	*>5% intl* 0.083	*<5% intl* 0.038	*>5% intl* 0.032
Factors that explain performance	Profitability 1993 (ROS)		Profitability 1994–5 (ROS)	
Greater internationalization of sales	*<5% intl* 0.075	*>5% intl* 0.133	*<5% intl* 0.023	*>5% intl* 0.086

of the factors that contributed to company performance can be gleaned from analyst reports and company statements during the 1990s. Several of them are sketched in this section.

11.5.1. *Gigante*

Like other retailers, Gigante suffered from the national recession that followed the peso devaluation of late 1994. Sales dropped 25 percent the following year. Its problems were aggravated by demands from the owners of the acquired Blanco chain for payments due. Grupo Gigante dismissed some 6,000 workers and closed some of its stores. To pay its debts it borrowed money at high rates of interest and sold 20 percent of its shares to two banks: Banamex and Inbursa. The founder of Gigante retained a fortune valued at US$800 million, but this sum was down from US$1.3 billion in 1993.

Grupo Gigante gradually recovered from the crisis. Sales rose from 11.8 billion pesos in 1995 (about US$1.8 billion) to 19.07 billion pesos (US$2.04 billion) in 1998. Profits, which dipped to a low of 270 million pesos (US$41.3 million) in 1995, increased each year to 870 million pesos (US$93 million) in 1998.[6]

11.5.2. *Controladora Comercial Mexicana (CCM)*

The company's improving performance came to an end with the capital flight of late 1994, followed by the devaluation of the peso and the consequent severe recession of 1995. CCM's sales dropped by 18 percent in 1995 and another 5 percent in 1996. Moreover, because of the devalued peso, the company's dollar-denominated debt of US$300 million took on critical proportions. In order to make payments on the debt, Comerci had to lay off staff and scale back expansion plans. In order to cut costs, the Price Costco stores shifted their stock from about half domestic, half foreign goods, to 70 percent domestic, 30 percent foreign. Nevertheless, the company continued to add more stores and restaurants and in late 1996 declared plans to spend US$260 million over the next two years to open thirty-four new stores. In 1997, Comerci purchased Kmart Mexico, S.A. de C.V. for US$148.5 million. In spite of the still-sour Mexican economy, Comerci remained profitable in every year following 1994.

11.5.3. *DESC*

Desc continued to do fairly well in the early 1990s, although its profit margin dropped. In 1992, the company had net income of 354.09 billion pesos (US$114.4 million) on net sales of 5,158 billion pesos (US$1.67 billion). The currency crisis and peso devaluation of late 1994 resulted in a net loss of 1.44 billion pesos (US$411.4 million), primarily because of heavy losses in noncash foreign exchange. During 1995, an outstanding performance by the chemicals sector, largely because exports doubled, enabled Desc to record a modest net profit of 329 million pesos (US$48.4 million) on net sales of 11.46 billion pesos (US$1.69 billion). The company had invested heavily in Grupo Irsa, raising its output to 100 percent of capacity and capitalizing on cheap raw materials and low labor costs to dramatically build sales in the United States and Europe. High- interest rates and continuing recession took a heavy toll on Desc's auto parts and real estate sectors.

Sparked by the North American Free Trade Agreement, the Unik auto parts division did very well in 1996. Exports accounted for almost half of its sales as the division became a premier supplier to Detroit's Big Three. In October 1996, Spicer agreed to purchase Borg-Warner Automotive Inc.'s unprofitable North American manual transmission business for about US$40 million. This business was expected to have sales of about US$105 million for the year. Spicer, in July 1997, purchased Dana Corp.'s transmission division. Desc was planning to move the purchased Borg-Warner and Dana plants to its automotive center in Queretaro.

Desc recorded net sales in 1996 of 11.98 billion pesos (US$1.53 billion) and net income of 1.90 billion pesos (US$241.7 million). Chemicals accounted for 44 percent of net sales; automotive parts for 36.8 percent; agribusiness for 13.6 percent; consumer products for 4 percent; and real estate for 1.8 percent. Exports accounted for 31 percent.

11.5.4. CEMEX

Cemex's foreign operations gave the company a hedge against the weakening peso, down 7 percent against the dollar in the first half of 1994, and then by more than 90 percent in the following twelve months. The recession had the effect of paralyzing mortgage loans in Mexico, which in turn affected the housing sector and the demand for cement. Still, net sales dropped only 2.3 percent, offset somewhat by a decline in the costs of sales and operating expenses derived from lower fuel and electric energy prices (a major expenditure in the cement industry), a decrease in personnel, and a 23 percent increase in worker productivity. (This is all a quote taken from Business and Company Resource Center.)

11.5.5. DINA

Mexico's highway-construction program came essentially to a halt with the capital flight of late 1994 that resulted in the devaluation of the peso and a severe economic recession. Dina's net sales plummeted to 5.25 billion pesos (about US$687 million) in 1995. Bus sales fell from 2,040 to 169 and truck sales from 30,644 to 5,219. This catastrophic drop was not only due to the

Mexican recession but also to the effect of the North American Free Trade Agreement (NAFTA), which opened wider the Mexican market to US competitors.

NAFTA, however, also had positive aspects for Dina, because it could now buy US components at lower cost. In addition, it could more easily penetrate the US and Canadian markets through its alliance with Navistar and its acquisition of MCII, which became MCII Holdings (the United States) Inc. in 1996 and absorbed Dina Autobuses, S.A. de C.V. in 1997. In 1998, only 23 percent of Dina's revenues came from Mexico, and 83 percent of its profits were in dollars. MCII had an installed base of about 75 percent of the bus coaches operating in the United States and Canada. More than half of Dina's trucks were being exported. In 1998, Dina severed its alliance with Navistar and unveiled a new lineup of medium- and heavy-duty trucks.

Nevertheless, although Dina made money in 1996 and 1997, it remained in serious financial difficulty. Although sales reached about US$1.14 billion in 1998—the first time it had topped the billion-dollar mark since 1994—the company incurred a net loss of about US$85.14 million because of large interest payments on its debt, which was about US$700 million at the end of 1998. By June 1999, Dina's ADRs had fallen from their January 1994 high of US$31 a share on the NYSE to US$1.25.

11.5.6. *Herdez*

The collapse of the peso in late 1994 resulted in both opportunities and challenges for Grupo Herdez. Although exports to the United States became cheaper, about 60 percent of the company's costs—for cans, cartons, and jars, for example—had to be paid in increasingly expensive US dollars. Herdez's profits fell, but the company remained in the black and in early 1996 formed Herdez Corp., a US joint venture, with Hormel Foods Corp. Hormel's grocery-products division began distributing Grupo Herdez's salsas, refried beans, *mole,* and other products under the Herdez, Bufalo, and Doña Maria names, as Mexican food became increasingly popular in the United States. In 1995 a Mexican joint venture had begun distributing Hormel's spam, chile, stew, deviled ham, vienna sausage, and other meat products in Mexico.

11.5.7. *FEMSA*

Fomento Economico Mexicano, S.A. was formed in 1988 in the restructuring of the major Mexican group, VISA. FEMSA became the main operating subsidiary of VISA, holding the group's businesses in beer (Cervecerias Cuauhtémoc y Moctezuma) and soft drinks (Coca-Cola FEMSA). This restructuring resulted from the group's near-bankruptcy during the Mexican debt crisis of the 1980s, and it separated Banca Serfin, Mexico's third largest bank, from these industrial businesses.[7] FEMSA continued to be approximately half devoted to the soft drink business and half to beer through the early 2000s.

In the mid-1990s, with the Tequila Crisis, FEMSA was hit hard in Mexico, but not significantly in other Latin American countries where the company sold beer and Coca-Cola products. Just before the crisis hit, FEMSA bought 51 percent of the shares of Coca-Cola Argentina, thus becoming the largest Coca-Cola bottler other than the parent company.

11.5.8. *Grupo Salinas*

Grupo Salinas was formed in 2001 from a group of subsidiaries which included Grupo Elektra which was founded in 1950. During the 1970s, Grupo Elektra was hit hard by a peso devaluation and made major shifts in its strategy. The 1990s and beyond have been a period of rapid growth for the companies that now comprise Grupo Salinas. For example, TV Azteca was launched after being purchased from the Mexican government in 1993. Todito.com was established in 1999. Unefon and Banco Azteca were launched in the early years of the 2000s. It does not appear that the 1994–5 peso devaluation had a major impact on Salinas companies. However, deregulation has had major impacts on the companies in Grupo Salinas' strategy. For example, privatization of a government television channel led to the creation of TV Azteca and related media companies. Deregulation in the cellular phone industry has led to the launch of two Salinas cellular phone companies, Iusacell and Unefon. Additionally, Salinas has taken advantage of changes in the banking industry to launch Banco Azteca. Salinas has also changed its internationalization strategy. Its media, banking and retail companies have expanded into international markets, including the United States.

From another perspective, it is useful to examine the Mexican groups' strategies and performance in relation to the impact of deregulation of the market. While this deregulation has occurred somewhat gradually since the mid-1980s, there was one major change that can be used as a turning point in the past decade. This was Mexico's entry into NAFTA, which took place on January 1, 1994. This event occurred just before the Tequila Crisis, so separating out the two impacts is somewhat difficult. Our interest in the economic integration issue can be explored by comparing the performance of firms before the entry into NAFTA (1992–3) with their performance after NAFTA began and after the Tequila Crisis was over. We used data from 1999–2000 as the with-NAFTA period of comparison. Results are shown in Tables 11.3a and 11.3b.

Table 11.3a shows that joining NAFTA (along with other deregulation of the Mexican economy) had more dramatic impact on the more-diversified firms in our group. That is, it appears that the choice of a more focussed (sectoral) strategy produced a smaller reduction in profitability than a conglomerate

Table 11.3a. Product diversification and performance relative to deregulation

	Low diversification	High diversification
	Bimbo; Gigante; Dina; Herdez; FEMSA; Televisa; Elektra; Cemex; Comercial Mexicana	Desc; Carso (+);
Factors that explain performance	Profitability 1992–3 ROA 0.071 ROS 0.085	Profitability 1992–3 ROA 0.084 ROS 0.127
Factors that explain performance	Profitability 1999–2000 ROA 0.060 ROS 0.065	Profitability 1999–2000 ROA 0.056 ROS 0.076

diversification strategy—though the diversified firms still had slightly higher profitability than their more focussed counterparts in the post-NAFTA period when measured by return on sales, and just slightly worse performance when measured by ROA.

Table 11.3b shows that joining NAFTA (along with other deregulation of the Mexican economy) has had much greater negative effect on the firms that were more internationally oriented. Both domestically and internationally oriented firms suffered reduced profitability in the 1999–2000 period compared to the pre-NAFTA period, but the more-international firms were hit harder than those that concentrated on the domestic market. Still, the more-international firms had superior performance than the more-domestic group using either measure of performance.

In another study, Thomas (2006) found that Mexican firms' degree of internationalization showed a curvilinear impact on firm profitability during the 1990s. Initially, Mexican firms experienced, on average, negative performance when expanding internationally. This is presumably because of inexperience and the 'liability of foreignness'. However, over time, Mexican firms learned from their international experiences, and their performance began to turn positive as they continued to expand internationally. These results suggest

Table 11.3b. International diversification and performance relative to deregulation

	<5% international sales	>5% international sales
	FEMSA; Bimbo (92); Gigante; Dina (92); Herdez; TV Azteca (02); Elektra; Comercial Mexicana	Desc; Cemex, Carso; Bimbo (02); Televisa; Dina (02)
Factors that explain performance	Profitability 1992–3 (ROA) 0.070 (ROS) 0.062	Profitability 1992–3 (ROA) 0.080 (ROS) 0.153
Factors that explain performance	Profitability 1999–2000 (ROA) 0.049 (ROS) 0.043	Profitability 1999–2000 (ROA) 0.056 (ROS) 0.077

that greater internationalization will correlate with superior performance, but that measuring this performance requires more than a one-time observation of the relationship. The rewards from internationalization were not seen initially but took time to appear in the companies' financial performances.

Thus, our findings that the more-diversified and the more-international firms tended to be hit harder by deregulation than their more-concentrated and more-domestic counterparts require careful interpretation. The more-diversified firms still had superior performance than the more narrowly focussed firms; it was just that their superiority was diminished under the economic opening of Mexico.

11.6. Conclusions

The firms in our sample of large Mexican grupos demonstrated various degrees of diversification across industries. The firms that had greater amounts of business outside of Mexico clearly survived the Tequila Crisis more successfully than those that had less overseas business. This is not particularly surprising, because most overseas business involved exporting, and the Tequila Crisis made Mexican exports much more competitive internationally, as the peso dropped to about half of its precrisis value relative to the dollar.

More diversified firms across industry sectors appeared also to outperform the more narrowly focussed firms during the Tequila Crisis, supporting an argument that the Mexican market is more like the markets of other Latin American and Asian markets, where sectoral diversification provides an important hedge against market, cost, and regulatory problems. This feature continues to differentiate the Mexican economy from the United States—though Mexico is more similar to most other countries of the world where such sectoral diversification provides important benefits to the firms.

Results of the comparison of our groups of firms before and after the economic opening of Mexico showed reasonably similar effects. The more-diversified firms tended to demonstrate superior performance than their more-focussed counterparts. However, the overall impact of deregulation seems to have decreased the performance differential between the types of firms, so that the more-diversified (sector-wise and internationally) firms have a smaller edge over more narrowly focussed firms.

Obviously, these results should be taken with caution, due to the small number of firms included. Still, our discussions with managers in the firms tended to support the same conclusions—broadly speaking, that spreading business across sectors and outside of Mexico made for more-stable, and more-sustainable performance.

Notes

1. Mexico's move toward an open market can be dated to 1984, when the country joined the General Agreement on Tariffs and Trade (GATT). In addition, the Government removed limits on foreign ownership of Mexican companies in 1987 (repealing the 1973 law on that subject, which had limited foreign ownership to 49% of a Mexican company), and in 1993 opened almost all industries (except oil, electricity, and real estate) to foreign ownership.

2. This opportunistic strategy is epitomized by the Grupo Luksic in Chile, where leaders of the family have stated on several occasions that their strategy is to 'buy low, sell high', i.e., to buy businesses in weak condition, fix them up, and sell them at a higher price. This strategy implies no core business other than management of diverse organizations, looking for undervalued assets and improving them for resale. See e.g. 'The Luksic Group: A Chilean Conglomerate in a Global Economy', INSEAD case no. 302-059-1. (2002).

3. The Tequila Crisis was the financial crisis that hit Mexico when the government allowed the peso to devalue abruptly in December of 1994, producing a market-driven devaluation from about 3.5 pesos per dollar to 7 pesos per dollar in a few months. This triggered a wave of company failures and bank failures, leading to a drop in national income of 6.5% in 1995 and subsequent shock waves that lasted for several years. See, e.g. Calvo, G. A. and Mendoza, E. G. (1996). 'Mexico's Balance-of-Payments Crisis: A Chronicle of Death Foretold', *Journal of International Economics* 41 (November): 235–64; and Sachs, J., Tornell, A. and Velasco, A. (1996). 'The Mexican Peso Crisis: Sudden Death or Death Foretold?', *Journal of International Economics* 41 (November): 265–84.

4. We were unable to explore this hypothesis, because the firms that had low-cost strategies in one business did not follow that same strategy across all businesses. Thus, we could not use overall company performance to judge whether the low-cost strategy in one business segment was superior to rival strategies in that segment.

5. Cemex and Dina had less than 5% international sales in 1992–3, and more than 5% international sales in 1994–5. We categorized these firms in the appropriate category for each of the years.

6. The company sketches are taken largely from company information available from Thompson-Gale, at the website: http://www.gale.com/BusinessRC/. This information was supplemented by additional facts taken from the company websites.

7. Interestingly, FEMSA's principal shareholder, Eugenio Garza Laguera, lost Banca Serfin to the government nationalization of the banks during the 1982 debt crisis, and then bought Mexico's second largest bank, Bancomer, in 1991. This holding, in turn, was sold to Banco Bilbao Vizcaya in 2000 after the Tequila Crisis.

References

Amsden, A. H. (May 1991). 'Diffusion of Development: The Latin Industrialization Model and Greater Asia', *American Economic Review*, pp. 282–6.

Dawar, N. and Frost, T. (March–April 1999). 'Competing with giants: survival strategies for local companies in Emerging markets', *Harvard Business Review*. pp. 119–29.

Grosse, R. (2000). 'Transformational Management', in Robert Grosse (ed.), *Thunderbird on Global Strategy*. New York: Wiley.

—— (2004). 'The Challenges of Globalization for Emerging Market Firms', *Latin American Business Review*, Vol. 4., No. 4, pp. 1–21.

—— and Fuentes, C. (July 2002). 'LanChile—The Globalization', Thunderbird Case Series No. A-09-02-0013.

Guillen, M. (2000). 'Business Groups in Emerging Economies: A Resource-based View', *Academy of Management Journal*, Vol. 43., No. 3, pp. 362–80.

Khanna, T. and Palepu, K. (2000). 'Is Group Membership Profitable in Emerging Markets: An Analysis of Diversified Indian Business Groups', *Journal of Finance*, Vol. 55., pp. 867–91.

—— —— (July–August 1997). 'Why Focussed Strategies May Be Wrong for Emerging Markets', *Harvard Business Review*, pp. 41–51.

Kumar, K., and McLeod, M. G. (eds.) (1981). *Multinationals from Developing Countries*. Toronto, Canada: Lexington Books.

Lall, S. (1984). *The New Multinationals*. New York: Wiley.

Leff, N. (1978). 'Industrial Organization and Entrepreneurship in the Developing Countries: The Economic Groups', *Economic Development and Cultural Change*, pp. 661–75.

Peres, W. (ed.) (1998). *Grandes Grupos y Empresas Industriales Latinoamericanos*. Santiago: CEPAL.

Robles, F.(1999). 'Grupo Editorial Norma: Formulating a Vision for the Next Century', company case study, xerox.

Thomas, D. and Grosse, R. (2005). 'Explaining the Inward and Outward Internationalization of Emerging Market Firms: A Focus on Mexico', Working Paper.

Thomas, D. E. (2006). International Diversification and Firm Performance in Mexican Firms: A Curvilinear Relationship?, *Journal of Business Research*, 59(4): 501–7.

Wells, L. T. (1983). *Third World Multinationals*. Cambridge, MA: MIT Press.

Part IV

Competing in Emerging Markets

12

'Multilatinas' Go to China: Two Case Studies

Andrea Goldstein and Omar Toulan

12.1. Introduction

In a global economy where barriers to the circulation of capital, goods, services, and talent—while still present—do not shield anyone from competition, Latin American firms can only compete against domestic and foreign rivals by building specific competitive strengths. Although a few such companies have truly managed an evolutionary process in which technological capabilities were being developed, their numbers are not large enough to generate a new pattern of specialization. Case studies, however, are useful to illustrate specific dynamics and the embeddedness of corporate trajectories in history.

Building up a multinational presence through direct ownership of production subsidiaries abroad is obviously a key component in this 'package' that may enable multinationals from Latin America (*multilatinas*) to beat out the competitors from abroad—in their own markets as well as elsewhere in the world. Focussing on Embraer and Techint—the two South American firms that arguably best epitomize world-class manufacturing based not only on the intensive use of natural resources, but also on technology and human capital[1]—the intent of this research is to identify those characteristics and strategies that will enable firms from Latin America to compete successfully domestically and overseas in the years ahead.

More specifically, the chapter zooms in to analyze their experiences in China. This choice reflects three rationales. First, China has been the world's

We thank Henrique Rzezinski at Embraer and others for their kind collaboration and other participants to the 'How Can Latin American Firms Compete?' research project for useful comments on earlier drafts. The usual caveat applies: in particular, the opinions expressed and arguments employed are the authors' sole responsibility and do not necessarily reflect those of McGill University, the OECD, the OECD Development Centre, and their Members.

fastest-growing market for quite a few years. In 2004, it was the third largest FDI recipient in the world, surpassed only by the United States and the United Kingdom (UNCTAD 2005). No multinational (MNC) claiming to be a global player can shy away from its huge population, high-skilled low-wage workforce, and relative political stability. Acting as they are in concentrated industries, to respond competitively to new challenges, these firms are obliged to go to China.

Second, complementarities between China and Latin America have been identified by other scholars (e.g. Santiso 2004) and fast growth in the former has been an important driver behind the extremely good economic performance in the latter in 2004 (CEPAL 2004). China has traditionally maintained friendly, if distant, relationships with Latin American countries, (possibly with the exception of some Central American nations that recognize Taiwan). Brazil, in particular, was courted assiduously by the Chinese in the years following the 1989 Tiananmen Square protests, when Beijing was seeking out nonideological business partners.[2] Economic and political ties have gained a much reinforced momentum in recent years as China took off and found in Latin America an ideal source for its seemingly unbound appetite for raw materials.

Some Chinese MNCs have made investments in the region. Shanghai Baosteel, China's largest steel maker, already has a joint venture with CVRD, the world's largest iron ore producer, which is also negotiating with Chinese investors to build slab plants in northern Brazil. Nonetheless, only a few *multilatinas* have taken the plunge (see Appendix, Table 12A.1 for a partial list). There is a feeling that Latin America, mired in its own economic problems, failed to seize opportunities in China. Brazil, for example, does not have a significant role in China's Three Gorges Dam project, despite several visits by Chinese delegations to Brazil's giant Itaipu hydroelectric plant over the past decade. In Mexico the fear is that companies are being too averse to risk and are putting excessive emphasis on the opportunities in the US market.[3]

Third, and possibly the most interesting factor for looking at *multilatinas* in China, is that many Western MNCs have been misled by the apparently unlimited opportunities in China (Studwell 2003; Yan and Libeberthal 2004; Clissold 2005).[4] As China undergoes two major transitional phases—from a command economy to a market-based one, and from a rural, agricultural society to an urban, industrial one—the business environment remains characterized by structural uncertainty, structural complexity, and structural deterrence (Luo 2000). The caprice of the government, pervasive corruption, and other malpractices also limit the ability of firms to predict risks and protect themselves against them, although these factors are probably of less relevance for large MNCs, with their strong bargaining power vis-à-vis the Chinese government both at local and central levels. The success of foreign companies depends on the extent to which they can maximize economic benefit derived from industrial decentralization, the opening up of new sectors, the elimination of supply or price control in certain industries, a loosening of government intervention over market demand, a realization of pent-up demand, and an industrial life cycle transition. MNCs also need to evaluate organizational learning capabilities to overcome the hurdles of foreignness. The greater the effort made by top managers to stress the importance of their Chinese businesses in relation to their global operations, the higher their success in China (BCG 2003). While expatriates still hold the most senior positions, in the medium run Chinese locals are assuming a greater role in both middle- and senior-management ranks.

Could it be the case that *multilatinas*, accustomed as they are to operate in a volatile environment where rules are not always respected (Sull 2005), are better positioned to weather those basic cultural factors that make the domestic Chinese market so difficult for others to penetrate? The chapter follows a simple structure. The next Section, 12.2, succinctly describes the history of the two companies in order to identify the sources of their success. Section 12.3 then examines the experience of Embraer and Techint in China, trying to shed light on two specific issues—which resources have they used to replicate their global success in China? And, have their experiences in China differed from those of their global competitors? We then conclude with a summary and synthesis of our findings.

12.2. Building Latin American Firms into Global Leaders

12.2.1. *The Case of Embraer*

Embraer was established by the Brazilian government in 1969 as part of its import-substitution-based industrial policy (Goldstein 2002*a*). Early strategies concentrated on aircraft design, assembly, and fuselage production. Although strongly supported by procurement from the government, the company focussed on export markets, which brought it longer production runs, new ideas for technical change, and exacting performance standards. In the course of its 25-year history as a state-owned enterprise, Embraer used licensing and cooperation agreements to bring new resources and knowledge into the firm and develop a strong core competence—system engineering for producing aircraft. But while this learning process was initially accompanied by progress on other fronts—such as organizational and marketing skills—by the mid-1980s engineering considerations overtook other criteria in the mindset of senior management.

In 1994, the company incurred a loss of US$30 m. In the same year, the company was privatized. It was bought by three Brazilian investors, jointly owning 89 percent of the company's shares. The Brazilian state still retained a 7 percent holding. Embraer's best-selling plane, the 50-seat ERJ-145, was presented at the 1996 Farnborough fair and secured its first contract with Continental Express, a subsidiary of Continental Airlines. The ERJ family, also composed of the 37-seat ERJ-135 and the 44-seat ERJ-140, share 95 percent commonality among all models, with low operating, crew training and maintenance costs.

Since 1996 more than 800 aircraft of the original ERJ family have been delivered to more than thirty airlines in twenty countries. Embraer returned to profitability in 1998 after eleven consecutive years in the red. The following year's devaluation of the Brazilian real was both positive and negative. On the one hand, it helped Embraer, as the wage bill fell from 13 to 9.7 percent of production costs between 1997 and 1999. On the other hand, the financial costs of raising new debt, as well as servicing outstanding dollar-denominated liabilities, both rose and the dollar-value of the funds budgeted for government export programs decreased.

Exports now make up 95 percent of total sales and Embraer claims to lead unit sales in the world market for regional aircraft. In 1999, Embraer also became Brazil's largest exporter, accounting for 3.5 percent of total Brazilian sales abroad, although it fell to the fourth place in 2003, with a 2.6 percent share. A new manufacturing and test site in Gavião Peixoto enables airworthiness flights of high-speed military aircraft in Brazil, instead of sending airplanes to the United States for that service.

In July 1999, Embraer announced the launch of a new family of larger jets, marketing it chiefly outside the United States. The 70-seat ERJ-170 won FAA and EASA certification in February 2004 and a month later the first production example was delivered to Poland's flag carrier LOT. In November 2004, the company received its first order for the larger ERJ-175 from Air Canada. In December 2004, the first Asian customer, Hong Kong Express Airways, ordered four ERJ-170s. Deliveries were set to start in late 2005, supporting Embraer's overall goal of delivering 145 aircraft in 2005. As of 30 September 2005, Embraer had a total workforce of more than 14,000, and a firm order backlog, including the Airline, Business, and Defense markets, totaling US$ 10.4 billion.

Over the past five years, Embraer has also become more global. In October 1999, a consortium of French aerospace companies acquired 20 percent of its equity, thus reducing the Brazilian shareholders' total stake to 69 percent, and in July 2000, Embraer was listed on the New York Stock Exchange. In 2003, the firm opened a maintenance facility in Florida to perform modifications and heavy repairs. Embraer has had a certificated repair facility at its Brazilian factory, but almost all maintenance had been done through a fairly comprehensive worldwide network of third-party facilities (either in-house at operating airlines or by authorized maintenance centers). In December 2004, Embraer bought from the Portuguese government a 65 percent stake in Ogma, a maintenance, repair, and overhaul (MRO) firm, for €11.4 m. Ogma employs 1,700 people and had a 2003 turnover of €107 m.

The post-privatization recovery owes much to the actions implemented by management, which injected a new corporate strategy to ensure alignment between Embraer's core competence and market signals (Goldstein 2002a). Various forms of organizational change have led to innovation and improved performance. The hierarchy was flattened by cutting the number of managerial levels from ten to four, and performance-related remuneration was also introduced for all employees. Most importantly, a number of activities— such as strategic planning, total quality management, market intelligence, the *kaizen* workforce empowerment strategy, and the analysis of system performance feedbacks—were formalized and endogenized in the company's routines.

The process of organizational change has involved 'vision', trial and feedback learning, and consensus-building. All such elements have played a role, although it is not easy to rank order them. Vision has probably been the most important. In 2001, Mauricio Botelho, Embraer's CEO since 1994, won the annual Laurels Award granted by the industry's leading magazine for 'correctly reading the transformation of the commuter airline industry from turboprops to jets—an insight not gleaned by many established European and American manufacturers—and by focussing on a single overarching objective: customer satisfaction'.[5] It is important to remember that at Embraer the formal creation of a market intelligence function came after, and not before, the launch of the ERJ family. Botelho, while a mechanical engineer by training, did not have any background in aerospace, and this may have made it easier to spot the transformation in the industry. The Transforming the Organization for Results (TOR) Program launched in 1997 stands at the core of the learning process.[6] In a phase of rapid growth, it aimed at integrating the development of new activities with a constant review and improvement of operational processes. As regards the personal development and professional training of its workforce, Embraer has implemented a Career and Salary Plan, an Industrial Integration Program, and a Supplementary Retirement Plan.

Crucially, Embraer has rapidly developed the systems integration skills necessary to assemble a modern airliner. The company has focussed on designing, assembling, marketing, and servicing the final aircraft, while research and development activities have been outsourced to the Centro Técnico Aeroespacial (CTA), a government-run training and research center. All key components, including the avionics, flight controls, engines, wings, tail units, and fuselage segments, are bought from outside suppliers. Several aerospace component-suppliers from Europe and the Americas chipped in as 'risk-sharing partners' for the ERJ-145, directly investing R$64 m (over a total equal to R$593 m, roughly US$300 m) in cash and materials and providing liquidity via deferred payment provisions. In the case of the new ERJ family, development costs are even larger (about US$850 m) and by far the largest investment ever started by Embraer. No less than one-third of such costs are being contributed in cash by risk-sharing partners, who are responsible for developing, producing, and delivering entire systems as well as major components. Embraer will be responsible for the forward fuselage, nose cone, center fuselage II, and wing to fuselage fairings. This strategy should not only reduce Embraer's development costs and risks, but also, by reducing the number of its suppliers and easing logistics, allow it to concentrate in what it does better, that is, design, assemble, market, and service the final aircraft. Several of Embraer's foreign suppliers have set up operations in Brazil as part of the effort, while others are planning to do so.

An additional element has been played by geographical location. São José dos Campos stands in the very heart of the Paraíba Valley, 43 municipalities that host 430 exporters and produce 3 percent of Brazil's GDP (Goldstein 2005). MNCs such as Ericsson, Volkswagen, Ford, and General Motors have established some of their largest plants there, attracting additional investments in the component and electronics industries. Embraer could tap into these existing investments, playing the role of fulcrum and coordinator in a network of specialized Tier II suppliers. While Embraer has not taken equity positions, some such firms had been created in the mid-1990s by skilled technicians laid-off by Embraer and other aerospace companies. A concerted effort to improve and deepen the articulation between different private and public partners is underway. Twelve specialized suppliers, organized in the High Technology Aeronautics (HTA) consortium, attended the Le Bourget Air Show in June 2005.

Finally, in this industry manufacturers have traditionally benefitted from helping government hands, whether through military tanker deals, airline handouts, launch aid, or direct orders from hands-tied state carriers. Public sector institutions such as the National Bank for Economic and Social Development (BNDES) and Financiadora de Estudos e Projetos (FINEP), part of the Ministry for Science and Technology, have actively supported this process. Embraer has also been the largest beneficiary of Programa de Desenvolvimiento Tecnológico Industrial (PDTI), a program of the Ministry for Science and Technology that provides fresh funding and tax holidays for innovating firms. Also important has been the extension of export subsidies. In this brutally competitive environment, the rivalry between Embraer and Bombardier has escalated from the firm to the national level (Goldstein and McGuire 2004). In May 2000 the government of Canada asked the WTO for permission to retaliate by blocking US$3.3 bn in goods and trade privileges over 7 years—the largest trade confrontation Canada has engaged in, and one of the largest disputes in the history of the WTO. Brazilian authorities responded that the threat of sanctions 'could make it difficult or even impossible for Brazil to seek alternatives which would prevent an irrational escalation of the dispute, with the capacity to set off counter-retaliations or other measures that would damage the economic and commercial relationship in different areas'. Since then, new WTO decisions have supported Brazil, and Canada has indicated it will implement the February 2002 ruling.

As such, Embraer's success at becoming one of the leading airplane manufacturers can be traced to a combination of factors, starting with its systems integration and management abilities. On top of this, the firm adds access to a sophisticated base of suppliers and strategic partners. And, as with all players in this industry government subsidies play an important role particularly when it comes to international expansion. Its decision in the late 1990s to invest in a larger regional aircraft has also placed it in an attractive position for future growth, providing it with a more expansive portfolio of aircraft sizes to offer its customers than its leading competitor Bombardier, which has yet to firmly commit to entering the larger regional aircraft market.

12.2.2. The Case of Techint

Organización Techint, with headquarters in Buenos Aires and Milan, is comprised of more than thirty operating companies and has offices in as many countries around the world. With its main focus and origins lying in the steel sector, Techint is widely considered to be 'the' leading industrial group in Argentina and to possess one of the best managements in all of Latin America. With over 50,000 permanent employees worldwide, the Group boasts 2005 revenues of roughly US$11 billion.

The Group was founded in the late 1940s by Agostino Rocca, who immigrated to Argentina from Italy where he had served as head of the Italian state steel sector. With seed capital provided by a handful of wealthy Milanese families, he established Siderca in September 1954 in Campana, 80 km outside of Buenos Aires. The facility was the first of its kind to produce seamless steel pipe in all of South America. Though it was only a semi-integrated facility until the mid-1970s, Siderca continuously received investment in expanding the productive capacity from the Group since its first days. The firm's rise to international preeminence, however, did not occur until the end of the 1970s and the 1980s when heavy capital investments were undertaken, including the backward integration of the firm into primary steel production (Toulan 1997).

The other major component of Techint's steel business lies in flat products, initially focussed around Propulsora, founded in 1968 in Ensenada as a downstream processor, buying the hot-rolled coils either from SOMISA (the former Argentinian state-owned steel complex) or via imports. As with Siderca, Propulsora also had a number of smaller specialized facilities, such as Arsa, Sidercolor, and Serviacero, that undertook galvanizing, electroplating, and pre-painting. Following the acquisition of SOMISA in 1993 by Techint, all of the individual finishing firms were incorporated into the new Siderar. Most

Table 12.1. Techint: major steel acquisitions, 1986–2005

Year	Company	Location	Division
1986	Siat	Argentina	Tubes
1993	Somisa (Siderar)	Argentina	Flat
1993	Tamsa	Mexico	Tubes
1996	Dalmine	Italy	Tubes
1997	Sidor	Venezuela	Flat
1998	Tavsa	Venezuela	Tubes
1999	Confab	Brazil	Tubes
2000	NKK Tubes	Japan	Tubes
2004	Algoma Tubes	Canada	Tubes
2004	Posven	Venezuela	Tubes
2004	Silcotub	Romania	Tubes
2005	Hylsamex	Mexico	Flat
2006	Maverick	United States	Tubes

Sources: Deutsche Bank (2005), 'Tenaris S.A.—Seamless success' and Techint internal presentations.

of the management of Siderar, however, came from Propulsora, and in fact the firm served as a breeding ground for top managers for the entire Group. The heads of Siderca's Italian and Mexican operations, for instance, both began in Propulsora (Toulan 2002).

Overall, Techint has an annual steel capacity of sixteen million tons (2005), making it the largest player in Latin America and among the top twenty producers worldwide. At the core of Techint's strategy is growth through acquisitions (see Table 12.1). With the global expansion of the Group came the need to reorganize so as to better leverage cross-border synergies from the various acquisitions and present to the customer one interface. This first began in the tubes area with the formation of Tenaris in 2002, which merged the operations of Siderca, Tamsa in Mexico, Dalmine in Italy (the firm which Agostino Rocca once ran), TAVSA in Venezuela, Confab in Brazil, NKK Tubes in Japan, and Algoma Tubes in Canada. Other acquisitions which followed in Romania and Venezuela were then integrated directly into Tenaris rather than being managed as separate entities.

Tenaris has an annual production capacity of over 3 million tons of seamless steel pipe products and 850,000 tons of welded pipes,[7] annual consolidated net sales in excess of US$4.1 billion, and 16,000 employees worldwide (2005). The firm is the largest seamless steel tube producer in the world, controlling upward of 20 percent of international trade in seamless tubes, and roughly one-third of the Oil Country Tubular Goods (OCTG) market.[8] It is also a leading provider of pipe handling, stocking, and distribution services to the oil and gas, energy, and mechanical industries. Tenaris enjoys both geographic and product diversification, with a strong presence in South America (20% of 2004 sales), Europe (30%), North America (27%), the Middle East and Africa (13%), as well as the Far East and Oceania (10%). In terms of its products, seamless steel pipes dominate the scenario (80% of 2004 sales) followed by welded steel pipes (8%), energy (10%), and other products and services (2%). Tenaris is 60 percent owned by the Techint Group and is listed on four exchanges: Argentina, Mexico, Italy, and New York (ADRs).[9]

Tenaris is further reorganized around customer segments rather than products, as had been the case in the past. These segments include:

- Oilfield Services: providing a complete range of casings, tubings, and accessories developed to function under extreme conditions and delivered directly to and installed at the oil well

- Pipeline Services: offering an extensive range of seamless and welded tubing for onshore, offshore, and deep-water pipelines

- Process and Power Plant Services: responding to the needs of refineries, petrochemical companies, and power plants

- Industrial & Automotive Services: producing a range of tubular and cylinder products, including design, delivery, and inventory management systems.

Nearly 65 percent of Tenaris' sales are to the oilfield services and oil processing industries; the other 35 percent is destined mainly for the European automotive industry and energy sectors. Therefore, its sales and earnings are highly correlated with the price of oil, which in turn supports E&P spending and a subsequent demand for Tenaris' tubular products. In OCTG pipes, the Group has established alliances with Repsol YPF, Chevron, Shell, ExxonMobil, Petrobras, Pemex, and Agip, each customer representing yearly sales of roughly US$80 million.[10]

The second half of the steel business is comprised of the recently formed Ternium, which merges Siderar, Sidor (based in Venezuela), and the recently acquired Hylsamex (based in Mexico). Together these facilities have a combined capacity of 12 million tons of flat and long steel products, and stand as the main steel complexes in each of their respective countries. The acquisition of Hylsamex in May 2005 was the Group's largest ever, with a purchase price of over US$2.2 billion. Starting February 2006, Ternium began trading on the New York Stock Exchange.

In addition to its core businesses in the steel sector, Techint also has an important set of engineering and construction companies specializing in the design and implementation of pipelines, oil and gas facilities, petrochemical plants, industrial plants, power plants, mining and metals complexes, and other infrastructure and architectural projects. They also design and supply advanced melt shop equipment, furnaces, strip process lines, and other types of machinery and equipment for industrial applications. Smaller investments of the Techint Group include energy businesses focussed around the E&P of oil and gas, the construction and operation of natural gas transmission networks, and energy and utility supply and trading. Dalmine Energie is a major supplier of electricity and natural gas to many industrial companies in Italy. In addition, Techint designs and builds hospitals, and manages a consolidated network of private health care institutions in Italy.

The rationale for recent acquisitions has been to focus on areas where Techint lacks presence. In particular, for Tenaris the United States is an interesting market because of its proximity to the Tamsa mill (Mexico), which is one of the most technologically advanced in the NAFTA region. Nonetheless, due to antidumping rules, Tenaris can only export to the US deepwater products market and to the auto and other non-OCTG industries. Hence the decision to acquire Maverick for US$3.2 billion in June 2006, adding two million short tons of steel pipes to Tenaris global annual capacity. As for Ternium, with its acquisition of Hylsamex, it is fortifying its role as the leading player in Latin America and opening the door for greater entry into the US market. It has also moved to acquire upstream suppliers of raw materials in countries such as Venezuela.

As alluded to above, there are a number of keys to Techint's success in international markets, some of which draw upon its history coming from Argentina and some of which stand as independent of the national context. On the one hand, the firm's extensive experience with governments and highly regulated industries has given it an advantage when entering newly liberalizing markets compared to firms from OECD countries. Its successful privatization of SOMISA served as a platform for other privatizations in which the firm participated in Mexico, Italy, and Venezuela. Techint's ability to effect major turnarounds in these formerly state-owned firms, however, is also a testament to the Group's excellent management skills and emphasis on market leading technologies to improve efficiency. This ability to initiate major restructurings has been tied to the firm's policy of acquiring management (if not always ownership) control when undertaking these acquisitions, an issue which entry into markets such as China challenges. Over one-third of the top management team has received graduate degrees from leading universities in the United States or Europe. Its high emphasis on training extends throughout the ranks of the firm and has been one of the fundamental pillars upon which it has expanded internationally. Seeking out lead customers and technological partnerships where needed has also contributed to the firm being able to compete at the high end of its businesses and resist the commodity segments to which firms from emerging markets are often relegated. Outsourcing noncore activities to world-class suppliers such as Air-Liquid and Portia and Clark Chapman has further allowed the firm to focus on what it does best, the actual production of steel. Finally, the role the Rocca family has played in the success of the firm cannot be underestimated. Making the decision to become a world-class player while their home market was still closed to outside competition took visionary leadership. By clearly spelling out different strategies for each division and taking into consideration the limitations given their geographic origins, Techint was able to become the global leader in a niche segment (tubes) and a major regional player in the larger flat products market. As such, the firm's success can be attributable to a combination of visionary leadership, heavy investments in management and human resources, experience with restructurings, and a strategy of focussing on its core and excelling technologically in it.

12.3. Investing in China

12.3.1. *The Case of Embraer*

The lure of China is as appealing for aircraft manufacturers as for any other global industry. The Civil Aviation Administration of China (CAAC) expects travel demand to grow an average of 10 percent annually through the end of the decade. With China presenting itself to the world at the 2008 Olympic Games in Beijing and the World Exposition in Shanghai, its air transport market is expected to trail only the US market by 2020. As far as Embraer is specifically concerned, China's regional airlines are still in their infancy, but the central government's commitment to the Great Western Development Strategy (GWDS)—an effort to improve the living standards of the 367 million Chinese who live far from prosperous coastal China—and the current reform and consolidation in the airline industry will lay a solid foundation for network rationalization (Findlay and Goldstein 2004).

It must be underlined, however, that many problems remain. The load factor is roughly 10 percentage points lower than in the rest of Asia (63% vs. 73%). Aircraft fly around only 5 to 6 hours a day and night flights are nonexistent, despite many domestic routes taking up to 6 hours. Given the large capital immobilized in an aircraft, 9–10 hours are estimated to be necessary for positive returns on investment. Moreover, half of airports are underused, as airlines do not have the correct aircraft type to operate many of the routes. Half of the country's airports (72 out of 143) handle fewer than 200 passengers a day, resulting in heavy losses for the airport operators. Moreover, on 466 of China's 795 air routes the number of daily passengers is lower than 120. Finally, minnow airlines will not get a fair chance to grow if legislation does not outlaw seat dumping, cross-route subsidization, and other anticompetitive practices.

In the Asian aviation industry, Korea and Indonesia looked at the regional jet sector in the 1990s, but for different reasons they could not build up the required capabilities (Goldstein 2002b). In the late 1990s Chinese authorities initially identified Fairchild Dornier, the smallest of the three main firms in this subsector, as the regional jet manufacturer most amenable to enter into negotiations to trade technology sharing and transfer for privileged market access. However, government approval for the deal was delayed and even a November 2001 visit by Germany's Chancellor Gerhard Schroeder to China could not accelerate the process. The Chinese wanted to push through demands of increased technology transfer.

Acknowledging that the local aviation industry lacked the capability to produce larger planes competitively, in November 2000 the Commission of Science, Technology, and Industry for National Defence (COSTIND) decided to commit CNY5 bn (about US$600 m) in research and development for the ARJ21, or Asian Regional Jet for the twenty-first century. AVIC I Commercial Aircraft Co. (ACAC) was created to oversee resources, production, certification, and marketing. Development costs are relatively low, partly because ACAC has shifted some of the costs on to its suppliers, and partly because labor is cheaper than elsewhere. Given that aircraft, unlike cars, are still largely hand-built, salaries account for a third of an aircraft's cost and the advantage of China in this respect is an important consideration.

Embraer has been busy in Asia since the mid-1990s, considering this market the big plum for its global expansion. The company is confident that its broad offerings of regional jets and turboprops—from the 30-passenger EMB-120 Brasilia turboprop to the 110-passenger ERJ-195—offer cost-effective solutions for local market needs and set Embraer apart as the only company with the ability to serve this market from the bottom to the very high end of it. Since May 2000, Embraer has had a permanent office in Beijing, staffed by about fifteen employees, with a Chinese-born and Brazilian-educated managing director in the person of Guan Dongyuan. Embraer clinched its first Chinese deal in 2000, when Chengdu-based Sichuan Airlines purchased five ERJ-145s and took options on several more. The following year Southern Airlines placed twenty firm and ten option orders and Wuhan Airlines an additional ten orders for the ERJ-145s. However, the sale, with an approximate value of US$1 bn, was stalled for months, as it still required final government approval. Brazilian President Fernando Henrique Cardoso personally intervened with his Chinese counterpart Jiang Zemin to speed up approval, but this did not change the situation. The bone of contention was the Chinese request to see Embraer produce some of the parts locally.

In 2001, the company established a major parts presence in China, working with China Aviation Supplies Import and Export Corp (CASC) to warehouse about US$20 m worth of inventory. The venture with CASC, China's fifth largest trading company with annual turnover exceeding US$1.5 bn, is seen as generally enhancing Embraer's aircraft sales capabilities in the region, as well as supporting the operation of Embraer aircraft.

At the 2002 Asian Aerospace Conference in Singapore, Embraer made it clear that its goal was to make its presence in China effective and permanent by establishing a final assembly line for its regional jets. In September the

State Council gave its approval for outline plans to assemble the ERJ-145 in China and later in the year Embraer signed a US$50 m agreement with two companies controlled by AVIC II—HAIG and its subsidiary Hafei Aviation Industry Company (HAIC). Claiming that it needed a majority equity stake to effectively transfer technology and managerial know-how, Embraer secured a special authorization from the government and has a 51 percent share in the joint venture.

The new company, Harbin Embraer Aircraft Industry (HEAI) Company Limited, is based in Harbin, capital of the north-east province of Heilongjiang, located 900 km north of Beijing. The plant manufactures some components as well as assembles and tests the planes, to be marketed primarily in China. The joint venture has a production capacity of twenty-four aircraft, worth about US$19.5 m each, per year and is planned to roll out between 250 and 300 aircraft over the next ten years. The facility has a 24,000 m^2 surface and a staff of over 180, including ten expatriates.

The first aircraft's maiden flight was in December 2003, a few months behind schedule. This was the first Embraer aircraft manufactured outside Brazil. In February 2004, Guangzhou's China Southern Airlines ordered six ERJ-145s, thus becoming the second local carrier to operate the aircraft. China Southern will deploy them on routes in the less-developed mountainous western region of the country. Embraer China sees the China Southern order as significant because it has raised hopes of other Chinese airlines ordering the aircraft for their hub-and-spoke routes. In June 2004, the customer took delivery of the first HEAI-made aircraft, with deliveries continuing through January 2005. Fourteen months later it was the turn of China Eastern to receive the first of five China-made ERJ-145s and in January 2006 China Eastern Airlines Wuhan Ltd acquired five more. Deliveries of these aircraft will occur between November 2006 and June 2007. Five more may be sold in 2006.[11]

Embraer debuted the ERJ-170 to local airlines at the second biannual Brazil–China Expo held in Shanghai in May 2004. The company believes there is potential in China's regional air carrier market, because many short air services and small airports are now served by larger planes, while smaller jets could help them raise efficiency and increase frequencies. The ERJ-170, however, may go into direct competition with the ARJ21.

What were, beyond the more immediate numerical targets, the expectations for Embraer in China? For both partners, the new company would provide customers with comparatively low-cost aircraft with low maintenance costs. Embraer had been looking to China to reduce the dependence on the United States, which accounts for 56 percent of its commercial aircraft sales. On the Chinese side there was a clear desire to develop its industry and, Brazil also being a Third World country, authorities thought that more than an assembly license could be expected from Embraer. The precedent had been set by Sino–Brazilian collaboration in satellite and space research, which culminated in a second successful launch in October 2003. It is important to bear in mind, however, that skepticism about the project has abounded from the beginning. In 2002, Pierre Lau, an analyst with Nomura Securities, argued that 'high fixed costs and a comparatively late start [are] likely to work against Embraer's joint venture. Unless they receive at least 20 orders a year, it would be difficult for them to be financially viable.'[12] The company expected HEAI to deliver six planes in 2004, or about half the number it had anticipated. 'The speed in which the facts are happening is not the speed that we expected in the very beginning,' said Botelho, who estimates the plant will make ten aircraft in 2005.[13]

The most accurate reading of the underperformance over the first 2 years seems to be that Embraer's expectations in terms of a more fluid access to the domestic market have not been fulfilled. Although local production avoids import duties of 24 percent, these are being cut by WTO agreements in 2006, so the tariff-jumping argument per se is not convincing. As reported above, in the past Embraer had signed several preliminary agreements to sell planes in China, only to fail to convince their customers to sign final accords. This way it learnt that—due to the still infant stage of market institutions and capitalist culture, no less than the interest on the part of buyers in extracting as many concessions as possible—doing business in China requires more patience and *guanxi* (relationship) than in other parts of the world. Ozires Silva, who was chief executive of Embraer from 1970 to 1986 and then again in the mid-1990s, said he could never close a sale to China because the company did not have a plant there. 'There is no other way. If you want to sell in China, you have to produce there'.[14] The Brazilians therefore thought that the willingness to engage in a not unsubstantial and long-term commitment would give them the edge over competitors like Bombardier which is still considering whether to build a plant in China as well.[15]

Without any guarantees for minimum orders, Embraer was confident that, with the right business sense, a product with the appropriate characteristics would easily find a place in the market. Government involvement in air transport, however, remains significant despite the gradual shift to a more hands-off Western approach. Airlines still need purchase approval from the state council and from China Aircraft Supply Corporation, a government-owned company that decides on the country's aircraft purchases.[16] Moreover, China may leverage its purchasing scale and gate-keep its economy to promote AVIC. AIG and GE, which want to expand their financial services business ever deeper into China, run huge aircraft leasing subsidiaries, ILFC and GECAS. The government may quietly pressure them to acquire ARJ21s in exchange for opening market gates to the parent firms.[17]

Botelho has also hinted at the slow progress in setting up a market for regional air transport—featuring new players, freedom to set tariffs at cost-recovery levels, and adequate taxes—as a key hindrance.[18] China still charges flat landing and cabin cleaning charges for all planes and China's Air Traffic Management Bureau lets large planes fly at the level where fuel can be used economically, while the feeder planes are often guided to lower levels where more fuel is consumed.[19] The prospects of setting landing fees and taxes according to the size of aircraft, which would reduce the cost of operating regional jets and boost demand for HEAI's products, remain uncertain.

Nonetheless, airport construction fees for regional aircraft have already been cut to CNY 10 (US$1.20) from CNHY 50 (US$6) per passenger.[20] In another promising development for Embraer, in early 2004 authorities refused Air China the authorization to use 180-seat aircraft to compete with Sichuan Airlines on the Chongqing-Chengdu 300-km route.[21] And the decision to invest in China seemed to pay when Embraer announced in August 2006 the sale of 100 commercial planes, half of which will be manufactured in China, totaling US$2.7 billion to Hainan Air. The contract was signed during an official goodwill visit to Brazil by Wu Bangguo, chairman of the Standing Committee of the 10th National People's Congress.

Down on the shop floor finding a suitable collaborator, politically and technically, in the right place needs careful homework. Commenting on the rival Chinese and Russian-built regional jets, Botelho said that while there can be no doubt over their technological competence, these ventures may have problems in building up a serial production operation and ensuring after-sales servicing.[22] Management also thought that majority ownership of HEAI would prevent the emergence of the programs that had plagued previous joint ventures.[23] AVIC wants larger subcontracting packages to be performed in China—the first couple of aircraft were kits flown in from Brazil and little more than the final stuffing and painting was done in Harbin. Embraer is currently evaluating possibilities for sourcing certain parts from HAIC, in substitution of some imports. Fuselage panels would be the natural next step, but two major preconditions must be in place. Embraer wants more sales before contracting more work to Harbin, and the machine tools to do so must be procured first. Location and infrastructure are other important considerations, especially in light of the summer 2004 power shortage.

Two years is obviously too short a period to assess an investment as complex as the one that Embraer has embarked upon in China. The first, more general point is that the race to China is not paved with instant gratifications and that Brazilian business is unlikely to fare much better than other global competitors. Hype remains the order of the day—for instance on the basis of the fact that Brazil had been listed by the government as a permitted travel destination for Chinese citizens, some thought that there would be a fully loaded Boeing 747 flying to Brazil everyday.[24] A long-term effort is required and Brazil is heading in the right direction (e.g. the visit by President Lula in May 2004), but the fruits will only be harvested down the road. Indeed, the Chinese ban on Brazilian soya bean exports in June 2004, which was justified on very tenuous grounds and had the desired result of cooling the international price for this particular commodity, lends support to this hypothesis.

Nonetheless, the market for regional jets remain a sellers' one. Although sluggish so far, orders will surely come through, for were these ventures to fail some investors in aerospace and other industries might lose heart, causing headaches for the government, which needs foreign investment to create sorely needed jobs and introduce new technology. Moreover, the heavy investment made to build new airports only makes sense if the new regional airlines have the proper type of aircraft to fly to such routes. And the current vintage is far too old for this. In this sense the upside potential for Embraer management—which at any rate proffers optimism and reminds skeptics that the Harbin investment is relatively small compared to the US$150 m that are destined to the Gavião Peixoto plant—is large, if the first-mover advantage allows it to tap into this huge market. In fact, in August 2006 the gamble seemed to pay off when Embraer finally secured a major deal to sell 100 aircraft (including 50 larger ERJ-190s) to Hainan Airlines Co. for U$2.7 billion. This deal substantially raises the company's firm order backlog, which had been stuck at around US$10 billion for some time. It also means Embraer will deliver more planes than the 150 that had been predicted for 2007 and increase deliveries in 2008.

HEAI's prospects are necessarily intertwined with those of Chinese aerospace more generally. It is difficult to foresee the joint venture succeeding if other Chinese-owned firms fail in their current plans. At the same time, authorities may be tempted to push the ARJ21 project ahead of HAEI. Despite the growing interest in the country's potential, skeptics remain doubtful about long-term prospects for aircraft manufacturing in China, citing past experiences.[25] It will take determination, commitment, and a lot more financial investment, but the Chinese aerospace industry may also achieve credibility for more and more aircraft parts and even larger aircraft to be built in China over the coming decade, dramatically reshaping global aerospace.

12.3.2. The Case of Techint

In steel production, Techint's presence in China is limited to Tenaris, and is reflective of the different strategies adopted by the two divisions as well as the differences in industry characteristics between the two. Ternium, competing in the flat steel sector, has adopted a regional approach, focussing on being one of the dominant players in the Americas. With a much larger and fragmented industry segment, the pressures as well as ability to enter the Chinese market are few, and as such it has not as yet been a focus for Techint's flat steel business.

By contrast, Tenaris operates in a global market in which relatively large economies of scale have resulted in a high degree of market consolidation. Its presence in China first started in 1976, when Siderca started exporting piping to large Chinese trading companies which would then disperse the product to the various oil fields they represented. In this period, the products which the firm sold were standardized both in terms of product specifications as well as price, and purchased in one or two lump orders per year. Direct contact with the end users, the oil fields themselves, was closely guarded by the trading companies. For 15 years, business remained more or less the same. It was not until 1990 that the firm set up a small office in Beijing. With this new physical presence in China, Techint slowly began having direct contact with the oil fields, visiting their facilities, and being better able to identify the specific necessities of each oil field. While in some cases purchases remained on an annual or semiannual basis, in others purchases began to be more regular and come directly from the oil fields themselves.

With the rapid growth of the domestic market, China has become the second largest consumer of oil piping in the world after the United States, with annual consumption of 8–9 million tons and an annual growth of 6 percent. Much of that market, however, is consumed by relatively simple products and is dominated by local Chinese players. By contrast, Tenaris focusses on the higher value added, more complex products, where it has a dominant position. Japanese players are also important in this segment and combined have a larger market share than Tenaris, but the latter remains the largest individual player.

Given the growing importance of China, Techint decided to make the country its own business unit in 2004 with the goal of growing the business and eventually establishing production facilities in the country. In expanding its operations in China beyond the initial commercial activities, Tenaris is using both expatriates and nationals. 'We started by sending expatriates with significant industrial knowledge and have begun forming the new management structures by searching for Western-educated professionals of Chinese origin. At the same time, however, because of localization, we understand the importance of cultivating the local workforce, so we will also focus on building entry-level programs with the hope that, in a few years, we will have a good layer of local people,' said Luis Albaine, Regional Human Resource Director (SpencerStuart 2004: 5).

Currently, Tenaris is working on the Nanhai Project, the largest petrochemical complex in China, and jointly owned by Shell and the Chinese National Offshore Oil Corporation (CNOOC). Tenaris is supplying not only the piping material, but also project management services. It has located a project manager onsite to work jointly with the BSF (a joint venture between Bechtel, Sinopec, and Foster Wheeler) project team. In addition, they have also been supplying pipes to Dongfang Boiler Works in China for more than 10 years.

Aside from selling piping, Tenaris is expanding its service offerings in China. It is currently providing a type of full pipe-management services for

Kerr-McGee's offshore activities from its Tanggu service yard at Bohai Bay.[26] Through this new service base in Tanggu, Tenaris' Chinese employees manage and coordinate all activities including the integration of local suppliers. As part of the pipe management service for Kerr-McGee in China, the company maintains 24-hour ready-to-run inventory that is dispatched offshore as the client requires. The full-pipe management program covers delivery of pipes, joints, and accessories, according to Kerr-McGee's very dynamic drilling plan. The program relieves the operator from performing multiple logistics tasks. Tenaris coordinates the preparation of float shoes and float collars for cementing in coordination with China National Offshore Oil Co. Services Ltd. (COSL) and the manufacture of the pup joints. Unique services from the mill to the well are provided which far exceed the simple delivery of pipe. Material is delivered to the docks for Kerr-McGee boats with 24-hour notice to ensure there are no delays or stoppages of rig operations. Local expertise in customs, languages, and procedures contributes to meeting these operational challenges. Kerr-McGee provides Tenaris with its drilling schedule, pipe specifications, and the required daily quantity of pipe. With that information, tables of monthly quantities are developed. Weekly meetings are held between the company's personnel in China and Kerr-McGee regarding changes that may occur either in the type or quantity of pipe needed. Coordination of the production and shipping timetables must be accurate and worked out long in advance to avoid any possible mishaps. For example, in the case of tubes manufactured at the Siderca mill, the supply process must be planned 4 months in advance, taking into account that the shipment itself to Tanggu takes about 40 days.

In the past few years, China has also become the most active market for Techint Technologies, which designs and assembles industrial plants locally, from both the installations and contracts point of view: roll grinders have been installed in China in the iron and steel plants of Anshan, Baotou, Guangzhou Zhujiang, Jiuquan, Lian Yuan, Maanshan, and Wuhan.[27] In April 2004, the firm also signed an order with Tianjin Pipe Company for a new traditional 90 tons EAF. Techint has also had exposure to Chinese oil companies outside of China, in places such as Kazakhstan and Sudan, where these firms have oil fields.[28] However, the Chinese presence abroad is still relatively small (roughly 1/20th the size of the domestic market). In 2004, it established a fully fledged engineering company in China under the name Techint Industrial Technologies Beijing Co. Ltd (TITBCO) to coordinate its activities in China.

In addition to providing engineering services to Tianjin, Tenaris is studying opportunities for a joint venture with Tianjin Pipe Corporation, China's leading producer of seamless OCTG casing, to produce tubes and accessories for China's growing oil and gas industry.[29] The initial goal of the project is to enter into a strategic alliance with Tianjin, where the two companies will work together to develop a joint venture pipe threading facility and an oilfield accessories plant with an investment of up to US$20 million. Products designed specifically for use in oil extraction and production operations will be the primary focus of these new facilities. Both facilities would be majority owned by Tenaris, and would be established in the Tianjin Free Trade Zone, bordering the Bohai Sea about 72 miles from Beijing. Tenaris sees this as an opportunity to enhance its participation in this prominent market and work with the leading local producer of OCTG casing and a company with a strong focus on manufacturing quality products (Tenaris News 2004).

Looking from the outside, however, the firm does face a number of challenges in addition to opportunities in order to develop a major production presence in China. As with the oil and auto sectors, steel is considered by the Chinese government to be a strategically important industry, and as such foreign majority ownership is restricted. The Chinese government recently came out with its National Steel Industry Policy (July 2005) which reaffirms its intent to regulate the sector. It states that foreign firms should not be allowed to control domestic companies and that if they want to invest in a minority form, they should have 'independent intellectual property in steel-making technologies and have an annual output of 10 million tons'. (Qi Xiangdong, Deputy Secretary General of the Chinese Iron and Steel Association, July 2005). This has not prevented some of the large flat steel firms from entering the market, such as Mittal and Arcelor. However, in the more sophisticated seamless tubular steel market, it has deterred entry by competitors on a major production basis in favor of imports. As alluded to earlier, Techint has in the past attributed much of its success to its ability to apply its management abilities through majority control. At the same time, Techint's presence in the high end of the market makes the issue of technology transfer an area of concern for the firm.[30] Though improving, the legal protection of patents and intellectual property rights makes it difficult to reach agreements with potential local partners. The firm appears to remain optimistic, however, that with time, it will be able to find common ground between the objectives of China's central government and those of the firm, which would eventually allow it to leverage its technological and managerial skills on a local basis in China.

12.4. Conclusions

Its 1.2 billion population, slow but steady transition into a fully fledged market economy, rapid economic growth, and WTO membership, all combine to make China a compelling subject for business executives, policymakers and scholars, including those in Latin America. The experiences of Embraer and Techint highlight that, notwithstanding the tacit know-how they may have coming from emerging economies themselves, these companies face the same challenges firms from OECD nations encounter when entering China. The starting requirements are the same. One needs to operate at world-class levels, as entering these markets implies competing not only against local Chinese firms but also the flood of foreign investment entering the country. Furthermore, as is widely cited, one of the principal goals of China's more liberal approach toward inward FDI is the authorities' desire to incorporate advanced technologies and upgrade local abilities. As such, even if one is accustomed to dealing with the institutional complexity of an emerging market, this is not a sufficient condition to succeed in the Chinese market. Knowing how to operate in an environment of weak institutional infrastructures (Khanna and Palepu 1999, 2002) can indeed serve as an added resource for firms from emerging markets to tap into, but at the same time this is counterbalanced by an often higher cost of capital, even if they are publicly listed in OECD countries.

The two companies that we have looked at do indeed operate at globally recognized standards. Both Embraer and Techint are leaders in their market segments, and while there are some differences in the source of that success, there are also a number of commonalities. Thus while Embraer has probably benefitted more from its close relationship with the Brazilian government than Techint has with the Argentinian government, both do indeed have very strong institutional relations abilities.[31] Furthermore, the two firms have shown to be excellent at managing supply chains, the boundaries of the firm, and relations with key international suppliers. And, possibly most important of all has been a clear and articulated global vision from the firms' top managements. These firms decided to look internationally while they still enjoyed domestic protection, and as such countered the pattern of most firms in emerging economies. By being proactive in their internationalization, they were able to reach quality standards earlier and under a less pressured environment than firms that were forced to quickly adapt to increased local competition in the 1990s, following the adoption of market liberalization programs in their home countries.

That being said, there are also differences in the approaches adopted by Embraer and Techint toward China. They, however, can be attributed more to the industry segment in which they operate and the source of their competitive advantages than to any specifics related to being *multilatinas*. Embraer has been relatively more proactive in establishing a production presence in China, whereas Techint has set up offices and provides services locally but still imports its products. If we look at the two companies, we see that Techint's expertise resides more in sophisticated process technologies, whereas Embraer's is rooted more in its ability to coordinate assembly and its access to critical suppliers. That being the case, the technology transfer demands imposed by the Chinese government are more of an issue for Techint than Embraer. As such, it is logical that the former would be more cautious when it comes to its entry strategy.

As has been described above, these firms do indeed have the foundations needed to be successful in a market like China. At the same time, they must also heed the advice given to all firms entering China (Lieberthal and Lieberthal 2003). Avoid irrational exuberance, get the local expertise you need (do not simply assume that all emerging market institutions are the same), and remember that this is an economy that is constantly changing (thus the conditions for which one negotiates an agreement today may not exist tomorrow). Furthermore, though some authors (Orr 2004) have noted that investment barriers are diminishing, this is not necessarily the case across the board. While intellectual property protection is gradually improving and the requirement for local partnering is being dropped in many industries, for firms competing in strategically important sectors such as the ones in which Embraer and Techint are involved, these issues are still of great importance.

Appendix

Table 12A.1. China investments projects by selected *multilatinas*

Firm	Strategy
Cemex	Although it considers China an interesting market, where its products would compete well with low-quality local cement, it is waiting for the industry to consolidate. In the meanwhile it considers entering Russia (where cement assets are owned by individual investors and acquisitions are smoother) and Turkey (where the export potential is higher).
Vitrocrisa (joint venture between Vitro of Mexico and Libbey of the United States)	Some large Vitro's customers, such as Sunbeam, already produce in China for the US market and Vitro is currently supplying them from Mexico. In September 2004 it launched a feasibility study to install a small US$10-to-15 million plant in China. This plant could also supply Mexican beverage producers (beer, tequila) which are already exporting to China.
Indústria Paranaense de Estruturas	IPE is a small producer of light, single-engine trainer planes, with fifteen employees and annual turnover of US$1 million. It considers opening a plant in China to produce the IPE-O6Aaircraft.
Aeromot	It manufactures small planes and aircraft parts, with 2005 turnover of US$17 million. In 2003 it signed an agreement with Guizhou Aviation Industry for a joint venture to produce the Ximango motorglider and the Guri two-seater trainer (of which it has already sold two units, which have not been delivered yet due to delays in payment). Twenty Chinese workers are being trained in Porto Alegre. According to initial plans, production in China will be equal to at least ten aircraft per month (2005 production in Brazil was 20 units) and Aeromot will hold 25 percent of the joint venture (although it is negotiating royalties on the planes to be sold in China). Components such as landing gear and wing fixation systems will be produced in Porto Alegre.

Sources: 'Reconoce Vitro la importancia de China', *Reforma*, 16 September 2004; 'Busca Cemex extender mercado', *ibid.*, 4 November 2004; 'Aeromot adia joint venture com chineses para 2007', *Valor Econômico*, 6 April 2005, and 'Embraer do futuro', *IstoÉ*, 29 May 2005.

Notes

1. Cemex from Mexico would be a third example, but it does not have a strong presence produce in China.

2. Six of the seven members of the Communist Party's recently retired Politburo visited Brazil, and President Jiang Zemin came twice. 'Cultivating a Partnership: Brazil Finds a Market for Exports and a Friend in China,' *The New York Times*, 23 April 2003.

3. 'Da miedo llegar a China,' *Reforma*, 1 June 2004.

4. For a few recent case studies, see also 'Getting a Foothold in China' and 'Kraft Foods Works on Improving Its Recipe for Distributing Goods', *Wall Street Journal*, 3 April 2004; 'Les multinationales menacées par le 'surinvestissement' en Chine', *Le Monde*, 9 March 2004, and 'It's Getting Hotter in the East' and 'How Cummins Does It', *Business Week*, 22/29 August 2005.

5. '2000 Laureate Awards', *Aviation Week and Space Technology* 7 May 2001.

6. TOR includes corporate initiatives such as Integrated Technological Development (in the areas of production, product engineering, and information technology), emergency projects, data cleaning, and implementation of the ERP (Enterprise Resource Planning) system.

7. Even though Tenaris has 3.32 billion tons of nominal seamless capacity, its effective capacity is 3.00 billion tons.

8. 'Techint no descarta crear otra sociedad', *La Nación*, 8 June 2002.

9. A very small 0.2 percent is in the hands of directors and senior executives and the remaining 39.8 percent is in the public's hands.

10. 'Techint no descarta', *cit.*

11. 'China negocia compra de mais cinco aviões da Embraer', *O Globo*, 8 September 2005.

12. Reuters.

13. 'Embraer Sees Rising Jet Sales to China as Costs Fall', *Bloomberg*, 30 July 2004.

14. 'Embraer Sees Rising Jet Sales to China as Costs Fall', *cit.*

15. 'Optimism despite airlines risk aversion', *Financial Times—Special Report Aerospace*, 19 July 2004. Bombardier Transport, on the other hand, is already operative in China through a joint venture with Sifang Power (Qingdao) Transportation, which has sold train and subway cars in the Shanghai region.

16. At the end of 2004, Boeing shares fell 2.2 percent in a day on the announcement by CAAC of a freezing of new commercial aircraft purchases in 2005, in an effort to curb 'over-heated' growth in the sector and uncontrolled capacity expansion by domestic airlines (see 'China to freeze aircraft orders in 2005', *Reuters*, 29 December 2004).

17. GECAS has agreed to lease four ERJ-170s to Hong Kong Express (HKE), the first of which was delivered in late September 2005. At the time the agreement was signed, HKE had hinted that the order could reach up to ten aircraft, but the 1 October (China's National Day) announcement that the ARJ-21 maiden flight will be in 2006 may scupper the deal. See 'China fará avião regional para competir com o jato 170', *O Estado de de S. Paulo*, 2 October 2005.

18. 'Diretor-presidente da empresa diz que canadense Bombardier atiçou "cachorros grandes" ao anunciar seus novos aviões', *O Estado de S. Paulo*, 19 Mar 2005.

19. 'Good times ahead', *Orient Aviation*, September 2004.

20. 'First China-built regional aircraft takes to skies', *China Daily*, 17 December 2003.

21. 'Leis ameaçam sucesso da Embraer na China', *Folha de S. Paulo*, 12 July 2004.

22. See 'Embraer hints at Russian ERJ-145 production', *Flight Daily News*, 17 June 2003 and 'Diretor-presidente da empresa diz que canadense Bombardier atiçou "cachorros grandes" ao anunciar seus novos aviões', *O Estado de S. Paulo*, 19 Mar 2005.

23. 'Nas asas da Embraer', *O Estado de S. Paulo*, 25 June 2004.

24. See 'Brazil to expand economic cooperation with China', *Xinhua English*, 1 September 2004.

25. Other transport industries tell a somewhat different story. Less than ten years ago China's shipyards were still turning out simple container vessels and bulk carriers and had a world market share below 1 percent. In 2003, they produced 13 percent of the world's new ships, behind only South Korea and Japan. In 2004, with a backlog of some 800 ships on order, including for sophisticated liquefied natural-gas carriers to mostly foreign specifications, the share is set to grow to 16 percent. Heilongjiang's Qiqihar Locomotive has also begun selling freight trains to Australia. As per the car industry, 'many feel that it is only a matter of time before vehicles assembled in China make significant inroads in the Japanese market' (Sturgeon and Florida 2004: 64), although growth is likely to be 'rapid, but uneven and painful' (Doner et al. 2004: 175).

26. 'Managing OCTG supply and delivery', *World Oil Magazine*, July 2004, vol. 225 (7).

27. New orders were also received from Baotou Iron & Steel (a fifth roll grinder, this time for the new CRM), China Steel Corporation (two Pomini roll grinders' revampings for the existing HSM), Guangzhou Zhujiang Iron & Steel (a fourth roll grinder for the CSP Mill expansion), Handan Iron & Steel (one roll grinder for the CRM), Jinan Iron & Steel (one roll grinder for the new CRM), Jiuquan Iron & Steel (three roll grinders for the new CSP Mill), Laiwu Steel (one roll grinder for the HSM), Maanshan Iron & Steel (a fourth roll grinder for the CSP Mill expansion), Tonghua Iron & Steel (two roll grinders and other roll shop equipment for the new DSP Mill), Yantai Nanshan (two roll grinders for the new Aluminum Mill) and Yieh Phui for SLTC (two roll grinders for the new CRM).

28. In January 1998 Techint International Construction put in a winning bid to build the Port Sudan marine terminal.

29. Tenaris Oilfield Services, News, May 2004.

30. Interview with Paolo Rocca, CEO and President, Organización Techint, Buenos Aires, 13 October 2005.

31. When needed, the Techint Group can also draw on the support of Italian authorities.

References

BCG (Boston Consulting Group) (2003). *China: The Pursuit of Competitive Advantage and Profitable Growth*.

Boletín Informativo Techint (2003). 'Tenaris. El rebranding del área tubos de la Organización Techint', No. 308.

CEPAL (2004). *Balance preliminar de las economías de América Latina y el Caribe*.

Clissold, T. (2005). *Mr. China: A Memoir*. Collins.

Dussel Peters, E. (2004). 'Oportunidades y retos económicos de China para México y. Centroamérica', *mimeo*, CEPAL, Mexico City.

Goldstein, A. (2002*a*). 'From National Champion to Global Player: Explaining the Success of Embraer', *CEPAL Review*, 77: 97–115.

—— (2002*b*). 'The Political Economy of High-Tech Industries in Developing Countries: Aerospace in Brazil, Indonesia and South Africa', *Cambridge Journal of Economics*, 26: 521–38.

—— (2005). 'Lead Firms and Clusters in the North and in the South: A Comparison of the Aerospace Industry in Montreal and São José dos Campos', in E. Giuliani, R. Rabellotti, and M. P. van Dijk (eds.), *Clusters Facing Competition: The Importance of External Linkages*, Ashgate.

—— and Steven McGuire (2004). 'The Political Economy of Strategic Trade Policy and the Brazil–Canada Export Subsidies Saga', *The World Economy*, 27(4).

Khanna, T. and Palepu, K. (1999). 'The Right Way to Restructure Conglomerates in Emerging Markets', *Harvard Business Review*, 77(4): 125–34.

—— —— (2002). 'Emerging Market Giants: Building World-Class Companies in Emerging Markets', *Harvard Business School Case*, No. 703–431.

Lieberthal, K. and Lieberthal G. (2003). 'The Great Transformation', *Harvard Business Review*, 81 (10): 70–81.

Luo, Y. (2000). *Multinational Corporations in China. Benefiting from Structural Transformation*. Copenhagen Business School Press.

Orr, G. (2004). 'What Executives are Asking about China', *The McKinsey Quarterly*, pp. 17–23.

Pitsilis, E. V., Woetzel, J. R., and Wong, J. (2004). 'Checking China's Vital Signs', *The McKinsey Quarterly*, pp. 7–15.

Rigzone.com (Dec. 4, 2003). http://www.rigzone.com/news/article.asp?a_id=9774

Santiso, J. (2004). 'Latin America's Friend across the Pacific', *Financial Times*, December 16.

SpencerStuart (2004). *Succeeding in China: Best practices in overcoming the war for talent* (http://content.spencerstuart.com/sswebsite/pdf/lib/Succeeding_in_China.pdf).

Studwell, J. (2002). *The China Dream*. Profile Books.

Suarez, F. and Oliva, R. (2002). 'Learning to Compete: Transforming Firms in the Face of Radical Environment Change', *Business Strategy Review*, 13(3): 62–71.

Sull, D. N. (2005). *Made in China: What Western Managers Can Learn From Trail-Blazing Chinese Entrepreneurs*. Harvard Business School Press.

Tenaris News: Oilfield Services (May 2004).

Toulan, O. (1997). 'Internationalization Reconsidered: The Case of Siderar', *Sloan Working Paper*, No. 3938.

—— (2002). 'The Impact of Market Liberalization on Vertical Scope: The Case of Argentina', *Strategic Management Journal*, 23(6): 551–60.

UNCTAD (2005). *World Investment Report*. Geneva.

Yan, R. and Libeberthal, K. (eds.) (2004). *Harvard Business Review on Doing Business in China*, Harvard Business School Press, Harvard Business Review Paperback Series.

13

Sustainable Management of Korean Firms: A Case Study of Yuhan–Kimberly and Its Implications for Latin American Firms

Dong-Sung Cho and Keum-Young Chang

13.1. Introduction

Hyundai Motors Co., POSCO, Samsung Electronics Co., and LG Telecom are major Korean companies that have grown into global players. Though these companies differ in the industries where they operate, they have one thing in common, which is that they are headed by powerful managers with superior business minds who have leveraged the Korean government's active industrial policies and aggressively responded to changes and challenges in the international market, and consequently, built an effective mechanism for success unique to each of the companies.

However, there is one company in Korea that is above all these globally famous companies in the respect and love it has earned from the Korean people. The Korean parent company of the firm in question is the fourth oldest company of the more than 1.5 million companies that operate in Korea. This company was selected as the best employer in Korea, as well as the company Korean consumers want most to repeat purchases with. In addition, this company was selected by the Corporate Longevity Forum[1] as the company with the best prospect for long life in the future.

Surprisingly, the company that is accompanied by such colorful adjectives and that has captured the heart and earned the respect of the Korean people is not a global name, but a local one called Yuhan–Kimberly, a joint venture between Yuhan Corporation, a Korean company and an American company named Kimberly-Clark. Yuhan–Kimberly is a household and sanitary goods maker that supplies diapers, sanitary pads, toilet paper, facial tissue, and nonwoven fabrics. The company may not look too glamorous nor its work rewarding just by looking at the products it handles, but it is the company that Korean college students want to work for most. The reason does not just lie in the fact that it is a profitable company with the largest market share in the industry. It is more because of its corporate image which reflects a corporate culture that encourages creativity and autonomy, innovation and challenge, people-focussed management and lifelong learning enabled by the 4 crews and 2 shifts working system, corporate social responsibility management and ethics management. Not surprisingly, Yuhan–Kimberly was the winner of the Best Corporate Image Award for Ethical Management and was selected as one of the top five companies with the highest social contribution in 2001 by the Federation of Korean Industries, an organization that consists solely of conglomerates, despite the fact that Yuhan–Kimberly is not a conglomerate itself. Yuhan-Kimberly's feats do not end on the domestic soil. Its reputation has spread overseas and in 2003, it was selected as the sixth *Best Employers in Asia* (No. 1 in Korea) by *The Asian Wall Street Journal* and Hewitt Associates.

However, the road to success has not always been smooth for Yuhan–Kimberly. Once, its market share in its main business plummeted from 100 to 18 percent and the company endured no less than 13 years of labor strife and inner disruption. However, since CEO Kook-Hyun Moon took the helm in 1995, it has been successfully transformed into a company commanding the largest market share for all of its products as of the end of 2004, just nine years since he took office. Yuhan–Kimberly is committed to ethics, corporate social responsibility and environment management, which not only drive up financial performance but also enable sustainable prosperity, thereby making Yuhan–Kimberly the best model for firms in the twenty-first century.

In order to analyze the drivers of Yuhan–Kimberly's success in financial performance as well as in social reputation, we have used the SER-M model with a focus on the mechanism of the interaction among subject, environment, and resource to systematically and comprehensively identify all of the success factors.

We believe that by identifying the success factors of Yuhan–Kimberly, we will not only provide implications for managers working in other regions of the world and possibly, in other times on the 'right' way of managing but also present various hypotheses on the successful achievement of sustainable management through the pursuit of new values such as respect from the market and love from the consumers, rather than the blind pursuit of sales and profit that is traditional of the existing firms.

The success factors of a company, in particular, for creating a new form of sustainable management that we hope to find through Yuhan–Kimberly, will provide the basis for Latin American firms to develop a sustainable management model that is appropriate for the Latin American environment, which is different from the standard global model that is generally based on the American model.

13.2. Holistic Approach to Analysis of Corporate Competitiveness: The SER-M Model

Strategic management theory has long focussed on finding the source of competitive advantage of a company which generates excess profit and has either focussed on the internal or on the external aspect of a company (Hoskisson, Hitt, and Wan 1999). The earliest theory was influenced by Simon (1945) and Cyert and March (1963) and focussed on the decision-making process and the role of the manager inside a company. Later theories developed by scholars who studied industrial organization theory shifted their focus to the external aspect of a company, thereby highlighting the industrial organizational view such as that of Porter (1980), which focusses on the structure of the industry in which the company operates. However, when industrial organization theory failed to explain the gap in performance among the companies operating in the same industry, scholars once again began turning their eyes to the internal aspect of a company. The new internal-focussed theory is the RBV initiated by Wernerfelt (1984), which forms the core of strategic management theory today that has given birth to diverse views and debates which consequently have expanded the concept of resource.

Though the focus of strategic management theories has shifted from inside to outside, and back to the inside of a company, the theories shared a common trait in that their methodologies were rooted in reductionism, or mechanical philosophy represented by Descarte and Newton. And though some scholars have recognized the importance of an integrated approach, and some have even attempted to pursue the approach (Palmer and Wiseman 1999; Bate, Kahn, and Pye 2000; Flamholtz and Aksehirli 2000; Nonaka, Toyama, and Konno 2000; Lähteenmäki, Toivonen, and Mattila 2001), to date, the mechanism-based view (MBV) is the only framework that presents a common theoretical view or approach to investigating the importance of an integrated and holistic approach.

Although various scholars in the field of strategic management have shifted their focus from leadership to industrial organization to resource over time, they were basically oriented toward individual factors in explaining corporate performance. Naturally, a new approach was proposed in the name of the 'SER-M framework' as a replacement for the existing approaches. This approach has two characteristics. The first characteristic of the SER-M model is eclectic, as it claims a need to simultaneously study the 'S'ubject (leadership), the 'E'nvironment, and 'R'esources. The second characteristic of the SER-M model is integrated, claiming a need to study the fourth variable, that is,

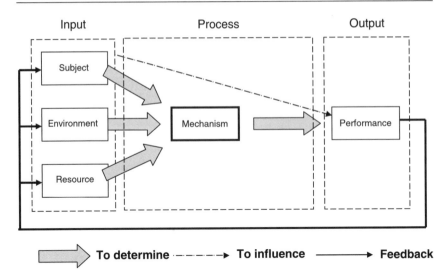

Figure 13.1. The concept of the SER-M model

interactions among the three key variables through the 'M'echanism (Cho and Lee 1998). Cho and Kim (2005) made a detailed documentation of all the statistically tested empirical papers on firms' financial performance that were published from 1990 through 2004, and confirmed the increasing frequency of resources, and more recently of mechanisms that were proven as independent variables. The SER-M model is graphically illustrated in Figure 13.1.

Entering the twenty-first century, 'Mechanism', the fourth variable of the SER-M model, has been explored as the single most important determinant of corporate performance (Cho 2004). Cho (2005) argued the importance of Mechanism as a source of the sustainable competitive advantage of a firm, replacing Barney's VRIN-based resources (1991). The MBV is now borne through a series of these papers on the mechanism.

The discussion on the MBV to date has been two-pronged—(a) the mechanism as a source of competitive advantages of a firm and (b) the mechanism as a tool for studying the various phenomena of strategic management.

First, in the theory that claims the mechanism as a source of the competitive advantages of a firm, a business phenomenon is created as a result of a process in which a subject creates a resource within a certain environment. Mechanism is the dynamic interaction of the subject, resource, and environment and the repetition of the process of interaction. Cho (2004) asserts that the existing strategic management theory cannot properly identify the source of competitive advantage of a firm since it only studies individual factors, such as leadership, industrial organization, or resources, separately when the mechanism that forms the foundation of a competitive advantage of a firm is created through the interaction of the three factors. A deeper look into mechanism shows that it consists of three factors—composition of resources, sequence, and timing (Cho 2005). That is, even companies with similar resource and environment will have different mechanisms depending on how the subject mixes the three factors with what strategic purpose. The main factors that determine the composition of resources, sequence and timing are subject, resource, and environment.

Second, the MBV is viewed as a methodology or an approach for understanding business phenomena. In order to properly identify business phenomena, the causes or factors that drive the business phenomena need to be identified and the mechanism of interaction of the factors that ultimately create the phenomena need to be understood. The best way to identifying the mechanism is to classify the factors into S, E, R, and M based on the SER-M model (Cho and Chang 2005).

13.3. Case Study of a Korean Firm: Yuhan–Kimberly's Mechanism for Success

As of February 2004, Yuhan–Kimberly's products were No. 1 in market share, with diapers, feminine pads, tissue, paper towels, and moist wipes accounting for 67, 62, 55, 55, and 48 percent of the market, respectively. However, behind this success lies countless adversity and challenges overcome. Since Yuhan–Kimberly's birth as a joint venture between Yuhan Corporation and Kimberly-Clark on March 30, 1970, it has grown into a health and hygiene product company. However, a number of prominent conglomerates like Ssangyong Group, CJ, and Amore Pacific began jumping onto the household product bandwagon. Later, many international firms like Procter & Gamble rushed to tap the local market after foreign investments were liberalized in 1989. Brutal competition from new entrants and their aggressive market advance tactics bore down heavily on Yuhan–Kimberly, which was ultimately forced to give up its market-leading position. However, with 1995 as a turning point, Yuhan–Kimberly bounced back, and managed to take back the No. 1 spot in the market. And now, nine years into CEO Moon's leadership, the company enjoys a phenomenal growth.

In this chapter, we attempt to analyze Yuhan–Kimberly's success by using the SER-M model, taking the MBV as the most important framework of analysis.

(1) CEO Kook-Hyun Moon's Leadership: S: CEO Kook-Hyun Moon with his challenging spirit, passion, and execution power is one of the most important factors that have made the success Yuhan–Kimberly enjoys today possible. In order for a company to achieve innovation, a CEO who presents a vision for innovation and who promotes the vision with passion and commitment is absolutely vital. In this aspect, CEO Moon's challenging spirit and aggressive leadership served Yuhan–Kimberly well in creating and building a corporate culture that pursues autonomy and responsibility, innovation and challenge, expression of creativity, free discussion, and consideration for the society and the nation.

More specifically, Yuhan–Kimberly encourages the employees to take ownership and responsibility for their jobs, which, while guaranteeing the autonomy of each of the employees, also encourages them to personally find ways to achieve harmony with the organization to which they belong. Job delegations and empowerment are considered very important, and delegated authorities are taken very seriously. The organizational structure at Yuhan–Kimberly consists of twelve division heads with different titles ranging from director to senior managing director reporting directly to the CEO. Despite the difference in their titles, the division heads have a horizontal relationship in which each one assumes the full responsibility of a division head. Proposals from the working level are approved by the department heads, and the division heads only intervene when there are issues that cannot be resolved at the department head level. As such, the organization structure guarantees freedom in judgment and activity while imposing strong accountability and authority on each member of the company.

Second, Yuhan–Kimberly was floundering in the early 1980s when it first began its diaper business, so much so that profit from other businesses had to be poured into the business. Thanks to these efforts which were grounded on a firm belief in the growth potential of the business, it has grown to become one of the most important businesses for Yuhan–Kimberly. In 1983, Yuhan–Kimberly introduced Korea's first-ever panty-shaped diaper, Huggies. Since then, Huggies has commanded the largest market share for the past two decades and has literally become synonymous with paper diapers in Korea. The fearless spirit that welcomed new challenges, the aggressive and the positive attitude and the belief in success that were demonstrated in the process were values that CEO Kook-Hyun Moon has enrooted in Yuhan–Kimberly.

Third, Yuhan–Kimberly encourages experimental and creative behaviors from its employees. To prevent wasting time developing plans for new ideas and strategies which sometimes consumes an unnecessary amount of time that could instead be used more effectively for implementation and action-taking, Yuhan–Kimberly encourages experimenting with new ideas consistently to respond speedily to the rapidly changing environment.

Fourth, Yuhan–Kimberly creates video newsletters that enable the management to share detailed business information with the employees. CEO Moon personally appears in each of the video newsletters and gives a detailed explanation on management issues that the employees are curious about using PowerPoint. After the management discloses detailed information transparently through the video newsletter, the employees discuss the issues among themselves and present their opinions to the company so that the management can reflect them in running the company. As such, Yuhan–Kimberly creates a culture in which the management and the employees run the company together.

Fifth, CEO Moon stresses to the employees the importance of accurately understanding the position of not only the company but also of the society and the country and furthermore, the global market. According to CEO Moon, understanding the society and the country, and the world in which a company operates is extremely important not only because it is essential for achieving its goals and survival but also because changes in the global market impact every aspect of a company.

(2) The Environment: E: The Korean economy has grown rapidly at an annual average rate of 9.7 percent since the beginning of the government-led economic development in the early 1960s until 1997 when the economic crisis hit the nation badly. The ensuing phenomenal growth driven by qualitative and quantitative labor, robust entrepreneurship, and the government's export-oriented development strategy built self-confidence in the Korean people and bore fruit to economic feats that have propelled the country on to becoming the world's 11th largest economy and 12th largest in trade volume in just three decades. The economy that had been agriculture-oriented shifted its focus to heavy chemicals and services, and the country's status was raised significantly in international society. All these achievements drew the attention of the international society, and the world came to regard Korea as a success case of economic development.

It was commonly viewed that economic development spearheaded by the government enabled Korea to rise from the ashes of the Korean War to achieve phenomenal economic growth. The government's economic development plan focussing on the expansion of industrial production capability was constantly at the heart of the government's industrial policy which has changed over time along with the changes in the domestic and international environment. From the 1960s to the 1970s, the government directly intervened in the market and made decisions on distribution of investment by sector. The government undertook large-scale investments in the form of public-sector projects. In large-scale projects conducted by the private sector, the government personally selected highly skilled entrepreneurs or developed the land required for a project or provided funding. The government also aggressively promoted an export-focussed growth strategy and nurtured export and heavy chemical industries. During the 1980s and 1990s, the government reduced its hands-on direct intervention and focussed on encouraging creativity from the private sector and stressed competition and opening of the domestic market (Kyung Tae Lee 1996). The launching of the World Trade Organization in 1995 further expanded world trade and strengthened multilateralism. Korea joined the OECD in 1996 as its 29th member and proactively joined in the effort to create international economic order (1996 White Paper on Trade and Industry 1997). However, the economic crisis that hit Korea at the end of 1997 devalued the Korean currency, resulted in the bankruptcy of many companies, and caused the sovereign rating to plunge, which ultimately placed the country under the stewardship of the International Monetary Fund (IMF). To overcome the economic crisis, the government aggressively pursued corporate restructurings and attracted foreign direct investments and on August 23, 2001, succeeded in repaying the entire IMF fund which amounted to $19.5 billion (2002 White Paper on Industry and Resource 2003).

(3) Reputation as a Resource (R): Yuhan–Kimberly's reputation as Korea's most ethical company has its roots in the culture and reputation of its parent companies, Yuhan Corporation and Kimberly-Clark.

Yuhan Corporation was founded by an independent activist and social worker, Dr Il Hwan Yu in 1926. It is a national company that has consistently emphasized and practiced the spirit of volunteering, thereby earning the love and respect of the Korean people. The management philosophy of Yuhan Corporation is grounded on the value proclaimed by Dr Il Hwan Yu, who said, 'the profit earned by a company must be returned to the society that has nurtured the company'. Dr Il Hwan Yu was a pioneer in management and adopted advanced management tactics—Yuhan Corporation went public, a first for a pharmaceutical company in Korea and separated ownership from management, and also introduced the Employee Stock Ownership Plans (ESOP) and professional manager system for the first time in Korea. Yuhan Corporation, which has consistently adopted cutting-edge management methods during the eighty years of its history, has remained faithful to its three corporate philosophies consisting of production of the best products, dutiful tax payment, and contribution of business profit to the society.

Yuhan–Kimberly's American partner, Kimberly-Clark, has achieved phenomenal growth under the leadership of CEO Darwin E. Smith. During the twenty years when Smith, the soft-spoken CEO turned in-house attorney, led the company, Kimberly-Clark achieved an astounding growth and transformed itself from a good company to a great company. Kimberly-Clark achieved a cumulative stock return that was 4.1 times higher than the market, easily overtaking its competitors, Scott Paper, and Procter & Gamble, and even surpassing some of the powerful players such as Coca Cola, Hewlett-Packard, 3M, and General Electric. He was a man with a strong ambition on the business level, but he was also a man with extreme humility, which is the fifth level of leadership, on the personal level (Collins 2001).

Yuhan–Kimberly, strongly influenced by the corporate culture of its parent companies, has established five business philosophies—respect for human beings, customer satisfaction, social contribution, value creation, and innovation—as its corporate values.

(4) The Mechanism: M: Mechanism as a source of a company's competitiveness is created in the process of a subject (S) using resources (R) to respond to the environment (E). During this process, these factors interact with one another. At Yuhan–Kimberly, the mechanism for success is formed through the *composition* of various IMT, the *sequence* by which these techniques are implemented, and the *timing* of each IMT being implemented. These various IMTs are the Neway model, Loc-balization (aimed at building global competitiveness through the accumulation of competitiveness in the Northeast Asian region), lifelong learning through the 4 crews 2 shifts working system, the domestic R&D center that has enabled differentiated product competitiveness, social responsibility, and ethics management.

On the *composition* dimension, Yuhan Corporation's Il Hwan Yu's and Kimberly-Clark's Darwin E. Smith's corporate philosophies were effectively synthesized to create Yuhan–Kimberly's corporate philosophies, which are social responsibility management and ethics management. In terms of *sequence*, Yuhan–Kimberly established a system for promoting innovation within the company called 'Neway', which is founded on its corporate philosophies, and then encouraged the employees to actively participate in the system based on which the company developed products with differentiated competitiveness and dominated the domestic market after which the company pursued its global strategy. As far as *timing* is concerned, in 1997, when the world was mired in economic crisis, while most Korean companies were busily reducing R&D expenditure on product development, cutting down on training and advertising that are necessary for developing new markets, Yuhan–Kimberly developed ultra-slim sanitary pads and diapers that let fresh air in which were highly demanded by the Korean consumers then. In addition, Yuhan–Kimberly provided regular training of up to 183 hours annually per person and adopted a lifelong learning system, a system that had not been heard of in Korea, let alone abroad. Also, Yuhan–Kimberly invested 1 percent of its annual sales to open a summer camp as part of the 'Keep Korea Green' campaign, where teenagers participating in the program planted 150 million trees, thereby enabling the company to fulfill its social responsibility while promoting the company at the same time. These efforts finally paid off and Yuhan–Kimberly gained an average 98 percent in customer loyalty.

13.3.1. *Bold Management Innovation Model: Neway*

Yuhan–Kimberly set up the Neway team with the surplus resources left after pursuing innovation in the organizational structure. The Neway provided an opportunity for the employees to take rest and to capture lifelong learning opportunities and to come up with new ideas for working in an innovative way. People who have worked in the Neway team or those who were sent overseas for training were promoted, which gave them opportunities to develop their capabilities and to spearhead innovation within the company. The Neway drove the streamlining and transformation of the organization structure at Yuhan–Kimberly and became the central point of internal and external activities.

Through Neway, Yuhan–Kimberly established an organizational culture that was efficient and that pursued lifelong learning. In the first stage of change management, unnecessary reporting lines were eliminated and inefficient and overlapping jobs were reduced. By streamlining the organization and standardizing work process, the company granted appropriate autonomy and authority to each of the employees while strengthening responsibility at the same time. In addition, inter-departmental cooperation increased to enhance internal communication and enable speedy completion of tasks. Yuhan–Kimberly also adopted Kimberly-Clark's work process, HPWS, and integrated departments with high similarity into one and provided training to the drivers and engineers. The equipment at the plants was reallocated which also prompted the redistribution of human resources and created a more efficient and safe working space, and when one production line was closed after the equipment was moved, the employees who had worked at the closed line were either given the opportunity to work in another line or to study further to transfer to another department.

If Neway was the tool for achieving companywide management innovation, Functional Excellence Teams (FETs) drove changes in the specific areas within the company. In areas that the FET perceived required change, the FET developed plans for change management and ran various data analysis to identify whether the specific area was ready for change and implemented the plan by using the results of the analysis. To transform the working processes and methods in line with the new system, organization structures were redesigned and plans for creating a desirable organizational culture were newly established. In order to promote the projects, the FETs set up project teams, created environment, and provided training to successfully complete the projects. Many companies, in promoting new changes, send many messages to the employees but most of the time the employees either do not understand the messages correctly or are indifferent to them. To prevent this, Yuhan–Kimberly set up teams by organization to conduct the project for the survival of the company, thereby inviting the employees to actually participate in the process of innovation.

Yuhan–Kimberly, recognizing the need to shift the management paradigm from production-focus to customer-focus, carried out transformation to standardize internal process and to maximize the efficiency of the supply chain as well as enabling real-time information sharing both internally and externally.

13.3.2. *Loc-balization*

On March 1, 2003, CEO Moon headed up business collaboration among five Northeast Asian countries—Korea, Japan, China, Hong Kong, and Mongolia— as Kimberly-Clark elected him president of the company's North Asia region and its business forum. This was a clear affirmation of Yuhan–Kimberly's position as a solid corporate leader in North Asia. The objective of Kimberly-Clark's collaborative forums, which are made up of (CEOs) managing directors from K-C subsidiaries worldwide, is to facilitate the sharing of information and knowledge as well as an exchange of human and material resources between subsidiaries, which is why Yuhan–Kimberly has been given the responsibility of serving as a connecting hub for all the K-C subsidiaries in the North Asian region. At the same time, it also serves as an incentive for Yuhan–Kimberly to start reaching out to the wider Kimberly-Clark global network to share its signature 'Yuhan–Kimberly style of doing business'—born out of years of accumulated knowledge and know-how—with other subsidiaries, as well as an opportunity for Yuhan–Kimberly to understand the business environment in the other countries to obtain knowledge helpful for developing global strategy. For example, Yuhan–Kimberly tapped into a new business area of consulting service while deploying its employees to support factories in each country, thereby providing Yuhan–Kimberly with the opportunity to experience global markets as a global leader which subsequently prompted Yuhan–Kimberly to promote new changes.

The basic principle behind Yuhan–Kimberly's business management in North Asian factories is to lead with utmost respect for local management. It fundamentally planned to commit to play a supportive role instead of playing 'boss'. The plan was to provide technical support and training to factories in the region to help them maintain a high level of productivity like Yuhan–Kimberly's and never to exercise direct control over anybody. In terms of management, the goal was to delegate responsibilities and powers to representatives from each region so they could strengthen their stand-alone independent capabilities. At its core, Yuhan–Kimberly's one-of-a-kind style of management is all about enhancing self-empowerment of an organization. Although Yuhan–Kimberly put forth the long-term vision and strategic action plans for operations, it was up to each subsidiary to carry out their own actual implementation with full ownership and responsibility, which gave them a chance to naturally improve their leadership skills and assertiveness. Yuhan–Kimberly's North Asian team was a combination of a vertical management structure and a horizontal support structure. A local management team from each of the subsidiaries was responsible for the vertical management of its own company.

13.3.3. *Lifelong Learning through the 4 Crews 2 Shifts Working System*

When demand for its products dropped drastically during the economic crisis in 1998, Yuhan–Kimberly had to close down some of its production lines for more than six months. The plant operation ratio slumped to below half its usual level and products continued to stock up. To make matters worse, 4 out of 10 of the employees worked under full capacity. When the pressure for restructuring which would entail massive lay-offs had reached a peak, CEO Moon reorganized the crew system from 3 crews to 4 crews and promoted job-sharing which would increase the number of workers by 33 percent. Although the 4-crew work system had the potential of incurring high financial risk due to increase in labor cost, the system generated unexpected results. The machines were operated year-round and the productivity of the employees improved drastically thanks to sufficient rest and training on new technologies.

The 4 crews 2 shifts system which has been implemented across all of Yuhan–Kimberly's factories divides all the employees into 4 crews. Each crew works for four 12-hour days then has 4 days off (including 1 day for training), another crew works four 12-hour nights then takes 4 days off. The crews work in a 16-day cycle. The shift changes at 7 a.m. and 7 p.m. every day and the net working hours per week are 42 hours and 45.5 hours when including training hours. Among the hours, 1.5 hours in overtime is paid. The annual regular training hours are 183 hours and holidays and days off are used as necessary for additional training. The system enables the company to have 33 percent more employees than other companies that implement 3 crews with an added bonus of training on top of employment. In addition, the 4 crews 2 shifts system provided training and rest, enabling the workers to have both a healthy head and mind. This enabled the workers to take time to recharge themselves, which enhanced the workers' loyalty toward the company and consequently led to a significant increase in company performance.

13.3.4. *Global-Level R&D Center that Sources Differentiated Product Competitiveness*

The sanitary pad and diaper industry is very sensitive to fluctuations in population. Consequently, the drop in Korea's birth rates meant a cutback on the local market for Yuhan–Kimberly. To respond to the projected decline in population going forward, Yuhan–Kimberly not only built a new business strategy, but also started pursuing a global advance strategy to find opportunities abroad and overcome the limitations of the domestic market. To this end, Yuhan–Kimberly has built up world-class R&D capabilities thanks to huge investments in research and development and the accumulation of all the technical know-how in its organization. Right now, time-to-market for new products is about nine months. The bigger advantage on top of the speed is that the products are advanced high-quality goods that give it a global competitive edge.

13.3.5. *Corporate Social Responsibility and Ethics Management*

Yuhan–Kimberly has been strongly committed to social contribution and has gained an image and reputation as the most respected and trusted company in Korea and a company that practices ethics management. The positive reputation and credibility of Yuhan–Kimberly has led to creating an equally positive image for its products. Yuhan–Kimberly's social campaign, 'Keep Korea Green, Green' promoted under CEO Moon's strong initiative since 1984, is recognized as the best environment campaign that boasts twenty-one years of history. The campaign is aimed at developing forests and consists of fundraising, a model forest development project, environment education, and support for discovering natural resources and cultural heritages. In addition, Yuhan–Kimberly publishes environment-related books, supports R&D activities for finding ways to maintain a sustainable environment and is currently planning to establish an environment-friendly production system inside the company.

CEO Moon did not merely stop at stressing the importance of ethics management and aggressively put theory into practice. He has maintained a frugal lifestyle and eliminated supportive functions for the management such as secretaries and received reports directly for approval. With the CEO setting an example, the management had no choice but to change; they also set out to personally correct 'wrong' practices. They eliminated entertainment expenses and congratulations and condolence expenses and placed a ban on the practice of giving presents to and entertaining customers. Yuhan–Kimberly's ethics management is a top-down effort that is the foundation of sustainable management.

13.4. Conclusion

Yuhan–Kimberly, which has grown amidst the rapid changes in the Korean economy, has emerged as a lean and efficient company through drastic innovation. As a result, Yuhan–Kimberly offers differentiated products and services to the customers and has an organization that is horizontal and that practices innovation to create value, and consistently tries to realize people-focussed management by providing lifelong learning opportunities.

In addition, Yuhan–Kimberly has proven the importance of sustainable management by practicing ethics, corporate social responsibility, and environment management, which are becoming the buzzwords in the twenty-first century. To Yuhan–Kimberly, investment made outside the company is not money down the drain but on the contrary is an investment that generates higher return on investment than money spent on any of the traditional marketing activities such as advertisement. Yuhan–Kimberly discloses business information, promotes transparent and credible management through delegation of authority and autonomous management, establishes environment management systems internally and externally, while at the same time sharing social vision through the social campaigns.

Moreover, Yuhan–Kimberly's Loc-balization is a successful demonstration of a creative management that does not exist in any other part of the world, thereby making it the benchmark for companies throughout the world.

Yuhan–Kimberly's innovation, ethics, corporate social responsibility, environment, and creation management have culminated in making it the most respected and loved company, the most preferred employer for college graduates and the company with the highest customer loyalty in Korea. In addition, considering that the Corporate Longevity Forum has projected Yuhan Corporation with the longest lifespan in Korea and that Yuhan–Kimberly accounts for the largest sales and profit of the Group, Yuhan–Kimberly's mechanism for success created through innovation, ethics, corporate social responsibility, environment, and creation management is a clear demonstration of 'sustainable management'.

There are many global companies that made significant investment in corporate social responsibility, such as environment protection measures, in Latin America. These companies are examples of sustainable management not only in terms of their economic performance, but also corporate social responsibility. These companies, therefore, offer good comparisons with Yuhan–Kimberly in Korea.

Based in Mexico, CEMEX is the world's largest ready-mix cement company with operations in more than fifty countries. CEMEX emphasizes continuous innovation for strong economic performance with unwavering commitment to society and environment. Since 1994, CEMEX has been implementing an environment protection program, which includes minimizing electricity use, introducing a control system of atmospheric emissions, preserving raw materials, and cooperating with NGOs. CEMEX has also supported some seventy environment protection projects in thirty countries. (www.cemex.com)

Companhia Vale do Rio Doce (CVRD) is the second largest global producer of manganese and iron alloys and the largest provider of logistics services in Brazil. CVRD considers the environment to be a fundamental component for the quality of its products and services and commits itself to sustainable development involving a balance between environmental protection and economic growth needs. For this reason, CVRD adopted economically viable and compatible environmental protection measures such as maintaining the Environmental Management System, educating and training its employees to act in an environmentally correct manner, and setting requirements for its suppliers' products and services to prove environmental quality. (www.cvrd.com.br)

AmBev is the largest beverage company in Latin America and the sixth largest beverage company in the world. In the past five years, AmBev invested US$36 million in environmental programs. Eight of its 50 units are ISO 14001 certified by Bureau Veritas Quality (BVQI), which assesses environmental quality. The company is also one of the founders of the CEMPRE (Compromisso Empresarial para Reciclagem—Corporate Commitment to Recycling) initiative, a nonprofit organization composed of a group of private companies that promotes and improves recycling processes in Brazil. (www.ambev.com.br)

To enhance the completeness of the SER-M framework for sustainable management, we need to study further the 'sequence' and the 'timing' of the sequence in deploying the five IMTs that compose the mechanism of sustainable management identified through the case study of Yuhan–Kimberly. It goes without saying that more sophisticated and empirical research should subsequently be conducted to validate the mechanism that consists of composition, sequence, and timing.

Note

1. The Corporate Longevity Forum is a study group composed of doctoral students in the field of business strategy at Seoul National University. Strategic management researchers have been mainly interested in the origin of corporate performance. Nowadays the lifespan of a company is an important research topic because a company's longevity contributes to meeting the company's stakeholder interests and society as a whole. Through exemplary cases of long-life companies, the Corporate Longevity Forum tries to identify the mechanism that enables corporations to prosper longer, and to find its strategic implications.

References

1996 White Paper on Trade and Industry (1997). Ministry of Trade and Industry.
2002 White Paper on Industry and Resource (2003). Ministry of Commerce, Industry and Energy.
Barney, J. B. (1991). 'Firm Resources and Sustained Competitive Advantage', *Journal of Management*, 17: 99–120.
Bate, P., Khan, R., and Pye, A. (2000). 'Toward a Culturally Sensitive Approach to Organization Structuring: Where Organization Design Meets Organization Development', *Organization Science*, 11(2): 197–211.

Cho, D. S. (2004). 'The Mechanism-Based View: Strategic Paradigm for the 21st Century', Working Paper series of the Society for Mechanism Studies.

—— (2005). 'The "Mechanism" as an Alternative Source of Sustained Competitive Advantage: Case Studies of Japanese Sogo-shosha and Korean Chaebol Groups', Working Paper presented at the Faculty Seminar of Fuqua School of Business, Duke University, July 6th, 2005, Durham, NC.

—— and Chang, K. Y. (2005). 'The Mechanism-Based View of the Firm: A New Holistic Approach to the Strategic Management Research', Paper presented at the 2005 Summer Conference of Korean Academic Society of Business Administration, Phoenix Park, Korea.

—— and Kim, B. (2005). 'Longitudinal Study on the Use of Independent Variables in Strategy Research', Working Paper presented at the Faculty Seminar of Fuqua School of Business, Duke University, July 6th, 2005, Durham, NC.

—— Lee, D. H. (1998). 'New Paradigm in Strategy Theory: "ser-M",' *Monash MT Eliza Business Review*, 1(2): 82–98.

Collins, J. (2001). 'Good to great: Why Some Companies Make the Leap . . . and Others Don't', Jim Collins c/o Curtis Brown, Ltd., New York.

Cyert, R. M. and March, J. G. (1963). *A Behavioral Theory of the Firm*. Englewood Cliffs, NJ: Prentice-Hall.

Flamholtz, E. G. and Aksehirli, Z. (2000). 'Organizational Success and Failure: An Empirical Test of a Holistic Model', *European Management Journal*, 18(5): 488–98.

Hoskisson, R. E, Hitt, M. A., Wan, W. P., and Yiu, D. (1999). 'Theory and Research in Strategic Management: Swings of a Pendulum', *Journal of Management*, 25(3): 417–56.

Lähteenmäki, S., Toivonen, J., and Mattila, M. (2001). 'Critical Aspects of Organizational Learning Research and Proposals for Its Measurement', *British Journal of Management*, 12: 113–29.

Lee, T. K. (1996). 'Theory and Reality of Industrial Policy', Institute for Industrial Policy Studies.

Nonaka, I., Toyoma, R., and Konno, N. (2000). 'SECI, ba and Leadership: A Unified Model of Dynamic Knowledge Creation', *Long Range Planning*, 33: 5–34.

Palmer, T. B. and Wiseman, R. M. (1999). 'Decoupling Risk Taking from Income Stream Uncertainty: A Holistic Model of Risk', *Strategic Management Journal*, 20: 1037–62.

Porter, M. E. (1980). *Competitive Strategy*. New York: Free Press.

Simon, H. A. (1945). *Administrative Behavior*. New York: Macmillan.

Wernerfelt, B. (1984). 'A Resource-Based View of the Firm', *Strategic Management Journal*, 5: 171–80.

www.ambev.com.br

www.cemex.com

www.cvrd.com.br

14

National Financial Systems in Latin America: Attributes, Credit Allocation Practices, and Their Impact on Enterprise Development

John C. Edmunds[†]

14.1. Introduction

In Latin America very few large, globally integrated multinational firms have arisen. In its 2005 survey, the magazine *América Economía* lists the twenty-five largest firms in Latin America. The list has behemoths on it but very few of the firms are integrated or global. Eleven of the region's twenty-five largest firms (ranked by turnover) are in the primary producing sectors of oil and gas, mining, and steel. Three telecommunications companies and two electric utilities also appear among the top twenty-five. Most of those companies operate in a single country. They are vertically integrated, but nowhere near as globally integrated as many other big companies headquartered in the industrial countries. Among the top twenty-five companies there are only two, TELMEX and CEMEX, that have extensive operations in many countries.

This chapter puts forward an explanation for the pattern of enterprise development: *national financial systems* in Latin America have held back the development of firms in the region. Access to capital was a constraint that discouraged them from some of the paths of expansion that firms in the rich countries and firms in the Asian Tiger countries followed with extraordinary success. The largest Latin American firms grew large in their own home countries, but the financing they were able to obtain restricted all but a very few

[†] The author received generous support for this research from the W.F. Glavin Center for Global Management at Babson College and is grateful for Mario Gutierrez (M.A., Brandeis University) for many valuable contributions to this project.

of them from becoming large, globally integrated multinational firms. This explanation focusses on the attributes of Latin American financial systems, and assembles piece by piece a compelling, but not exclusive, explanation for the pattern of business enterprise development. There are many other reasons why so few of the world's large multinational companies have arisen in Latin America. Many of those other explanations are also compelling, and hopefully this explanation focussing on the national financial systems will join with the other compelling explanations to constitute a more complete explanation of the region's distinctive pattern.

14.2. Hypotheses

This research hypothesizes that six attributes of Latin America's national financial systems have diminished their capacity for financing global-scope multinationals and have also predisposed them to channel credit to other sorts of uses. The research presents data supporting the assertion that each attribute is an accurate description of Latin American financial systems. It does not prove that each attribute has a damaging effect on the growth of globally integrated firms, and it does not quantify how much damage each attribute caused. Further research may reveal other attributes, but the six given below have been present in Latin American national financial systems. The six attributes, taken as a whole, indicate why those financial systems were not able, and were not set up, to provide the kinds and amounts of financing that a nascent multinational would have needed in order to become an integrated world-class player.

The six attributes are that Latin American national financial systems have been:

1. *Too small* to provide the amount of financing needed to support the growth of large, globally integrated multinational firms;
2. *Often embroiled in crises of liquidity*, so they could not provide steady infusions of capital to firms that might have been able to become global if, at pivotal times in their development, they had been able to rely on raising capital;
3. *Weak in providing equity capital to firms*, so the firms often had to rely on their own internal profits as their primary source of equity capital, and often had to look to the debt markets for financing, when equity financing would have been more appropriate to their needs;
4. *Too focussed on traditional forms of lending, i.e. financing exports and imports*;
5. *Too inclined to loan money to the national governments*, more than was the custom in other parts of the world, instead of lending to private firms; and

6. *Designed in a way that gave preference to local, single-stage firms engaged in commodity production and export,* instead of preferring to finance the growth of firms with far-flung, integrated operations.

For the first three of these attributes, evidence is abundant and relatively easy to gather. Also the damaging effect of these three attributes on enterprise creation and expansion is obvious. This chapter provides recent evidence showing that Latin American financial systems do have the first three attributes.

The fourth, fifth, and sixth attributes are also damaging; however, evidence is harder to gather and will not be as convincing to skeptics, because other national financial systems outside Latin America have also suffered from those attributes at times. Companies in those other parts of the world were sometimes able to become global players, so the fourth, fifth, and sixth attributes are not as assuredly damaging to the growth of world-spanning enterprises. Consequently, it will be harder to argue that the presence of the fourth, fifth, and sixth attributes caused the underperformance in creating world-spanning enterprises. With regard to the last three attributes, therefore, the objective in this chapter is only to show that they are accurate characterizations of Latin American national financial systems. Some readers will infer causality but others will remain skeptical.

By showing that six attributes are accurate characterizations of Latin American national financial systems, this research seeks to draw attention to the role that national financial systems have played in the pattern of business development in Latin America, and particularly in the development of large enterprises in the region. That is a part of the explanation for the chronic underperformance of Latin American economies, and merits full consideration along with the other components of the explanation. In the sections that follow, there is a discussion of the existing literature; then the existing literature is cited in providing evidence that the six attributes do accurately describe Latin American national financial systems; then there is a discussion bringing in relevant supporting topics, including the savings rate, comparisons to the Asian Tigers, and the recent rise in the region's savings rate; then there is a brief conclusion.

14.3. Review of Existing Literature

There is an extensive literature on Latin American economic development, and also an extensive literature on monetary policies and exchange rate policies in the region. Topics include the role of central banks, price controls, exchange control, and currency boards. There is not, however, such an extensive literature on how the national financial systems in Latin America gather and allocate capital. There are entire books on capital flight, and an extensive literature on informal economies. There are not as many articles that dig deeply into the motives of people who move money out of Latin America, nor why so many people in the region choose to operate in the informal sector.

The literature is surprisingly silent on how national financial systems in Latin America gather the savings of the local wage earners. It is easy to find references to the region's low savings rate. Most of the articles tacitly assume that the savings rates really are low, but some mention that the true savings rates may be higher than the reported figures, because some savings leak out, to be deposited in financial institutions outside the region.

The literature is even more silent on how the national financial systems allocate capital. There is now a growing literature on venture capital in Latin America, and on micro-lending, and there are also studies of the Chilean-style private pension fund schemes that have spread through the region. There are, however, very few studies documenting which kinds of projects got financing and which ones did not get financing. A possible explanation for this gap in the literature is that the post–World War II efforts to spur economic development in Latin America emphasized industrialization and export development. Capital was an input to both, and was chronically scarce. The existing financial institutions did not provide enough financing, and often perversely directed capital to activities like cattle raising, which were seen as less dynamic and less productive than industrial projects. In consequence, there was a tendency to dismiss the existing financial institutions as part of the old, tradition-bound economic order. The existing financial institutions were interesting to researchers who wanted to lay bare the mechanisms by which rich families controlled the levers of power in Latin American countries. But they were not interesting to many experts on economic development, who often argued for leapfrogging the existing financial institutions and setting up government entities to finance the new manufacturing enterprises that the industrialization and export promotion policies required.

For this research the need, in view of the gaps in the literature, has been to cast a wide net, extending the search to related fields, to find relevant sources. The approach we have taken is to cite the sources that we have found in the sections of the paper that discuss each attribute of Latin American financial systems. In providing evidence and citations to support the discussion of each of the six attributes, we have used the most recent sources, and the best that we could find. Further research may uncover additional sources, but we do not expect to find sources that make specific causal links between the attributes of the region's financial systems and the types of large enterprises that emerged.

14.3.1. *Small Size as a Limiting Factor*

National financial systems in Latin America have been small for the entire history of the region. They were small during the colonial period, in the decades following independence, and continue to be small during the modern era. At the end of the colonial period, national financial systems were so subordinate and insignificant that the standard histories of the region scarcely mention them at all. Those histories treat the national financial systems as part of the set of institutions that the new elites took over after freeing themselves from their Spanish and Portuguese overlords. The financial systems are mentioned only in passing in those histories, and the few comments dedicated to them indicate how little importance authors attach to them. For example, Herring (1968) states that 'much of the chief business in banking and trading had been in the hands of *peninsulares* who were now banished' (p. 284). The author points out in many passages how the underprivileged were mistreated, and how the many countries of the region enacted new constitutions, or formed new governments, but makes no further comment about national financial systems until he describes the high inflation rates of the post–World War II commodities boom.

At the time when Latin American countries achieved their independence from Spain and Portugal, the large financial centers were London, Paris, and Amsterdam. Madrid was still repaying the debts that the Spanish monarchy incurred during previous generations, so it was not a place where large amounts of money could be raised. Lisbon was not the center of a large enough economic zone, and much of the zone under its financial suzerainty was poor. In consequence it could not offer large amounts of financing for ventures in Brazil. In the richer Latin American countries, during the colonial period the national financial systems facilitated the pattern of development that was in fashion, and that pattern did not require the financial systems to be proactive or large. Their small-sized and subordinate role was consistent with the mercantilist trading paradigm that assigned a conventional and delimited economic role to the Latin American colonies during those years. The focus of the colonial economies was to export commodities, and the merchants in the capital cities who exported those commodities were a key constituency for the monarchy's designated local representative. Much of the financial paperwork was done in Spain, and the creoles were prohibited from doing that kind of work.

Another function those colonial financial systems performed was to finance the imports that the commodity production system needed, and the imports of luxury goods that the elite consumed. There were some instances when manufacturing in the colonies took place, but there was no financing for it from the official financial systems. As suggested by Chapman (1938) and Harding (1947), the colonial paradigm explicitly prohibited manufacturing enterprises in many parts of Latin America, and the financing of them was therefore also prohibited.

Data from the 1980s indicated that the region's financial systems were still small, but by that time there was more awareness of how much damage they could cause. Writers no longer dismissed them as insignificant. The policy of relying on foreign capital and foreign financial institutions appeared to aggravate cyclical downturns, causing them to spiral into fully fledged depressions. There was an outpouring of research on financial systems after the Third World debt crisis broke out in August 1982. In the Eighties, there were careful attempts to measure capital flight. Everyone knew that it existed, and had a vague notion that it was harmful, but they did not attribute to it as much causality as it deserved. Then the economic stagnation persisted for almost a full decade, and when attention turned to the financial system, researchers uncovered some striking facts. Williamson and Lessard (1987) express one illustrative fact very clearly. They state that 'much of the accumulation of foreign assets by the domestic private sector in Latin America in recent years has coincided with external borrowing by the sovereign' (p. 20). That finding confirmed the suspicion that Latin American governments borrowed foreign currency in London and New York, which then 'leaked' away into Swiss bank accounts belonging to wealthy individuals who enriched themselves. The Latin American countries found themselves with large debts and little new capacity to service the debts.

The track record of the national financial systems of Latin America has not always attracted as much attention as it did from those two researchers, but those systems, whether under scrutiny or not, have continued to underperform compared to the systems in the rich countries.

Data from the IMF's Global Financial Stability Report (2005) give a measure of how small these financial systems have remained despite their recent rapid growth. For 2004, total bonds, equities, and bank assets in Latin America were US$2,739.4 billion, an amount equal to 136 percent of the region's GDP. That percentage compares unfavorably to the proportions of the financial systems in the industrial countries, which range from 358.6 percent for Canada to 413.0 percent for Japan.

The comparison with rich countries like Canada and Japan shows how small the region's national financial systems are in comparison to the systems in the rich countries. For this discussion it is more relevant to compare the Latin American systems to the ones in other emerging countries, particularly the countries that were able to nurture companies that have become integrated global giants. This comparison will reveal whether the small size of Latin America's financial systems was a plausible explanation for the region's underperformance in spawning large multinationals.

This comparison with other emerging countries reveals that the national financial systems of Latin America have performed worse than the ones emerging in Asia and Eastern Europe in the key tasks of gathering and allocating capital (IMF 2005). Aggregate figures for the size of the capital markets show this clearly. For example, the IMF (2004) reported that in the emerging Asian countries total bonds, stocks, and bank assets were equal to 242.2 percent of GDP at the end of 2002 and 250.6 percent of GDP at the end of 2004. That is surprising because the national financial systems in emerging Asia and Eastern Europe have had very well publicized problems that have hampered their performance.

It should have been easy to outperform the national financial systems of emerging Asia because the Asian Crisis of 1997 revealed such deep flaws in the design of those countries' financial systems. The Asian Crisis was severe and recovery from it was slow, so its lingering effects should have allowed Latin American financial systems to outdistance their counterparts in emerging Asia. The crisis caused the financial systems of the Asian Tigers to shrink, then to spend time repairing the damage. But that is not the only reason why Latin American financial systems should have been able to surpass the ones in the Asian Tiger countries. The financial systems in the emerging Asian countries continue to be bank-dominated. During the years before the Asian Crisis, companies in emerging Asia relied on bank financing and did not issue bonds very frequently. Stock markets were small and volatile and companies did not use them very often to raise equity capital. By 2002, the real economies of the Asian Tiger countries had recovered from the crisis, but the bond and stock markets in those countries were still not the dominant providers of capital. As of the end of 2002, bank assets constituted 58.4 percent of the total of bonds, common stock, and bank assets in emerging Asia (IMF 2005). Stock markets in emerging Asia rallied in the years 2003 and 2004, but as of the end of 2004 banks still remained the largest providers of capital, with bank assets accounting for 50.8 percent or the total of bonds, stocks, and bank assets (IMF 2005).

The comparison with emerging Asian countries indicates that the financial systems in emerging Asia were larger in comparison to GDP than their counterparts in Latin America. They achieved this size advantage despite being bank-dominated, and despite remaining excessively reliant on banks as allocators of capital longer than the Latin American systems did. The Latin American national financial systems became capital-market-dominated quite rapidly. That is a step forward, because capital market dominated systems are more transparent, suffer less from moral hazard, and are less vulnerable to domino-like collapses. The transformation to capital market domination happened rapidly in Latin America. Data for 2002–4 are illustrative. Bank deposits in Latin America at the end of 2002 were 44.9 percent of the total of bonds, stocks, and bank deposits. By the end of 2004 that figure had fallen to 33.6 percent of the total (IMF 2005).

In Eastern Europe, central planning gave way to market systems. This was a difficult transition, and the procedures for gathering and allocating capital went through a painful overhaul. The capital markets in that region are still small, and have grown slowly. Total bonds, stock, and bank assets were 81.8 percent of GDP at the end of 2002, and declined to 69.8 percent by the end of 2004 (IMF 2005). Bank assets grew more slowly, dropping from 33.4 percent of GDP at the end of 2002 to 27.1 percent by the end of 2004 (IMF 2005).

The evidence above indicates that the *size* of Latin American capital markets was *small* compared to the rich countries and to the countries of emerging Asia. The size of capital markets gives an indication of how much capital is available to be allocated during each time period. When capital is more abundant, economic growth can be higher, and large enterprises can get more financing to take advantage of growth opportunities. When capital is abundant enough, the allocation process can be inefficient and can still result in high economic growth. Also, large enterprises have a better chance of getting enough capital to achieve global standing.

In assessing these data, it is clear that Latin America's financial systems performed better in 2002–4 than they did in the Eighties. But they did not grow fast enough to outpace the Asian Tigers, despite the huge stumble that the Asian Tiger financial systems took in 1997. The Latin American financial systems did manage to stay ahead of the ones in Eastern Europe, at least in size. The comparison with the emerging countries of Eastern Europe shows that those systems have not yet been able to gather and allocate comparable amounts of capital. The Latin American financial systems also have another accomplishment to their credit. In the aggregate they were more successful than the Asian Tigers in diminishing the degree of dominance of commercial banks in the capital allocation process.

14.3.2. *Crises of Liquidity as a Limiting Factor*

During the past two centuries, every country, with the possible exception of Switzerland, has had financial crises. The frequency and severity of these crises have affected the amounts of financing that growing companies can obtain. Liquidity crises have also had a less obvious effect. The more frequent and severe they are, the more they bias companies against using debt financing. To see why, consider two risks of using debt financing. One is that the income stream of the business may be inadequate to repay the company's debts. This happens during the most typical type of financial crisis, in which the money supply shrinks rapidly, and prices of goods and services often fall, so the borrower's output may not bring in enough revenue to pay the debt. This also happens during hyperinflation, when the borrower has a hard time maintaining the profit margin needed to service debt. The second risk is that the company's short-term lenders may be unwilling to renew their loans to the company. Because of those two risks, in countries where financial crises are frequent, companies that survive are careful not to expand faster than their rate of internal cash generation permits.

In Latin America, there are many examples of family-controlled businesses that choose not to expand as much as the market will allow. They grow by reinvesting some of the profits, but do not seek debt or equity financing to expand faster. A sociological explanation is that the owners are engaging in 'satisficing' behavior—that is, they have reached a level of income where the marginal utility of more income falls so low that they choose to spend more time on leisure activities instead of working longer hours. An explanation from the theory of finance is that their business is vulnerable to downturns, so they are wary of using debt financing, because sooner or later debt turns out to be very expensive or very risky.

If Latin American businesses are indeed vulnerable to cyclical downturns and crises in the national financial systems, the observed aversion to using debt could be the result of *survivorship bias*. This bias distorts many statistical studies of financial performance because investigators inadvertently ignore the firms that did not survive, and so put too much weight on the behavior and performance of the ones that did survive. In the Latin American context, it could have happened that firms with the most conservative financial policies had a higher rate of survival. If the ones that shunned debt survived and the ones that used too much debt perished, an observer would, at any point in time, see more companies that shun debt. If that description corresponds to reality, an implication would be that older Latin American business executives would display a visceral aversion to debt, because they would have seen many good businesses fail as a result of owing too much money and being unable to repay it.

This possibility suggests an explanation for the observed pattern of enterprise development in Latin America. A worldwide macro-level version of survivorship bias may have been in operation. Suppose that one group of countries found a way of designing its financial systems so that they are more stable, and suppose that another group of countries does not improve the design of its financial systems, so that in that group of countries frequent financial crises continue to occur. Also suppose that in both groups of countries at some starting date in the past there were family businesses that potentially could have become globally integrated multinational firms. In the countries with stable financial systems, the firms that expanded are more likely to be the survivors, and at some point in their development they may have gained an advantage by expanding overseas. In the countries with unstable financial systems, the firms that were more cautious about using debt financing are the ones that were more likely to survive. Those cautious firms expand only using internally generated funds, and do not venture abroad. An observer who arrives several decades after the starting date would find that, with several striking exceptions, globally integrated multinationals arose in the countries that developed stable financial systems sooner.

There would be two sorts of exceptions to this pattern. In the natural resources sector there would be large quasi-government enterprises, which arose in the countries where the natural resources are located, and used their political leverage to obtain the capital they needed. The other sort would be the globally integrated multinationals from South Korea, Taiwan, India, and China. These multinationals arose despite being headquartered in countries with national financial systems organized along traditional lines—bank-dominated, or centrally planned, and vulnerable to crises. The Asian countries where they arose put high national priority on supporting the growth of large multinational firms, and succeeded by overriding every obstacle, including the tradition-bound lending practices of private banks. The evidence indicates that these Asian countries steered capital to the companies that became large, world-class players. Describing South Korea, Martin Hart-Landsberg (1988) wrote, 'South Korea went through an extended period of domestic industrialization.... It was a forced march, directed by military dictatorship, but it did raise living standards'. The Latin American countries, with the exception of Brazil, did not have such centrally directed policies of industrial development.

For the Asian Tiger countries, the regional financial crisis of 1997 was a severe blow, which called into question the feasibility of building an economic miracle in the goods producing sector without remedying the inadequacies of the national financial systems. Many high-ranking people in the Asian Tiger countries felt that the severity of the crisis was out of proportion to the sins that some borrowers and lenders in the Asian Tiger economies had committed.[1] The financial systems in the Asian Tigers had been handmaidens of the industrialization process. Their sudden collapse was doing so much damage that for several months skeptics were questioning the viability of the Asian Tiger economic growth strategy.

The response to the crisis varied. India and China escaped financial contagion because their financial systems were closed. Malaysia instituted capital controls. Thailand's and Indonesia's financial systems crashed, and their recovery was slow and painful. South Korea was a long way from the epicenter of the crisis, and many South Koreans felt that their country should not have been engulfed in it. South Koreans understood their financial system, and at first believed that the world financial market was overreacting. Later they acknowledged that the chaebol had expanded too rapidly, and had borrowed too much. South Koreans grudgingly accepted the need for consolidation in the banking sector and better disclosure regulations. They did not fully accept the need for the subsidiaries of a chaebol to cease guaranteeing the debts of the other subsidiaries.[2]

The South Korean response to the financial crisis was instructive and contrasts sharply with the Latin American response to that same crisis. Several of the South Korean chaebol were in financial distress after the Asian Crisis broke out. If South Korea had adopted a pure laissez-faire policy, the damage to the country's carefully constructed industrial powerhouse might have been profound. The South Korean response was to circle the wagons and preserve as much of the existing structure of corporate entities as they could. The de facto national economic policy was to negotiate debts while ramping up exports. The country also subjected its financial system to careful scrutiny, first to understand what caused the vulnerability, and then to reform it. Meanwhile, the top priority for financial policy was to direct the export revenues to paying debt. In that fashion South Korea weathered the Asian Crisis (Lodge and St. George 1998).

The Asian Crisis spread across the Pacific and affected Latin America. It is revealing to compare how Chile, Brazil, and Argentina responded to the financial contagion from that crisis. Chile found that it had become a dumping ground for Asian manufactured goods, particularly South Korean goods. Chile's response was to allow its currency to weaken 10 percent versus the US dollar. That was not the only response. For the preceding decade Chile had regulated inflows of foreign portfolio investment by imposing a penalty if the foreign portfolio investor withdrew the money before one full year had elapsed. This regulation was called the *encaje*. It had the effect of raising the real interest rate in Chile, and is one of the reasons why that country's famous retirement system delivered such strong returns.

Toward the end of 1997, Chile lowered the encaje to zero, in effect eliminating it. Short-term portfolio investment then flowed in, and quickly lowered the real rate of interest in Chile. This might sound like a boon to the economy, but it was not. Capital became cheaper to obtain in Chile, but the companies that had access to it did not take the opportunity to expand. Instead the economy stagnated. Large Chilean companies, which had expanded into other South American countries in the early Nineties, did not continue expanding abroad. Manufacturing companies that had survived the Seventies and Eighties, when Chile repealed tariffs on imports, suffered, and many disappeared. There were 60,000 manufacturing jobs in the shoe industry, and they disappeared, with the last ones going away after 1997.[3]

The real rate of interest remained low in Chile from 1998–2002, but did not have the hoped-for effect of stimulating economic growth. Borrowers were cautious, and government incentives to invest in new export-oriented businesses did not coax many companies to undertake new investments. According to the Central Bank of Chile (2003), returns on pension accounts fell, and the country's real growth rate was between 0 and 2 percent per year from 1998–2002. The Chilean economy did not resume its 6 percent real growth rate until 2003. By that time, South Korea's exports were 42 percent above their 1997 level (ISI Emerging Markets Database 2003).

Brazil and Argentina both suffered following the Asian Crisis. They each were trying to impose monetary discipline and each had set a fixed parity with the US dollar. Each country succeeded in maintaining the fixed parity after the Asian Crisis broke out, but Brazil wavered after the Russian default of August 1998. Brazil struggled to stem the outflows of foreign exchange and the speculative pressure on the fixed parity in the last four months of 1998, and then abandoned the fixed parity in January 1999. The Brazilian real, which was at par with the US dollar in mid-1996, had weakened to 1.20 per US dollar by the beginning of 1999. Then, in the middle of January 1999, it shot up and reached 2 reales per US dollar by the end of February (Federal Reserve Bank of St. Louis 2000).

Brazil was powerless to prevent the sudden weakening of its currency. The effects on its large companies were damaging because they owed foreign currency. The effects on Argentina were delayed but ultimately more serious. Argentina's famous fixed exchange rate ultimately could not survive the devaluation in Brazil.

Chile, Brazil, and Argentina each responded to the one-two punch of the Asian Crisis and the Russian default in different ways. Their responses, however, were similar in that they all allowed local firms, including large ones that operated internationally, to suffer. The South Korean response was strikingly different. In South Korea the priority was to preserve the large manufacturing companies that were the country's leading exporters, and to keep the whole structure of large firms as intact as possible. In Latin America, the priority was not as focussed on maintaining the health of the large firms. In Chile, many of the large companies were controlled by Spanish companies, so there was not a strong sense of ownership or national interest when the large companies stopped expanding internationally or withdrew their listings from the Santiago Stock Exchange. At the time when these large Chilean companies were suffering from the financial aftermath of the Asian Crisis, other priorities in Chile were more pressing. In Argentina, the collapse of the convertibility plan left the big public utilities with a mismatch. Their revenues in devalued pesos were no longer adequate to service their debts. The effect was to make the common shares of those companies almost worthless. For example, the market price of Telefónica de Argentina shares in New York reached US$50.00 on March 3, 2000, and then crashed to US$2.00 on October 9, 2002.[4] For comparison, shares of Korea Electric Power traded in New York at US$21.37 in February 1997, and fell to US$6.27 on June 16, 1998.[5] That is a 96 percent drop for the Argentinian stock and a 61 percent drop for the South Korean stock. The severity of the price declines is only one indication of each country's response to the financial crises, but the comparison does measure the losses that shareholders suffered.

Crises of liquidity, in summary, have had a deleterious effect on the growth of large companies headquartered in Latin American countries. The comparison with the effect of crises on the large companies in the Asian Tiger countries, and how those countries tried to preserve their large companies, is noteworthy, and deserves to be an important part of the conventional explanation for the paucity of large integrated Latin American multinationals.

14.3.3. *Equity Offerings as a Limiting Factor*

From 1988 to 1993 Latin America was experiencing a stock market boom. During that time there was a wave of initial public offerings, and Latin American stock markets rallied strongly. Then, following the Tequila Crisis of December 1994, those equity markets crashed, trading volume declined, and initial public offerings came almost to a complete halt. From 1995 to 2002 many companies went private because the paperwork associated with maintaining the public listing was more trouble than it was worth (Chong and Lopez-de-Silanes 2003). Data from Chile show this pattern very clearly. There was a burst of initial public offerings in 1990–2 in response to a tax incentive, and by 1994 there were 335 companies listed on the Santiago Stock Exchange. This number gradually declined to 288 by 2001. The volume of trading fell by 45 percent from 1995 to 2002. Stock market capitalization stagnated, rising from the post-crash low of US$27.3 billion at the end of 1994 to only US$34.3 billion at the end of 2002.[6]

Figures for initial public offerings in Chile reveal that the stock market had become insignificant as a source of capital. The number of initial public offerings in 1999 was three. There were four in 2000 and three in 2001. Then in 2002 there was only one! In 2003, the number rose to two (Abuhadba 2004). Finally, in 2004 the market took off and there were ten that year and several high profile ones in 2005. Stock market capitalization and trading volume boomed. But by then many Chilean companies which had been on track to become multinationals had pulled in their horns. Chilean companies had been expanding internationally, particularly to other South American countries in the early Nineties. They pulled back, and shelved their international aspirations, except in the retail sector, where Chilean companies were expanding aggressively in Peru and laying plans for expansion into Colombia.

ENDESA Chile, a large electric utility, was becoming a multinational in the early 1990s, and then pulled back. Its American Depository Receipts trade on the New York Stock Exchange. In 1994, they traded as high as US$14.58 on October 18, 1994. At that time ENDESA Chile was actively bidding for electric power plants that were being privatized in Argentina, Brazil, and Colombia. When ENDESA Chile won the bid, the company would send Chilean personnel to manage the power plants.

Then three events intervened. First, the Tequila Crisis hit, and ENDESA Chile's stock price stagnated. For most of 1995 and 1996 it was in the US$11 to US$12 range. Second, the Asian Crisis hit. The company's stock had struggled up to the $19 level when the crisis hit, only to sag down to US$7.80 by October 1998. The company's stock struggled back up after 1998, but slid again because of a corporate governance scandal, falling as low as US$6.84 in March 2003. From that point it climbed steadily, reaching US$30 on November 17, 2005.

This lackluster stock market performance was surprising. Chile's advantages made ENDESA Chile an obvious candidate to become one of South America's dominant electric utilities. It shied away from that role. Chileans gave many reasons for the company's disturbing unwillingness to continue developing into a continent-wide dominant player.

One reason they gave was the company's personnel policy. Mid-career engineers took two-year assignments managing the power plants the company had acquired in other South American countries, but then had a hard time reintegrating themselves into the management of the company when they came back from these foreign assignments. Two of them complained that when they accepted the foreign assignment they thought it would be a feather in their caps, but after they came back they felt that the foreign assignment had been a detour in their progression to top positions in the company.[7]

Another reason that Chileans gave why ENDESA Chile pulled in its horns relates to the control of the company. The corporate structure is complicated, but there was a master block of stock that gave the holder effective control. During the second half of the Nineties, the control block was pledged to lenders in Madrid. The owner of the control block ordered the company to direct a large part of its cash flow to dividends, to pay the lenders in Madrid. In effect, the owner of the control block turned the company into a cash cow.[8]

The third and most well-publicized reason why ENDESA Chile shied away from additional expansion opportunities in South America is that there was a corporate governance scandal. This was known as the Enersis scandal in Chile. To summarize a convoluted matter, one of the company's officers arranged to transfer control of the company. Most of the shareholders received too little, because Chilean corporate law did not yet give tag-along rights to minority shareholders. But the person who arranged the deal managed to obtain a price for his shares that was 11,000 times higher than the price the other shareholders received.[9] As of 2005, litigation was still continuing about this transaction.

This history of a large Chilean company, which had a very highly qualified engineering staff, and had access to the most modern capital market in South America, is sobering. The growth opportunities were there, and the company was taking advantage of them, then it stopped. The reasons it stopped relate to the financial system, to its management development policy, and to the defects in its corporate governance. The story is not entirely discouraging, because the company is now doing well, and anyone who bought the stock in 2003 or 2004 has done well, but the company is still not expanding abroad.

In Brazil, the pattern of equity market development was similar, with slight variations in chronology. The commercial banks competed successfully with the stock market until a change in tax treatment in 2002 made investing in mutual funds more attractive. Around the same time the Novo Mercado was created. This was a new section of the Brazilian stock market. New issues of common stock had to be floated on the Novo Mercado, except in special cases, and the rules of corporate governance in the Novo Mercado made the shares floated there more attractive.

Under the Novo Mercado rules, all shares had to have one vote each, and there could not be any shares with more than one vote. The pattern in the past had been for controlling families to keep a huge percentage of voting control. They did that by creating a class of shares with many votes and keeping those shares for themselves, and offering shares with only one vote or no vote to the public. That practice circumvented one problem but created another. It allowed the controlling families to keep control of the companies without having to subscribe to their pro rata share of each new issue of shares that their companies made. The drawback of that practice was that the shares offered to the public were unattractive. The public did not invest very much in the stock market. As recently as the year 2000, individual investors accounted for only 20.2 percent of the transactions on the Bolsa de Brazil. Institutions (including mutual funds) accounted for only 15.8 percent of the transactions. Foreigners, businesses, and financial institutions including commercial banks accounted for the rest of the transactions.[10]

Understandably, when the old set of rules was in place, the stock market remained small. Its total capitalization stagnated during the period 2000–2. It was R$441 billion as of the end of 2000, and R$436 billion as of the end of 2002. The amount of equity capital that firms were able to raise there was small compared to the GDP and compared to the opportunities for expansion that Brazilian firms had available to them. Meanwhile, the stock markets in the industrial countries were raising larger amounts of equity capital for firms that could then expand and become global players.

The combined effect of the Novo Mercado legislation and the rise of mutual funds had a dramatic effect from 2003 onward, and by the end of 2004, the picture was different. Stock market capitalization had risen to R$905 billion and the participation of individual investors and institutions including mutual funds in the total volume of trading had risen to 27.5 and 28.1 percent respectively.[11] There were eight initial public offerings, by law all in accordance with the Novo Mercado standards of corporate governance, and those offerings raised a total of R$4.5 billion reales.[12]

This impressive upsurge in stock market activity creates new possibilities for Brazilian firms. Previously, the controlling shareholders could raise equity capital only by putting their control at risk or by issuing shares at low multiples of earnings per share. Many of them chose not to expand or to expand only by using debt financing, which carries its own well-known risks. If Brazilian firms had been able to obtain more equity financing, a larger number of Brazilian firms might have expanded and become globally integrated multinationals.

14.3.4. *Focus on Traditional Forms of Lending as a Limiting Factor*

In every country the national financial system develops, evolves, and reforms itself concomitant with the struggles among groups that are vying for preeminence. Beginning from the time of independence, there were long-running rivalries in several Latin American countries. These rivalries played a role in focussing the financial systems on particular kinds of economic activity. There was a consensus that the national financial systems should perform routine functions, for example, provide currency in the form of coin and paper money to lubricate the wheels of local commerce. That consensus, however, was superficial, and masked a deeper discord. The motivations for issuing local currency included, in addition to the familiar ones of providing a means of payment and gaining seigniorage, also to assert authority over each entire country, to preempt provincial *caudillos* and *hacendados* from issuing their own scrip or coins.[13] The central governments were concerned that provincial strongmen and landowners would become too powerful, and disavow fealty to the central government, so issuing national currencies was a way of asserting the authority of the capital city over the provinces.

The national currencies were legal tender, with privileged status over the local scrip that *hacendados* in the hinterland sometimes issued. That privileged status created a *moral hazard* problem. Powerful people in the capital city had an incentive to issue too much of the national currency, relative to the central government's tax revenues, as a way of extending the capital city's economic power and military dominance over the hinterland. The elite in the capital city also had an incentive to restrict the convertibility of the national currency into foreign exchange, and to keep control of the country's reserves of foreign exchange in their own hands.

The historical rivalry between ruling elites in the capital cities and local strongmen running their own fiefdoms is one possible explanation why the national currencies of Latin America often suffered from high rates of inflation and occasional massive devaluations. The monetary policies were sometimes expansionary, both in the sense that we use the term today, and in the sense that would have seemed logical one or two centuries ago: the creation of money in excess of tax revenue would have been seen as an attempt to stimulate commerce, and as an attempt to extend the geographical range over which the national currencies ruled as the sole means of effecting transactions. The goal was not only the one that comes to the modern reader's mind, that is, seigniorage; it was more ambitious, seeking to unify each entire national economy, and bring all its far-flung regions under the sway of the central government. The goal was also to gain profits from all trade within the country, and especially to skim profits from trade involving the country's commodity exports, and to concentrate those profits in the hands of the elite in the capital city, which before independence had to be shared with the Crown.

This view of the role of currency, and the set of institutions that it engendered, is of course a caricature, and did not exist in such manifest form in all Latin American countries for the entire postcolonial period, and might not have existed in such pure form anywhere in the Latin American region. This caricature, nevertheless, is useful because it suggests that several countries committed the error of setting up their financial systems to help win a power struggle. The caricature is also useful in this argument, because it points out how the management of the currency and the chartering of financial institutions could have influenced the path of enterprise development. In this argument, it is useful to introduce the concept of *risk aversion,* which plays an important part in finance theory. Risk aversion is a rational response to unstable conditions in financial markets. Applying the concept helps explain decisions that investors and managers made in Latin America during several time frames since independence. A currency regime that is predisposed to inflation can inadvertently tilt the national economies toward commodity production, by favoring the known export-oriented businesses, whose products are priced in foreign currency. It can also raise the economic power of the capital cities, by apportioning a large share of the profits to financiers and exporters in those capital cities.

A differently conceived national financial system might have induced many Latin American economies to become diversified and entrepreneurial, and might have fostered geographical decentralization, with many regional sub-centers of wealth and economic power. Financial risk, however, was always present, and access to capital was always difficult, except for projects that had strong sponsorship. Risk aversion therefore argued for investing in activities that central government favored. Brazil's industrial development is a good source of examples of how risk aversion operated. The history of Brazil's industrial development is a lengthy story, with many promising starts that fizzled, and many tantalizing moments of opportunity that did not deliver the results which seemed possible. There were many beginnings in Bahia, Minas Gerais, Rio, and Sao Paulo. If these beginnings had developed fully, they would have given Brazil a geographically decentralized manufacturing sector, and might have transformed Brazil into an exporter of manufactured goods in the early years of the twentieth century. Exports of manufactured goods would have shifted economic power away from the landowning families, and would have diminished Brazil's extreme reliance on coffee as its main source of foreign exchange. All that might have happened many decades before the government-sponsored industrialization policy that accelerated during the 1951–4 presidential term of Getulio Vargas and continued during the 1956–61 presidential term of Juscelino Kubitschek. It is easy to imagine alternative histories for Brazil, but the glimmering possibilities did not materialize. What happened in reality was that the country opted for the centrally directed style of industrialization that these presidents adopted. That style delivered more lasting accomplishments than the de facto laissez-faire policy that had prevailed during earlier periods. It is tantalizing to speculate what prevented the happy developments that did not occur. The assertion here is that the financial system's focus on traditional forms of lending is partly responsible.

14.3.5. *Too Inclined to Lend Money to Their National Governments*

Another form of traditional lending was to lend to the government. This would also deprive nascent firms of the capital they needed to become global players. Data compiled by the IMF show that for several Latin American countries during the time frame 1957–70 the local commercial banks increased their lending to their national governments. IMF data also show that during those same years, commercial banks in other countries such as the United States and Singapore were decreasing their lending to their governments, and increasing their lending to private borrowers.

To show that the region's commercial banks were systematically depriving private firms of access to capital and giving preferential access to government borrowers, there needs to be a strong statistical pattern, particularly during a time frame when large multinationals were emerging in other parts of the world. Ideally, this time frame would be a period when there were no big distortions happening in the world economy that would influence lending decisions in Latin American countries. For the statistical evidence to be most convincing, it would be important to choose a time period when there was no pan-Latin American financial crisis, no boom in commodity prices, no worldwide depression, and no world war. It would also be important to choose a time frame when there was no major shift in the dominant economic growth model.

Unfortunately every time frame for which data are available is contaminated to some degree by confounding influences.[14] The time period chosen, 1957–70, was not a period of financial crises, world war, world depression, nor particularly high commodity prices. It was a period when the Asian Tigers were laying the groundwork for their economic rise. Lee Kwan Yew, the architect of Singapore's legendary economic transformation, became prime minister in 1959. It was also a period when the European and Japanese economies grew rapidly, having fully recovered from World War II.

In Latin America the complicating factor in 1957–70 was the widespread adoption of import substitution policies. These policies biased lending decisions in favor of investments in manufacturing for the domestic markets. The companies that arose during this time frame were infant industries that depended on preferential access to local markets. They were not oriented toward foreign markets, nor toward foreign expansion.

The import substitution policies, however, should have induced a shift in lending toward the private sector. The IMF data that exist show an unexpectedly contrary pattern. In several Latin American countries there were shifts in lending *away from* the private sector during this period. Governments borrowed a growing portion of the total capital that was provided by commercial banks. In Peru from 1964–70, Brazil from 1965–70 and in Mexico from 1964–8 this pattern was particularly strong.[15] The IMF database does not provide data about commercial bank lending patterns for all Latin American countries for the 1957–70 time frame. The data that the IMF does provide show a disturbing pattern. The data indicate that nascent multinationals in the region, if they existed, would have had difficulty obtaining large amounts of financing from local commercial banks.

Comparisons with commercial bank lending patterns in countries outside the region indicate that the Latin American pattern was not unique. A cross-sectional analysis for all countries in the world would not reveal a very strong pattern because the data are incomplete. Also in every country commercial banks routinely lend money to their national governments from time to time. Indeed, many are required to hold government bonds in their portfolios. Ideally, the evidence would indicate that Latin American financial institutions loaned more to their national governments, and did it more often, depriving their private firms of access to capital, and so impeding their growth. The evidence is too incomplete and too mixed to show a decisive result, but the data for several countries outside Latin America do support the assertion.

In two rich countries during that time frame the commercial banks were reducing their loans to their governments and increasing loans to private borrowers. In the Unites States, commercial banks reduced their loans to the governments steadily from 1957 to 1969, and then increased them slightly in 1970. In Switzerland, commercial banks reduced their loans to the government from 1967 to 1970, in a steady downtrend that was interrupted each year by a slight seasonal uptick.[16]

To compare what was happening in another emerging country outside Latin America at that time, IMF data for Thailand were considered. In Thailand, the pattern of commercial bank lending in 1957–67 was similar to the pattern in Peru for the same time frame. Commercial banks increased their lending to the government.[17] This is provocative, because Thailand grew rapidly enough to be classified as an Asian Tiger, but Thailand's devaluation was the triggering event for the Asian Crisis of 1997. Subsequent revelations about the lending practices of Thailand's commercial banks made its financial system look like a hotbed of cronyism.[18] Thailand's economic growth has been enviable, if volatile, but it is worth noting that Thailand has not given rise to many global multinationals. Perhaps its lending practices are an explanation.

The evidence given here is consistent with the assertion that commercial bank lending patterns had influence on the kinds of business enterprises that arose in each country. It would be premature, however, to state a definitive conclusion. The data are too fragmentary, too many of the time series have gaps in them, and in all the cases discussed here there may be problems of data quality and consistency. The most that can be said is that the evidence supports the hypothesis, but does not support it strongly enough to override other explanations for the observed composition of business enterprises in Latin America.

14.3.6. *Design as a Limiting Factor*

The centralized, commodity-export-focussed way of organizing and running the national financial systems had unintended consequences. These consequences were hard to see at the time but in retrospect are more obvious. The exporters in the capital cities probably did not see the damaging side-effects of the financial systems that existed in their countries, and might not have been able to imagine any other way of organizing the national financial systems, but modern readers can appreciate what the effects were. One was to discourage small merchants and manufacturers from relying on the local financial institutions. Inflation and devaluation were too severe and too frequent to ignore. Also there was another type of moral hazard that scared away many small potential users of the financial system. The national financial systems were dominated by classic family-controlled commercial banks. Those banks tended to lend to their affiliated businesses, basing their lending decisions on family ties or the borrower's social standing. That led to dangerous levels of what Latin Americans call *préstamos vinculados (loans to related parties)*.[19] The moral hazard was that the entire financial system was vulnerable to collapse, so relying on it would be suicidal in the long run. A national financial system dominated by banks that have too many loans of that sort on their books is unstable, and from time to time collapses, causing losses to depositors, a general contraction of credit, and a lingering distrust of financial institutions.

Lending to related parties is not the only practice that causes the instability of a bank-centered financial system. Classic commercial banks seem legitimate because they have existed in Europe since at least 1100, but they are unstable. The managers face so many conflicts of interest that it is difficult to give a complete enumeration of them. When a classic commercial bank is the centerpiece of a group of family businesses, in a financial system that depends on self-regulation, the result is too often a domino-like collapse that spreads to every province and to every sector of the entire economy.

In the past quarter century, the national financial systems in Latin America have become diverse. Some are now market-centered with independent central banks, while others remain bank-centered, with central banks under the direct control of the chief of state, but in the decades following independence they were strikingly similar to one another. They all had been established during the colonial period in accord with instructions coming from Spain and Portugal, and after independence they all sought to replicate features of the European-style national financial systems. In particular, they replicated features of the financial systems of Spain, Portugal, the Italian city-states, and Paris. They took the idea of merchant banking from Italy and the idea of the stock exchange from the Paris Bourse (Covarrubias 2004).

They did not copy every feature of European financial systems. They did not copy several institutions and practices that were already in widespread use in northern Europe. Surprisingly, they did not copy the idea of issuing government bonds in their local capital markets, which the Dutch had pioneered around 1500. They also did not copy the idea of a central bank, which the Swedish and the English had pioneered prior to 1700. Latin American countries floated bonds in European capital markets within a few decades of independence, but did not try to float bonds in their home markets until much later, and they established central banks as late as 1925 and 1926.[20] As for regulation, they relied on the code of the gentleman and self-regulation. The prevailing view was that financial activity was a private matter. It was like running a non-financial business. Finance practitioners who acted imprudently or dishonestly would suffer loss of reputation. For a century after independence, that informal pressure was the main mechanism of social control that many countries had over their national financial systems. There were sporadic attempts to treat the financial system as a public good. These sought to fix prices, control the allocation of foreign exchange, and to channel loans to sectors or strata that were not obtaining enough financing. There was tacit recognition that financial booms and collapses have externalities, that is, secondary effects that reach far beyond the parties directly involved. But the efforts to find the right mix of regulation and laissez-faire lurched and sputtered. In some countries, the usual set of checks and balances are still not fully in place.

The legal system always gave protection to loans secured by mortgages on land (inmuebles and inmobiliaria). Loans secured by circulating assets (enseres and muebles) did not enjoy the same level of protection, so there was a bias against lending for working capital. There were letters of credit and bills of lading, so finished goods for export could serve as collateral, but work in progress did not qualify for financing.[21]

329

These legal biases must be considered in combination with two facts. First, there was always a shortage of capital compared to the opportunities to invest it profitably. Second, rich families that had extensive landholdings were often in control of commercial banks. The result was that new kinds of activity, different from what the rich families knew best, did not qualify for much financing. Also, there was no market for general-obligation corporate bonds, secured only by the full faith and credit of the issuing company.

These institutional arrangements denied capital to companies that wanted to integrate vertically, diversify into new lines of business, or expand abroad. Vertical integration shifts the mix of assets, so that the company has more work in progress, and less immovable tangible collateral per unit of value added. Diversifying into new lines of business is riskier than expanding production of an export commodity, which has a cash price in Seville, Amsterdam or London. The returns to investing in new lines of business can be high on average, and still not attract capital in a financial system like the one described. The downside risk is too great, so the riskier sorts of ventures require equity financing, with upside participation.

There were no mechanisms in the national financial systems to bankroll companies that wanted to expand abroad. Overseas assets, in theory, could serve as collateral, but in practice they would not have been able to qualify for financing in competition with local fixed assets. In consequence, if there had been Latin American companies wishing to expand abroad they would have had to find innovative ways of financing their international expansion.

A comparison with financial practices that were typical in Amsterdam, Paris, and London illustrates the difference. In Amsterdam, joint-stock companies appeared as early as 1520, to finance shipping ventures to the Spice Islands. These ventures often established trading posts in faraway places. Investing in these overseas trading ventures was riskier than investing in letters of credit or government bonds, but offered upside potential. London had its famous money market, where short-term commercial paper was discounted.[22] In Paris, there was a large market for international bonds before World War I. French companies and Latin American governments floated bonds in that market. Latin American companies raised some capital there, but did not use it to finance expansion into other countries. In London, and later in New York, Latin American railroad bonds were issued, but the Latin American railroad companies did not invest in other countries.

Two reasons for the differences in financial practices are (a) in Europe there was more capital and fewer land-intensive or resource-intensive opportunities to invest in; (b) in Europe the capital markets allocated a larger portion of the total amount of credit.[23] The profits from risky ventures were very high and conventions for distributing the profits gave a large enough share of the gains to the people who took the risk.

The national financial systems of Latin America, according to this simplified characterization, gave loans to borrowers who could pledge land, to finance the production and export of primary products. Other feasible investments did not conform to the design of the national financial systems and so did not obtain as much financing.

14.4. Discussion

14.4.1. *Recent Success in Gathering Savings*

According to Duesenberry (1949), in every society there are people who save and others who do not. He suggests that savings behavior, however, is not absolutely hardwired in the brain of every individual. Savings behavior can be induced, coerced, or discouraged. In recent history, there have been many forced-savings schemes, and many countries that have become known for their high savings rates. There have also been many schemes that have discouraged savings. Latin America has seen an abundant number of schemes that have discouraged saving, or pushed it into the shadowy world of the parallel economy, such as in the case of Brazil in 1997 (Amann and Baer 2003).

The region's savings rate has always been cited as a reason for its slow economic growth, for its overdependence on foreign borrowing, and for its surprising inability to diversify into more promising kinds of economic activity, whether manufacturing, or skill-intensive services, or creating globe-spanning enterprises.

Until recently, official statistics supported this low-savings characterization, but anyone who has lived in the region for a long time has had personal experiences that call into question the validity of the low-savings statistics. A stroll through the downtown of many Latin American cities brings one into contact with money changers, who are always anxious to buy dollars. The ultimate buyers of the dollars include many local citizens who are seeking to protect their savings from inflation or devaluation. Another fact is that people who go from Latin America to the United States are often asked to carry envelopes full of greenbacks to relatives living in Miami, who then deposit the cash into an FDIC-insured bank account in the United States. Those savings are not reported in the statistics. When the money is eventually deposited in a US financial institution, the savings are incorrectly attributed to North Americans. The reality has been that for many years Latin Americans have gone to the trouble of moving their savings out of their home countries, to financial systems in the rich countries, where the risk of inflation, devaluation, or outright dispossession is not as great.

To an outside observer, it appears that the objective of these laws was to force the local citizens to hold the local currency against their will. The

Table 14.1. Gross national savings rates by region (percentage of GDP)

	1970–81		1982–9		1990–4	
	Average	Median	Average	Median	Average	Median
Industrial countries	23.8	23.4	20.6	20.2	20	19
Latin America	17.9	17.3	15.5	15.2	17.1	16.7
Southeast Asia	22.9	21.3	30.2	30.7	33.2	34.2

Source: IMF Database.

governments that imposed the laws never explained their motivations in such coercive terms. Instead, they would speak earnestly of the need to channel resources to high-priority domestic investment projects, or the need for all citizens to be loyal to nationalist ideals. It often happened, however, that the local currencies would lose some or all of their value. The people who were compelled to hold the local currency would lose and would be resentful. They would often jump to the conclusion that the national financial system was rigged against them. They saw themselves as chumps, and believed that bigger, better-connected players received prior warning of the devaluation and converted all their holdings of local currency just ahead of it. The victims can be forgiven for forming a negative attitude toward saving, and for swearing that they would not be victimized again.

Very recently several Latin American countries have reformed their national financial systems. These reforms have rewritten those countries' social contracts to include commitments to maintain stable currencies and to provide adequately designed and managed financial institutions where savers can put their money and expect to earn a positive return on it. The results have been dramatic. Table 14.1 illustrates how stark the difference was between Latin America's savings rate, as it was reported in the official statistics, and the famously high savings rate in Southeast Asia during the years 1970–94. Subsequent to the time periods reported in Table 14.1, official savings rates in a few key Latin American countries have risen, and so the regional average has also improved.

14.4.2. *Comparisons to Other Emerging Countries*

Latin American countries are diverse, and their paths of development have diverged. Nevertheless, it is sometimes helpful to view them as a group. It is also customary and convenient to consider other emerging countries in groups. The Southeast Asian Tigers are the group that has achieved the highest rates of economic growth, for example, 7.8 percent per year for 1987–96. Latin American countries achieved only 2.7 percent per year during that same period, beating Africa, which averaged only 2.2 percent, and trailing the Middle East, with 3.4 percent.[24]

The national financial systems of the Southeast Asian Tigers and the emerging countries in the Middle East were bank-dominated, as were the financial systems in Latin America. That is, commercial banks allocated more capital than the local stock markets and bond markets did. Despite this similarity, the Southeast Asian emerging countries have been able to foster the growth of more globally integrated multinational companies, and have consistently scored higher in export diversification, skill content of exports, and other categories of competitive success (De Gregorio and Wha Lee 2003).

Data for these groups of emerging countries show clear differences in savings rates and debt service ratios that outweigh the similarities in the design of their national financial systems.

Savings rates in Latin America are still low, but no longer so much lower than the world average. For the period 1983–90, world average savings were 22.8 percent of GDP. The Southeast Asian Tigers achieved an average savings rate of 34.6 percent, while the Middle East and Latin America achieved only 18.4 and 19.8 percent during that period. By 2004 and 2005, Latin America had achieved savings rates of 21.1 and 21.5 percent respectively, not far below the world average of 21.5 and 22.1 percent for those years, but still far below the 33.0 and 32.5 percent savings rates of the newly industrialized Asian countries for 2004 and 2005.[25]

There is also a striking difference in debt service ratios. The developing countries in Asia spent only 5 percent of their imports of goods and services on debt service payments during the period 1983–90, while the Middle East countries spent 3.1 percent and Latin America and the Caribbean paid 15.6 percent.[26] This burdensome ratio has made exports a high priority. At the same time, it biased business decisions against projects that would take large amounts of foreign exchange, or take too many years to reach fruition, even if the projects would ultimately bring in much more foreign exchange than they cost to develop.

Latin America's lower savings rate and higher debt service ratio are possible reasons for the low number of globally integrated firms headquartered in the region. Capital has been chronically scarce and expensive, and the high dependence on foreign capital magnified the instability of the region's economies, which in turn made large capital investment projects riskier, especially if they depended on private sources of capital.

14.4.3. *The Recent Rise in Savings and its Implications*

The rise in savings has happened very rapidly. The most rise has produced the surprising result that since 1999, the Latin American region has been a *net supplier of capital to the world financial market*. World financial statistics show this clearly. At the end of 1999, Latin American countries in the aggregate owed US$807.1 billion to lenders outside the region. By the end of 2005, this amount was US$842.4 billion. During the 1999–2005 period, the region's foreign exchange reserves increased from US$143.4 billion to US$249.5 billion.[27] Subtracting foreign exchange reserves from the amounts owed shows that in 1999 the region's net debt was US$663.7 billion, and by 2005 it had fallen to US$592.9. That is a decline of US$70.8 billion.

This remarkable reduction in net foreign debt was accomplished while local savings were flowing into the national financial systems. Local borrowers, including the governments, were able to replace foreign financing with local financing. In Brazil, for example, the foreign debt has fallen from US$242 billion in March 2000 to US$178 billion in July 2006.[28]

The rise in savings has often been attributed to the high commodity prices since 2002. A more complete explanation includes the financial reforms that several countries have implemented. Another reason for the rise is the reaction to the Asian Crisis. When that crisis broke out in 1997, it may have prodded many Latin American countries to accelerate the financial reform process. Latin American countries had just recovered from the Tequila Crisis of 1994–5. To their dismay, they found themselves once again over indebted to foreign banks, and again had to suffer another bout of contagion, credit contraction, and economic hardship. It was especially galling that the triggering event had not even occurred in Latin America! Latin American countries were being castigated for sins that they had not committed.

The international financial system was a harsh and capricious taskmaster. It punished Latin America once again for its past sins, and was deaf to the region's protestations that it was innocent this time. The need to repay foreign banks, coming such a short time after the Tequila credit crunch, prompted several Latin American countries to reform their capital markets and to overhaul their financial institutions. The reforms gave the local institutions the capability of attracting local savings. Privatized pension schemes took off in Mexico and Peru during this period. The pension schemes fueled the growth of local bond markets, which had been tiny and had mediated mostly government bonds before then. For example, as of year-end 2001, the total value of Latin American corporate bonds was only US$23.4 billion; by the end of 2004 that amount had risen to US$215.1 billion.[29] After the capital market reforms went into effect, borrowers in many Latin American countries were able to borrow locally by issuing bonds, and thus they no longer needed to borrow abroad.

The economic stagnation that the Latin American region suffered from 1998–2002 was a consequence of the pressure from foreign lenders seeking repayment. The classic way that Latin America has repaid foreign debt has been to create a trade surplus and a surplus of local savings over local investment. Devaluing the local currency creates the trade surplus by making exports more profitable and imports more expensive. Lack of alternative uses for money accomplishes the surplus of savings. New capital investment projects look unattractive because there is excess capacity, so citizens put their money into local financial institutions. This harsh corrective mechanism brings the foreign debt back into line with the capacity to service debt, but imposes hardship and austerity on local populations.

This explanation of Latin America's prudent financial performance is harsh and skeptical because it implies that the recent rise in the region's savings rate may be nothing more than an artifact of the imperative to repay foreign debt. If this skeptical view is correct, savings rates in the region will not stay high and will not keep rising. In that case, there would be no permanent improvement in the availability of capital, so Latin American globally integrated firms would not arise in the future.

A more optimistic view of the rapid rise of saving is that local pressures were already at work before the Asian Crisis. Contagion from Asia accelerated reforms that were already in progress. Latin American countries never liked having to rely so heavily on foreign debt, and saw a way of breaking the cycle of dependency. The way was to become more successful in gathering and allocating local savings. There was clearly room for improvement in the national financial systems, and that has been the avenue that several countries have followed with growing success. Aggregate statistics indicate that Latin American financial systems were not only bad at gathering savings. They were also bad at allocating those savings to the most promising uses. Data from the Eighties and Nineties show that for the entire Latin American region, economic growth averaged 2.9 percent per year for 1984–93 and 2.5 percent for 1994–2003. During the overall 20-year period savings rates were in the 18–19 percent range. That implies a marginal capital/output ratio much higher than the normal acceptable range of three to five. The ratio for the Southeast Asian Tigers was around four during that time period. The implication is that in Latin America capital was being allocated inefficiently. There were probably better uses for that capital. What might have happened is that the same mature, low-technology sectors continued to attract a large portion of the available capital, while other sectors got less than they could have used productively.

The encouraging implication of the rise in savings is that in the new environment of market-centered capital allocation, innovative firms may obtain more capital, and may be able to expand and diversify in ways they have been unable to do until now. Reforms to the national financial systems are moving forward in a handful of countries, and soon we will be able to see if this optimistic view is valid.

Until this point we have ignored the handful of Latin American firms that managed to become world-class multinationals despite the severe limitations of the national financial systems in the countries where they arose. CEMEX is the best-known example. It arose in Mexico, and managed to become one of the most dominant companies in a capital-intensive business. That is a remarkable accomplishment, and it shows how a truly exceptional entrepreneur can overcome seemingly insurmountable obstacles. CEMEX obtained capital from international markets and found innovative ways of paying for acquisitions, using national capital markets in the countries where its targets were located.[30]

Another success story has been Cencosud, the Chilean retail conglomerate. It started in 1952 and became an innovator in retailing, but did not need large amounts of capital until 1982, when it expanded into Argentina. Its expansion in Argentina is consistent with the argument put forward in this chapter: Chile's national financial system has functioned better than Argentina's, and consequently the Chilean company has been able to expand into Argentina. Other Chilean retail conglomerates have expanded into Peru and (to a lesser extent) into Colombia.[31]

14.5. Conclusion

There are many reasons why so few large, globally integrated companies have arisen in Latin America. The assertion put forward here is that the national financial systems of those countries are partly to blame because they were not set up properly to finance the growth of those companies. Assuming that there had been Latin American companies that possessed all the other preconditions necessary to become large, global-spanning enterprises, the small-size and idiosyncratic practices of their national financial systems would have prevented them from attaining their potential.

This chapter has given an argument consisting of many related parts, and has provided evidence in support of all the parts. The evidence for the first three parts of the argument is strong. For the other three parts, the evidence is indicative but not absolutely definitive. There can be little doubt, however, that national financial systems played an important part in creating the mix of economic activities and the kinds and sizes of business enterprises that we observe today. The objective here has been to draw attention to the role that national financial systems played. If this research achieves its purpose, the debate on Latin American business development will henceforth include the question of how the credit allocation practices in the region have operated, and how they are being reformed, so that the Latin American region will, from now on, be able to create its share of the large, globe-spanning companies in the world.

Notes

1. Famously, Mahathir Mohamad, prime minister of Malaysia, blamed the crisis on George Soros and other currency speculators, not on lending practices in the Asian

Tiger countries. 'Mahathir vs. Soros: A plan to weaken the region's currencies?' Asia Week, August 8, 1997, Web edition http://www.asiaweek.com/asiaweek/97/0808/nat2.html

2. South Korean bankers expressed this view to the author during a banking seminar in Seoul, South Korea in December 2003.

3. Professor Francisco Arroyo of the University of Chile cited this figure in conversations with the author in 2004.

4. Quotes are for the American Depository Receipt. Source: Yahoo Finance Website.

5. Quotes are also for the American Depository Receipt. Ibid.

6. Data from the Superintendencia de Valores y Seguros (Chile) website, Mercado Accionario statistics.

7. During the summer of 1997, the author taught at the Universidad Adolfo Ibanez and these two people were students in the author's class. They were studying for their MBAs with a view toward changing careers.

8. In 2002, Professor Roberto Darrigrandi and the author were teaching a class session in the MBA Program at the Universidad del Desarrollo in Concepcion, Chile. This explanation was provided by a student in the class. Other students confirmed this explanation.

9. Professor Roberto Bonifaz of the Universidad Adolfo Ibanez explained this long-running scandal to me in those terms. The full details were very complicated and some of them are in dispute.

10. Bovespa.com:br/Relatiorio Annual 2004, p. 23.

11. Ibid.

12. Bovespa, op. cit., p. 31.

13. Modern practices differ from the ones that were considered normal at the time of independence from Spain. The idea of the 'money supply' scarcely existed, and what today we call macroeconomic policy was a very minor part of the responsibilities of central government. Governments maintained peace and protected citizens from foreign invasion. Weather and crop yields were the key determinants of macroeconomic conditions. For a detailed view of what motivated heads of state to issue currency in previous centuries, see Alexander del Mar, History of Monetary Systems, (facsimile reprint of the edition published by Charles H. Carr and Company, Chicago, 1896), passim.

14. The author is indebted to Professor Harvey Arbelaez of the Monterey Institute of International Business for this insight.

15. Data collected from the IMF International Financial Statistics by Vinay Kaza.

16. Ibid.

17. Ibid.

18. 'Mid-Year Economic Review 2002,' *The Bangkok Post*, Web edition, http://www.bangkokpost.net/midyear2002/banking.html

19. For a recent article on 'préstamos vinculados' see *'La Falta de Educacion Financiera en el Ecuador'*, *Amalia Verdezoto Vidal, Americ Economia on-line edition, July 5, 2002, http://www.americaeconomica.com/numeros3/168/reportajes/amalia168.htm*

20. Bolivia and Chile.

21. An early reference to this distinction between classes of collateral, and the way that European financial systems dealt with them, is provided by Frederic L. Nussbaum,

'A History of the Economic Institutions of Modern Europe', originally published in 1935, reprinted by Augustus M. Kelly, Publishers, New York: 1968, pp. 297–298. This distinction between mortgage financing and various mechanisms for lending secured by inventory or accounts receivable was an important feature of the system that Latin American countries imported from Spain and France.

22. Walter Bagehot, the first editor of *the Economist*, describes this market in his classic book *Lombard Street*, referenced in the following note.

23. In the classic book *Lombard Street: A Description of the Money Market*, (New Edition, New York: E. F. Dutton and Company, 1910) Walter Bagehot gives a description of the commercial paper discounting process which he says operated in London during the years 1870–1910 on a much larger scale than anywhere else. With regard to the developing countries he wrote, 'there is no large sum of transferable money; there is no fund from which you can borrow, and out of which you can make immense works... it is certain that in the poor states there is no spare money for new and great undertakings, and that in most rich states the money is too scattered...' pp. 7–8.

24. International Monetary Fund, *World Economic Outlook*, September 2005, p. 211.

25. International Monetary Fund, *World Economic Outlook*, September 2005, p. 277.

26. International Monetary Fund, *World Economic Outlook*, September 2005, p. 273.

27. Data from the International Monetary Fund, *World Economic Outlook*, September 2005, pp. 269 and 273.

28. ISI emerging markets Database.

29. Data from the IMF World Financial Stability Report, 2002 and 2005.

30. The remarkable success of CEMEX and its financial policies have been profiled many times. Ravi Sarathy and David T. A. Wesley wrote one of the best accounts of the company's financial expertise, CEMEX: The Southdown Offer, 2003, case number *903M13*, Richard Ivey School of Business.

31. The history of Cencosud has been a favorite topic for MBA students in Chile to study and debate. The 'retail war' that has been going on among the top Chilean chains (including Falabella, D&S, and Ripley) was front-page news in Chilean financial newspapers during 2004 and 2005. The expansion into Peru and Colombia was portrayed as a way of gaining advantage in that war, by making forays into virgin territory. For a history of Cencosud, see its corporate website www.cencosud.cl. For a discussion of the retail wars, see El Diario Financiero and Estrategia, Chile's two daily financial newspapers.

References

Abuhadba, M. (2004). *IPOs en Chile: Salfacorp y el Underpricing*. (Informe Área de Negocios No. # 25). Santiago de Chile, Chile: Universidad Santo Tomás.

Amann, E. and Baer, W. (2003). *From the Developmental to the Regulatory State: The Transformation of the Government's Impact on the Brazilian Economy*. (Session 309/ECO 002, Congress of the Latin American Studies Association). Dallas, TX.

Chapman, C. E. (1938). *Colonial Hispanic America: A History*. New York: Macmillan.

Chong, A. and Lopez-De-Silanes, F. (2003). *The Truth about Privatization in Latin America.* (Research Network Working Paper No. R-486). Washington, DC: Inter-American Development Bank.

Covarrubias, I. (2004). *La Economía Medieval y la Emergencia del Capitalismo.* Texto completo en http://www.eumed.net/cursecon/libreria/index.htm

De Gregorio, J. and Wha Lee, J. (2003). *Growth and Adjustment in East Asia and Latin America.* (Working Paper No. 245). Santiago, Chile: Central Bank of Chile.

Duesenberry, J. (1949). *Income, Saving and the Theory of Consumer Behavior.* Cambridge, MA: Harvard University Press.

Harding, C. H. (1947). *The Spanish Empire in America.* New York: Oxford University Press.

Hart-Landsberg, M. (1998). *The Asian Crisis: Causes and Consequences.* Against the Current, 73 (March/April).

Herring, H. C. (1968), *A History of Latin America, from the Beginnings to the Present.* Random House; 3rd edition.

International Monetary Fund Global Financial Stability Report September 2003, Statistical Appendix, p. 143.

International Monetary Fund Global Financial Stability Report September 2005 http://imf.org/External/Pubs/FT/GFSR/2005/02/index.htm.

International Monetary Fund Global Financial Stability Report, September 2005, Statistical Appendix, p. 171.

Lodge, G. and St. George, A. (1998). *Collapse in Asia—1997–98.* (HBS Case study No. 9-798-084). Cambridge, MA: Harvard University.

Williamson, J. and Lessard, D. R. (1987). *Capital Flight and Third World Debt.* Washington, D.C.: Institute for International Economics.

15

Beating the Paradoxes of Emerging Markets: Strategies for Reaching the Consumers at the Bottom of the Pyramid

Guillermo D'Andrea

'What is good does not need to be more expensive'. This basic principle inspires the strategies of a number of firms which have successfully attempted to reach the BOP, trying to prove wrong the myth that anything cheap will end up costing more. Here we present the conclusions of various studies on the markets at the BOP, and of companies targeting them.

The picture of scarcity that characterizes the poorest segments of emerging markets conveys the assumption of a series of simplistic myths about these consumers' reality, and the persistence of some misconceptions regarding the real possibilities for companies to effectively address their needs. The examples of a few firms are intended to illustrate how to overcome those prejudices and reach the vast markets at the BOP. They also illustrate the magnitude of the challenge and the profound perspective required to generate creative solutions, innovative in its own way.

15.1. A Complex Picture of Scarcity

In the complex world of the twenty-first century, a number of trends coexist but not necessarily converge. Large corporations, a result of the concentration of increasingly mature industries, coexist with and generate more business through a myriad of small companies, which they need to carefully sustain in order to keep the efficiency of their increasingly decentralized strategies. The growing commoditization of products, such as home electronics, gives way to an economy based more on relationships than on mere negotiating power between manufacturers and their channels of distribution. Greed and the constant search for profitability combine with a growing sense of social responsibility among businesses. And in a world defined in more than one aspect by the 80/20 relation—80 percent of the population have only 20 percent of the purchasing power worldwide—strategies designed for mature markets need to be adapted in order to address this 80 percent of the world population living in emerging markets.[1]

The scarcity that typically characterizes emerging markets also prevents the surge of world-class leaders. However, we will see how some companies are able to break this traditional pattern and address the needs of the markets at the BOP, and by doing so achieve global leadership, joining world leaders who, through a change of perspective, also access these vast markets.

15.1.1. *Strategies Focussed on the Bottom of the Pyramid*

The reality at the BOP is pretty different from the traditional myths. They are a very important market, with a significant economic value, and they prefer well-known brands—many times more than buyers from segments in a better economic situation. In Argentina, 70 percent of these households represent 75 percent of the population and they account for 58 percent of the food products market. Their access to communications is growing—35 percent have a cell phone; 47 percent, cable TV; 65 percent, a fixed line telephone; 16 percent possess a computer.[2] And they prefer to buy in neighboring stores that do not have any bargaining power with wholesalers or the leading manufacturers, but have the trust of their customers, who are also grateful for their recommendations.[3]

Some companies have understood this reality and developed business models according to these segments' needs, managing even to conquer leading positions in the more advanced markets. *Corona* Beer of Mexico enjoys a leading position among the imported beers in 122 countries; its sales in the high-price segment are mainly due to the fact that they link their image to the pleasure of vacations in Mexico.[4] *Arcor* of Argentina is the top world candy producer. It sells its many products in 110 countries based on a strong presence at local fairs and chambers, supported by local executives and factories distributed in several countries. *Cemex* is the third largest world manufacturer of cement, with presence in thirty countries, based on a system of just-in-time delivery that the competition finds hard to imitate. But these—and other companies that we will analyze—have a fundamental component of their strategies at the BOP.

Cemex's[5] strategy relies heavily on its just-in-time system of distributing concrete, inspired on the method used by the 911 emergency number, which allowed them to reduce delivery time from 3 hours to 20 minutes, of a highly perishable product like concrete. A lower requirement of working capital together with a greater turnover resulted in increasing profits and an extraordinary source of financial resources. But not less important is its access to the self-construction market at the BOP, by far the largest buyer in emerging countries. The creation of the *Construrama* franchise to cater to this segment provided a better access, making it easier to grant credits to small suppliers of building materials (*corralones*) which also received advisory assistance to improve their business. The profound understanding of this segment of buyers led to establishing ways to attract remittances from exiles in the United States for their relatives, ensuring that these funds arrive in the country and that they are safely invested in building materials that help reduce the 5-year period it usually takes to build their simple dwellings. Brand advertising via popular soccer teams strengthened its relationship with this segment,[6] where having their own house is priceless, not only for its material value but also to the self-esteem of those who have built a home for their family at great effort.

Corona beer enjoys a premium price in international markets, partly due to a selective distribution and an image of attractive holidays. But in Mexico its strategy was based on extensive distribution, placing emphasis on a strongly competitive price for a product of good quality. Unlike its international positioning, its focus in its home market is the mass market, and it has not hesitated to take part in price wars to defend its share among the lower segments.

Arcor[7] originally based its strategy in Argentina on the extensive distribution of its products of competitive quality at lower prices, manufacturing under a model of vertical integration that encompasses raw materials, production of energy, its own packaging and distributing through its own network of wholesalers. Only in the 90s, they added a communications component to reinforce its brand image and improve the quality perception, on top of adding other brands through takeovers, but always being careful of not losing its presence in the popular BOP market segments.

Bimbo sells its bread and other quality bakery products like salted snacks, sweets, and chocolates, based on a large fleet of 22,000 trucks and 400 distribution warehouses and over 600 distribution agencies that ensure the delivery of fresh products to an extensive network of 450,000 retailers in Mexico. As bread lasts for 12 days, Bimbo recovers it from the shelves on the third day to ensure its maximum freshness at home, and redistributes it among a network of stores as 'Pan de Ayer' (yesterday's bread) at a price that is lower by 25 percent. Another alternative is to put together certain products in promotion packages and sell them in 'Cold Bread Routes' on the cities' outskirts, with an average discount of 35 percent. In 1984, the company started direct distribution in the Unites States, and in 1990 they acquired a factory of bread and sweet rolls in Guatemala, which was the first step toward the expansion across Latin America.

Kola Real is the company founded by the Añaños brothers looking to diversify out of their agricultural business by manufacturing soft drinks in their city of Ayacucho in the south of Peru.[8] Since the very beginning they offered a low-price product, which was distributed extensively through an informal, unstructured, and growing network of carriers, supported with local brand presence as they opened new markets. This presence was aimed at the needs of their popular customers, such as the setting up of first-aid posts in poor areas, obtaining a high brand recognition with a significantly lower investment than any other manufacturer in the same category. Based on this focussed strategy they earned close to 20 percent of market share, before repeating the formula in Venezuela where they achieved 14 percent and more recently 5 percent in Mexico but under the Big Cola brand. By these means, their revenues have mounted up to over $300 million.

Jabon La Corona commands 80 percent share of the Mexican soap market with its Zote brand, successfully competing with giants such as Procter & Gamble, Unilever, and Colgate.[9] Fabric softeners, detergents, and olive oil have been added to its product line, always answering to the principle of offering good quality products at low prices. The company does not invest in advertising, relying on customers' recommendation, nor in R&D, trusting product innovation to their own employees, who belong to the same social class as their target customers.

But not all the innovations aimed at the BOP were designed by companies that originated there. Some multinational companies have managed to overcome their own paradigms and develop successful solutions.

Coca-Cola Venezuela boosted the creation of 30,000 'productive homes' (hogares productivos), giving small refrigerators to housewives, therefore improving its distribution in remote neighborhoods and supporting the creation of new microbusinesses.[10] This followed a similar line to what it had done in India in 2002, where it added to its formal traditional distribution system any available means—rickshaws and carriages—to supply to the small rural towns that until then it had not been able to properly reach.[11] It distributed more than 2 million fridges among rural retailers and created 200 ml bottles which were sold at Rs 5, half the price of the previous 300 ml one. Furthermore, it adapted its image to local culture, employing a Bollywood star to communicate the price cut, in three advertisements especially made for rural and semiurban populations.

Unilever's approach to the BOP in Brazil caused a modification in the Omo soap, replacing the powder for soap bars in order to sell the product in the Northeastern markets.[12] Women in that region, lacking washing machines, go to the river to wash the clothes, where they socialize with other women while devoting themselves to their families' care, which is shown in their family members walking around in clean clothes.

343

SC Johnson in Argentina examined the progress of its furniture polish Blem after the 2001 economic crisis. A shift from the spray formula to the paste allowed the company to diminish the cost of the container by 60 percent, so even though it doubled its cost of direct labor it reduced the selling price by 30 percent.

In Mexico, Procter & Gamble redefined the characteristics of its Always sanitary towels and launched Naturela to successfully compete in the B-brand market, based on a product that keeps its main characteristics. In a similar fashion, in Brazil it redefined the quality of disposable diapers to reach a 12 percent share in the market's lower segments.[13]

These last examples show that, in spite of their local origin and strong bonds with their markets, understanding the BOP is not an asset belonging only to local companies. Executives joining MNCs but coming from emerging markets are also cracking the locks to access these markets, and local companies will need to be aware of this growing competition in their own markets. As MNCs also discover the value of the markets at the BOP, these could well become the next competitive arena.

15.1.2. *Aiming at the Middle*

The cases analyzed show variations regarding the traditional strategic approaches. In the first place, those strategies based on skimming the markets by introducing the brands through the upper segments in order to generate an 'aspiration' positioning, prove to have a limited effect when trying to reach farther than the upper segments, to those with more or less limited possibilities of buying them. The inability to purchase them may turn aspiration into frustration and even anger, as we have already seen, and consequent brand rejection. Some companies have sensibly decided to aim at the middle of the pyramid, placing their products within the reach of middle-class consumers.

The case of Bodegas Lopez in Argentina illustrates this 'aimed at the middle' strategy.[14] Its Lopez brand is shown in the opening price level for fine wines, and it offers three more brands—Rincon Famoso, Chateau Vieux, and Monchenot—with increasing levels of price and quality, and two others—Traful and Vasco Viejo—for lower price points. It is interesting to point out that this winery's brand is not at the top of the pyramid of prices and brands, but in the middle, but outsells by far its competitors in the fine wine segment.

Likewise, Nazca Cosmeticos of Brazil decided to broaden its line of quality hair care products at medium-to-high prices, targeting the population of African origin which has clearly different characteristics than those buyers of European origin.[15] Research revealed not only these evident differences but a desire of recognition of their own specific characteristics instead of having to adapt to using products designed for customers with different needs. Nazca decided to risk its brand prestige by aiming at this neglected segment, becoming the dominant player of this significant segment without losing sales among their previous customers.

The strategies aimed at the middle of the pyramid have several aspects in common: quality products, extensive distribution, and affordable price. There are three principles that appear to guide them: accessibility, affordability, and availability. They are based on attractive products that create buying impulse. Both design and size facilitate product access, and finally, extensive distribution places products within easy reach of consumers.

15.1.3. *Designing Strategies for the Bottom of the Pyramid*

These examples show us that developing these strategies entails significant innovation in more than one aspect, to modify the offer to cater to the needs of those consumers who are in greater need.

A deep understanding of their actual needs, purchasing, and consumption habits was applied in the first place, to be able to distinguish the varying behaviors of the segments comprised within this large group of consumers, as the case of Jabon La Corona showed.

Secondly, innovation is often more related to the business process than to the products themselves.[16] Their needs are more associated with simple access than to more advanced technological developments, which in many cases buyers cannot apply and do not require. Technological innovation is more directed at modifying processes in aspects like production, logistics, marketing, and service. By these means access is facilitated not only in terms of the product's cost but through other factors that relate to its availability, like in the case of Bimbo's 'yesterday's bread'.

Finally, innovations come not only from analyzing their own sector, as in the case of Cemex with the application of the 911 technology. It is necessary to explore other regions and business sectors with an open mind in order to find responses that can be adapted to one's own business.

It is essential that these product innovations and service adaptations intended to broaden the product offer show a solid respect for the dignity of the chosen segment and convey the necessary trust so as to build long-lasting relationships—something that was properly interpreted at Kola Real.

To promote these innovations key process areas were identified—such as logistics, marketing, or service—and then selected to carry out experiments. Some of these adaptive process variations generated enough differential value and were therefore selected in order to disseminate them into the organization, spreading the implementation. Essential to the success of these innovation processes was the dedication of cross-functional teams for the search for improvements throughout the whole business process. These teams also facilitate further implementation, since they knew each function peculiarities and how to respond to the different objections that would arise to the suggested changes.

15.1.4. *Changing the Vision Along the Value Chain*

As the innovation process comprises logistics, service, and marketing aspects, it requires a broad business perspective, including the links in the industry's value chain. The examples of Cemex' Construrama and Coca-Cola's 'hogares productivos' show that to develop strategies based on business models that create value for emerging consumers, it is necessary to ensure the sustainability of other participating businesses by aligning the strategies of all parties involved.

Value creation is at the top of the agenda when catering to emerging consumers, and value is not only created through innovation and individual cost reduction, but also by improving efficiency along the supply chain. Consensus and coordinated actions along the supply chain are required if the costs to reach the market are to be improved. Suppliers, wholesalers, and retailers must build a dialogue in order to boost the efficiency for reaching end-customers. Aspects such as the efficient use of logistics or presence in points of sale require this type of participation and coordination.

In some cases, the government and other incumbent institutions that affect the consumption sector may have to participate in this forum. Aspects such as tax evasion, very common in the entire region with the exception of Chile, affect every player's performance in one way or another. However, the solution to this problem that hinders the growth of the best players and affects society as a whole cannot be solved by some well-intentioned participants: it requires an overall and coordinated approach.

But this will not happen as long as some of the major players believe that they can generate more by their own means, to the detriment of their competitors, than collaborating with other participants of the sector's chain in a more transparent fashion. Working along sector chains requires setting aside the vision of sheer competition to an evolved concept of competitors and collaborators. This approach allows formulating and implementing a common agenda of feasible and controllable action plans.

These agreements are intended to increase the productivity and innovation of every member of the sector chain, promoting the sustainability of each player's business. The broad concept is to enlarge the pie rather than sustain a dispute to see who gets a bigger slice—of a total pie that keeps shrinking with each crisis! Opportunities need to be identified and seized, but under the condition of sharing the benefits among the supply chain's participants.

The broadened focus is on understanding what boosts the industry's development as a whole, how each player gains and loses competitiveness and how they can develop together a greater capacity of innovation.

15.1.5. *Managing Deceiving Perspectives about the Bottom of the Pyramid*

These misconceptions hide rigidities and a lack of vision that work similarly as the myths on emerging consumers, restraining the access to these segments.[17]

1. It is not our segment, they cannot afford the quality and level of innovation of our products: The statement hidden behind this statement is that the cost structure is taken as a given, with little chances of being reduced, and consequently costs are too high for these segments. The cases of *Blem* and *Omo*'s product redefinition and *Coca-Cola*'s distribution reconfiguration reveal that these companies not only revised their costs but the entire product concept and manufacturing processes as well in order to reach these customers.

2. They do not have use for advanced products: When redefining products executives realized that the functionalities were different. The price of a top brand training shoe is comparably much higher for an emerging consumer than for a high-income buyer, but it is for this very same reason that the first one is likely to use it more carefully and not for the purpose it was originally designed for.

3. Only consumers in more advanced markets appreciate and pay for technological innovation: Even though this may be true to some extent, it is also a fact that they do not require such an advanced technology, and consequently they do not consider that innovation worth the cost of a higher price. Hutchinson Telecommunications Argentina set its Port Hable communications network to address the poorest segments around Buenos Aires. They offer cellular telephones with a limited coverage of a few blocks. In doing so, they provide means of communications to places out of the reach of ground network lines necessary to install fixed phones, and through a cell of limited scope the company offers service to the cellular telephones that are under their range of influence. In a way, it is a wireless telephone with a greater coverage. The much lower cost of the required technology opens access to these areas that have been ignored by traditional communications companies that stick to the model of fixed telephones served by wire lines.

4. Their total volume being low, they are not key to the company's long-term success, for they do not generate enough profitability: As we have seen in the first myth, a more detailed and deeper analysis shows this

statement to be false, but sustaining it drives us to consider them as an eventual, sporadic opportunity, almost a distraction. Bimbo's 'yesterday's bread'[18] shows how they can be aggregated to the business on a permanent base, and not as an addition more connected to social responsibility issues but to the business itself.

5. The true intellectual challenge lies in developed markets: It is there where the most significant progress regarding innovation takes place. As a consequence of this, one cannot recruit or appoint the best executives to work at the BOP, since it is not stimulating enough to lure them. Companies, such as *Fabrica de Jabon La Corona*, prove that solving the challenges to cater to the BOP requires sometimes a complete redefinition of the business processes, something that only the most experienced and flexible managers are able to do. If it is not taken as the real challenge it represents but rather as a secondary objective, attracting the best candidates to devote their time to this segment turns out to be extremely difficult.

15.2. The Mythology of Scarcity

The scarcity of low-income consumers reflects a number of variations. Not just their income varies in terms of amount and frequency, but also their level of equipment, from car availability to common home goods like refrigerators, and in their access to energy, communications, and running water. Expensive and scarce capital availability has a negative impact in R&D private budgets, and also reflects in a weak technological platform, due to the lack of world-class universities that would provide well-trained scientists.

Scarcity goes along with dense populations with deeply rooted habits, such as daily shopping and cooking. Families comprise three, four, or five persons per household, seasonal workers with variable and unpredictable incomes resulting from high unemployment rates. This combined with the lack of appliances for keeping food fresh, among other things result in the need to cook daily. But income variations are also due to the peculiar characteristics of self-employment in jobs such as plumbers, painters, electricians, taxi drivers and the like. Therefore shopping is done daily and sometimes twice in the same day, in low volume and with special emphasis on freshness since food will be consumed shortly after. To this the neighboring store becomes the best option, not only for convenience but also because it allows rounding down the purchase if available cash is insufficient, acquiring only the strictly necessary amounts of products, getting the best affordable quality of freshness, and the brands that best fit their particular needs. It is money that is lacking, not time that can be used to optimize the value of their spending. In these cases, time-saving products are not economical, given their higher price.

Out of a limited understanding of their reality, the picture of emerging consumers at the BOP is filled with misconceptions. They would like to buy products but cannot afford them, their purchasing power is too low to become a significant market, and their preferences go straight to the lower price, and so on. Myths like these condition the development of strategies that could effectively address their specific needs. The resulting paradox is a limited access to products and services for an enormous group of consumers who require them to satisfy their very basic needs.

During 2003, a research project was ordered by The Coca-Cola Retailing Research Council—Latin America, to better understand consumers' preferences in the region with regard to their purchasing habits. While setting the project it became clear that it should focus on the vast majority of less favored consumers that make the biggest portion of the market: the emerging consumers. Our research covered six countries: Argentina, Brazil, Colombia, Costa Rica, Chile, and Mexico. Four focus groups were conducted in each country for a total of 208 participants. Target consumers were women from the emerging socioeconomic strata who (*a*) typically make the bulk of household purchases for food, beverage, personal care, and cleaning product categories and (*b*) shop regularly in at least one type of small-scale retail format. Among the secondary sources consulted were Socio-Economic Strata (SES) profiles from local marketing research associations and previously published, relevant consumer studies from organizations such as Latin Panel, A. C. Nielsen, and local retail-oriented associations like Mexico's ANTAD. Fieldwork carried out in each country included 217 store checks and 190 in-depth interviews with small retailers.

Its focus was to understand not only *what* and *where* these consumers buy, but *why* they make these choices. While there are many salient differences between emerging consumers across the six countries in this study, several common themes emerged that contradict the conventional wisdom about these consumers. We will look at the 'truth' about emerging consumers, in relation to six common myths—or preconceptions—about lower-income segments.

15.2.1. *The Myths on Emerging Consumers*[19]

1. Emerging consumers have little money to spend: In spite of being perceived as 'poor,' emerging consumers in fact have a considerable amount of money as a group to spend on consumer products. And, while incomes are indeed lower and less stable, these consumers dedicate a larger portion of their income to household purchases.

Consumer products are the number 1 consumption category across Latin American countries, with housing/rent, transportation, and communication typically absorbing a large part of the remainder. However, while consumer products make up roughly 30–35 percent of consumption for the 'average consumer' in a given country, emerging segments spend a disproportionately bigger share on these products—anywhere from 50–75 percent, with the lowest SES claiming to spend nearly all income on these purchases. Hence, while it is true that their incomes are lower and overall they buy less, the net effect is that household purchases can still amount to substantial sums over time, and therefore represent a significant share of the consumer goods markets (see Figure 15.1). Two separate studies by A.C. Nielsen and ANTAD suggest that average tickets for emerging segments may reach up to 50 percent of what middle-class and higher-income consumers spend in *supermarkets*. It should be noted that the reported average ticket sizes by SES do not take into account frequency of shopping and that emerging consumers shop much less frequently in large supermarkets.

Furthermore, the vast majority of lower-income consumers can hardly be described as 'destitute'. It is true that Latin America has its share of poverty, and that there are social classes who have the misfortune to earn the descriptive label of 'marginal' or 'indigent'. But many households today have running water, electricity, and basic appliances that have an impact on purchasing behavior. Nearly all 'C' and 'D' households have a television, radio, and refrigerator (e.g. 90–100 percent household penetration)—and in countries like Mexico and Costa Rica, penetration of washing machines, VCRs, and access to cars in urban areas is relatively high with the exception of Colombia, where penetration of TV, stoves, and radio lowers to 65–85 percent.[20]

Beyond the rather large fraction of the budget these purchases represent, household expenditures have a much greater meaning to emerging consumers. For the women that control the majority of these purchases, consumer products are a key mechanism by which they fulfill the overlapping roles of 'wife', 'mother', 'economist' and 'self'. Focus groups revealed that considerable self-esteem is derived from managing these expenses in the best way possible to care for the family—a task that, as we next observe, can be rather complex.

2. At the base of the pyramid the needs are simple, and the lowest price prevails: Their lower and less stable incomes mean emerging consumers need simple, affordable products, and low cost retail formats. Yet emerging consumer product and format needs are better described as 'basic' rather than 'simple'. These consumers overwhelmingly purchase more basic foodstuffs and perishables, but they are willing to pay for intermediate and leading brands in basic categories. And they also may shun low-cost retail formats such as hard discount stores.

Overall, very few of the focus group participants stated they shopped at hard discount supermarkets (especially in Mexico and Colombia, where almost

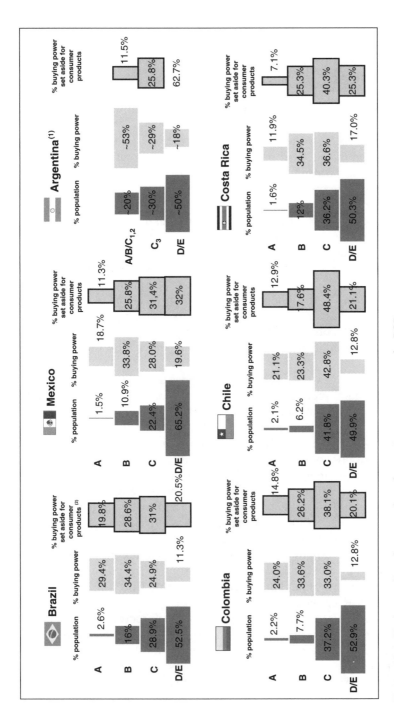

Figure 15.1. Understanding the true value of emerging consumers at the BOP

all participants claimed they 'never shopped' at discount supermarkets—in Argentina, shopping incidences were the highest observed for this format). It should be noted that sample size is not sufficient to make a quantitative assessment and that many consumers interviewed may not happen to live or work near these stores. That said, issues with this format were expressed in each country, indicating that there is some dissatisfaction with this store format for at least a subset of emerging consumers.

Certainly, there is a well-established link between affordability and category penetration of consumer products in low-income households. The shopping basket of these consumers *is* weighted toward staple products—some of which are common across countries while others are not (see Table 15.1). Typically, the more expensive, higher value-added categories like frozen foods, ready-to-eat meals, yogurt or flavored milk drinks, and fabric softener have lower penetration in these households, driven in part by the low penetration of household appliances like freezers and microwaves. Undoubtedly, relatively low penetration of freezers and microwave ovens in emerging segments partially explains the low penetration of ready-to-eat meals and frozen foods. But also many of the group participants expressed enjoying preparing meals from 'scratch' as an extension of caring for the family and it is not clear that they would 'panty load' frozen meal components (e.g. chicken, meat, and vegetables) even if they owned freezers and enjoyed incomes that permitted stocking.

In looking at emerging consumer attitudes toward brands, there is tension between brand preference and consumers' economic reality. We found that these consumers have a strong preference for intermediate and leading brands and not buying them can generate frustration. Overall, discussion group participants stated that they regularly purchase intermediate and leading brands; we also noted an unwillingness to try new brands. In many categories, emerging consumers showed more loyalty to 'brands' in general than to a single, preferred name. The consumer will have a relatively small set of brands that are considered acceptable substitutes, and switching does occur within this set. In many cases, this switching was driven by promotional prices. However, these attitudes toward brands are not a lemming-like response to advertising campaigns or blindly ignoring economic constraints—consumers *are* keenly aware that leading brands carry a price premium. But perhaps more importantly, brands embody backing, confidence, and quality for these consumers as a group.

It is worth noting that brand loyalty (for the purposes of this study, defined as *purchasing* a brand as opposed to just *preference* or *purchase intent*) differs by category. Interestingly enough, we found the highest loyalty to brands on staples like rice and cooking oil. Loyalty was also high for aspirational categories like soft drinks, or categories that impact self-esteem as a caregiver (e.g. laundry detergent), but economic reality overrode purchase intent

Table 15.1. What do emerging consumers buy?

	Staples	Secondary	Luxuries
Packaged foods	Rice, beans, dry pasta, oil, salt sugar, tomato sauce, cookies and snacks for kids (value brands) Br.: flours (wheat, manioc, corn), canned fish (Class C) Col.: lentils	Sweet and salty snacks, some canned food Mex: cereal, snacks Arg.: salty snacks, sweets, candy Ch.: dressings, mayonnaise	Canned foods, chocolate candy, cookies (leading brands), cereal Arg.: tuna, olives, 'alfajores' Br.: condensed milk, cake mix Ch.: heat of palm Col.: salty snacks (adults)
Perishable Foods	Fruits and vegetables , eggs, bread, margarine/butter Arg.: jelly, cold cuts Mex./Br.: class C: yogurt	Cold cuts, meats Arg/Ch.: sausages Br.: yogurt, cheese, chicken Mex.: ground hamburger meat Ch/Col.: margarine, chicken	Frozen foods, icecream Br.: frozen lasagna, fried potatoes, hamburger patties Br./Mex.: ready-to-eat pizza Mex./Col.: seafood
Beverages	Coffee, Juice concentrate Col.: chocolate bars Br.: value brand sodas Mex.: powdered drink mix Ara/Ch.: tea	Value brand sodas (Arg, Col), Br.: powdered drink mix Arg./Br.: beer	Coca-Cola Arg/Col.: wine Mex.: tequila, rum CR: gatorade sports drinks Ar/CR: tang powdered drink
Cleaning products	Powdered laundry detergent, bleach, disinfectant Br./Col.: bar laundry soap Mex.: softener, steelwool Arg.: floor cleaner	Softener Arg.: multi purpose cleaners, air freshener Col.: liquid dish detergent	Leading brands in detergent and softener Br.: furniture polish
Personal care	Toilet paper, soap, toothpaste, sanitary napkins, deodorant, family shampoo Mex.: diapers Arg./CR: conditioner, cotton	Leading brand shampoo (Arg. Br.), conditioners	Leading brands, perfume Br.: personal shampoo, facial lotion Ch.: makeup Mex.: body lotion

Source: IBOPE Solution, BAH analysis.

more often. Overall, less loyalty was observed in personal care and cleaning products, even though brand preference was still high (especially in personal care categories that appeal to consumers' sense of vanity). Hence, brand attitudes and purchasing patterns represent quite rational and savvy behavior on the part of emerging consumers, who are fulfilling their need for performance in categories that make up the bulk of the daily diet or that showcase capabilities as a caregiver. Similarly, the risk aversion of these consumers in trying new brands makes sense given that there is less room to experiment or 'fail'— selecting an underperforming product has greater financial implications when incomes are lower. These observations are in line with existing theory, which holds that a consumer's 'level of involvement' with a category is positively correlated with loyalty. In many categories, emerging consumers are more loyal to 'brands' in general than to a single, preferred name. The consumer will have a relatively small set of brands that are considered acceptable substitutes, and switching does occur within this set. In many cases, this switching is driven by promotional price points.

Acceptance of dramatically lower priced (and low cost) 'value brands' is growing in some countries; nevertheless, emerging consumers are still drawn to brands. In Brazil and Argentina, emerging consumers were more open to trying value brands, especially in cleaning products. Economic necessity clearly plays a role in increasing trial of these products, as do word of mouth testimonials from friends and family about performance. However, intermediate and leading brands still represent the largest share of purchases and emerging consumers hesitate to try value brands. Low-price points are attractive but can also generate mistrust and skepticism about product quality—'Lo barato sale caro' ('What is cheap ends up being expensive') a frequently heard comment.

Another way in which the 'lowest cost' myth does not play out relates to package sizes. Subsets of emerging consumers have lower or less stable incomes, and they prefer to smooth consumption over time rather than go without products. Lower incomes mean that larger sizes represent a much larger portion of available income, so consumers knowingly incur higher per unit costs (e.g. price per gram) on smaller sizes to keep ticket sizes down and in line with cash on hand.

3. Emerging consumers are overwhelmingly attracted by lower prices: Emerging consumers are certainly 'price sensitive', as evidenced by the meticulous tracking of price benchmarks, the exercise of self-constraint while shopping, and aversion to debt and credit when purchasing consumables. Their response to the recent deterioration in economic conditions shows that they do scale back spending in response to decreased incomes or increasing prices (if incomes do not also rise). However, purchasing decisions are more driven by a desire to minimize 'total purchasing cost'—which is entirely different from retail shelf price.

'Total purchasing cost' represents a fully loaded cost for a basket of goods, and retail shelf prices naturally make up an important part of the equation. However, we found that emerging consumers mentally factor in transportation costs to arrive at a final price for the shopping basket—that is, the 'total purchasing cost'. In addition, they have a strong awareness of 'hassle factors' (such as finding child care or policing/coping with children's demands while in the store), logistical constraints for bringing purchases home, and time spent commuting or (to a lesser degree) standing in line. This makes the *interplay* of physical proximity and pricing a top criterion for selecting a retail format.

Format needs do differ for 'daily' and 'large/stocking' purchases, but physical proximity is the first order determinant of store choice in both cases. Consumers do not like to travel very far and they consider the transportation costs of even round trip bus fare or a short taxi ride to be significant. Most discussion group participants did not consider public buses and subways to be a viable means of transportation for bringing purchases back home when heavy or numerous packages/bundles were involved; instead, consumers tended to reference the price of a pirate taxi ride, 'collective' or shared van/taxi service when referring to the transport expenses they were factored into the 'total purchasing cost'. When asked to explain the difference between a store that is considered 'close by' versus 'far away', most consumers define both of these extremes within a relatively small physical distance—'one block' versus 'seven to ten blocks away', or 'within a 5 minutes walk' versus 'three or four bus stops away'. Most emerging consumers in urban areas (by far the bulk of the population in these segments) have numerous store formats nearby and thus need travel only minutes to make daily or even stocking purchases. Usually, the nearby stores are small-scale retail formats such as traditional, over-the-counter shops, small independent supermarkets, or street/open air formats.

The smaller average ticket sizes resulting from both lower incomes overall and greater prevalence of 'daily' shopping behavior in emerging consumer segments have relevant implications. Proximity translates into significantly lower 'total purchasing cost' for emerging consumers if shopping at geographically close-by, small retailers. An estimate of the 'break even' price discount required to recover just the cost of a bus trip to and from a store located further away throws more light over this point. Given the low ticket size associated with a 'daily needs' shopping trip, the price discount would have to reach from 25 to 55 percent only to justify the trip transportation costs. Not surprisingly, emerging consumers require significant discounts on a complete shopping basket to choose a store for a 'stocking' trip—not just one or two items.

4. Emerging consumers should prefer shopping at supermarkets: Following this 'Modern Trade Myth', emerging consumers are often looked at as junior versions of their higher-income compatriots, who should naturally flock to the modern infrastructure shopping experience, and the variety and value that large supermarkets provide. (This myth presupposes that there are specific barriers to this happening, as we discuss in the next section.) Emerging consumers may not be all that distinct from higher-income segments in that all consumers tend to look for 'good' prices at stores they consider to be within an acceptable distance. In many categories, emerging consumers are more loyal to 'brands' in general than to a single, preferred name. The consumer will have a relatively small set of brands that are considered acceptable substitutes, and switching does occur within this set. In many cases, this switching is driven by promotional price points. But the similarities probably stop there. Other distinct format characteristics beyond the proximity/price combination seem to distinguish emerging from higher-income consumers.

Product assortment is certainly a relevant store choice criterion for all consumers, but in the emerging segments, product variety can be a double-edged sword. Emerging consumers do not like to feel their choice is restricted and consequently they value a wide assortment—although admittedly as a point of interest or form of entertainment. As an example, many emerging consumers described how they like to browse the wide variety of personal care and general merchandise items found in larger stores—but that they did not necessarily buy. Furthermore, the entertainment value of a wide assortment was clearly associated with 'stocking' trips—which occur much less frequently in these segments. In fact, a wide assortment sometimes has a negative effect because it is either too tempting or time consuming to shop, or because it reinforces feelings of restriction and having to do without. Thus, emerging consumers value the 'right' product assortment—a mix that is carefully tailored to needs for performance brands, economy, *and* feelings of validation. This is a decidedly more abstract concept than simply filling a store with thousands of SKUs.

'Operational Characteristics of Street Markets in Brazil'

In Brazil, metropolitan street markets or 'feiras' are quite common. They are licensed by the city governments and operate from Tuesday to Sunday. For each day of the week, several different feiras occur in different locations. The items sold to consumers at the feira are mostly fresh produce, beef, fish, and poultry. Within each category, it is common to find many grades of product or hard to find 'local specialties.' There may also be a very limited selection of grocery items, housewares, clothing, and shoes. In São Paulo, they are responsible for 70 percent of the overall supply of fresh food for the city.

Feiras take place in predetermined streets, which are closed for traffic, and later cleaned by city employees. They consist of portable stalls or modified vehicles, from which products are sold. Stalls are set up early in the morning—between 5:00 and 6:30 a.m. The public starts to arrive around 7:00 a.m., but customer movement peaks around 10:00 a.m. and by 1:00 p.m., most of the crowd is gone. In the early hours of the feira, prices tend to be higher, and no discounts are offered. As the morning progresses, prices are reduced and discounts are offered. Stall owners, or 'feirantes', seek to sell all their merchandice since in many cases product is fully ripe and highly perishable.

Note: paraphrased from 'The Structure of Sao Paulo Street Markets: Evolving Patterns of Retail Institutions', Journal of Consumer Affairs, vol. 33(1).

For some product categories like fresh fruits, vegetables, meats, breads, and milk, emerging consumers in fact do not prefer large chain supermarkets at all (see Figure 15.2). Instead, there is a strong association of fresh categories with street and open air formats where quality is perceived to be higher, prices are substantially lower, products may be sampled, and the customers can actively manage the price/quality trade-off by choosing the time of day at which they buy. It is important to note that for these consumers, the definition of 'quality' in fresh categories is not necessarily consistent with the uniformly shaped and colored product typically offered for sale in large supermarkets.

Whereas there is a feeling that the stocking and ripening process employed at large supermarkets is unnatural and even worsens the taste, street and open air formats are seen as wholesome and 'farm fresh'. Incidentally, there is evidence that higher-income consumers have similar attitudes since although they do purchase more 'fresh' categories in large supermarkets than lower income SES, overall penetration is relatively low compared to other categories.

As it turns out, 'modern' infrastructure is attractive to emerging consumers but relatively unimportant as a store selection criterion when it comes to fresh produce. Aspects of store physical appearance are secondary, with infrastructure and hygiene used as a screen rather than a driver of choice. Services associated with the shopping experience at large chain supermarkets (e.g. promotional flyers, delivery with minimum purchase, loyalty cards, and extended operating hours) are similarly less important. A portion of emerging consumers are attracted to large supermarkets, but by and large, these large chain formats lack a key element: the emotional proximity and feeling of community that comes as a result of personal relationships with shopkeepers or store personnel. Personal relationships are usually the top factor for differentiating between outlets with comparable prices and distance for this group. And it almost always enters into store choice when making daily purchases in small-scale retail stores. These relationships typically result from a history of positive interactions and experience—providing customers with a sense of familiarity and belonging. Personal relationships—rather than formal processes—are the mechanism by which this group generally resolves issues like exchanging a product, coming up short at the cash register, selecting a product during a stock-out, or feeling confident that produce and meats are fairly weighted. In comparison, emerging consumers report poor treatment by staff while shopping at large chain stores. In large chain stores, treatment was usually described as 'professional' when seen in a positive light, but not 'personal' or 'caring'—words that were used to positively describe small-scale retailers. Sometimes this is the result of extra scrutiny from security personnel, or clerks who show visible frustration when economizing consumers ask to weigh small purchases or inquire after promotions. The 'cold' treatment is often said to come also from other customers in the store.

5. 'It's only a matter of time and money' for emerging consumers to flock into large supermarkets: Building on the previous discussion, this myth assumes that emerging consumers cannot act on their natural preference for larger supermarkets for a number of reasons—for example, they have lower incomes, they do not own cars, or they may need the credit that is offered by small retailers.

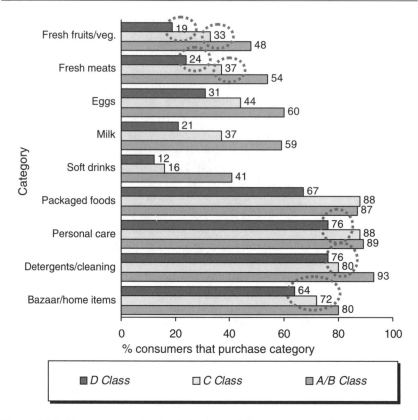

Figure 15.2. Consumer purchasing behavior in Mexican supermarkets (percent consumers' purchasing category, by SES).
Source: ANTAD.

Today, emerging consumers infrequently shop—if at all—at large supermarkets or hypermarkets. We observed extremely low penetration with these consumers in Colombia, Mexico, and Argentina (a more recent phenomenon). In Brazil, a moderate number of consumers shopped at supermarkets but these tended to be small independents or local chains with no more than four or five stores. Penetration was higher in Chile and Costa Rica, where consumers noted that large supermarkets happen to be located close by.

Other strong factors deter emerging consumers from switching away from small-scale stores—but the need for credit is not typically one of them. Some do take advantage of credit out of necessity on occasion, and consumers who rely on 'fiado' credit do have strong barriers to switching stores. Yet, generally speaking, lower-income segments are averse to spending beyond their means and they prefer to pay cash as a means of controlling expenditures. Credit is viewed as more appropriate for major purchases (e.g. appliances, back-to-school supplies, and uniforms) rather than for funding day-to-day consumables.

That said, emerging consumers commonly 'come up short' on small purchases and rely on their 'virtual wallet' at small-scale retailers who essentially offer a type of informal credit by allowing regular customers to make up these small differences on their next shopping trip—usually the next day or shortly thereafter.

'Special Forms of Consumer Credit in Latin America'

One type of credit that is available in Latin America is commonly known as 'fiado'. When a consumer purchases 'fiado', no cash is exchanged at the time of sale and the owner notes the amount of purchase in a record or notebook under the customer's name. The customer returns on a later date (e.g. on payday) to pay down the balance due or retire the debt entirely. 'Fiado' is not available at chain retail supermarkets.

Typically, no interest charges are levied. But customers who take too long to pay or renege on debts are likely to have their names and how much they owe posted on a sign for all in the neighborhood to see. There are strong social incentives for customers to make good on balances to retailers, but there is still considerable risk. Small-scale retailers typically offer this type of credit only to a subset of their customers.

Other types of credit used by emerging consumers vary by country. For example in Brazil, checks are more commonly used than in other countries to make purchases, and some emerging consumers do have accounts. Chain retailers and some small independent supermarkets will allow customers to postdate checks, thereby granting short-term credit. The consumers who participated in our focus groups very rarely used credit cards.

This is a critical service for this group, since having to remove purchases at the time of payment is considered extremely embarrassing and to be avoided at all costs. Furthermore, it allows parents to send their children to make daily purchases with the least amount of money possible—considered a valuable means to control impulse spending on candy and snacks. Technically speaking, this is a form of short-term credit. But it is more like an extension of the personal relationship between the consumer and the shopkeeper, rather than a transaction or service. Also, since the amounts in question are extremely small, the benefit of this 'virtual wallet' to consumers is one of financial flexibility, rather than needing the credit per se.

We have seen that credit is not a driving force behind this behavior. Furthermore, given emerging consumers' distinct values and needs, it is not clear that increased incomes and access to transportation would cause them to 'graduate' to different retail formats at all. The lack of personal relationships, a modern but 'out of element' shopping experience, and negative perceptions about some categories (like fresh goods) would more than likely keep them

Figure 15.3. Emerging consumer values.

away. Figure 15.3, emerging consumers values, summarizes their needs and preferences with regard to retail selection.

6. 'The popular class'—Emerging consumers may be addressed as a single group: In mature markets, numerous terms have entered the common vocabulary to describe the unique characteristics and behavior of the middle and upper income classes—yuppies, buppies, DINKs, BOBOs, and more. Typically, lower-income consumers are unceremoniously lumped into the 'blue collar' or 'working class', as if no notable differences existed among these consumers. Similarly, Latin America's lower-income consumers are often collectively referred to as the 'popular class'.

The qualitative research for the referred study, however, indicates that there are probably many meaningful differences between emerging consumers—a basis for further study and segmentation. Clearly, demographic variables such as size and stability of income matter: some subsegments have incomes that afford 'stocking' occasions, greater experimentation, and breadth of purchases while other consumers are more focussed on daily needs and tend to avoid changing brands or stores. Emerging class consumers, even though they may share a relatively homogenous profile in demographic/socioeconomic variables, could be differentiated by psychographic variables. Specifically, there appears to be a range of lifestyle and shopping attitudes along a continuum of practicality/control/traditionalism and emotion/impulse/innovation. These differences in lifestyle and attitudes have an impact on shopping behavior, manifested in characteristics such as brand loyalty, store loyalty, willingness to innovate, price sensitivity and responsiveness to promotions, and breadth of categories purchased. Economic crisis also shows its impact, as newly constrained consumers seem to act differently from structurally low-income groups—many of the 'newly poor' are struggling with the ordeal of defining what they can do without.

In summary, research across six Latin American countries breaks six common myths about emerging consumers. Although 'poor' relative to upper the SES, these consumers spend a great deal of money on consumer products and constitute a significant portion of these markets. When shopping, they follow a quite rational and sophisticated behavior as they seek to reconcile preferences with their economic reality. They have a distinct set of product and format needs—which does not necessarily include whatever is lowest cost, credit, or responding to shelf prices. The personal relationships and sense of community they seek is a strong incentive to shop in small-scale retail formats. Furthermore, differences within emerging consumers imply that retailers need a differentiated proposition to address the needs of this group.

Research conducted in Argentina by Grupo CCR in 2004[21] also shows a rich complexity that demands a more careful treatment of these groups. The impact of the economic crisis in 2001 showed different impacts depending on the extent of the economic deterioration experienced at each household. Two groups could be observed at first sight: those who had been able to adapt to it—eventually their economic misadventures had started before—and those who still long for their previous status and were living in aguish. Among the first, chances to recover their projects were observed, while the melancholic or anguished showed differing attitudes, ranging from staying alert to keep from further deterioration, to the anger of who cannot fit to the new reality.

These differing attitudes are less associated with the actual economic level, and more to the size of the deterioration, or the extent of the downfall. A greater degree of affinity was observed among consumers that had experienced a larger variation in their status, than with those living at—and sharing—the same economic level.

15.2.2. *Solving the Paradoxes*

Cemex, Arcor, Corona Beer, Jabon La Corona, Kola Real, Nazca Cosmeticos, and many other companies, some cited here and others that are not, have found ways to successfully deal with the Bottom of the Pyramid. Some proudly rank among the global players, while others limit themselves to their local markets. Nevertheless, they all share a strong bond with the Latin American consumer, through their understanding and respect of their needs, and the intelligent adaptation of their business models in order to access the vast markets at the Bottom of the Pyramid. Their management has been able to look past the typical misconceptions regarding the poor, and revise their business processes under a fresh perspective. And they are not tied to business models and strategies that have originally proved their success in developed markets, but whose adaptation to emerging environments requires changes that challenge that original success formula. All of these are reasons for betting that they will be around for quite a while, in spite of the general trend toward the globalization of markets.

Notes

1. Charles Handy, Understanding the Shifts, CIES, Rome, 2004.
2. CCR Report, Comprendiendo la Base de la Piramide, Buenos Aires, 2004.
3. Creating Value in Retailing, The Coca-Cola Retailing Research Council, 2003.
4. Rohit Deshpande, Corona Beer, Harvard Business School case 9-502-0223.
5. Innovating Around Obstacles, Donald Sull, Alejandro Ruelas-Grossi and Martin Escobar, Strategy & Innovation, Nov.–Dec. 2003.
6. Why Mexicans mix cement with football, Financial Times, July 8, 2004.
7. G. D'Andrea, Arcor International Expansion, IAE case, 1995.
8. Miguel Ferre, Kola Real case, PAD, Lima. 2000.
9. Fabrica de Jabon La Corona, Working Paper, IPADE, 2003.
10. John Ireland, Como han ganado las multinacionales en los mercados populares de Venezuela, Debates IESA, Vol. VIII, N. 3, 2003.
11. K. Subhadra and S. Dutta, Coca-Cola India's Thirst for the Rural Market. ICFAI Center for Management Research, 2004.
12. P. Pacheco Guimaraes and P. Chandon, Unilever in Brazil: Marketing Strategies for Low-Income Consumers. Insead, 2004.
13. Thomas Weinrich and Renata Ribeiro, Negocios de primera con marcas de segunda, Harvard Business Review, May 2004.
14. Fernando Robles, Francoise Simon, and Jerry Haar, Winning Strategies for the New Latin Markets, Financial Times–Prentice Hall, 2003. Chapter 5, p 175: An Emerging Approach: Convergence to the Center.
15. Nazca Cosmeticos. Working Paper, IAE, Division of Research, 2001.
16. Alejandro Ruelas-Grossi, innovar en mercados emergentes: El paradigma de la T grande. Harvard Business Review América Latina, February 2004.
17. Adapted from C. K. Prahalad and Stuart Hart, The Fortune at the Bottom of the Pyramid, Strategy + Business, Issue 26, 2002.
18. Grupo Bimbo, Working Paper, IPADE, 2003.
19. The Myths on Emerging Consumers is taken from the study by The Coca-Cola Retailing Research Council: Creating Value in Retailing for Emerging Consumers. 2003.
20. According to researcher Napoleon Franco & Cia., Bogotá, Colombia.
21. Los sectores de menores recursos, un gran mercado de consumo. Research presented at 3rd. Conference on Consumer Products, December 2004, IAE, Buenos Aires.

References

Chattopadhyay, A. and Dawar, N. (2000). Rethinking Marketing Programs for Emerging Markets. Working Paper. Insead.

D'Andrea, G., Stengel, A. y Goebel-Krstelj. Nov. (2003). *Creating Value for Emerging Consumers. Harvard Business Review.*

Gomez Samper, H. and Marquez, P. Business Challenge: Encouraging the market of the masses. Discussions IESA, Vol. VIII, N. 3

Hart, S. and Christensen, C. (Fall 2002). 'The Great Leap. Driving Innovation from the Base of the Pyramid'. *MIT Sloan Management Review.*

Ireland, J. How the Multinationals Have Penetrated into the Popular Markets of Venezuela. Discussions IESA, Vol. VIII, N. 3.

——Marketing in Venezuela Today: Searching for the Majorities. Discussions IESA, Vol. VIII, N. 3.

Malave, J. The Popular Consumer: A Vast and (almost) Unknown Market. Discussions IESA, Vol. VIII, N. 3.

Prahalad, C. K. and Hammond, A. (Septermber 2002). Serving the World's Poor Profitability. *Harvard Business Review.*

Other Case Studies

Bodegas López. Guillermo D'Andrea, IAE, 2003

Carrefour Chevere! Iana Torres and Ashok Som. Essec, 2004

Carrefour in Malaysia's Retailing Industry. M. Sadiq Sohail. King Fahd University, 2004

L'Oreal Thailand. Dominique Turpin IMD, 2003

Tupperware in India. Swapna Kingi. ICFAI, 2004

LG: Rural Marketing in India. Dakshi Mohanty. ICFAI, 2004

16

Conclusions: So . . . *Can* Latin American Firms Compete?

Luiz F. Mesquita

Can Latin American firms compete? This is the question that drove not only our debate throughout this book, but also during the conference we organized to discuss the competitiveness of Latin American firms. At the end of this conference, the authors had enthusiastically concluded that the answer to such a question was a *qualified* 'yes'. In their research, the authors unearthed abundant evidence demonstrating that a number of successful private and public enterprises from Latin America have developed unique strategies to cope not only with the broad scope and quickness of economic and political change in the region but also with the challenges of going global *from* Latin America. On the other hand, the answer above also indicates that much work remains to be done in regard to broadening this competitiveness to other firms and sectors. As pointed by Robert Grosse in Chapter 1, Latin American firms still have little representation in the list of the largest, most aggressive, and most competitive multinationals from emerging economies. It is with the intent of helping broaden this competitiveness that we put together this book. As such, my goal in this last chapter is to weave common threads across the various studies included here, with the intent of distilling common strategic factors and decisions used by these successful Latin American firms.

Latin America as a region stretches from the Southern tip of South America in *Tierra del Fuego* all the way up to Mexico, where it borders the United States. The languages spoken there are various, including not only the obvious Spanish and Portuguese, but also French, Dutch, English, and many other native tongues. Culturally, although most people tend to see Latin Americans in stereotypical frames, the region encompasses immense differences in heritage and managerial habits (see recent study by Friedrich, Mesquita, and Hatum 2006, for a thorough review). Given this diversity, one could question our attempt to speak of a *Latin American Firm*. However, as Frachia and Mesquita

(Chapter 9) pointed out, the region has shared some common economic and political elements in the past 100 years which enable one to find patterns that help explain common strategies and decisions that link the various successful firms portrayed throughout this book. Such events include, but are not limited to roller-coaster bouts of economic development boom and bust; massive presence of the state in the economy, inducing power relations and bureaucratic controls; failing markets for labor, capital, and many other intermediate production goods; underdeveloped and unstable institutional environments, especially in the financial and judicial areas; as well as radical changes in foreign trade conditions, especially during the 1990s, as many governments pursued the precepts of the *Washington Consensus*. All in all, the resulting environment became one characterized by higher levels of uncertainty and risk for investments, property rights, competition, resource acquisition, and strategic decision-making.

Throughout our book, the authors have looked at specific pieces and levels of these Latin American challenges and sought to understand their nature, as well as how firms have geared up to cope with and overcome them, as these firms strive to compete not only locally (with local and foreign opponents) but also globally. The evidence we have about the formal strategies and activities developed by these firms seems at first to be composed mostly of context-specific activities, where particular firms perform particular strategies. The academic challenge that results from this chapter involves weaving common threads that contain these idiosyncrasies, while still providing general principles for understanding Latin American firm strategies. As such, my goal in this chapter is to unify such important idiosyncrasies in simple, yet understandable principles, to help understand the uniqueness of Latin American firms. To weave these threads, I examine the various studies presented throughout this book under the lenses of three leading theoretical perspectives in management research—institutional theory, transaction cost economics, and the resource-based view of the firm, within the context of Latin America. Below I first introduce these concepts, and later discuss Latin American firm strategy commonalities within these theoretical frameworks. This discussion is parallel to, but offers a differentiated view from, the analysis in Chapter 1 of this book.

16.1. Institutional Theory, Transaction Cost Economics, and the Resource-Based View

Institutional theory summarizes the influences of systems surrounding people and organizations that influence their behavior (Shapiro 1987; Zucker 1986). In a way, organizations (i.e. mostly the people within them) operate according to expectations that are based on guarantees, safety nets, or simply safeguarding structures they observe within the environment they operate in. As such, institutional settings have an impact on behavior as members of a system act according to the expected, where such expectations have symbolic representations that everything is 'customary' (Baier 1986: 25), 'normal' (Garfinkel 1963: 188) and 'seems in proper order' (Lewis and Weigert 1985: 974). Institutional theory is useful for examining phenomena in Latin America, as it permits one to understand firm behavior and strategy under institutional constraints. For example, North (1990) explains that institutions provide the rules that structure people interactions in societies and that organizations react to such formal and informal rules. As such, institutions enable the reduction of both transaction and information costs as they reduce the uncertainties surrounding behavior of partners, and facilitate interactions.

Transaction cost theory helps examine the boundaries of the firm (i.e. what the firm internalizes vs. what it outsources) through an analysis of trade-offs between the internal costs of bureaucracy versus the external costs of transaction (Williamson 1985; Masten 1996). Under exchange hazards, such as increasing uncertainty and asset-specific investments, at the margin, such trade-offs are likely to favor vertical integration. Transaction cost economics is useful for examining phenomena in Latin America, as it permits one to understand why firms integrate businesses and supplies which in a developed context would simply be procured in the market. In a way, where markets are efficient in ways to offer competitive prices for the goods procured, the trade-offs mentioned above favor outsourcing, whereas where markets fail (due to high uncertainties, and small numbers bargaining), these trade-offs favor vertical integration.

The RBV of the firm is often seen as a more recent development vis-à-vis the above-mentioned two. It purports to explain why firms are different and how they achieve and sustain competitive advantages (Wernerfelt 1984; Barney 1986, 1991; Dierickx and Cool 1989; Peteraf 1993). This stream of literature is specifically concerned with how firms acquire capabilities, as well as how these capabilities are associated or not with competitive advantages. For example, Barney (1986) explained that key resources differ in their 'tradability' and that managers can identify these resources and their prices through factor markets. Dierickx and Cool (1989) supplemented these views by indicating that some special resources do not find themselves easily in such markets; firms must instead painstakingly develop them internally through path-dependent investments. Later, Barney (1991) and Peteraf (1993) indicated that resources may lead to competitive advantages when they are valuable, rare, and costly to imitate.

The RBV of the firm is a particularly useful theory perspective for understanding resource acquisition difficulties and their association with competitive advantage within the context of Latin America. Particularly, factor markets in Latin America are known to be deficient, whereas the concept of path dependence explains the difficulties Latin American firms have in establishing coherent path-dependent, resource-developing investments. Thus, the development or acquisition of resources which would otherwise be easy to obtain in developed economies becomes a severe constraint for these firms.

16.1.1. *Weaving Common Threads of Strategic Decision-Making by Latin American Firms with Institutional Theory*

As discussed above, institutions represent rules and signals that provide a framework within which members of a society interact. As such, actions of firms and people within them are oriented based on anticipation that others will behave as expected. Otherwise, firms cannot coordinate actions (North 1990). In Latin America, such rules and signals (or the lack of them) operate at several levels such as cultural, judicial, as well as financial, labor, and capital markets. It is interesting to notice how successful Latin American firms have operated under the premises of the above theoretical perspective. Marcia Tavares (Chapter 3), for example, highlights that FDI by Latin American firms has been more likely to earn them advantages in international markets where firms are able to transfer their experience to handle business dealings to other contexts of similar cultural and linguistic settings. By operating in markets offering similar cultural institutions, Tavares argues, these Latin American multinationals accrue similar advantages to those acquired in the domestic markets, in regard to serving particular patterns of customer demand for quality and technology. Where foreign markets differ significantly in regard to such cultural and linguistic heritages, Tavares argues that such Latin American firm advantages are not necessarily sustainable.

The institutional environment is also relevant to explain the patterns of investments in locally developed technologies. In this regard, Jorge Katz (Chapter 4) looks at the government policy environment surrounding Latin American firms. Unlike what was observed across Asian emerging economies, he explains, the dramatic changes in overall country developmental policies implemented across the region have exacerbated uncertainties and risks, as opposed to creating more assuring environments for firm investments in research and development for new technologies. His recommendations for rectifying such institutional surroundings include government investments in overall infrastructure, such as information and telecommunications systems as well as the development of more transparent regulations and longer-term investments in technology incubators and subsidy programs for small and medium enterprises. In the same line, Wood and Caldas (Chapter 10) and John Edmunds (Chapter 15) explore the difficulties imposed by the uncertain institutional environment. Wood and Caldas, in particular, highlight the economic turmoil Brazilian companies faced through the past few decades, with a sequence of inadequate inflation-stabilizing plans that resulted in one of the most volatile economic environments in Latin American history. Similarly, Edmunds demonstrates how the financial institutions of a country can foster investments. Particularly, he explores how weaknesses in the financial institutional environment (e.g. financial markets are small, often illiquid, too focussed on financing the expansion of traditional commodity production and exports, as opposed to financing innovation and new technologies) have often held Latin American firms short of becoming internationally competitive. The underlying message here is that where the institutional settings provide incentives for private initiative, innovation is fostered (see Jefferson and Rawski, 1995).

The liberalizing reforms that swept Latin American markets during the 1990s aimed at, among other things, creating free market institutions that would help create just the sort of stable institutional context to support greater levels of development and competitiveness. However, the extent to which such institutions change across various economic sectors differs, and such difference is likely to affect firms differently across these economic sectors. In that respect, Eduardo Frachia and Luiz Mesquita's (Chapter 9) debate on how such changes developed more rapidly in some sectors vis-à-vis others and how this variance helps explain the competitiveness of Argentinian firms in foreign markets is very illustrative. Their study highlights that where economic reform had a faster impact on curbing failures in labor, capital, and supply markets; firms were more likely to focus on their product corporate strategy and become more aggressive in their international expansion.

In contrast to the studies that highlight how firms *passively* adapt to their institutional surroundings, many scholars debate that enterprises can react more dynamically and play a more active role within such an institutional environment if they have adaptive abilities that allow them to maneuver beyond institutional constraints (Oliver 1991). Here, Hatum and Pettigrew's (Chapter 12) study illustrates how organizational flexibility indeed supports such maneuvering abilities, enabling firms to more successfully navigate through the maze of institutional uncertainties observed in Argentina, throughout the past twenty years. I will return and discuss such organizational flexibility in depth further in the section on the resource-based view, but the lesson that this study brings to our understanding of strategy-making under diverse institutional settings is one of firms *actively* overcoming their surrounding limitations.

Another example of such *active* approach to dealing with institutional shortcomings is the process of helping create one's own institutions to govern the expectations of investors. Firms that can help create rules that foster strong institutions, help form expectations, and therefore help foster investments by the larger industrial community with positive externalities for all involved. One fine example of such a process is offered in the study by McDermott (Chapter 5). Here, the author contrasts the creation of government institutions across the wine-producing regions of Mendoza and San Juan in Argentina. As richly illustrated in this chapter in the province of Mendoza, producers were able to establish a strong collaboration with the provincial government, and create a more innovation inductive environment by exploring the privatization of a previously government-owned winery and transforming it into a regional federation of cooperatives that provided modern technical training, credit and many other services to the winery entrepreneurial community at large. As such, McDermott links the internationally successful presence of Mendoza wineries (in contrast to the less successful San Juan ones) to the development of these institutional factors. To help further contrast what can happen when firms lack the ability to work together and help form institutions, one can turn to Michael Penfold's (Chapter 7) account of the shrimp cluster in Venezuela. This country is known to have suffered through disastrous changes in private investment institutional settings recently, where the federal government has geared toward a communist form of socialism, taking direct control of any economic sector it deems *strategic* (The Economist 2007). As firms in this sector lack appropriate government-supported market institutions as well as abilities to create a cooperation-inducing environment, they are eventually unable to overcome common problems such as the *Taura* virus that threatened the entire industry.

All in all, the underlying lesson arising from the debate of our chapters, in regard to institutional settings is that *yes*, governments do have an important role in shaping appropriate innovation-inducive institutional settings. *However*, as it became clear across the various chapters, firms *can* and *must* help shape their institutional environments by developing strategic responses instead of adapting passively. *Additionally*, firms can also *actively* develop resources to cope with weak institutional environments. Firms can develop growth-oriented responses from an active strategic choice perspective instead of just constrained strategic choices. The studies included here demonstrate how relevant it is to see competitive advantage from a firm and entrepreneurial perspective as opposed to a 'waiting for the government to do something' perspective. Even with regard to investing in foreign markets, where Latin American firms find themselves to be new players in an inhospitable market, firms are still able to choose institutional settings that are more similar to those they are accustomed to in their domestic markets.

16.1.2. *Transaction Cost Economics*

Transaction cost economics, as traditionally applied, often takes the institutional environment for granted. As such, this theoretical perspective has mostly been applied to developed market contexts, characterized by strong legal regimes, and binding social norms. Less is known about governance structures for transactions in emerging economies (Hoskisson et al.

2000: 254). Latin American institutional settings, as explored above, bear some important characteristics which affect how firms are organized as well as how they transact with each other. Particularly, measurements of outcomes from agreements as well as judicial enforcement of contracts are important factors that hinder efficient transactions among business and economic actors in Latin America (Carrera et al. 2003). Additionally, in a country where the institution of transparent market pricing does not often accurately provide signals for efficient resource allocation, measurement costs are known to be quite high. Here, resource markets are affected, and consequently the ease with which firms obtain competitive inputs is strongly affected. (See my more extended debate on resources in the section that follows.) Similarly, in countries where official discretion rather than the rule of law seems to define property rights, enforcement costs are high (la Porta at al. 1997). As such, transaction cost economics often suggests that firms develop a preference for hierarchical governance over the private market.

What this means for Latin American firms is that the most successful enterprises are often those diversifying into new product markets to greater extent vis-à-vis successful firms operating in more developed markets. In a way, transaction cost economics explains the incidence of unrelated diversification. Khanna and Palepu (1997) argue that unrelated diversification by large business groups is efficient in emerging economies because of their underdeveloped capital and labor markets. This argument connects closely with Williamson's arguments (1985) that market failure leads to diversified hierarchical firm development. To exemplify how successful firms have manipulated these forces, authors of several chapters in our book explore the strategies employed by diversified organizations, the so-called business groups.

Grosse (Chapter 2), for instance, highlights how close-knit groups of stakeholders (e.g. families or groups of families) have held tight ownership control of organizations, even where these organizations have outstanding shares traded in domestic or foreign exchanges. By vertically integrating, and forming larger capital and labor pools, Grosse explains, these firms form advantages that confer them an edge over other domestic and foreign competitors in this Latin American environment, which is characterized by failing markets for these very resources.

Another good example of successful unrelated diversification, which follows the transaction cost economics rationale, is Héctor Ochoa's study of the Colombian GEA (Chapter 6), as well as Grosse and Thomas' study of fifteen of the largest Mexican economic groups (Chapter 11). These organizations are known to have pursued very high levels of business diversification. In the particular case of GEA, its activities ranged from a chocolate, cookies, and crackers company, going through cement all the way through finance and insurance. Ochoa's debate of GEA's internal organization demonstrates that firms can not only take advantage of scale and scope economies in related business activities (as explored by Grosse in Chapter 2) but also accrue advantages of risk diversification and resource pooling in unrelated business activities. As an example of the advantages of related activities in the foods division, GEA consolidated thirty-three food companies, giving this division scale and consumer identity power to dominate the local market vis-à-vis local and foreign competitors. On the other hand, an example of the advantages it gains from unrelated diversification include market power and a larger capital pool that enable it, for example, to develop its powerful distribution channels—which as Ochoa highlights, lies at the heart of GEA's competitive advantage—in the local market as well as abroad. The same type of rationale applies to Grosse and Thomas's Mexican business groups. By amassing larger pools of resources, these firms develop sprawling distribution channels which lie at the center of these Mexican success stories. Such advantages also played a central role in helping these firms expand abroad; such an expansion further solidified these firms' resistance to economic volatility in their domestic market, such as that observed in the Tequila Crisis of 1994 and 1995.

Although it may sound as if larger degrees of diversification into unrelated businesses may seem the pattern in Latin America, Frachia and Mesquita (Chapter 9) explain that this is not always the case. Business groups in fact may take very diverse forms; some of them pursuing only limited levels of diversification. At first, Frachia and Mesquita's study of Argentinian business groups may sound as if practice defies theory, that is, that the precepts of transaction costs discussed above are not always correct. However, as Frachia and Mesquita explained, the concepts apply equally here. The catch is that, the competitive landscapes across various economic sectors, as well as capital and labor markets, developed differently over time, following the implementation of market-liberalizing reforms in those countries (as it was the case in Argentina and several other Latin American countries throughout the 1990s). Particularly, despite expectations that market-liberalizing reforms guided by the so-called *Washington Consensus* would turn failing capital and labor markets into more fluid environments, and as a result, according to the transaction cost perspective, fewer firms would pursue larger degrees of diversification, the fact is that several of these spot markets take longer to develop. As a consequence, one is likely to observe a mix of business groups pursuing different strategies. According to Frachia and Mesquita's analysis, business groups operating mostly in business segments least affected by the liberalizing reforms were likely to continue pursuing larger degrees of diversification (so as to defend themselves from higher transaction costs); on the other hand, business groups operating mostly in business segments most affected by the liberalizing reforms were more likely to decrease their degrees of diversification, now that risks of transaction costs were lower.

As one can see, by carefully analyzing how likely particular markets are to fail, firms can devise different organizational forms so as to cope with the home environment. The examples and analyses included in our book indicate that by carefully crafting their corporate strategies (i.e. levels of diversification) according to the concepts discussed here they are more likely to succeed vis-à-vis local and foreign competitors unaccustomed to such market circumstances.

16.1.3. *The Resource-Based View of the Firm*

The main precept of the RBV, as summarized in our early discussion above, is that where firms are able to amass valuable, rare, and costly to imitate resources they are to earn a competitive advantage. The studies we included here that highlight the value of particular types of resources for competitive advantage of Latin American firms differ from other traditional RBV studies in at least two very important ways. First, the value of resources is intrinsically based on a particular context. Depending on the characteristics of such context, a focus on certain resources is actually known to create strategic inflexibility and core rigidities for the firm, leading to negative returns (Leonard-Barton 1992). Second, the ease with which resources can be acquired, an issue first discussed in Barney's debate of factor markets (1986), is often taken for granted in several RBV studies, particularly those involving developed markets. Indeed, the very fact that factor markets often fail in emerging economies, and in particular in Latin America, indicates that resource acquisition may be one of the most difficult tasks for top managers of Latin American firms to handle. In sum, in the context of Latin American firms competing at home or abroad, any discussion of resources as sources of advantage have to be combined with a characterization of the institutional environment and market failing characteristics surrounding the firm. Firms therefore have to manage the social and market context of their resources and capabilities in order to generate rents.

To this point, little research using an RBV framework has examined strategy differences in the social context of emerging economies (Hoskisson et al. 2000: 256). Like most resources that create competitive advantage in emerging economies, on the whole they are intangible. However, they are not necessarily product market resources, as suggested by the knowledge-based view of the firm (e.g. technologies or patents). Some resources are especially more valuable in the context of emerging economies. Thus, firms in emerging economies are often known to reap the benefits of first-mover advantages that include being the first participants in new product markets, reputation effects, and economic advantage of sales volume, and dominance of sprawling distribution channels.

One of the best examples of the intricacies involved in resource development and deployment in Latin America is presented in the study of Andres Hatum and Andrew Pettigrew (Chapter 12). Through an ethnographic-like study of two Argentinian champions respectively leading the pharmaceutical and food industries, Sidus and AGD, Hatum and Pettigrew explore the value of organizational flexibility as an intangible resource in helping firms to cope with the constantly changing environmental conditions that characterize Argentina's (and most of Latin America's) economy. Their study highlights the important match that exists between environmental conditions (i.e. unstable context) and the value of resources and capabilities (i.e. organizational flexibility). This study is particularly rich in detailing the types of capabilities that allowed these firms to have organizational flexibility, and therefore, differentiate themselves from local and foreign competitors. Such capabilities included know-how on acquisition processes as well as an uncanny drive to learn from experiences of successful firms in other industries.

The match between context and resource value also seems to drive new resource investments, as firms recognize the nature of their surrounding institutional environments. In fact, in emerging economies, such as those in Latin America, local competitors may develop capabilities for relationship-based management in their environment that substitute for the lack of institutional infrastructure. These assets may be used domestically or in transferring abroad to other emerging economies where such assets would also be useful. Such is the case of Tavares's study (Chapter 2) of foreign direct investments and competitiveness of Latin American firms. In a way, her analysis confirms that as firms develop resources and capabilities to operate within a certain cultural and political context, as they expand geographically, the most likely foreign markets they are bound to succeed in are those of similar institutional surroundings. In a similar vein, Goldstein and Toulan's analyses of Brazilian *Embraer* and Argentinian *Techint* highlight that global competitiveness of Latin American firms rely not only on the unique technologies and product-related capabilities (i.e. aircraft manufacturing and industrial steel products, respectively) that these firms developed but also on organizational capabilities. Such organizational capabilities, similar to those described by Tavares in Chapter 2, relate to these firms' abilities in maneuvering through the maze of bureaucratic and political environments of an emerging economy. This is obviously not to say that these firms' product technologies are not valuable outside their home institutional context. In fact, these authors highlight that both *Embraer* and *Techint* seem to demonstrate that Latin American firms, though not always known for their technical capabilities, are indeed able to compete globally, with a competitive edge, based on their having developed superior product technologies and know-how.

As far as competing in the local markets against multinationals is concerned, it seems that successful firms have not only relied on their superior flexibility and technological know-how, but also on first-mover advantages in the possession and dominance of strategic resources. For example, Grosse (Chapter 1), Ochoa (Chapter 8), Frachia and Mesquita (Chapter 9), Grosse and

Thomas (Chapter 11), and D'Andrea (Chapter 16) all highlight the importance of dominating distribution networks in the local markets. Here, brand name and familiarity with the local consumer give these local firms a significant edge over foreign firms which are often unfamiliar with not only habits of local consumers but also with how to operate within this particular cultural institutional setting. All in all, it seems early relationships with distribution channel gatekeepers, governmental agency officers, as well as opinion-leader customers seem to be a valuable intangible resource for local firms. In fact, early relationships, an intangible asset, can be said to give tangible benefits, such as access to the limited number of government licenses, as well as limited distribution channel shelf-space.

Still in the matter of contexts that enhance the value of resources, several successful Latin American firms have pursued niche strategies. The underlying logic is that of seeking positions that have not yet been subjected to the highly rivalrous context of globalization, therefore helping dodge the landslide of aggressiveness often seen coming from multinational corporations entering emerging markets. In this regard, D'Andrea (Chapter 16) gives us a very rich description of retailing successes to the consumers known to be at the 'bottom of the pyramid'—BOP (i.e. very low-income consumers)— as opposed to those at the 'top of the pyramid'—TOP (i.e. higher income consumers). Because BOP shoppers make up the overwhelming majority of consumers in Latin America, and also because these consumers are often forgotten by large foreign multinationals who are often only able to target wealthier Latin American consumers who are more similar in profile to those found in their home markets, several key abilities seem to give local firms a strong advantage in the competitive landscape. D'Andrea lists several of these, including relationships with small local *mom-&-pop* retail outlets, packaging that is more suitable for very low-income consumers (e.g. selling cigarettes in smaller quantities than the traditional 20-cigarette pack), as well as developing abilities to produce at low cost, but still maintaining a strong brand image. By managing these capabilities, indigenous firms, unknown to the globalized world, have taken on multinational giants. Just to cite two classic examples from D'Andrea's research, Peruvian *Kola Real* maintains a significant edge over colossal competitors Coke and Pepsi in the low income market segment. Likewise, through such key capabilities in retailing *Jabon La Corona* has beaten Proctor & Gamble, Colgate, and Unilever in the Mexican soap market.

In regard to resource acquisition, my discussion above on transaction cost economics highlighted the difficulties one may suffer when handling resource-bundling activities in contexts characterized by failing capital, labor, and inputs markets. Other than vertically integrating, firms have several other options to ensure their ready access to key competitive resources. For example, many competitive advantages in Latin America seem to be based on network relationships and close business–government ties, such that firms become effective monopolies in their home markets. The research by McDermott (Chapter 5) and Penfold (Chapter 7) seem to take us in that direction.

A valuable example of successful resource acquisition and development is offered in the study by Dong-Sung Cho and Keum-Young Chang (Chapter 14). Using experience from company strategy in Korea, they bridge the path to our context with resource-development lessons that can be useful to Latin American firms. Their examination of the Yuhan–Kimberly joint venture demonstrates how local firms must face foreigners not only as competitors but also as potential partners, from whom they can amass lacking resources and capabilities, and learn how to become more competitive. Among the intangible resources this joint venture has created, one can appreciate the value of reputation for fair people management and ethical behavior and the fostering of innovative management techniques. Lastly, the theoretical model offered here (the SER-M model) enables one to link leadership, environment, resources and mechanisms through which these factors interact to help the joint venture sustain its advantage vis-à-vis its competitors.

In a similar vein to that of Cho and Chang, Wood and Caldas also carefully lay out a conceptual model (SCAR, for sustainability, cost, attractiveness, and return) that help firms identify one's particular strengths and weakness versus foreign firms, especially in regard to resources and capabilities. As they high-light, the most challenging difficulties Brazilian firms face relate to amassing capabilities that help domestic firms overcome failing institutional settings and market contexts, much in the same way Hatum and Pettigrew discussed the value and importance of organizational flexibility.

In essence, the research presented here demonstrates that a firm must understand the relationship between its company assets and capabilities, and the quickly changing nature of the institutional infrastructure as well as the characteristics of its industry. In so doing, the emerging economy firm may be able to become an aggressive contender domestically or globally by using its resources as sources of competitive advantage. As the markets are liberalized and globalized further, managerial expertise derived from experience with closed economies seems unlikely to provide a resource in emerging economy environments, as such large conglomerates are likely to have to change their approach to diversification and resource acquisition.

As a concluding remark, in this book we aimed at studying not only the unparalleled circumstances Latin American firms face in regard to their sur-vival and competitiveness but also the unique challenges they go through to develop strategic decisions that enable them to overcome such distinctive difficulties and attain an advantage vis-à-vis local and foreign competitors. We obviously do not offer answers to all problems, but it has been our hope that our small effort will help light new avenues for further academic and professional inquiry into the competitiveness of Latin American firms.

References

Baier, A. (1986). Trust and Antitrust, *Ethics*, 96(2): 231–60.

Barney, J. B. (1986). 'Strategic Factor Markets: Expectations, Luck, and Business Strategy', *Management Science*, 32: 1231–41.

Barney, J. B. (1991). 'Firm Resources and Sustained Competitive Advantage', *Journal of Management*, 17(1): 99–120.

Carrera, A., Mesquita, L., Perkins, G., and Vassolo, R. (2003). 'Business Groups and Their Corporate Strategies in the Argentinian Roller Coaster of Competitive and Anti-Competitive Shocks', *Academy of Management Executive*, 17(3): 32–44.

Dierickx, I. and Cool, K. (1989). 'Asset Stock Accumulation and Sustainability of Competitive Advantage', *Management Science*, 35: 554–71.

The Economist (2007). 'With Marx, Lenin, and Jesus Christ', *The Economist*.

Friedrich, P. M., Mesquita, L. F., and Hatum, A. O. (2006). 'The Meaning of Difference: Beyond Cultural and Managerial Homogeneity Stereotypes of Latin America', *Management Research*, 4(1): 53–71.

Garfinkel, H. (1963). 'A Conception of, and Experiments with, "Trust" as a Condition of Stable Concerted Actions', in O. J. Harvey (ed.), *Motivation and Social Interaction*, New York: Ronald Press, pp. 187–238.

Hoskisson, R. E., Eden, L., Lau, C. M., and Wright, M. (2000). 'Strategy in Emerging Economies', *Academy of Management Journal*, 43(3): 249–67.

Jefferson, G. H. and Rawski, T. G. (1995). 'How Industrial Reform Worked in China: The Role of Innovation, Competition, and Property Rights', in M. Bruno and B. Pleskovic (eds.), *Proceedings of the World Bank Annual Conference on Development Economics*. Washington, DC: World Bank, pp. 129–56.

Khanna, T. and Palepu, K. (1997). 'Why Focussed Strategies May Be Wrong for Emerging Markets', *Harvard Business Review*, 75(4): 41–50.

la Porta, R., Lopez de Silanes, F., Schleifer, A., and Vishny, A. (1997). 'Legal Determinants of External Finance', *Journal of Finance*, 52: 1131–50.

Leonard-Barton, D. (1992). 'Core Capabilities and Core Rigidities: A Paradox in Managing Product Development', *Strategic Management Journal*, 13 (Summer special issue): 111–25.

Lewis, J. D. and Weigert, A. J. (1985). 'Trust as a Social Reality', *Social Forces*, 63: 967–85.

Masten, S. E. (1996). *Case Studies in Contracting and Organization*. Cambridge, MA: Oxford University Press.

North, D. C. (1990). *Institutions, Institutional Change, and Economic Performance*. New York: Cambridge University Press.

Oliver, C. (1991). 'Strategic Responses to Institutional Processes', *Academy of Management Review*, 16: 145–79.

Peteraf, M. A. (1993). 'The Cornerstones of Competitive Advantage: A Resource-Based View', *Strategic Management Journal*, 14: 179–91.

Shapiro, S. P. (1987). 'The Social Control of Impersonal Trust', *American Journal of Sociology*, 93(3): 623–58.

Wernerfelt, B. (1984). 'A Resource-Based View of the Firm', *Strategic Management Journal*, 5: 272–80.

Williamson, O. (1985). *The Economic Institutions of Capitalism*. New York: Free Press.

Zucker, L. G. (1986). 'Production of Trust: Institutional Sources of Economic Structure 1840–1920', in B. M. Staw and L. L. Cummings (eds.), *Research in Organizational Behavior*, Vol. 8. Greenwich, CT: JAI Press, pp. 53–111.

Index

Index

household appliances 350
imported beers 341
institutional conditions 10–11
large groups 18, 250–66
leading banks with major local operations
    in 22
low-income consumers 22
manufacturing production 70
maquila production 34
oil 40
privatized pension schemes 334
shrimp exports to 157
SMEs export to 52
soap market share 23, 343, 374
strategy based on extensive distribution 342
tilapia 15
vehicle industry 72
see also América Móvil; ANTAD; Bimbo;
    CARICOM; Carso; CCM; Corona; Femsa;
    Hylsamex; Jabon La Corona; Telmex;
    Tequila Crisis
Miami 331
microbusinesses 343
microclimates 90, 92
    detailed mappings of 104
    diversity of 105
microeconomic behavior 76
microeconomic conditions 222
    changes in 223
    influence in shaping of corporate
        strategies 225
    shifts in 201
micro-lending 312
micro-level strategies 14–16
Middle East 276, 332
    savings rate 333
middle-income classes 360
Milan 275
Miles, M. 207
military dictatorship 318
mimetic behavior 173, 179
Minas Gerais 325
Minetti 216
minimal government 205
mini-mill steel 48
mining 35–9, 47, 48, 277, 309
    gold 127
    largest companies in the world 53
minority shareholders 130, 322
    transparent relations with 138
mistakes 246
mistrust 162
Mitsubishi 126, 135
Mittal 287
MNCs (multinational corporations), *see* MNEs
MNEs (multinational enterprises) 3, 11, 17, 20,
    22, 23, 31, 40, 69, 111, 253, 321

ability to outperform 236
advantages in comparison with 252
attempts to enter Chinese market 19
challengers successfully fended off from 254
competing against 21, 35, 220
discovery of value of BOP markets 344
entry into local/domestic markets 216, 217,
    219
European 15
foreign affiliates 32, 41
forward integration 162
global 145, 328
globally integrated 309, 310, 318, 324
important competitors 14
investment in shrimp industry 151
largest emerging market 12
misled by apparently unlimited
    opportunities 270
nascent 327
products branded by 250
risk of losing ownership to 145
sectors less attractive to 223
significant difference between size of 246
taking advantage of low local costs 34
target of entry of 221
US-based 15
world-class 335
modernization 236, 247
    technological 125
molecular biology 77
monarchy 313
Monchenot 344
monetary policy:
    expansionary 324
    lax 204
    stable 205
money 319, 324, 349
    creation in excess of tax revenue 324
    deposited in financial institutions 331, 335
    lack of alternative uses for 334
    lacking 348
money supply 316
Mongolia 303
monitoring:
    environmental 74, 242
    mutual 83, 104
monocropping 84
monopoly 9, 35, 58, 77
    imminent end of 56
    market 204
    state, privatizing and/or deregulating 206
    suppliers to government organizations 252
Monsanto 73
Montenegro, Rodolfo 95, 105
Moon, Kook-Hyun 294, 297–9, 303, 304, 305
moral hazard 315, 328
Morck, R. 32

Index

resources (*cont.*)
  shared 110
  socioeconomic, legal and inherited 92
  structural transformation strongly biased in
    favor of activities 70
  tangible 204, 219–20, 223
  technological 140, 220
  training 106
  upgrading 104
  valuable 8, 239
  vital 99
  VRIN-based 296
  wasting 106
  see also financial resources; human resources;
    natural resources; resources and
    capabilities
resources and capabilities 209, 214, 217,
  219–21, 222
  common core 224
  path dependent 225
respect 301, 303, 305
  love and 300
  market-leading 21
responsibility 298
  delegation of 303
  strengthening 302
  see also social responsibility
restaurants 56, 131, 258
restructuring 97, 99–101, 109, 145, 244–5, 260,
  279
  aggressively pursued 300
  major 278
  post-privatization 57
  see also participatory restructuring approach
retail-oriented associations 349
retail sector 38, 48, 188, 253, 254, 261
  expansion of 70, 321
  innovator in 336
  see also small-scale retail stores
retention 169, 245
retrenchments 243, 246
revenues 40, 51, 104, 343
  devalued 320
  dispersed 214
  fiscal 153
  not enough to pay debt 316
  tax 324
rickshaws and carriages 343
rigidities 347
Rincon Famoso 344
Rinker 48
Rio de Janeiro 325
risk 316–17
  credit 53
  downside 330
  exchange rate 53
  financial 304, 325

inflation devaluation 331
inherent 165, 244
market cycles 53
opportunities and 239
perception of 209
rating 240
significantly diluting 244
well-known 324
risk aversion 52, 245, 270, 325, 353
risk diversification 51, 52, 53–4, 216
  incentives to 150
risk management 51–4, 243
  unusually high standard in 244
risk reduction 50, 51, 52–3, 142, 257
risk-sharing 73, 128, 140, 156
  partners 273, 274
RMC Group 47, 48, 53, 54
Rocca, Agostino 38, 275, 276
Rocca family 278
Rodrik, D. 85
Roemmers 186
Roggio 224
Roman 224
Romania 276
rotation 60
rule of law 154
rules of inclusion 87, 104, 110, 111
Rumelt, R. P. 214
Russian default (1998) 320

Sabel, C. 86
SABMiller 125
Sabó 18, 54, 244–5
Sadia 56
Safford, S. 95
SAG 74
St Martin 176, 191
salaries 280
sales 151, 252, 253, 260, 272, 277
  dropped 258
  export 157
  foreign 256
  plummeted 259
  return on 256, 257, 262
Salinas, Ricardo 253
Salinas Rocha, Hugo 253
Salinas Group 253–4, 256, 261–3
salmon 15, 16, 67, 70
  major farming countries 73–4
  world prices for 75
salsas 260
Samsung Electronics Co. 293
San Juan 13, 14, 82, 83, 86, 87, 369
  Mendoza vs. 92–101, 104, 109, 111
  number of vineyards 90
  registered and active wineries 91
Sanborns 38, 252

410